Brief Treatments
for the Traumatized

Recent Titles in
Contributions in Psychology

Modern Perspectives on B. F. Skinner and Contemporary Behaviorism
James T. Todd and Edward K. Morris, editors

Chaos Theory in Psychology
Frederick David Abraham and Albert R. Gilgen, editors

Classifying Reactions to Wrongdoing
R. Murray Thomas

Prevent, Repent, Reform, Revenge: A Study in Adolescent Moral Development
Ann C. Diver-Stamnes and R. Murray Thomas

Post-Soviet Perspectives on Russian Psychology
Vera Koltsova, Yuri Oleinik, Albert R. Gilgen, and Carol K. Gilgen, editors

Multicultural Counseling in a Divided and Traumatized Society
Joyce Hickson and Susan Kriegler

Cognitive Psychology in the Middle Ages
Simon Kemp

Adolescence: Biological and Psychosocial Perspectives
Benjamin B. Wolman

Soviet and American Psychology During World War II
Albert R. Gilgen, Carol K. Gilgen, Vera A. Koltsova, and Yuri N. Oleinik

Counseling the Inupiat Eskimo
Catherine Swan Reimer

Culturally Competent Family Therapy: A General Model
Shlomo Ariel

The Hyphenated American: The Hidden Injuries of Culture
John C. Papajohn

Brief Treatments for the Traumatized

A Project of the Green Cross Foundation

Edited by
CHARLES R. FIGLEY

Foreword by Paul Pedersen, Series Editor

Contributions in Psychology, Number 39

GREENWOOD PRESS
Westport, Connecticut • London

616.85210651
B765

Library of Congress Cataloging-in-Publication Data

Brief treatments for the traumatized : a project of the Green Cross Foundation / edited by
Charles R. Figley ; foreword by Paul Pedersen, series editor.
    p.   cm.—(Contributions in psychology, ISSN 0736-2714 ; no. 39)
    Includes bibliographical references and indexes.
    ISBN 0-313-32137-X (alk. paper)
    1. Brief psychotherapy. 2. Psychic trauma—Treatment. 3. Post-traumatic stress
disorder—Treatment. I. Figley, Charles R., 1944– II. Series.
RC480.55.B775 2002
616.85'210651—dc21   2001054715

British Library Cataloguing in Publication Data is available.

Library of Congress Catalog Card Number: 2001054715
ISBN: 0-313-32137-X
ISSN: 0736-2714

First published in 2002

Greenwood Press, 88 Post Road West, Westport, CT 06881
An imprint of Greenwood Publishing Group, Inc.
www.greenwood.com

Printed in the United States of America

The paper used in this book complies with the
Permanent Paper Standard issued by the National
Information Standards Organization (Z39.48–1984).

10 9 8 7 6 5 4 3 2 1

Every reasonable effort has been made to trace the owners of copyright materials in this
book, but in some instances this has proven impossible. The editor and publisher will be
glad to receive information leading to more complete acknowledgments in subsequent
printings of the book and in the meantime extend their apologies for any omissions.

For my loving wife, Kathleen "Kat" Regan Figley

Contents

Foreword

One of the consequences of globalization has been the breakdown of village and primary group support systems and increased tolerance for violence. This book by Charles R. Figley reviews a variety of innovative and well-documented approaches to managing trauma through clinical interventions. One interesting example is the "reciprocal inhibition hypothesis" (RIH). The fifteen chapters describe a comprehensive variety of approaches, most of which are not adequately described in other books about clinical intervention. While various types of post-traumatic stress disorder (PTSD) are often acknowledged elsewhere, this book provides the best comprehensive review of brief treatment strategies for PTSD.

The book is divided into three parts. The introductory chapters of Part I identify the solid psychological theories on which the book is based. Both the more established treatment strategies and the more experimental approaches are addressed primarily from the perspective of cognitive-behavioral theory. Several approaches that are not typically associated with the cognitive-behavioral approach are described and analyzed. Some of the challenges facing providers of treatment are identified and matched to a variety of treatment strategies in a very practical and applied perspective. Patterns of PTSD behavior, as well as patterns of response to treatment, are discussed in detail. The careful reader will receive a framework for both the diagnosis and treatment of PTSD.

Generic treatments for typical presenting problems by traumatized clients are emphasized in Part II. The treatments described here and throughout the book provide the clinician with enough detail to begin using the treatment strategies in practice. This practical and applied emphasis is perhaps the most valuable feature of the book. A second, equally important emphasis in Part II is the importance of "relationship" to brief treatment strategies. A good therapeutic relationship is described as a necessary but not sufficient condition for positive outcomes, as documented throughout the research literature. Narrative therapy, Thought Field Therapy, and Eye Movement Desensitization and Reprocessing (EMDR) are some of the practical and applied approaches described. This book provides the best comprehensive and readable description of EMDR that I have found anywhere in the published literature.

Trauma-focused treatments, focusing on cutting-edge and more experimental treatment strategies, are described in Part III. These approaches include Multi-sensory Trauma Processing (MTP) in a variety of different populations. The effect of "frozen memory" is described, for example, and treatment strategies are documented in brief case examples. Neuro-Linguistic Programming (NLP) and Emotionally-Focused Therapy (EFT) are reviewed and evaluated as treatment strategies, compared with typical psychoeducational models. The Multiple Family Group Model and the Family Solutions Program (FSP) approach are also evaluated for use in a variety of different settings. The Traumatic Incident Reduction (TIR) approach is also applied to different situations. Each of these brief treatment strategies is followed by guidelines for debriefing and evaluating the treatment effects according to established guidelines.

Psychology is to this millennium what theology was to the previous millennium as an "engine of change." The fields of psychology are going through rapid and radical alterations to match the changing society in which psychology is applied. While there is some disagreement about that paradigm shift, there is almost universal agreement that profound changes are taking place in the field of psychology. This book is unique in demonstrating practical applications of psychology to the unique problems of violence and PTSD in this millennium.

Paul Pedersen, Series Editor

Acknowledgments

We would like to acknowledge with gratitude and appreciation the members of the Academy of Traumatology, who provided useful feedback and guidance in the development of this book; and the Green Cross Foundation, who provided financial support and inspiration.

Introduction

This book fills a void. There is no book available that focuses on brief treatments for the traumatized. There are other works on brief treatment, but the focus is on a general clinical population; there are also books that focus on single-treatment approaches aimed at the traumatized that purport to be brief.

There is an acute need for a handbook given the emergence of an extraordinary number that claim to desensitize or eliminate symptoms of post-traumatic distress. Moreover, managed care and the growing need for psychotherapy require brief treatments.

Brief treatments are those that have a focused, time-sensitive program of intervention that are guided by sound assessment methods, and can be verified empirically. Generic treatments are those originally designed for other presenting problems, but are effectively applied to the traumatized.

Part I, "Theoretical Overview," contains three chapters. Collectively, they provide the theoretical basis for the book. Chapter 1, "Theory-Driven and Research-Informed Brief Treatments," written by the editor of this book, emphasizes the importance of theory and research as the bases for all treatments including, but not limited to, mental health services and traumatology. It is noted that evidence-based brief treatments offer considerable reassurance to the general public, but are becoming vital to practitioners, who must justify what they do for reimbursement by insurance and other managed care systems. The latter section of the chapter includes a discussion of the role of experimental or neoteric treatment approaches within an evidence-based culture. One solution is theory-driven innovations. One example is the utility of the reciprocal inhibition hypothesis (RIH) first proposed by Joseph Wolpe (1958), recognized as one of the most studied and proven precepts in cognitive-behavioral therapy (CBT). CBT approaches enjoy more empirical support than any other in eliminating the symptoms of PTSD and related disorders and symptoms. It is suggested that some of the less-tested brief treatment approaches discussed in this book can be explained by and are consistent with the RIH thesis.

Chapter 2, "Behavioral/Cognitive Approaches to Post-traumatic Stress," by Lizabeth Roemer, David S. Riggs, and Nicole T. Harrington, provides readers with an introduction to the clinical theory that characterizes a behavioral approach to the treatment of post-traumatic psychological sequelae. The authors point out that clinicians often develop a treatment plan that is little more than a series of clinical techniques, devoid of a systematic theory or theory-based protocol. In this chapter the authors attempt to supply the theory for behavior therapy appropriate for working with the traumatized. Specifically, they focus on the theoretical foundations of behavior therapy and behavioral conceptualizations of post-traumatic stress in order to introduce readers to the concepts that underlie behavior therapy for trauma survivors. They argue that behavioral/cognitive theories of post-traumatic stress provide a useful foundation and guide for a range of therapeutic interventions including, but not limited to, those traditionally considered cognitive or behavioral. (In Chapter 4, these same authors provide detailed guidance in using behavior/cognitive techniques found to be effective in helping the traumatized.)

In Chapter 3, "Active Ingredients in Trauma-Focused Brief Treatments," Anne M. Dietrich notes that busy practitioners are often not able to easily sort them out to match which approach is best suited for them and particularly for a client at any particular stage of treatment. As a way of helping in this sorting process, she addresses the most fundamental challenges facing those who wish to help the traumatized. First, she discusses the issues associated with methods of exposure of clients to their traumatic experiences. The strict behaviorists argue that exposure is the single most important active ingredient, and often admonish practitioners for using any form of relaxation for fear that it would distract from and limit the power of exposure effects. Dietrich makes a convincing argument that practitioners should be discouraged from using prolonged exposure with fragile clients. Rather, there should be more opportunity for gradual exposure so that clients have ample time to process the material and develop their own effective and more long-lasting coping methods. Exposure, she argues, is only a means to an end and the end is integration of dissociative systems, drawing on a new theory of the traumatization process. Thus, it is proposed that effective trauma treatment involves assisting clients to overcome their fear of trauma stimuli/memories, using relaxation and safety induction methods while integrating their experiences into their existing cognitive schemas or structures. "That is, new information is integrated into memory, which might enable the individuals to modulate their distress more effectively through the use of contextual information that is discrepant from the original trauma." Second, Dietrich notes the additional risk factors for PTSD and how practitioners should attend to these risks. Among the risks is overlooking clients who may be exhibiting the symptoms of PTSD without apparently having witnessed a traumatic event. However, she argues that the same treatment approaches should apply. Also, she notes other risk factors: The severity, duration, and proximity of an individual's exposure to the traumatic event are most prevalent. However, practitioners should also consider the lack of social supports, traumatic family histories, traumatic childhood experiences, personality variables, and preexisting mental disorders. The third section is a reexamination of the entire etiology of PTSD. She first discusses the diathesis-stress theory, which posits that outcome is a function of an interaction between pre-dispositional (i.e., risk) factors (including, but not limited to, genetics) and environmental factors. From this perspective, neither environmental factors (the traumatic event) nor pre-dispositional factors, in isolation, are sufficient for PTSD. She then discusses the possible combination of magnitude and risk and the implications for diagnosis and treatment. In the section "The Role of Risk Factors," Dietrich discusses how risk factors themselves can affect outcome in terms of the person's characteristics (e.g., women are at a higher risk of rape than men), their subjective experiences (e.g., stoic acceptance in the face of uncontrollable stressors), and their reactions to their symptoms (e.g., sleep distress). In the final section, "Issues of Classification," she suggests that diagnosis depends on the particular risk factors involved in a given case, regardless of the severity or type of stressful event. Thus, a treatment plan that involves treating the client in "brief treatment blocks" may be most suitable for stabilization and treatment of the complex symptoms. Multiphasic approaches are wise, she suggests. Fragile clients require considerable patience, safety, and stabilization prior to confronting traumatic memories. Summarizing the arguments associated with classifying PTSD as an anxiety disorder, a dissociative disorder, or a stress disorder, she argues that because PTSD is nearly always co-morbid with other DSM diagnoses, it is wise to make a careful pre-treatment assessment. In the section "Treatment Targets," she contrasts treating simply PTSD with treating more complex and chronic PTSD. Here too, she suggests that treatment will depend on the nature of the event, the presence and severity of the particular risk factors in a given situation, and the particular form that the resultant symptoms take. Clearly, some of the risk factors (e.g., genetics, family history of disorder, gender, intelligence, biological alterations, and temperament) are not amenable to treatment, or are less amenable to treatment than others. Treatment outcome may thus depend, in part, on the presence of these risk factors. In the final section Dietrich provides a gift to practitioners who wish their approach had some research exposure: She suggests a systematic clinical (case) study. This is followed by a few brief suggestions for empirical study in relation to the roles of various etiological pathways and variables.

Part II, "Generic Treatments," includes five chapters that describe brief treatments drawn from approaches designed to treat a variety of presenting problems but adapted to focus on those issues most often presented by traumatized clients. Each chapter discusses how the treatment approach emerged and was applied to the traumatized in sufficient detail to allow the practitioners to try it out with their clients. Also, there is sufficient detail to enable trialists and other researchers to devise the necessary treatment manual to test the efficacy of the approach with traumatized clients or research participants.

In Chapter 4, "Behavioral/Cognitive Approaches to Post-traumatic Stress," Lizabeth Roemer, Nicole T. Harrington, and David S. Riggs build on their earlier theory in Part I. Here they provide an overview of their behavioral/cognitive approach. The first section of the chapter focuses on the initial phase of treatment. This includes the initial assessment, monitoring of behavior, psychoeducation, and establishing a therapeutic relationship. This section is followed by separate sections on exposure-based, cognitive, and skills-training interventions as well as relapse prevention. Here the authors note the primary goals are establishing a therapeutic relationship, establishing safety, assessment of strengths and weaknesses, formulating a behavioral conceptualization, and sharing with the client the formulation and plan for treatment. The psychoeducational component of treatment is emphasized throughout the initial phases and reemphasized throughout therapy. The middle section of the chapter focuses on specific intervention strategies, including exposure-based methods such as Direct Therapeutic Exposure (DTE), adding an in vivo element to exposure, and a discussion of the cognitive elements of adjustment and cognitive therapy generally. This section also discusses skills training. The latter section of the chapter focuses on the later stages of treatment, including relapse prevention and termination.

In Chapter 5, "The Use of Narrative Therapy with Couples Affected by Anxiety Disorders," Neil C. Headman provides an overview of the narrative approach and illustrates how it can be helpful for anyone with an anxiety disorder including, but not limited to, those caused by trauma. The first section of the chapter discusses the presenting problem of anxiety disorders then notes the common treatment approaches. Much of the chapter focuses on describing, justifying, and illustrating the use of the narrative therapy approach with anxious clients. The author points out that, unlike many traditional therapies, narrative therapy is not held up as a talking cure but as a therapeutic relationship. That is, the therapist and client work together to create more beneficial and preferred ways of knowing and being, particularly with regard to their perceived anxiety problems. He notes that this approach is designed to help clients free themselves from the demeaning and constrictive discourses prevalent in culture/society and to help them realize new and preferred ways of being. After discussing the basic assumptions of the approach, the author presents the assessment and treatment procedures and provides many illustrations in explaining and applying the approach with clients. The author admits there is little evidence of effectiveness of this approach but hopes that this chapter will lead to further studies that investigate its effectiveness. The final section provides an illustration of the application of narrative therapy in a case where parents were originally concerned about their daughter. The author illustrates that narrative therapy is a useful approach for externalizing the problem from the client and his/her relationship(s); decreasing interpersonal conflict and eliminating the need for blame; counteracting problem-induced, self-defeating beliefs clients have about themselves and others; opening the way for mutual respect and communication between partners/family members and uniting them against the problem; freeing individuals, couples, and families from limiting cultural discourses; and opening space for clients to construct new self-knowledge and ways of interaction.

Chapter 6, "Using Thought Field Therapy to Help Survivors of Destructive Cults" by Monica Pignotti, focuses on an extremely challenging group of clients. Survivors of destructive cults report a number of symptoms resulting from the aftereffects of traumatic experiences of physical, sexual, emotional, mental, and spiritual abuse, which include: depression, anxiety, panic attacks, flashbacks, nightmares, guilt, self-blame, anger, shame, humiliation, and a variety of other distressing emotions. The author explains that current approaches are helpful but limited. They are limited to educating the person about the cult experience and giving the survivor coping strategies for dealing with the emotional distress. Yet, symptoms often last at least 24 months after the person leaves the cult and sometimes far longer. There appears to be no program that reports more immediate symptom relief. The author argues that Thought Field Therapy (TFT) is a revolutionary treatment for psychological problems of the traumatized, including those traumatized by cults. In contrast to conventional treatments for trauma, TFT does not require painful reliving of traumatic experiences, and offers real help for the emotional distress commonly experienced by the cult survivor. Most of the chapter describes the approach and explains what to do with various clinical presentations. The latter portion of the chapter includes a case illustration, a 30-year-old woman who had been a member of an Eastern guru cult for 10 years, from the ages of 18 to 28. The treatment helped her with her anxiety, anger, and other negative emotions. The length of the entire session was 40 minutes, although the actual time for each TFT treatment was approximately five minutes. The beauty of the approach is that the reader has enough guidance in this chapter to try TFT for him/herself.

Chapter 7, "Sensorimotor Approach to Processing Traumatic Memory," by Pat Ogden and Kekuni Minton, is the latest generic treatment approach applied to the traumatized. Traditional psychotherapy addresses the cognitive and emotional elements of trauma, but lacks techniques that work directly with the physiological elements, despite the fact that trauma profoundly affects the body and many symptoms of traumatized individuals are somatically based. Altered relationships among cognitive, emotional, and sensorimotor (body) levels of information processing are also found to be implicated in trauma symptoms. Sensorimotor Psychotherapy is a method that integrates sensorimotor processing with cognitive and emotional processing in the treatment of trauma. Unassimilated somatic responses evoked in trauma involving both arousal and defensive responses are shown to contribute to many PTSD symptoms and to be critical elements in the use of Sensorimotor Psychotherapy. By using the body (rather than cognition or emotion) as a primary entry point in processing trauma, Sensorimotor Psychotherapy directly treats the effects of trauma on the body, which in turn facilitates emotional and cognitive processing. This method is especially beneficial for clinicians working with dissociation, emotional reactivity or flat affect, frozen states or hyperarousal, and other PTSD symptoms. In this chapter, the authors discuss Sensorimotor Psychotherapy, emphasizing sensorimotor processing techniques that can be integrated with traditional approaches that treat these symptoms. Because therapists' ability to interactively regulate clients' dysregulated states and also to cultivate clients' self-awareness of inner body sensations is crucial to this approach, three sessions are described illustrating the clinical application of this method.

Chapter 8, "Eye Movement Desensitization and Reprocessing in the Treatment of Post-traumatic Stress Disorder" by Louise Maxfield, is a comprehensive description of EMDR, the most researched psychotherapy in the last 10 years. Maxfield explains that EMDR is "a comprehensive treatment protocol in which the client attends to emotionally disturbing material in short sequential doses while simultaneously focusing on an external stimulus (therapist-directed eye movements, hand-tapping, auditory tones)." She first provides an overview of how EMDR was developed and the current theoretical description of how and why it works with the traumatized. She suggests that EMDR works by linking elements of traumatic memories with adaptive information contained in other memory networks, leading to a cognitive shift. Perhaps the most important contribution of this chapter to the field is Maxfield's careful examination of the best 12 outcome studies of EMDR. The conclusions are impressive and consistent. The summary notes that EMDR with civilian research client/participants experienced a 70%–90% decrease in PTSD diagnosis after three to four EMDR sessions. Results were even more promising among client/participants who were traumatized in war and who experienced a 78% decrease in PTSD diagnosis after 12 sessions. This is especially promising since VA Medical Center treatment programs report far less significant decreases with the same population. Most of the chapter describes and discusses the classic eight phases of EMDR treatment process, for those not familiar with the EMDR protocol. The latter portion of the chapter includes several useful case illustrations of the application of EMDR in the treatment of PTSD.

Part III, "Trauma-Focused Treatments," includes seven chapters. In contrast to Part II, these chapters feature hybrid treatment approaches that were drawn from existing therapies and modified to work with a particular presenting problem. In Chapter 9, "The Use of Multi-sensory Trauma Processing to Treat Post-traumatic Stress Disorder in Law Enforcement Officers," Nancy Davis emphasizes how modern-day law enforcement is not only under considerable distress, but also under constant and considerable danger. Although facing and talking about one's distress and trauma is vital to recovery, law enforcement officers learn not to do so for a variety of reasons. They fear, for example, that they will be viewed as deficient in their performance and abilities; that they will risk defense attorneys having access to their disclosures and using them used against them at the trials of perpetrators they helped prosecute; that the culture of law enforcement disdains emotional responses of any type, other than aggression. Based on these assumptions, Davis developed and describes in this chapter an approach that does not rely on the expression of feelings to assess and treat law enforcement officers presenting with PTSD, after she first describes the current array of treatment programs for this population and problem. Most of the chapter includes a description of her Multi-sensory Trauma Processing (MTP) approach. She describes MTP as a short-term treatment technique designed to deal with many common problems that arise in more long-term therapeutic interventions. Eye Movement Desensitization and Reprocessing (EMDR) is a critical element of this therapy. MTP uses the alternating stimulation that is the foundation of EMDR; however, MTP simultaneously uses three alternating stimulations consisting of alternating sounds and tapping, as well as eye movement. Although it is unclear exactly how this alternating stimulation creates positive change, Davis describes two theories that most explain its efficacy. The adrenaline thesis suggests that during hyperstresses the memories of the incident become "frozen" or unprocessed in the right brain, particularly the hippocampus. This frozen memory apparently leads to the symptoms of PTSD. Alternating stimulation may enable both hemispheres of the brain to process the traumatic memory, moving it from being "stuck" to an appropriate memory of the past. The REM sleep theory suggests that bilateral stimulation, as with eye movements during REM sleep, is disturbed by hyperstress. By replicating what the brain does naturally in REM sleep, the natural ability of the brain to process a memory may be reactivated. Davis reviews and discusses the solutions to 19 separate problems in working with traumatized law enforcement officers. The latter section of the chapter describes a 17-step

MTP treatment protocol, starting with an assessment of the extent and severity of the officer's reactions to one or more traumatic events, along with an orientation about how the symptoms and events are linked. The final step is a follow-up to the treatment. This is followed by a case history example of Officer John Day.

In Chapter 10, "The Use of Neuro-Linguistic Programming and Emotionally-Focused Therapy with Divorcing Couples in Crisis," Jeanne M. Bertoli provides an interesting and potentially powerful combination of neoteric treatment approaches to helping traumatized couples in crisis. Hostility between parents has yet to be dealt with quickly and effectively in the traditional models of divorce therapy. This hostility often dominates those divorcing or recently divorced and interferes with parents making decisions that are in their children's best interest. A new model has been offered in this chapter. It combines Neuro-Linguistic Programming (NLP) and Emotionally-Focused Therapy (EFT) in an attempt first to replace the attachment to the ex-spouse (and thereby remove the emotional connection), and then to reengage ex-spouses to form new interactional patterns aligned with their new roles as co-parents. EFT, which is based on systems theory and attachment theory (each will be discussed below), has been shown to be effective in many empirical studies. NLP, although not as theoretically or empirically sound, is based on physiology and cognitive processes, and offers hundreds of cases of anecdotal evidence of effectiveness. The Bertoli model is based on both systems and attachment theories, which are described briefly. After discussing the traditional approaches to divorce therapy, especially psychoeducational models, solution-focused models, the Bloom-Feshback divorce therapy model, and Gottman's approach to treating conflictual couples, she describes the NLP-EFT model. She describes it as a way of offering divorcing couples a process by which they might create a new, more superficial level of attachment that is safe. Upon completion of NLP, EFT focuses on reworking the dynamics of the interactions between the parents. The goal is to have parents communicate the underlying meanings rather than the specifics of any problem, thereby allowing for more positive interactions. For example, an ex-husband might be encouraged to tell his ex-wife that he is scared that if she remarries the children will not need him anymore, rather than insisting that it is inappropriate for her to bring men into her home in front of their children. This combination of therapies deals effectively with the emotions and restructuring necessary for functional post-divorce relationships. Studies must be conducted to show the effectiveness of these treatments together. The final section of the chapter uses the case of Tim and Sue to illustrate Bertoli's divorce therapy model.

In Chapter 11, "A Brief Multiple Family Group Model for Juvenile First Offenders," William H. Quinn, David J. VanDyke, and Sean T. Kurth note that most juvenile offenders have been traumatized and that this must be considered in any effective treatment approach. In contrast to most of the other treatment approaches for the traumatized, this chapter discusses not only family therapy but group treatment of families with children being treated stemming from being first offenders. The first section of the chapter describes their Multiple Family Group Therapy Model and a rationale for using this approach on juvenile offenders. Among other reasons, the authors argue that group work can create a caring and accountable community that can cut through the defensiveness of both children and parents in the presence of others like them. Moreover, the authors note that families who thrive in their treatment program are often disempowered and marginalized. They had become distrustful of the educational and legal systems and found little use for mental health professionals. Much of the chapter focuses on their Family Solutions Program (FSP) approach. As the name implies, they mobilize families to help their children, the juvenile offenders, "find solutions that will assist them in preventing repeat criminal offenses and achieving personal and family well-being." The program is 10 sessions (most often once a week) with the objectives of reducing juvenile crime, encouraging parental involvement and responsibility; increasing parenting skills that value the child and place parents in control; increasing youth's life skills in making decisions and acting responsibly; utilizing and building on families' strength and resources; increasing family communication skills; and increasing good school performance. The latter portion of the chapter includes an interesting case study of a family with a mother and her 14-year-old son, who was referred to the FSP for assaulting another child at school. The authors conclude that the program appears to be cost-effective. They report that the recidivism rate for first-time youth offenders who complete the FSP is only 20% lower than a control group.

In Chapter 12, "Traumatic Incident Reduction," Pamela Vest Valentine describes Traumatic Incident Reduction (TIR) as a brief, memory-based, therapist-directed, client-respectful intervention that has been empirically proven to reduce symptoms of depression, anxiety, and PTSD. She and others have found TIR to be effective in both the increase of self-efficacy and the reduction of depression, anxiety, and PTSD. In contrast to existing brief treatments, TIR sessions are open-ended. Once the procedure begins, it will continue until desensitization (elimination of the distressing trauma symptoms). Valentine also notes that TIR is highly structured and replaceable. Instead of the traditional dialogue between client and therapist, TIR uses a script consisting of both questions and directions. Valentine notes that TIR's theoretical foundation rests primarily in an understanding of cognitive and catharsis theories. However, she also discusses the hologram theory of traumatic experiences: Memories, emotions, and decisions might be "frequency-specific" to the state the brain was in when the incident occurred. What is vital, however, is that the client is guided to focus on the new decision, not just reliving the event or the supportive qualities of the therapist. After reviewing the existing empirical support for TIR, Valentine presents a detailed case example: Nancy, a 41-year-old Latino-American woman. In addition to illustrating the TIR protocol, the case illustrates what TIR clients often feel following treatment: A sense of ownership of and responsibility for the improvement.

In Chapter 13, "Interventions for Couples with Post-traumatic Stress Disorder," Victoria Tichenor, Keith Armstrong, Vickie Vann, and Robert-Jay Green begin with a case study of a couple seeking treatment, Martin and Marie. The authors point out that the case is an example of the challenges that exist in working with families struggling with PTSD. The authors collaborate to treat families of war veterans with combat-related trauma. After discussing what is known about how trauma affects systems like families and setting the stage for couple therapy, they describe their treatment approach. The Beginning Stages include setting the ground rules for the couple (e.g., confidentiality, restrictions against violence), and establishing the goals, conducting the assessment, and agreeing on the treatment plan. After the treatment plan the team focuses on psychoeducation, the use of homework, and other activities. The Middle Stage of Therapy, according to the authors, can be rather straightforward, such as increasing some behavior that already exists (e.g., spending more enjoyable time together). The authors discuss various blocks to achieving the goal (e.g., maladaptive interaction patterns) including, for example, teaching new ways of communicating. Talking about the trauma, and the role of feeling safe and feeling alone or distant in the process are discussed by the authors. They also discuss the importance of coordinating the therapeutic systems, such as the involvement of other health care providers, and if, when, and how to refer clients to other professionals. Finally, they discuss the Ending Stage of Therapy, specifically, getting stuck and unstuck with clients. The latter part of the chapter is an orientation to the reader in understanding how PTSD is manifested within a couple relationship. Specifically, they discuss intrusions, avoidance, and arousal and provide very useful case illustrations for each.

In Chapter 14, "Crisis Debriefings for Emergency Service Workers," Cheryl Regehr and John A. Hill focus on the challenges of emergency service work and their approach to helping these professionals process especially stressful work experiences. Emergency responders have long been aware of the stresses they experience as a result of encountering trauma, death, and life-threatening situations. Traditionally, however, acknowledging symptoms of distress has been viewed as evidence of a personality deficit or inadequate skills to perform in the job. More recently, research has highlighted traumatic reactions in workers which span emotional, physical, and cognitive areas of functioning. In response to concerns about the mental health implications of exposure to work-related trauma, the Crisis Debriefing model has arisen as an early intervention strategy designed to mitigate stress reactions. Utilizing a brief group treatment approach, this model aims to normalize reactions to events; it allows for ventilation of feelings and enhances the natural support system within the organization. After providing an overview of emergency service worker trauma, the chapter reviews the current, traditional treatment approaches, particularly those used in Canada. The majority of the chapter is devoted to a description of the Crisis Debriefing model with its roots in early crisis intervention theory. The latter section of the chapter focuses on a useful case illustration: Debriefing of police officers responding to a locked psychiatric admissions unit when a male patient who was acutely psychotic became violent and aggressive toward staff. The authors conclude by addressing the recent criticisms of the Crisis Debriefing model. They acknowledge the fact that debriefing does not protect individuals from post-traumatic stress reactions. Indeed, left to poorly trained professionals, such a powerful intervention may exacerbate severe symptoms in a few individuals. The authors, therefore, remind the reader that crisis intervention by definition cannot and should not deal with severe emotional distress. The authors note that "while the intervention is effective in increasing the sense of support that workers feel and enhancing mutual aid, it must be seen as part of a more comprehensive organizational plan that includes an enlightened and supportive work environment and individual assistance for workers experiencing extreme levels of distress."

In Chapter 15, "The Rewind Technique in the Treatment of Post-traumatic Stress Disorder," David C. Muss describes and justifies a rapid method of eliminating the symptoms of PTSD. The Rewind Technique is based on Visual-Kinesthetic Dissociation (VKD), a Neuro-Linguistic Programming technique devised to treat phobias. (See Chapter 6 for a more detailed description of VKD.) Muss, a physician, began to experiment with the technique with the local police force, reporting subsequently a two-year follow-up of no relapses in 19 police officers treated for PTSD. He named the technique the Rewind Technique because it accurately described the essence of the treatment. The author first discusses the benefits of this approach (e.g., how draining talk therapy is for the therapist working exclusively with the traumatized) and how it is also more client-friendly. "The beauty of the Rewind Technique is that it is the client that goes through all the details of the horrific event in his or her mind, usually in just one session in a couple of minutes." Much of the chapter includes a description of the exact protocol with the traumatized, including emergency workers. He starts by explaining what it will *not* do.

Collectively, these chapters provide direction for practitioners working with the traumatized. For too long the traumatized have given up on conventional psychotherapy. This book enables practitioners to select the best treatments for their particular clients, drawn from approaches originally designed for non-traumatized clients. This book provides critical and new ways of helping the traumatized by informing practitioners of ways to apply existing treatment approaches to meet their special needs. The traumatized may find relief from their traumatic symptoms, but, more than that, the treatment approaches have the potential for saving lives, saving marriages, and enabling the traumatized to draw on their experiences and their recovery as a source of inspiration rather than distress.

Part I

Theoretical Overview

Chapter 1

Theory-Driven and Research-Informed Brief Treatments

Charles R. Figley

> The stress of war tries men as no other test they have encountered in civilian life. Like a crucial experiment, it exposes the underlying physiological and psychological mechanisms of the human being. (Grinker & Speigel, 1945, p. ix)

What are the physiological and psychological mechanisms for detecting, responding to, and recovering from highly stressful events? Although the last five years have seen remarkable progress, this fundamental question still eludes traumatologists today. Yet these and other theory-driven questions in the quest to understand the fundamental nature of being traumatized and becoming untraumatized should guide the field. The chapters in this book focus on briefer ways of enabling the traumatized to overcome the especially debilitating, unwanted consequences of their traumatic experiences. The intention of this chapter is to discuss the importance of theory and evidence in the development of brief treatments of the traumatized.

TRAUMATOLOGY

Traumatology, originally called *traumatic stress studies*, refers to both the investigation and application of knowledge about the immediate and long-term consequences of highly stressful events and the factors that affect those consequences (Figley, 1989). The area emerged from a sub-area of medicine (now described as *trauma surgery*) (Donovan, 1991). The application of the term evolved to incorporate a much wider field that includes, but is not limited to, the traumatology of medicine, dentistry, and nursing. Traumatology now incorporates also traumatic stress studies, thanatology, victimology, disaster studies, rape trauma/sexual assault trauma studies, holocaust survivor studies, and many others (Donovan, 1991; Figley, 1988).

This field emerged over the last 20 years, yet its origin can be traced to the earliest medical writings that discussed the symptoms and treatment of hysteria (Veith, 1965). Indeed, theories and explanations of traumatic stress symptoms are found throughout history. Ellenberger (1970), for example, noted that symptoms such as flashbacks, dissociation, and startle responses were variously viewed as acts of God, the gods, the devil, and various types of spirits. One of the most important innovations, though, was the work done at La Salpetriere Hospital in Paris. There, Jean-Martain Charcot was the first to demonstrate that hysteria had psychological origins (Trimble, 1981).

In the literature that has emerged since the third edition of the *Diagnostic and Statistical Manual of Mental Disorders* (American Psychiatric Association, 1980) was introduced, most traumatology contributions have been in the area of clinical practice. As with most fields, traumatology is composed of a body of scientific knowledge that is based on research, careful observation, and guided by theory. As will be noted in the next section, the latter has received much less attention than the other elements that make up the literature of traumatology.

This volume presents a collection of treatment approaches that appear to be worthy of attention by traumatologists and other professionals who work with the traumatized, because the approaches attempt to provide the most efficient and brief treatment. Being efficient and brief is vital in the mental health marketplace today. The role of managed care and the demand for cost-effectiveness have acquired enormous power, and will likely continue to govern how the majority of health and mental health practitioners practice. What constitutes *sufficient evidence* to assure the public and the managed care industry that a particular treatment is efficient and worth the cost? In the immediate absence of such evidence, are there extenuating circumstances that could render some treatment approaches exempt from such evidence, at least on an experimental basis, until sufficient evidence accrues?

The central tenet of this chapter is that *brief treatments that enable the traumatized to become desensitized (non-anxious) to their traumatic experiences, without any apparent side effects, deserve the attention of practitioners to the extent that they pass the theory test.* The theory test refers to the determination that the treatment approach utilizes active ingredients that have heretofore been scientifically validated. As a result, these treatments are theoretically validated.

THE VITALITY OF THEORY-INFORMED BRIEF TREATMENTS

The scientific method can be conceptualized as a process in which the cycle of creating, testing, revising, retesting, and then reformulating theories is repeated over and over again. The job of scientists is to posit theories of the underlying processes that both account for and find expression in observed events. This is as true for Einstein's theory of relativity (Cassirer, 1923) as it is for the emerging field of traumatology (Figley, 1989).

The first step in constructing a theory is to determine the phenomenon for which it is to account. Throughout this book the authors attempt to offer strategies for helping the traumatized change and become symptom free. In contrast to pure practitioners,[1] traumatology scientists are concerned with understanding, among other things, "the underlying physiological and psychological mechanisms" of the traumatized human being; traumatologists also study the more complicated social and systemic mechanisms that both affect and are affected by trauma.

To do this, these scientists develop theoretical constructs, identify relations among the constructs, and note the connections between the constructs and potentially observable events representing the mechanisms noted earlier. The theory is a representational model of an unseen reality posited to underlie and account for observed events. A theory of the traumatization process, for example, should suggest how the theoretical constructs and potentially observable events are to be measured.

Looking at Both Negative and Positive Consequences of Trauma

Unfortunately, the field of traumatology evolved based primarily on observable events that were largely limited to the negative consequences of trauma. A majority of research has focused on clinical symptoms, most often PTSD symptoms. Yet, there is an emerging force in the professional literature that emphasizes strength-based assessment and treatment approaches—Seligman's *Learned Optimism* (1998). The antonym is learned helplessness (Petersen, Maier, & Seligman, 1995). Thus, the "underlying mechanisms" should account for how people thrive from potentially traumatizing experiences. The field should be able to account for why some people, under certain conditions (both internal and external to the person and her or his social network), respond immediately and in the long term to traumatizing experiences. Moving away from a pathological, medical model is a natural consequence of building a theory of the underlying mechanisms of trauma.

Results Follow Theory or Beauty Is in the Eye of the Beholder

At the same time, the theory you choose should dictate the way you interpret your results—be they research or clinical results. A recent series of reports on the effectiveness of treating clients with chronic, long-term PTSD concluded that the treatments were ineffective. Based on his review of these reports, Shalev (1997), among other things, pointed out that the reports *"reflect shortcomings in the theory of traumatization and PTSD"* (p. 422; emphasis added). He asserted that if our theories focus exclusively on dysfunctional healing we will not learn about normal healing. If our theory does not differentiate among stages of PTSD, we will not look for them in our research; our assessments will not be comprehensive. If our theory views reactions to traumatic events as hierarchical, rehabilitative, then that is how our treatments will be structured. If our theory expects major changes in "recovery," our treatments will fail if they are unable to affect such changes. If our theory is based on processing the past, then the treatment will ignore the future. Therefore, we must use a critical eye in investigating the "theory behind the treatment approach."

Theoretical Models and Schools of Thought

Throughout this volume, authors of innovative treatment approaches discuss either or both theory and research support for their particular approach. Most often there is a school of thought or representational model of the unseen reality of trauma and the traumatization process that is assumed, but unstated.

Ruth Leys (2000) provides a brilliant genealogical analysis of the concept of trauma and argues that there are two rival models that help explain why people do or do not suffer from a trauma-induced problem. Leys suggests that the Mimetic Theory camp embraces the notion of trauma, or the "experience of the traumatized subject," and can be understood as involving a kind of hypnotic imitation or identification. Precisely because the victim cannot recall the original traumatogenic event, she or he is compelled to act it out or in other ways imitate it. "The experience is an affront to common norms and expectations, shatters or disables the victim's cognitive and perceptual capacities so that the experience never becomes part of the ordinary memory system" (p. 298). The Mimetics would also argue that those who can remember are several steps toward recovery, though the process of recovery is long and difficult. Part of the challenge is "working through" the trauma in order to change their thoughts, feelings, emotions, and social relationships in ways that are not "obsessed" by the trauma.

Thus, the *Mimesis School* of thought argues that trauma and trauma reactions exists; that to eliminate the former requires desensitization or unlearning the relationship between the symptoms and the traumatic experience that caused them. In contrast, the *Antimimesis* proponents argue that without attending to the root causes of these symptoms, eliminating them will only lead to other symptoms that represent the basic disharmony.

Leys (2000) notes that Mimesis-informed therapy is a matter of changing the client's "simulation." She suggests that treatment success occurs when the link is eliminated between reminders of the event and unwanted emotions and behaviors, and then in replacing disturbing and self-defeating self-talk with more constructive and resilient self-statements. Yet, eliminating the pain of remembering sometimes leaves emptiness and confusion about how to put one's life back together with a new "simulation." Therefore, what is vital is developing a theory for the entire trauma induction, reduction, and recovery process. Chapter 4 in this volume, on behavior/cognitive therapy, is an illustration of Mimesis-informed therapy. Other illustrations in this volume are found in Chapters 12 and 14.

The *Antimimesis School*, according to Professor Leys, includes those who do not believe that trauma or traumatic reactions exist and therefore find far more data that support the lack of existence of trauma and traumatic reactions than the existence thereof. Members of this school argue that the symptoms viewed by some as traumatic stress reactions are in actuality a far more complicated system of causes. The Antimimesis thesis holds that traumatic events can and may cause either positive, negative, or neutral (no) consequences. Similarly, persons who view themselves as victims of a traumatic event may change their minds about their victimhood over time. Indeed, a person may display the symptoms of PTSD yet may never have experienced a traumatic event, and may or may not believe that his or her current predicament is a direct result of the event. The Antimimesis thesis suggests open mindedness about both the cause and the consequences of what is viewed by the Mimesis School as "trauma reactions."

Practitioners who adopt a more Antimimesis Theory believe that the traumatic event and its apparent consequences in the presenting problem are only a starting point. Bonanno (1998), for example, challenges the value of both mourning and especially the role of "grief work." He argues that the research shows very clearly that a considerable number of people do better avoiding grief work and, rather, use avoidance to help control the dosage of emotionally draining traumatic stress. Bonanno describes the grief work assumption as a summary heuristic for contemporary beliefs about the importance of working through thoughts and emotions associated with loss. Yet, he points out that there is considerable discrepancy between what is known about the bereavement process and what grief therapists do. For example, practitioners' maladaptive bereavement tests are often signs of good coping (e.g., avoidance of negative material, the use of denial). Bonanno asserts that the few empirical studies that test the (Mimesis thesis) assumption of "working through" (i.e., grief work) fail to demonstrate support. In contrast, working from another theoretical perspective, Bonanno's own program of research focusing on the factors that appear to help or hinder the loss accommodation of a large group of widows living in the San Francisco area, found that any event can be stressful to the extent that it overwhelms the person and strains one's stress management abilities. Sometimes avoidance is the best strategy. Humor, benign distractions, companionship, and other methods of stress management are often more important than being encouraged to talk about the loss.

Shalev (1997) notes that at times our naive views (read theories) may blind us to the reality that some clients get better and some do not. Exploring and understanding trauma, looking backwards, was the way toward healing its consequences. This is what he calls the "explorative-reconstructive therapy" (think Mimesis thesis) and those therapies that do not focus on exploration and reconstruction (non-Mimesis thesis). The latter adopt meaning propositions that "distort the rules of the psyche (or destroy the brain, or the hippocampus, or other memory systems)" (p. 420). Reactions according to the Antimimesis thesis would include symptoms that are iconic or procedural and *not conditioned*. They would support therapies that would *avoid* remembering and reliving because it is not a matter of (or even possible to provide an) explanation, but rather management and containment of the anxiety and fear.[2]

Another example of an Antimimesis School of thought is from family systems theory and used by "systems-informed" practitioners. Distress and stress indicators are also important. However, they assert that it is a systemic effect, not just one originating with a traumatic event. They most often look for distress in relationships that are linked to the dynamics of the family or other system. Rather than focusing on the traumatized, they assume that the entire family system is traumatized in some ways and, collectively, its members are enacting what they need to do in order to feel safe, connected, bonded, and loved by others for their own protection and well-being.

Proponents do not conceptualize prior sexual abuse as the genesis of the couple's presenting problem, but rather as an important piece to the couple's complex systemic puzzle. Other examples of the Antimimesis School of thought adopted by more systems-oriented practitioners also can be found in this volume (see Chapter 11).

By way of contrast, Chapter 13, though focusing on couples, illustrates the Mimesis School. Here the authors assume that the couple will not be able to fully recover from their difficulties until the traumatized partner can work through her or his trauma experiences with some kind of desensitization procedure.

Energy Psychology is another example of the non-Mimesis School within traumatology. It focuses on the imbalances within the energy system that can be caused by a trauma or memory of a trauma. This new subspecialty in psychology is part of a larger field of energy studies that includes energy medicine and energy nursing, and of other fields that include acupuncture and other treatment models (Figley, 1998a). The fact that a person is obsessed by a traumatic event means little to those who practice in this field. What is important is understanding how and where energy is stored and how to release it. Examples of Energy Psychology can be found in Chapters 6 and 15 in this volume, which focus on Thought Field Therapy; Chapter 10, which describes a Neuro-Linguistic Programming technique known as Visual-Kinesthetic Dissociation (VKD); Chapter 15, on the Rewind Technique; and Chapter 7, on the sensorimotor approach. Each focuses primarily on the presenting symptoms as a guide to eliminating them without assuming that "working through" the trauma is necessary through talk therapy.

Speaking theoretically, therefore, it appears to be possible to provide relief from the symptoms of trauma by focusing either on the original trauma and working it through, by focusing on the energy of the presenting symptoms, or focusing on the relationship system that maintains the symptoms. What, then, is the active ingredient in all of these approaches that may account for their effectiveness, irrespective of the theories that drive and direct them?

Desensitization and the Reciprocal Inhibition Hypothesis

Most practitioners from the Mimesis School agree that desensitization, the elimination of the conditioned trauma response (e.g., most PTSD symptoms), is a major goal in trauma treatment. Wolpe (1958) was one of the first to offer a hypothesis regarding the desensitization process. In 1952, Wolpe noted that Pavlov's[3] contribution to psychology, among other things, was the idea that neurosis is learned and not a result of a damage, disruption, or conflict.[4]

Inspired by Pavlov,[5] Wolpe (1958) reported the results of a series of experiments in South Africa. It was an effort to challenge the prevailing view (psychoanalysis) that relief from anxiety can come only through a careful analysis of family dynamics. Wolpe attempted to test an alternative hypothesis: "successful treatment of the neuroses must also depend upon the learning process." This classic program of research provided support for the hypothesis that learning is the active ingredient in dramatic change involving the reduction of unwanted subjective distress and other symptoms.[6]

Wolpe (1958) states his general principle in the following hypothesis:

If a response antagonistic to anxiety can be made to occur in the presence of anxiety-evoking stimuli so that it is accompanied by a complete or partial suppression of the anxiety responses, the bond between these stimuli and the anxiety responses will be weakened. (p. 71)

Applied to the traumatized, the hypothesis could be stated as follows: If a response antagonistic (e.g., low SUDs due to laughter, sex, or some other relaxation method) to the traumatic stress reaction (as measured by at least three physiological metrics) can be made to occur in the presence of anxiety-evoking stimuli (reminders of the traumatic event) so that it is accompanied by a complete or partial suppression (for a particular minimum amount of time that a SUDs reading is 0) of the traumatic stress responses, the bond between the trauma and the traumatic stress reactions will be weakened (p. 71).

Thus, if eating (especially when one is hungry) when one is feeling anxiety acts to inhibit the anxiety (i.e., reduces stress), food therapy would be the logical approach to the treatment of anxiety. Indeed, for some people, food is therapeutic in terms of self-soothing.[7] Unfortunately, there are heavy (weight) consequences.

Instead of using food with humans, Wolpe turned to alternative techniques that would, he hoped, be as self-soothing as food and still serve as a "natural antagonist" to anxiety. The one most preferred was the Jacobson (1938) relaxation method. Wolpe would train clients to use this relaxation method in combination with anxiety-provoking thoughts or other cues at a "dosage" (degree of distress) the client could comfortably tolerate. The dosage was increased until the client completely overcame any and all anxiety associated with the cause of the anxiety. This is now called the "desensitization" process.

Wolpe (1958) discovered the essence of distress and some simple ways of eliminating it. He suggested more than 45 years ago that what can be learned can be unlearned/relearned. Wolpe explained his rather elaborate theory or "neurophysiological view" as follows. He believed that there are anatomical relations among behaviors, such as those associated with fear and pleasure. Wolpe spent considerable space in his book describing the neural connections that are associated with learning and unlearning reactions. Regarding the latter, he noted extinction as a conditioned inhibition associated with fatigue (reactive inhibition). Of greater importance, however, was his introduction of the concept of reciprocal inhibition.

Wolpe noted that the application of this reciprocal inhibition to clinical settings is contingent on two issues: the utilization of an anxiety antagonist (e.g., food), and a clinical setting acceptable to the clients. He argued that the most effective anxiety antagonists would most likely be among those evoking parasympathetic activation of the autonomic nervous system. The first three anxiety antagonists were assertive responses, sexual responses, and relaxation responses. The latter became the most useful in clinical settings with clients seeking relief from anxiety disorders.[8] The other two responses, however, deserve empirical investigations. If the hypothesis is correct and the client can be trained in assertiveness, for example, the client's anxiety about social settings can be weakened as a result of such training.

This Reciprocal Inhibition Hypothesis predicts that if, after traumatization (or sensitization) (i.e., the learning of the association between the traumatic event and subjective feelings of distress), the person breaks the association (desensitization), then there is no distress. This is spontaneous reciprocal inhibition or, as Wolpe called it "a conditioned inhibition, a 'permanent' weakening of the connection between the originally learned cure and its response" (Wolpe, 1958, pp. 30–31).

Eliminating the anxiety response or energy in this way goes a long way in enabling the client to recover. Being less distressed and reactive enables the client not only to remember more effectively but also to think more clearly about his or her goals—both in therapy and in life generally.

Thus, all the traumatized are stuck with the consequences of their learning to fear the trauma until they can feel relaxed while facing the fear-causing trauma reminders. Some become more relaxed as a result of talking about the trauma; some become more relaxed by not talking or even thinking about it. Some find a way to laugh about or find inspiration in their trauma and, therefore, the bond between the reminder and the fear response is weakened. What about the treatment approaches described in this book?

Chapter 2 in this volume provides the contemporary and much more fully developed view of Wolpe's thesis. Roemer, Riggs, and Harrington offer a "behavioral/cognitive" perspective on post-traumatic stress reactions. They point out that frequently, clinicians develop a treatment plan that is little more than a series of clinical techniques, devoid of a systematic theory or theory-based protocol. The authors attempt to supply the theory for behavior therapy appropriate for working with the traumatized. Specifically, they focus on the theoretical foundations of behavior therapy and behavioral conceptualizations of post-traumatic stress in order to introduce readers to the concepts that underlie behavior therapy for trauma survivors. They argue that behavioral/cognitive theories of post-traumatic stress provide a useful foundation and guide for a range of therapeutic interventions, including but not limited to those traditionally considered cognitive or behavioral.

CONCLUSION

What are the physiological and psychological mechanisms for detecting, responding to, and recovering from highly stressful events? In this chapter I have attempted to show that it depends on your focus, your school of thought, and the active ingredients in recovering from highly stressful events.

Traumatology is a new field with ancient roots, a body of literature, and a set of theoretical perspectives. The central tenet of this chapter is that theory matters and eliminating the distress (desensitization) is the sine qua non for treating the traumatized. The theory test is the extent to which one's theory actually explains and predicts desensitization.

If we agree that most theories of the trauma are either Mimesis or Antimimesis by their core set of assumptions, it is an important factor in determining which treatment is best for which client under what circumstances. For those who adopt the Mimesis thesis, the mechanisms are tied to learning theory and how stress reactions are learned, can be maintained, and can be unlearned. Wolpe (1958) understood the process of desensitization and his reciprocal inhibition hypothesis has been largely supported through more than half a century of investigation. Therefore, those approaches that combine exposure to the stressful event with a heavy dosage of relaxation (activating the parasympathetic nervous system) are theoretically validated. Most of the brief treatment approaches described in this book draw on this mechanism, among others.

Those who adopt the Antimimesis thesis apply an alternative approach. They regard the same symptoms others would label as "traumatic stress reactions" as a perturbation of the system that is maintained by more complex factors than trauma in origin. The strategy, therefore, is to enable the client to address those systemic, interpersonal, and/or intrapsychic dynamics that require the "traumatic stress reactions" symptoms to either represent or maintain these dynamics. The symptoms will be permanently eliminated when these fundamental dynamics change.

It is not possible to know which thesis prevails because no data exist that have compared these competing models. This is due in part to the challenges of measurement. Future generations of clinical investigators should have fun attempting to find common ground in determining a fair and appropriate metric; one that is not limited simply to symptoms but which attends to the enormously complex biophysiological and sociological contexts of traumatization.

NOTES

1. This excludes, of course, those who adopt the Bolder Model of clinical psychology, or other scientist-practitioner hybrid professionals in mental health professions.

2. Neurobiological studies represent an important exception, though even brain scans results were linked to clinical symptoms (e.g., van der Kolk, Burbridge, & Suzuki, 1997).

3. Pavlov's discovery of conditioning principles ushered in the age of behavior

therapy that started in the 1950s and continues today. He discovered and confirmed that neurotic behavior can be created and eliminated by virtue of conditioning. It was discovered that dogs' salivation could be counter-conditioned.

4. Today we know that it is both. Yet, when one is changed the other diminishes in importance.

5. Wolpe (1952) was the first to effectively apply Pavlov's method. However, Mowrer (1939) postulated that fear and avoidance was maintained by a two-stage process and applied to phobias and other anxiety disorders. As later elaborated (Mowrer, 1947), fear is provoked both by the direct cause (stressors that should cause fight or flight) and associated cause (conditioned stimulus or stressor). An example would be an ambulance or some other warning device; and any and all things one associates with danger, that are inadvertently linked, such as "triggers" of our troubling memories). This is called classical conditioning.

6. Sherrington (1947, pp. 83–107) first introduced the term "reciprocal inhibition." Sherrington's work (e.g., 1906) on the nervous system was well-known to medical students and research physicians during the period of time that Wolpe was studying anxiety reduction. He found Sherrington's idea of inhibition of one spinal reflex by another, such as occurs when stimulation of an ipsilateral afferent nerve causes relaxation of a vastocrureus muscle contracting to a contralateral stimulus. He chose to expand the application to all "situations in which the elicitation of one response appears to bring about a decrement in the strength of evocation of a simultaneous response" (Wolpe, 1958, p. 29). Wolpe also credited Hilgard and Marquis (1940, pp. 108–114) with the finding that enabling new habits to develop in the same general situation often eliminates habits; and Wendt (1936) is credited with his finding that temporary reciprocal inhibition of an activity caused a permanently weakened strength of reaction. Wendt and others convinced Wolpe that there was a "competition between reactions" (Wolpe, 1958, p. 29) as the basis for this occurrence. Yet, he sought to describe the mechanism accounting for it.

7. *Why Do I Eat When I'm Not Hungry?* (Callahan, 1991) illustrates this well, suggesting that many people overeat in an effort to reduce their anxiety.

8. The RIH is an explanation for the weakening of old responses by new ones. Wendt (1936) first recognized this. However, he did not suggest a permanently weakened strength of the fear reaction. This historic contribution came from Wolpe (1958). He asserted that it is the process of *unlearning* through reciprocal inhibition.

REFERENCES

American Psychiatric Association. (1980). *Diagnostic and statistical manual of mental disorders* (DSM-III) (3rd ed.). Washington, DC: Author.

Beck, A. T. (1984). Cognitive approaches to stress. In C. Lehrere & R. L. Woolfold (Eds.), *Clinical guide to stress management* (pp. 37–51). New York: Guilford Press.

Bonanno, G. A. (1998). Emotional dissociation, self-deception, and adaptation to loss. In C. R. Figley (Ed.), *The traumatology of grieving: conceptual, theoretical, and treatment foundations* (pp. 98–108). Philadelphia: Brunner/Mazel.

Callahan, R., with Perry, P. (1991). *Why do I eat when I'm not hungry?* New York: Doubleday.

Cassirer, E. (1923). *Substance and function and Einstein's theory of relativity*. New York: Dover.

Donovan, D. (1991). Traumatology: A field whose time has come. *Journal of Traumatic Stress, 4*(3), 433–436.

Ellenberger, H. F. (1970). *The discovery of the unconscious: History and evolution of dynamic psychiatry*. New York: Basic Books.

Figley, C. R. (1978). Introduction. In C. R. Figley (Ed.), *Stress disorders among Vietnam veterans: Theory, research, and treatment* (pp. i–xi). New York: Brunner/Mazel.

Figley, C. R. (1988). Toward a field of traumatic stress studies. *Journal of Traumatic Stress, 1*(1), 3–11.

Figley, C. R. (1989). *Helping traumatized families*. San Francisco: Jossey-Bass.

Figley, C. R. (1998a). Editorial Note. In F. Gallo., *Energy psychology: Explorations at the interface of energy, cognition, behavior, and health* (pp. vii–viii). Delray Beach, FL: St. Lucie Press.

Figley, C. R. (1998b). Psychological debriefing, troubled children, and homophobia: toward a multidisciplinary, multidimensional field of traumatology. *Traumatology* [online], 4(2). http://www.fsu.edu/~trauma/art4v4i2.htm.

Figley, C. R. (2001). Origins of traumatology and prospects for the future, Part I. *Journal of Trauma Practice, 1*(1), 5–10.

Gallo, F. (1998). *Energy psychology: Explorations at the interface of energy, cognition, behavior, and health*. Delray Beach, FL: CRC Press.

Gallo, F. (2000). *Energy diagnostics and treatment*. New York: W. W. Norton.

Grinker, R. P., & Spiegel, J. P. (1945). *Men under stress*. Philadelphia: Blakiston.

Hilgard, E. R., & Marquis, D. G. (1940). *Conditioning and learning*. New York: Appleton.

Jacobson, E. (1938). *Progressive relaxation*. Chicago: University of Chicago Press.

Jacobson, E. (1940). Variation of pulse rate with skeletal muscle tension and relaxation. *Annals of Internal Medicine, 13*, 1619.

Lazarus, R. S., & Folkman, S. (1984). *Stress, appraisal, and coping*. New York: Springer.

Leys, R. (1994). Traumatic cures: Shell shock, Janet, and the question of memory. *Critical Inquiry, 20*(4), 221–235.

Leys, R. (2000). *Trauma, a genealogy*. Chicago: University of Chicago Press.

Meichenbaum, D., & Cameron, R. (1983). Stress inoculation training: Toward a general paradigm for training coping skills. In D. Meichenbaum & M. E. Jaremko (Eds.), *Stress reduction and prevention* (pp. 68–81). New York: Plenum.

Mowrer, O. H. (1939). A stimulus-response analysis of anxiety and its role as a reinforcing agent. *Psychological Review, 46*, 553–565.

Mowrer, O. H. (1947). On the dual nature of learning: A reinterpretation of "conditioning" and "problem-solving." *Harvard Educational Review, 17*, 102–150.

Petersen, C., Maier, S. F., & Seligman, M.E.P. (1995). *Learned helplessness: A theory for the age of personal control*. New York: Oxford University Press.

Seligman, E. (1998). *Learned optimism: How to change your mind & your life*. New York: Pocket Books.

Shalev, A. Y. (1997). Discussion: Treatment of prolonged posttraumatic stress disorder—Learning from experience. *Journal of Traumatic Stress*, 10(3), 415–422.

Sherrington, C. S. (1906). *Integrative action of the nervous system*. New Haven, CT: Yale University Press.

Sherrington, C. S. (1947). *The integrative action of the nervous system*. Cambridge: Cambridge University Press.

Trimble, M. R. (1981). *Post-traumatic neurosis: From railway spine to the whiplash*. Chichester: John Wiley & Sons.

van der Kolk, B., Burbridge, J., & Suzuki, J. (1997). The psychobiology of traumatic memory: Clinical implications of neuroimaging studies. *Annals of the New York Academy of Sciences*, 821, 99–113.

Veith, I. (1965). *Hysteria: The history of a disease*. Chicago: University of Chicago Press.

Wendt, G. R. (1936). An interpretation of inhibition of conditioned reflexes as competition between reaction systems. *Psychological Review*, 43, 258.

Wessler, R. L. (1982). Varieties of cognitions in the cognitively oriented psychotherapies. *Rational Living*, 17, 3–10.

Wolpe, J. (1948). *An approach to the problem of neurosis based on the conditioned response*. Unpublished Thesis, University of Witwatersrand, South Africa.

Wolpe, J. (1950). Need-reduction, drive-reduction, and reinforcement: A neurophysiological view. *Psychological Review*, 57, 19–23.

Wolpe, J. (1952). The formation of negative habits: A neurophysiological view. *Psychological Review*, 59, 290–299.

Wolpe, J. (1952b). Objective psychotherapy of the neuroses. *South African Medical Journal*, 26, 8–25.

Wolpe, J. (1958). *Psychotherapy by reciprocal inhibition*. Stanford, CA: Stanford University Press.

Wolpe, J. (1978). Cognition and causation in human behavior and its therapy. *American Psychologist*, 33, 437–446.

Wolpe, J., & Lazarus, A. A. (1966). *Behavior therapy techniques*. Oxford: Pergamon.

Chapter 2

Behavioral/Cognitive Approaches to Post-traumatic Stress: A Focus on Theory

Lizabeth Roemer, David S. Riggs,
and Nicole T. Harrington

Our goal in this chapter is to provide readers with an introduction to the clinical theory that characterizes a behavioral approach to the treatment of post-traumatic psychological sequelae. Clinicians unfamiliar with behavior therapy often view this approach inaccurately as a series of techniques to be applied atheoretically to people in distress. We will focus on the theoretical foundations of behavior therapy and behavioral conceptualizations of post-traumatic stress in order to introduce readers to the concepts that underlie behavior therapy for trauma survivors. In the course of this chapter, we hope that it will become apparent to the reader that behavioral/cognitive theories of post-traumatic stress provide a useful foundation and guide for a range of therapeutic interventions, not only those traditionally considered cognitive or behavioral. In a later chapter in this volume (Chapter 4), we will detail the specific techniques (derived from these conceptualizations) that have been found efficacious in treating the psychological sequelae of trauma. We will also illustrate how these procedures can be applied with care, empathy, and thoughtful flexibility so as to promote change in traumatized clients.

We intend these two chapters to be read together. We believe that much of the confusion over how to characterize behavior therapy has arisen because behavioral and cognitive techniques have been considered without attention to the theoretical foundations of these approaches. This separation may be partly due to behavior therapists' frequent use of manualized treatment protocols that fail to convey the complexity of behavior therapy. Such manualized treatment is beneficial in that it has allowed cognitive-behaviorists to establish empirical support for the efficacy of their treatments (support that is too often lacking in the mental health field). However, because they are devised for research purposes where standardization is essential, these manuals decrease the emphasis on individualized treatment plans that are critical to behavioral formulations (Goldfried & Davison, 1994). The advent of numerous trademarked protocols for the treatment of post-traumatic stress and other anxiety disorders that incorporate elements of a cognitive-behavioral approach but posit differing mechanisms of change further contributes to the confusion regarding what constitutes cognitive-behavioral treatment of a psychological disorder. Finally, the increasing characterization of interventions as purely cognitive, particularly in the popular press, which seems to depict "CBT" solely as rational thinking, or "how to think yourself to happiness," also contributes to misconceptions of cognitive-behavioral therapy. These characterizations inaccurately represent the cognitive element of behavioral approaches, and minimize what we feel is the crucial foundation of behavioral principles in cognitive-behavioral therapy.[1] We hope to correct these misperceptions here by focusing on what we consider to be the fundamental elements of behavioral approach to understanding the psychological sequelae of trauma.

In this chapter, we will present a description of the principles that guide our therapy with trauma survivors. We have chosen to reverse the usual naming convention (cognitive-behavioral) in our discussion in order to emphasize the primacy of behavioral principles in our approach. Behavioral approaches rest on the assumption that behavior is lawful and that one can specify its function through identifying relevant antecedent, organismic, and consequent conditions (Goldfried & Davison, 1994). The central task of therapy based in this theory, then, is to carefully assess the circumstances surrounding any given behavior, hypothesize the function(s) of this behavior, derive and implement interventions based on this functional evaluation, continually assess the effects of these interventions, and revise one's conceptualization and intervention strategies accordingly.

In the following pages, we first review some of the central concepts in behavioral/cognitive theory and then illustrate how these principles have been used to understand the psychological sequelae of traumatic exposure. In this chapter, and in Chapter 4, we include discussion of how behavioral theory can be applied to the range of post-traumatic difficulties clients experience, rather than limiting ourselves solely to symptoms of post-traumatic stress disorder (PTSD) (American Psychiatric Association, 1994). Finally, we will briefly discuss ways in which these principles and functional assessments can help to guide treatment. This link between behavioral principles and therapy will be discussed in more detail in Chapter 4.

CENTRAL TENETS OF BEHAVIOR THERAPY

The central tenet underlying behavioral therapy is that observed behavior is learned through the principles of classical and operant conditioning, modeling, and verbal information transfer; further, these principles may be used to modify or replace problematic behaviors.[2] A specific behavior can be understood as stimulus- or contingency-driven, or both. Stimulus-controlled behavior is thought to develop through classical conditioning, or association. When previously neutral stimuli are associated with emotionally meaningful stimuli (unconditioned stimuli), they often come to elicit similar emotional responses (and thus become conditioned stimuli). For instance, a Vietnam veteran who went through a terrifying firefight on a hot, muggy, rainy day might associate these environmental factors with the fear he felt at the time, and thus repeatedly experience fear on hot and muggy or rainy days. Such associations typically occur outside of conscious awareness so that these conditioned emotional responses are often experienced as unwarranted and surprising.[3] Once a response has been classically conditioned to a specific stimulus, additional stimuli may come to elicit similar responses through the mechanism of stimulus generalization. Stimulus generalization refers to the fact that stimuli that are similar to the originally conditioned stimulus will come to elicit similar responses (though perhaps of a lesser magnitude). So the Vietnam veteran might also come to experience fear in the shower or the boiler room, or any other hot or wet place.

Individuals also learn through operant conditioning based on the contingent consequences of their behavior. In this case, a behavior that results in a desired outcome (or the reduction of an undesired outcome) will be repeated and a behavior that results in an undesired outcome (or the reduction of a desired outcome) will be eliminated. Thus, a rape survivor who has a glass of wine following this horrifying experience might learn (again often without conscious awareness) from the ensuing reduction in distress she experiences to repeat this behavioral response (drinking) in times of distress. When desirable consequences follow a given response (or undesirable things are taken away) we are naturally inclined to repeat that response, even if rationally we are aware of long-term negative effects. Contingencies, particularly when they are strongly negative or positive, have a powerful influence on our behavior that can be hard to counteract rationally. These two relatively simple concepts interact in a variety of ways to produce patterns of behavior.

One potentially important distinction made in behavioral conceptualizations is between historical, etiological factors and current, maintaining factors for a given behavior. When developing treatments to encourage changes in behavior, it is important to recognize that the contingencies that may have led to the development of the behavior and those that serve to maintain it at the present time may be quite different. To bring about a change in current behavior usually requires an intervention aimed at addressing the maintaining factors. Take, for instance, a male client who does not display his emotions. We might learn that when he was a child he was consistently punished for any type of emotional expression. Although these contingencies are no longer present in adulthood, his behavior persists. This conceptualization of the historical factors for his current behavior may reduce his self-blame and help him see his behavior as a reasonable response in such conditions. However, those contingencies no longer account for this habit of emotional suppression. It becomes important to explore factors that contribute to the persistence of this behavior in adulthood. It may be that this emotional suppression is associated with a short-term decrease in distress that reinforces and perpetuates this style of responding. Further, the client may not have developed more effective means of affect regulation, so that to simply begin expressing his emotions would result in excessive emotionality and distress. These *maintaining* factors are of central importance in planning interventions aimed at this behavior.

Another layer of complexity in behavioral theory stems from evidence that individuals learn in ways other than direct experience. A series of studies has demonstrated that individuals learn through observing others (see Bandura, 1977, for a review). Observational learning appears to follow many of the same principles as direct learning. For example, studies have shown that individuals are more likely to exhibit a behavior if they have watched a model (another person) perform it and then receive a desirable consequence than if the model received an unwanted consequence (Bandura, 1965, 1977). Children who witness battering in their homes may learn that violence is a way of expressing anger, solving disagreements, or receiving subsequent affection. Individuals also learn from information that is communicated verbally by authority figures (e.g., a caregiver who says, "If you show your feelings you're not a real man!"). Once established, these verbal rules may persist even in the face of contradictory experience.[4] In addition to learning verbal rules, individuals learn to associate verbal material (spoken words or thoughts) with other stimuli or with consequences (i.e., through classical and operant conditioning). So words themselves can become associated with various emotions and verbal behavior is impacted by environmental contingencies. For instance, a girl might find that each time she says something self-deprecating she receives attention from her mother, and so may learn to self-deprecate more often and generalize the behavior so she thinks these thoughts even in the absence of external reinforcement.

Behaviorists agree that previous learning impacts subsequent learning. Based on learning history (including direct experience, observation, and verbal communication), individuals develop rules or expectancies regarding which stimuli are likely to co-occur and which contingencies are likely to follow particular responses. These expectancies then shape an individual's processing of information such that each person is more likely to attend to and remember information consistent with his or her expectations and ignore inconsistent information (e.g., Beck, Rush, Shaw, & Emery, 1979; McCann & Pearlman, 1990). In this way, one's current experience is shaped by what one has experienced, witnessed, or been told in the past. Thus, an individual who has had repeated experience with physical punishment preceded by anger might develop the expectancy that anger cues are a danger signal. This individual might attend closely to subtle facial and vocal indices of anger and ignore other stimuli that suggest safety. While this adaptation would be protective in an abusive situation, its generalization to other situations would likely result in an increased experience of interpersonal sensitivity, with elevated perceptions of others' anger, coupled with inattention to other interpersonal emotions. This would in fact intensify the perception that the world is a dangerous place.

A final important component of a behavioral conceptualization is recognition of potential behavioral deficits. An individual may have simply never learned how to exhibit a desirable behavior (Goldfried & Davison, 1994) or may be unable to enact a particular behavior in certain contexts. This can be a critical distinction to make in treatment. An individual who exhibits socially phobic behavior may not derive any benefit from extensive exposure to social situations (which would be a reasonable treatment from a classical conditioning conceptualization) if he or she does not know how to engage socially and cannot spontaneously exhibit these behaviors. Some form of skills training would be an essential ingredient of treatment for such a client.

A BEHAVIORAL/COGNITIVE CONCEPTUALIZATION OF POST-TRAUMATIC STRESS DISORDER AND ASSOCIATED DIFFICULTIES

Several behavioral/cognitive theories of PTSD have been proposed based on the concepts reviewed above. The reader is directed to these sources for a more comprehensive discussion of these theories (Chemtob, Roitblat, Hamada, Carlson, & Twentyman, 1988; Foa & Riggs, 1994; Foa, Steketee, & Rothbaum, 1989; Keane, Fairbank, Caddell, Zimering, & Bender, 1985; Litz & Keane, 1989). Here, we will only highlight the central elements in these conceptualizations, and touch on how behavioral principles can also be applied to those sequelae of traumatic exposure not encompassed in the diagnosis of PTSD as well.

Keane and his colleagues (1985) presented the first behaviorally based model of PTSD. This model used Mowrer's (1960) two-factor theory of fear development to account for the fear-based symptoms seen in PTSD (e.g., subjective fear, physiological arousal, avoidance). Briefly, during a trauma, individuals are classically conditioned to experience fear reactions to stimuli that were previously seen as neutral or positive (e.g., the combat veteran described earlier who comes to fear muggy, hot days). Keane and his colleagues also suggest that the intensity of the original conditioning experience (the trauma) leads to a broad generalization curve. That is, many stimuli that are similar to those that were originally associated with fear also come to elicit fearful responses. This principle of stimulus generalization helps account for the range of cues that evoke conditioned emotional responses among trauma survivors. For instance, strong reactions to the sound of gunfire might generalize to extreme reactions to a range of loud, unexpected noises. Higher order conditioning further contributes to the breadth of cues that elicit emotional responses. According to this behavioral principle, once a stimulus has been associated with a particular response (e.g., fear), it can function as an unconditioned stimulus to classically condition the response to other stimuli. For instance, a car backfiring, which serves as a conditioned stimulus in the example above, might occur in a given neighborhood, prompting a trauma survivor to become fearful of the neighborhood itself, or other sights, sounds, or smells that co-occur with the car backfiring.

Through classical conditioning and stimulus generalization, the trauma survivor may come to fear a wide range of situations and cues. The second component of Mowrer's theory focuses on the natural tendency to develop behaviors that avoid this conditioned fearful arousal. Behaviors that are successful at reducing fearful arousal are reinforced by the reduction in distress experienced by the individual (negative reinforcement). Thus, through the mechanisms of operant conditioning, the behaviors become more likely to reoccur in the future, leading to the extreme avoidance sometimes demonstrated by persons with PTSD. For instance, a woman who was raped in an elevator may experience extreme fear every time she approaches an elevator. If she turns and walks away from the elevator, she will experience immediate, welcome relief. This will increase the chances that she walks away from elevators in the future, or begins to avoid them altogether.

Many conditioned fears are short-lived because repeated exposure to conditioned stimuli in the absence of the unconditioned stimulus naturally leads to fear reduction. An individual may almost get hit by a moving bus, experience intense fear, and associate that fear with the bus. However, she will see many buses throughout the day that do not almost run her over, and the fear will decrease. When a previously neutral stimulus that has become associated with fear is presented repeatedly without the original fear-provoking stimulus, the fearful association diminishes (McAllister & McAllister, 1995). However, avoidance of the conditioned stimuli interferes with this process so that conditioned fear is maintained. In the example above, the woman who walks away from the elevator is not allowing herself to experience the elevator without an assault, so her fearful association with the elevator will not diminish. In fact, since she is likely to interpret her increased arousal in the presence of the elevator as confirmation of her fear, she only experiences corroboration of the danger she imagines. In this way, the avoidance associated with PTSD results in the maintenance of fearful responding to a range of cues. The avoidance component of this theory is central to the treatment strategies advocated for the fear-based symptoms of PTSD: A basic underlying principle of behavioral treatment of PTSD involves exposure to feared stimuli in order to diminish fear responses and eliminate threatening meanings.

Information/emotional processing theories of post-trauma reactions have expanded on this basic model by adopting network models of emotion to understand how fearful associations are maintained and how they can be altered. Foa and colleagues (1989) conceptualize PTSD using Lang's (1985) bioinformational model of emotions. In this model, information regarding associations between stimuli (e.g., sights, sounds, smells), responses (heart racing, palms sweating, running away), and meaning ("I'm going to die," "This is my fault") is stored in memory networks. Activation of one or more components increases the chances of activating associated components so that an increase in heart rate (e.g., from running upstairs) might lead to thoughts of death, thoughts of death might elicit recollections of traumatic images, and so on. Similar to the original behavioral conceptualization, stimulus generalization and higher-order conditioning broaden this associative network. This spread of activation may also occur through the meaning element: Stimuli that were once associated with safety meanings are likely to be present during a traumatic event, so their meaning elements will be altered to signaling danger. By association, other safety cues will similarly come to be reconstrued as danger cues. For example, a woman raped in her home (a place typically associated with a feeling of safety) may find herself afraid in numerous situations that used to feel safe (e.g., her place of work, her friends' homes, her car) because the meaning of these situations has changed from safety to dangerousness. Thus, traumatic exposure may result in a broad associative network that is easily activated by a range of stimuli, responses, and meanings.[5]

Based on extensive research on the mechanisms of exposure therapy in the anxiety disorders, Foa and Kozak (1986) propose that successful processing occurs when the memory network is fully activated (stimulus, response, and meaning elements are accessed and arousal is experienced) and new information is incorporated into the network (e.g., no negative outcomes occur; the individual experiences the safety of the therapeutic relationship rather than the danger of the traumatic event). Avoidance will reduce the chances that this network is sufficiently activated for new (nonthreatening) meanings to be incorporated; therapy must therefore target and reduce even subtle forms of avoidance.

Information-processing theorists have postulated that these trauma-related fear networks influence survivors' perceptions of their current experiences. Because these networks include salient danger and vulnerability meaning elements, they contribute to a tendency to experience the world as threatening. A host of empirical studies demonstrate clinically relevant individual differences in attention to and recall of emotionally salient information (see Litz & Keane, 1989; Mathews, 1990; Williams, Mathews, & MacLeod, 1996, for reviews). A person's expectations, predictions, and beliefs about what is likely to happen in the world, or to him or herself in particular, shapes what he or she attends to, recalls, and interprets from ambiguous situations. An individual who has experienced a traumatic event may be shaped by this event to expect, predict, and perceive threat and danger, more than a non-trauma-exposed individual. These ways of perceiving (schemas) then shape the experiences of this individual so that future learning may confirm perceptions of danger and vulnerability. A therapist must recognize and take into consideration these information-processing biases during treatment.

Behavioral or cognitive/behavioral theories of PTSD have tended to focus on the fear-related aspects of the disorder. However, many of the same principles may be used to account for many other symptoms of the disorder as well as co-morbid problems that are typically not conceptualized as part of the disorder itself. For example, it is often the case that the intense emotional reactions of persons who have been traumatized extend beyond feelings of fear to include other negatively valenced emotions such as anger, shame, guilt, and sadness. Behavioral models of PTSD account for these reactions in much the same way as conditioned fear reactions. That is, the principles of classical conditioning can work to associate stimuli present at the time of the trauma with any emotions experienced at that time. The processes of stimulus generalization and higher-order conditioning will operate to lead these emotional overreactions to occur in response to a wide range of environmental stimuli. As with fear, individuals also may engage in a variety of behaviors that serve to avoid the distress associated with these other emotional responses, but interfere with long-term successful processing of these reactions that would reduce their intensity (Rachman, 1980). For instance, a trauma survivor might experience anger in response to many trauma-related cues, but suppress these feelings and avoid these cues so that the anger is never sufficiently experienced, understood, and diminished.

Paradoxically, in addition to these kinds of excessive emotional responses, trauma survivors also experience deficits in emotional responding in certain situations. These emotional deficits, termed "emotional numbing," have historically been less well understood in the traumatic stress literature (see Litz, 1992, for a review). In general, behaviorally oriented theorists have conceptualized these deficits as an avoidance strategy aimed at reducing distress resulting from the cued emotional reactions that form the core of PTSD (Keane et al., 1985). However, many additional hypotheses have been proposed: Emotional numbing may be biologically mediated (van der Kolk, 1996); it may be comparable to freezing behavior observed among animals exposed to uncontrollable aversive stimulation (Foa, Zin-

barg, & Rothbaum, 1992); it may be a by-product of diminished atten-
tional resources due to hyper-responsivity to threat cues (Litz, 1992); it
may be a result of intentional suppression of emotional responses (Litz,
1992); and/or it may stem from skills deficits in emotional awareness and
regulation[6] (Linehan, 1993). In all likelihood, these deficits are multiply
determined, and the experience of emotional numbing is varied across individuals. While some survivors may experience emotions but choose not
to express them, others may experience undifferentiated arousal but be
unable to label and process it, whereas still others may not experience any
arousal at all when they feel "numb." For any given client, it is important
to assess these distinctions, as each possibility would have different implications for treatment.

Other problems associated with PTSD have been conceptualized as
avoidance-motivated behaviors. For example, alcohol and drug use are
thought to reduce the occurrence of intrusive thoughts and nightmares and
to limit the emotional distress associated with these symptoms when they
do occur. As with other avoidance behaviors, if the use of alcohol or drugs
proves useful in reducing distress, the behavior will be enacted more frequently. In some cases this will lead to diagnosable substance-use disorders
concurrent with the PTSD (see Ruzek, Polusny, & Abueg, 1998, for a more
in-depth discussion of co-morbid substance abuse). A similar conceptualization has been proposed to explain dissociative behavior among trauma
survivors (Wagner & Linehan, 1998). This model suggests that individuals
may develop a habit of dissociating that is negatively reinforced by the
reduced distress that accompanies it, leading to increased frequency of dissociation.

In behavioral models of trauma reactions, careful assessment is advocated in order to determine the exact nature of the relationship between
co-morbid disorders and PTSD. Often, disorders emerge as a direct result
of trauma-related symptomatology. For instance, individuals who have suffered with PTSD for some time may find themselves feeling hopeless and
helpless as a result of the seemingly uncontrollable, persistent distress they
experience. These feelings can be compounded by the trauma-related tendency to view the world as dangerous and themselves as vulnerable. Hopelessness may be further heightened by the environmental consequences of
post-traumatic symptomatology: Often, symptoms result in lost jobs and
ended or strained relationships. These stressful life events, coupled with
feelings of hopelessness and helplessness, set the stage for depression, which
is so often co-morbid with PTSD. On the other hand, recent data suggest
that depression may, in some cases, represent an alternative to PTSD as a
response to trauma (Shalev et al., 1998). It may be that individuals who
experience trauma primarily as a loss, with its associated sadness, develop
depression, while those individuals who experience the trauma as a threat
with a great deal of fear would be more likely to develop PTSD. The prev-

alent emotion experienced at the time of, or directly following, the event is likely to become more pervasive due to higher-order conditioning and stimulus generalization, and therefore might become characteristic of a subsequent disorder if one emerges.

Co-morbid anxiety disorders may also emerge as a result of PTSD symptomatology. Progressively increasing avoidance of a range of stimuli, along with a newly developed belief that the world is dangerous, may result in such marked avoidance of a range of situations that a co-morbid diagnosis of agoraphobia is warranted. Similarly, traumatic exposure is often followed by a host of negative social experiences (e.g., homecoming for Vietnam veterans, victim-blaming following disclosure of sexual assault) that may set the stage for the development of social phobia, as social cues become conditioned stimuli to be avoided (Orsillo, 1997). Alternatively, the heightened conditioned emotional responses among trauma survivors may take the form of full-blown panic attacks. This panic can come to serve as a conditioned stimulus itself, so that the experience of panic triggers traumatic associations, which heighten fear and exacerbate panic reactions (Resnick, 1997). In each of these cases, the functional association between various symptoms will help determine the appropriate sequencing of targets for intervention as well as when to consider concurrent treatments. For example, panic attacks may interfere with trauma-focused treatment because the experience of trauma-related distress may be a cue for a panic attack, resulting in avoidance of the emotional engagement needed for trauma-focused treatment. Thus, in some cases, treating the panic first, perhaps through interoceptive exposure, may be necessary (Falsetti, 1997). In other cases, however, such physical sensations might be overwhelmingly strong trauma cues, so that treatment of panic might need to take place after exposure treatment focused on the trauma itself, in order to reduce the strength of those associations.

Other difficulties that often present among individuals with PTSD have been conceptualized within the behavioral framework as skill deficits. For example, individuals with PTSD often experience difficulties in interaction with others. These problems have typically been seen as reflecting an inability to utilize appropriate social skills. It is not clear, however, whether this deficit represents a general deficit in the learning of skills (which may be particularly likely among those raised in a traumatic or invalidating environment), the loss (or disuse) of skills that were learned previously, or the inability to use skills when confronted with situations that are associated with emotional arousal similar to the trauma. As noted above, emotional dysregulation may also be due, in part, to deficits in the ability to identify, communicate, and regulate emotional reactions. It seems likely that within the large number of individuals with PTSD, individual cases of apparent skill deficits reflect any or all of these models.

As is apparent from the discussion above, trauma-related psychological difficulties are likely to be multiply determined. Specific factors (such as social skills or emotional deficits) may serve as both risk factors for the development of PTSD and consequences of the disorder. Clinicians should conduct a careful assessment of PTSD symptoms as well as of the associated features, and develop a conceptualization that considers these various functional relationships.

We have presented a brief overview of behavioral/cognitive theories as they can be applied to understanding trauma-related psychological difficulties. This overview provides a framework in which to conceptualize the diverse clinical presentations that characterize trauma survivors. In Chapter 4, we outline the key elements of therapy that emerge from this conceptual basis and have received empirical support.

NOTES

Preparation of this chapter was supported in part by National Institute of Mental Health Grant MH59044 to the first author. We wish to thank Carolyn Pepper and Amy Wagner for their helpful comments on an earlier draft of this manuscript.

1. Empirical studies support our view that behavioral elements are an essential, active ingredient in cognitive-behavioral treatments (e.g., Feske & Chambless, 1995; Jacobson et al., 1996).

2. This is not to negate biological or genetic influences on behavior; behaviorists acknowledge temperamental factors and include them as one component of the organismic variables they consider in case conceptualization. However, the therapy described here focuses on environmental factors as targets for intervention.

3. See Rescorla (1988) for a discussion of possible mechanisms underlying classical (Pavlovian) conditioning, which are beyond the scope of this discussion.

4. Hayes (1994) has argued that this persistence accounts for a majority of psychological difficulties, because rules interfere with new learning that would otherwise maximize adaptive behavior.

5. Foa and Riggs (1994) provide some suggestions for how to predict who will develop such elaborated fear structures and who will not, suggesting that individuals with rigid preexisting schemas regarding safety, self-worth, and meaning in the world will be most at risk for marked alterations in their associative networks/schemas.

6. Skills deficits may be particularly likely among those individuals who were raised in "invalidating" environments in which their emotional experiences were not acknowledged or were punished.

REFERENCES

American Psychiatric Association. (1994). *Diagnostic and statistical manual of mental disorders* (DSM-IV) (4th ed.). Washington, DC: Author.

Bandura, A. (1965). Influences of models' reinforcement contingencies on the acquisition of imitative responses. *Journal of Personality and Social Psychology, 1, 589–595.*

Bandura, A. (1977). *Social learning theory.* Englewood Cliffs, NJ: Prentice Hall.

Beck, A. T., Rush, A. J., Shaw, B. F., & Emery, G. (1979). *Cognitive therapy of depression.* New York: Guilford Press.

Chemtob, C., Roitblat, H., Hamada, R., Carlson, J., & Twentyman, C. (1988). A cognitive action theory of post-traumatic stress disorder. *Journal of Anxiety Disorders, 2,* 253–275.

Falsetti, S. A. (1997). Treatment of PTSD with comorbid panic attacks. *National Center for PTSD Clinical Quarterly, 7,* 46–48.

Feske, U., & Chambless, D. L. (1995). Cognitive-behavioral versus exposure only treatment for social phobia: A meta-analysis. *Behavior Therapy, 26,* 695–720.

Foa, E. B., & Kozak, M. J. (1986). Emotional processing of fear: Exposure to corrective information. *Psychological Bulletin, 99,* 20–35.

Foa, E. B., & Riggs, D. (1994). Posttraumatic stress disorder and rape. In R. S. Pynoos (Ed.), *Posttraumatic stress disorder: A clinical review* (pp. 133–163). Lutherville, MD: Sidran Press.

Foa, E. B., Steketee, G., & Rothbaum, B. (1989). Behavioral/cognitive conceptualizations of post-traumatic stress disorder. *Behavior Therapy, 20,* 155–176.

Foa, E. B., Zinbarg, R., & Rothbaum, B. O. (1992). Uncontrollability and unpredictability in post-traumatic stress disorder: An animal model. *Psychological Bulletin, 112,* 218–238.

Goldfried, M. R., & Davison, G. C. (1994). *Clinical behavior therapy* (2nd ed.). New York: John Wiley & Sons.

Hayes, S. C. (1994). Content, context, and types of psychological acceptance. In S. C. Hayes, N. S. Jacobson, V. M. Follette, & M. J. Dougher (Eds.), *Acceptance and change: Content and context in psychotherapy* (pp. 13–32). Reno, NV: Context Press.

Jacobson, N. S., Dobson, K. S., Truax, P. A., Addis, M. E., Koerner, K., Gollan, J. K., Gortner, E., & Prince, S. E. (1996). A component analysis of cognitive-behavioral treatment for depression. *Journal of Consulting and Clinical Psychology, 64,* 295–304.

Keane, T. M., Fairbank, J., Caddell, J., Zimering, R., & Bender, M. (1985). A behavioral approach to assessing and treating post-traumatic stress disorder in Vietnam veterans. In C. R. Figley (Ed.), *Trauma and its wake: The study and treatment of post-traumatic stress disorder* (pp. 257–294). New York: Brunner/Mazel.

Lang, P. J. (1985). The cognitive psychophysiology of emotion: Fear and anxiety. In A. H. Tuma & J. Maser (Eds.), *Anxiety and the anxiety disorders* (pp. 131–170). Hillsdale, NJ: Lawrence Erlbaum Associates.

Linehan, M. (1993). *Cognitive behavioral treatment of borderline personality disorder.* New York: Guilford Press.

Litz, B. T. (1992). Emotional numbing in combat-related post-traumatic stress disorder: A critical review and reformulation. *Clinical Psychology Review, 12,* 417–432.

Litz, B. T., & Keane, T. M. (1989). Information-processing in anxiety disorders: Application to the understanding of post-traumatic stress disorder. *Clinical Psychology Review, 9,* 243–257.

Mathews, A. (1990). Why worry? The cognitive function of anxiety. *Behaviour Research and Therapy, 28*, 455–468.

McAllister, W. R., & McAllister, D. E. (1995). Two factor-fear theory: Implications for understanding anxiety-based clinical phenomena. In W. O'Donahue & L. Krasner (Eds.), *Theories of behavior therapy: Exploring behavior change* (pp. 145–172). Washington, DC: American Psychological Association.

McCann, I. L., & Pearlman, L. A. (1990). *Psychological trauma and the adult survivor: Theory, therapy, and transformation.* New York: Brunner/Mazel.

Mowrer, O. H. (1960). *Learning theory and behavior.* New York: Wiley.

Orsillo, S. M. (1997). Social avoidance and PTSD: The role of comorbid social phobia. *National Center for PTSD Clinical Quarterly, 7*, 54–57.

Rachman, S. (1980). Emotional processing. *Behaviour Research and Therapy, 18*, 51–60.

Rescorla, R. A. (1988). Pavlovian conditioning: It's not what you think it is. *American Psychologist, 43*, 151–160.

Resnick, H. (1997). Acute panic reactions among rape victims: Implications for prevention of post-rape psychopathology. *National Center for PTSD Clinical Quarterly, 7*, 41–45.

Ruzek, J. I., Polusny, M. A., & Abueg, F. R. (1998). Assessment and treatment of concurrent posttraumatic stress disorder and substance abuse. In V. M. Follette, J. I. Ruzek, & F. R. Abueg (Eds.), *Cognitive-behavioral therapies for trauma* (pp. 226–255). New York: Guilford Press.

Shalev, A. Y., Freedman, S., Peri, T., Brandes, D., Sahar, T., Orr, S. P., & Pitman, R. K. (1998). Prospective study of posttraumatic stress disorder and depression following trauma. *American Journal of Psychiatry, 155*, 630–637.

van der Kolk, B. (1996). The body keeps the score: Approaches to the psychobiology of posttraumatic stress disorder. In B. A. van der Kolk, A. C. McFarlane, & L. Weisaeth (Eds.), *Traumatic stress: The overwhelming experience on mind, body, and society* (pp. 214–241). New York: Guilford Press.

Wagner, A. W., & Linehan, M. M. (1998). Dissociative behavior. In V. M. Follette, J. I. Ruzek, & F. R. Abueg (Eds.), *Cognitive-behavioral therapies for trauma* (pp. 191–225). New York: Guilford Press.

Williams, J. M., Mathews, A., & MacLeod, C. (1996).The emotional Stroop task and psychopathology. *Psychological Bulletin, 120*, 3–24.

Chapter 3

Active Ingredients in Trauma-Focused Brief Treatments

Anne M. Dietrich

Contemporary treatment approaches for Post-traumatic Stress Disorder (PTSD) include traditional approaches such as Cognitive-Behavioral therapy, Psychodynamic therapy, Group therapy, and Pharmacotherapy, as well as experimental approaches such as Body therapies (e.g., Sensorimotor Processing) (Ogden & Minton, in press) and other Asian-based approaches (often termed "Energy Therapies"). These approaches have varying degrees of data in support of their effectiveness, that range from anecdotal case reports to randomized and controlled studies (e.g., see Dietrich et al., 2000; Foa, Keane, & Friedman, 2000; Shalev, Bonne, & Eth, 1996; van der Kolk, McFarlane, & van der Hart, 1996).

Figley (chapter 1, this volume) states that desensitization (i.e., deconditioning the learned association between anxiety and a feared stimulus), through gradual exposure and reciprocal inhibition (RI), has received empirical support as an effective anxiety antagonist in the treatment of anxiety disorders. From this perspective, the learned response to the *original* feared stimulus (traumatic event) results in an anxiety or fear response that requires desensitization, as does the learned response that *maintains* the symptoms.

Note, however, that the view that desensitization and extinction involve unlearning the association between the conditioned stimulus and the unconditioned stimulus has been questioned. There is some evidence that emotional conditioning (e.g., involving the amygdala) is permanent, but can be modulated through contextual evaluation (e.g., see Bouton, 1994; Bouton & Schwartzentruber, 1991). Thus, although learning principles appear to be effective in the treatment of symptoms of PTSD (such as fear), it is not clear that the original emotional learning can be completely reversed.

GRADATED VERSUS PROLONGED EXPOSURE

In an early, well-controlled study, Brom, Kleber, and Defares (1989) found systematic desensitization (SD) to be effective for the treatment of PTSD. Rothbaum, Meadows, Resick, and Foy (2000) acknowledge the study by Brom et al., and also state that "although several studies have found that SD was effective in reducing posttrauma symptoms, the studies [other than that by Brom et al.] are not well controlled" (p. 75). Rothbaum et al. (2000) claim that, because prolonged exposure appears to result in better outcomes than shorter exposure and because relaxation during exposure does not contribute to treatment effectiveness, SD has fallen into disfavor.

Rothbaum et al. have not explicitly cited any empirical data in support of their assertion that relaxation *in combination* with gradual exposure fails to contribute to treatment effectiveness, however, and it is not clear as to how or why they have come to this conclusion. Moreover, they acknowledge that relaxation per se appears to have some "limited utility" for assisting clients with arousal (p. 79). One difficulty with prolonged exposure is that it is not well tolerated by some individuals (Rothbaum et al., 2000). For example, clinical data suggest that individuals with complex posttraumatic and dissociative disorders decompensate with prolonged exposure (e.g., Herman, 1992), and studies have also shown that direct exposure techniques result in deterioration for some proportion of clients (e.g., see Kilpatrick & Best, 1984; Litz, Blake, Gerardi, & Keane, 1990; Pitman et al., 1991; Pitman, Orr, Altman, & Longpre, 1996; Scott & Stradling, 1997; Vaughan & Tarrier, 1992; Watson, Tuorila, Detra, Gearhart, & Wiclkiewicz, 1995). Moreover, drop-out rates of participants with simple PTSD when using flooding and prolonged exposure techniques appear higher than with other approaches. Finally, empirical studies that compare prolonged exposure to other techniques frequently screen out those individuals with more complex forms of psychopathology. As such, prolonged exposure might be most effective with some proportion of traumatized people, and less appropriate for others.

As noted by Briere (in press), when exposure is too fast-paced with insufficient time to process the material, clients can easily become overwhelmed and resort to increased avoidance activities to modulate their distress. As such, they may utilize dissociation, cognitive avoidance, abuse of substances, and so on, and may drop out of treatment. In addition, effective treatment is believed to require information that is disparate from the original trauma (Briere, in press; Foa & Kozak, 1986). Disparate information includes the absence of danger, as well as positive components that are antithetical to danger (Briere, in press).

As such, the pacing that occurs with SD can function to prevent the excessive use of avoidance coping, whereas the relaxation response may provide disparate information from the original trauma (i.e., people are not in a relaxed state during a traumatic event). In relation to the latter, the relaxation or other disparate information, when repeatedly presented in conjunction with feared traumatic stimuli, acts in such a way that the original conditioned association is not reinforced (Briere, in press). Moreover, there is some evidence for the possible role of endogenous opioids with elicitation of opposite emotions (Solomon & Corbit, 1974). In other words, relaxation, although not sufficient in itself for the treatment of PTSD (Rothbaum et al., 2000), may not only help to attenuate arousal in response to exposure, but may function as positive information that is antithetical to the danger of the trauma.

Nijenhuis, Van der Hart, and Steele (Nijenhuis et al., in press; Steele et al., 2001) argue that recovery from PTSD and dissociative disorders involves the integration of traumatic memories, encoded and stored in a dissociative system metaphorically labeled the "Emotional Personality" (EP), into the "Apparently Normal Personality" (ANP), which has failed to perform this mental act. According to this theory, the EP is a psychobiological system dedicated to defense dedicated to bodily threat and life, and the ANP is a psychobiological system dedicated to fulfilling functions in daily life. Integration of the EP can be interfered with by excessive arousal during exposure, as well as by extreme lowering of the level of consciousness (e.g., entering trance states) of the ANP. If the ANP becomes overaroused during exposure to the traumatic memories, conditioned dissociative reactions can become reactivated. When the ANP engages in mentally avoiding the traumatic memory during exposure, exposure will be inhibited for that reason.

Therapy from this theory of structural dissociation involves concomitant activation of the dissociated traumatic memories and the ANP. Thus, exposure to these internal stimuli is required, as well as response prevention with respect to re-dissociation or mental avoidance that may hamper or block the effective exposure. Exposure is viewed as a means to an end (i.e., integration of dissociative systems), rather than as a therapeutic agent in itself. According to this theory, an ANP's fear and avoidance of traumatic memories maintains the dissociative organization of the personality, and the integration of dissociated material is key to recovery. It should be noted that not all individuals with simple PTSD are dissociative (Putnam et al., 1996), and thus this theory may not be applicable to all traumatized clients. With non-dissociative clients, painful memories may take the form of distinct cognitive schemata (such as in state-dependent memory), rather than as dissociated personality structures.

In summary, it is proposed that effective trauma treatment involves assisting clients to overcome their fear of trauma stimuli/memories and integrate them into their existing cognitive[1] schemas or structures. Gradual exposure/pacing allows clients to better tolerate the memories and affect, without the need for excessive cognitive avoidance or dissociation. The inclusion of disparate information (e.g., relaxation, safety, and so forth) and positive information assists the clients in modulating their memories such that the memories no longer have the power to elicit full-blown affective distress. That is, new information is integrated into memory, which might enable the individuals to modulate their distress more effectively through the use of contextual information that is discrepant from the original trauma. Readers may wish to keep these ideas in mind as they read through the various treatment chapters contained in this volumes.

In the next section, risk factors that are believed to contribute to the development of PTSD are summarized. It is suggested that, with an increase in the number of risk factors present for an individual client, active components of treatment may become increasingly more complex. Treatment interventions may thus need modification, depending on the nature of the risk factors present. Treatment outcome may similarly vary, depending on the presence, severity, and nature of various risk factors.

RISK FACTORS FOR PTSD: TREATMENT IMPLICATIONS

The construct of PTSD, as explicated by the *Diagnostic and Statistical Manual of Mental Disorders* (DSM-IV-TR) (American Psychiatric Association, 2000), includes two major etiological factors implicit in the diagnostic criteria. The first refers to the objective traumatic stressor event (Criterion A1), and the second refers to the subjective response of the individual to that objective event (Criterion A2). In the absence of an extreme stressor that involves, first,

actual or threatened death or serious injury, or other threat to one's physical integrity; or witnessing an event that involves death, injury, or a threat to the physical integrity of another person; or learning about unexpected or violent death, serious harm, or threat of death or injury experienced by a family member or other close associate (American Psychiatric Association, 2000, p. 463),

and second, the absence of the *specific* emotions of intense fear, helplessness, or horror, PTSD, by DSM-IV-TR definition, is not possible.

Research has shown, however, that some proportion of individuals appear to develop clinical symptoms of PTSD following normative life events (such as marital disruptions) (e.g., Burstein, 1985; Helzer, Robins, & McEvoy, 1987), leading some experts to question the wisdom of the A1 objective stressor criterion included in the DSM-IV. For example, Yehuda (2001), generalizing from Lazarus's (1990, 1993) notion of the role of subjective appraisal in *normal* coping, opines that weight should be given to subjectively distressing normative events, in the presence of risk factors, as etiological factors in *traumatic* coping or PTSD. That is, Yehuda appears to view stressful normative life events, in combination with certain risk factors, as etiologically sufficient for PTSD.

An alternative hypothesis, however, is that the risk factors in cases of low magnitude events are most predictive, not of a homogenous disorder of PTSD, but of preexisting disorder, or of another disorder that might mimic symptoms of PTSD (e.g., adjustment disorder, simple phobia). In this sense, symptoms or signs of other constructs (e.g., symptoms of depression, adjustment disorder, stress-induced phobias, complicated bereavement, dependent personality styles, etc.) are possibly being confounded with those of PTSD. These hypotheses require further empirical study. They also point to the importance of thorough assessment prior to treatment in the determination of treatment effectiveness. When clients who have experienced stressful normative events (and the absence of any trauma history) present for treatment with symptoms that resemble those of PTSD, practitioners should consider alternatives to PTSD as possible diagnoses. Desensitization techniques and trauma-specific techniques may still be appropriate for distress following normative events, however, depending on the specifics of the case and the symptoms in evidence.

The American Psychiatric Association (2000) discusses risk factors that affect the likelihood of developing PTSD:

The severity, duration, and proximity of an individual's exposure to the traumatic event are the most important factors affecting the likelihood of developing this disorder. There is some evidence that social supports, family history, childhood experiences, personality variables, and preexisting mental disorders may influence the development of Posttraumatic Stress Disorder. This disorder can develop in individuals without any predisposing conditions, particularly if the stressor is especially extreme. (p. 466)

Epidemiological studies (e.g., Kessler et al., 1999) have shown that event severity constitutes one of the most important risk factors for PTSD. The National Comorbidity Survey (as reported in Kessler et al., 1999) found that the risk of PTSD is highest for those male and female respondents who report rape, childhood physical abuse, and childhood neglect. Combat is also strongly related to PTSD for males (it should be noted that the effects of multiple traumas were not examined in this study).

McFarlane and de Girolamo (1996) note that traumatic stressors vary in terms of duration, severity of life threat, severity of injury, and loss of life and property, which may also function as risk factors for PTSD; however, there is little prospective research that looks at the role of these event factors in PTSD (McFarlane, 1999) and in dissociation (Ogawa, Sroufe, Weinfield, Carlson, & Egeland, B., 1997). According to Harvey and Yehuda (1999, p. 2), on the other hand, the finding that not all individuals develop PTSD after a severe traumatic event suggests "the failure to develop such symptoms is likely the result of subjective perceptions at the time of or subsequent to the event and not the impotence of the stressor."

According to Yehuda (1999a, p. xviii),

The dose–response relationship between severity of the trauma and the development of PTSD implies that vulnerability factors may be particularly important as one moves down along the spectrum of horror and catastrophe. Because there is a qualitative difference between being subjected to purposeful torture and being involved in a motor vehicle accident . . . vulnerability factors may be more relevant in the induction of PTSD in response to the latter (lower magnitude) trauma.

Thus, although the American Psychiatric Association, through the DSM-IV-TR diagnostic criteria, conceptualizes PTSD as a more or less learned response to a severe event that involves a subjective, affective component (which is partially borne out empirically by cross-sectional, epidemiological studies), empirical research has also suggested that the probability of occurrence is not only related to the severity, duration, and proximity of exposure (direct learning factors), but also to predisposing risk factors (Shalev, 1996; Yehuda, 1999a) that may or may not be learned, as well as to the type of traumatic event experienced (Davidson & Foa, 1991a; Kessler et al., 1999; McFarlane & de Girolamo, 1996). Moreover, not all individuals who are exposed to extreme stressful events develop PTSD (McFarlane & de Girolamo, 1996; Yehuda, 2001), which also appears to suggest that either (1) there is more involved in PTSD etiology than learning alone or (2) traumatic events can lead to PTSD or to other disorders (e.g., Dissociative Disorders, Mood Disorders, etc). The DSM-IV has included symptoms of other disorders in the "Associated Features" section to PTSD.

In practice, assessment of PTSD Criteria A1 (nature and severity of trauma) and A2 (subjective appraisal) during intake sessions can assist the clinician with treatment planning using brief treatments. Gathering data regarding the specifics of the event can assist the clinician in determining whether to utilize a simple exposure-based approach or a more phase-oriented treatment approach, and can assist the clinician when using traumatic memory exposure techniques. With regard to the latter, for example, if a client with simple PTSD uses avoidance due to fear of traumatic memories, the clinician can gently and carefully introduce specific details about the traumatic event to help trigger or elaborate on the client's memory (while carefully observing for and respecting the client's use of titration so as to not overwhelm the client) (see Briere, 1997a for a discussion on recognizing and working with clients' use of titration).

Similarly, thorough assessment of the client's subjective feelings and thoughts at the time of the event and after the event can assist the therapist with cognitive/affective reprocessing. For example, the therapist can gently challenge cognitive distortions that form during or following the trauma.

Moreover, the therapist can utilize information about the client's emotional state at the time of the trauma when doing desensitization (e.g., if the client reports intense helplessness, the therapist can monitor this during exposure, and provide or elicit discrepant information to assist in reprocessing and integration of the traumatic memory).

Traumatic Risk Factors. The following factors have been proposed as playing a role in the development of PTSD following exposure: Prior histories of other DSM disorders and gender (Kessler et al., 1999); genetic factors (McEwen, 2000; True et al., 1993; True & Lyons, 1999); family members who have PTSD or mood or anxiety disorders (Yehuda, 1999b); prior traumatization (Shalev, 1996); acute reactions at the time of the traumatic event, including the possible roles of peritraumatic dissociation, coping, and physiological stress reactions (McFarlane, 1999); biological alterations (Shalev, 1999; Yehuda, 1999b); neurocognitive factors (Orr & Pitman, 1999); impaired affect regulation or self-capacities (Briere, in press) and personality factors (Schnurr & Vielhauer, 1999).

Childhood maltreatment also constitutes a risk factor for the development of PTSD in response to a traumatic event (Briere, in press; Nijenhuis, van der Hart, & Kruger, submitted), which may be mediated by physiological sequelae following child maltreatment (e.g., see Glaser, 2000; Ito, et al., 1993; Ito, Teicher, Glod, & Ackerman, 1998; Putnam & Trickett, 1997; Teicher, Glod, Surrey, & Swett, 1993). That is, there is some evidence that child maltreatment results in physiological changes, which could increase the risk of exposure to traumatic stressors and/or developing PTSD in response to subsequent stressors.

During intake with new clients, it is suggested that therapists assess for risk factors and consider them as potential treatment targets or as factors that may affect treatment staging, progress, and outcome, as explicated later in this chapter (a checklist is provided for this purpose in Appendix A).

Reexamining PTSD Etiology

Harvey and Yehuda (1999) discuss diathesis-stress models of PTSD and other disorders. Diathesis-stress models posit that outcome is a function of an interaction between pre-dispositional (i.e., risk) factors (including, but not limited to, genetics[2]) and environmental factors. From this perspective, neither environmental factors (the traumatic event) nor pre-dispositional factors, in isolation, are sufficient for PTSD.

It would appear that there are several possible causal pathways leading to PTSD, each a function of variations in the type and severity of trauma and the degree to which risk and protective factors are present. Some possible pathways are depicted below.[3]

Low Magnitude Event and Low Risk Factors

With normative life events and low to moderate risk factors, it is hypothesized that the outcome would be temporary emotional distress that attenuates with time and/or supportive interventions. PTSD would not be an expected outcome.

Low Magnitude Event and High Risk Factors

With low magnitude events coupled with high risk factors, possible outcomes could be prolonged distress, adjustment disorder, complicated bereavement, phobia, single depressive episode, and so forth (depending on the specifics of the case), the symptoms of which could mimic PTSD.

High Magnitude Event and Low Risk Factors

With high magnitude events and low risk factors or high protective factors, an expected outcome might be distress with symptoms of acute PTSD or subclinical PTSD. In such situations, the distress and symptoms could attenuate with time and support, or might require some degree of exposure, desensitization, and/or cognitive processing (whether through formal treatment, or as a natural response to traumatic events) (e.g., Briere, in press).

High Magnitude Event and Moderate Risk Factors

In this scenario, an expected outcome could be simple to chronic PTSD, amenable to exposure and desensitization techniques and cognitive processing (e.g., CBT, EMDR, etc.). With more severe symptoms, other treatment modalities could be required, such as Dialectical Behavior Therapy (Linehan, 1993), Sensorimotor Processing (Ogden & Minton, in press), and so forth.

High Magnitude Event and High Risk Factors

When high magnitude events are coupled with high risk factors, the expected outcome could be severe and chronic PTSD, or complex PTSD (i.e., PTSD plus the associated features to PTSD). Interventions would consist of much stabilization and support prior to desensitization, and would likely involve other treatment modalities, such as interpersonal therapy, group treatment, skills training, body-focused treatments, and/or pharmacotherapy.

The Role of Risk Factors

The postulated pathways above are simplistic generalities in need of refinement (e.g., in terms of specific hypotheses regarding the interplay of relevant variables), and in need of empirical study. They also do not consider the type of trauma involved, or the explicit role of protective factors.

Risk factors may affect outcome in several ways. The actual outcomes of the above pathways are likely differentially determined, depending on properties of the stressor events, the risk factors present, the protective factors present, and the synergistic effects of their various possible combinations.

First, some risk factors can conceivably act to increase the probability that an individual is exposed to Criterion A1 (traumatic stressor) events (Kessler et al., 1999). For example, a child who has experienced emotional neglect may be at increased risk of interpersonal traumatization, such as extrafamilial sexual abuse. Similarly, women may be at higher risk of rape than men. A history of significant emotional neglect during childhood will in all probability complicate treatment. The client may have greater difficulty in feeling that she or he is worthy of self-care and/or care from others. Such clients may present with poor hygiene, lack of self-care, and a core belief of self as undeserving. She or he may have difficulty in trusting that the therapist is genuinely interested in his or her well-being. In such situations, the therapeutic relationship could require a significant amount of attention by the therapist, particularly during the early stages of treatment. Validation, support, empathy, and a non-judgmental stance on the part of the therapist can assist in the building of rapport and trust, and should be maintained over the duration of treatment. When the client is treated by the therapist in a respectful, validating manner, the client's schema of self as undeserving can begin to shift, which can assist the client in taking greater care to avoid possible re-traumatizing situations, even if she or he has a history of neglect or maltreatment. When clients present for brief treatments, an initial focus on assisting the clients in solidifying their sense of self as worthy of safety and care can set the stage for later trauma processing. Clients can take a break from treatment when desired, and can practice solidifying their gains in self-care and self-respect, in preparation for trauma treatment at a later date.

Second, as noted by McFarlane and deGirolamo (1996), the properties of the A1 Criterion (traumatic stressor) may function as risk factors that increase the probability of PTSD. For example, the severity of injury during a rape could determine the nature and degree of peritraumatic reactions, including the biological stress response (e.g., see Dietrich, 2000; McFarlane, 1999). With extended physical injury and stress, there may be excessive physiological dysregulation (McEwen, 2000). Stressors that result in significant tissue damage, therefore, could result in a longer latency to homeostatic baseline as the body attempts to recover (Dietrich, 2000). As noted by Yehuda (1999a), physiological alterations in response to traumatic stressor events may act to increase the risk of PTSD. With clients who have experienced physical injury at the time of the traumatic event, interventions relating to pain management and coping with loss might become an important treatment component. Adjunctive treatments, such as massage therapy, can also be recommended to clients. When there are significant immunological disruptions based in prior traumas (e.g., see Wilson et al., 1999), treatment interventions can be aimed, in part, at strengthening physical health.

Similarly, repeated occurrences of Criterion A1 events (frequency), the length of time exposed to the event(s) (duration), and the number of different traumatic events experienced, could also function to increase the risk of PTSD, independent of the nature of the subjective response. That is, the data at this point in time may not be conclusive that the events, per se, are insufficient to lead to PTSD. Although some studies have reported that experiencing the "same" trauma (e.g., the Holocaust) leads to differential response (i.e., some get PTSD, some do not) (e.g., Yehuda, 1999a), it is not clear that all Holocaust traumas, even when in the same camp, are objectively the same. The same would likely hold with traumas such as rape, combat, and so forth. One rape is not identical to another; one battle is not identical to another. As difficult as it may be to do so in a practical sense,[4] it is my view that well-designed study is needed that looks carefully at the stimulus properties of the event(s), while statistically controlling for the effects of subjective/risk factors.

Third, subjective factors, such as appraisal, may mediate between the event and outcome, affecting the response (Harvey & Yehuda, 1999). For example, appraising oneself as helpless in response to a traumatic event may lead to increased risk of PTSD, whereas an illusion or belief in control can lead to better outcome (van der Kolk, McFarlane, & Weisaeth, 1996). In this sense, risk factors may act on the subjective experience criterion (A2) of PTSD to mediate outcome. Treatment interventions that incorporate cognitive reframing or restructuring could be helpful. Adjunctive interventions such as self-defense courses can also increase a client's sense of power and control.

Risk factors could also conceivably affect subjective experience in a way that moderates outcome, by affecting the *experience* of the stimulus (traumatic event) properties. For example, McFarlane (1999, p. 176) posits "passive surrender, stoic acceptance, and cognitive-reframing are appropriate in situations where the stressor is uncontrollable." So, for example, a rescue worker who is removing bodies following a disaster might fare better if she or he (temporarily) cognitively reframes the bodies as something else (e.g., store mannequins). Although such reframing can assist individuals in coping with the immediacy of the trauma and enable them to function, clients may need to expose themselves to the actual memories if they are troubled by intrusions and other post-traumatic symptoms. The role of the therapist in this regard is to validate and normalize the coping response, while also gently challenging the client's cognitive framing of what happened. For example, if Joe continues to frame the bodies as mannequins for several months after the traumatic event, and experiences intrusive images of bodies with concomitant distress, it would be important to validate and empathize with Joe's experience, but also to expose him to the trauma so that he could integrate the dissociated emotional components into his conscious awareness, such as with the following intervention (when Joe is ready): "In order to get through that horror, you coped by viewing the bodies of those *people* as mannequins. You needed to do that to get through it. [Gently, softly:] I am wondering, Joe, how you feel when you look back and you see that those 'mannequins' are human beings."

Finally, risk and/or protective factors could conceivably affect outcome after a traumatic event, such as degree of tolerance of distress in response to memories of the event, openness to seeking treatment following a traumatic event, as well as to treatment responsiveness. For clients who have difficulties with tolerating the distress from traumatic memories, skills training (Linehan, 1993) can be advantageous in preparation for later processing. In addition, with chronic trauma (such as incest), normative healing processes (see Briere, in press) may be constantly impeded or interrupted because of repeated violations, resulting in increasing levels of avoidance over time becoming a habitual coping response. Avoidance as a habitual way of coping with trauma-related distress has important treatment implications. Skills training, such as teaching clients to practice mindfulness skills, emotional regulation, distress tolerance, and communication skills (Linehan, 1993), can assist clients with tolerating the painful trauma affect and thus reduce their tendencies toward avoidance coping.

ISSUES OF CLASSIFICATION: IMPLICATIONS FOR DIAGNOSIS AND TREATMENT

The DSM classifies PTSD as a homogenous anxiety disorder that is distinct from other disorders. However, empirical data concerning the presence of postulated risk factors, the heterogeneity of sequelae following traumatic events (e.g., see Dietrich & van der Kolk, in preparation), as well as the degree of symptom overlap among different diagnostic categories of the *Diagnostic and Statistical Manual of Mental Disorders* (DSM-IV-TR) (American Psychiatric Association, 2000),[5] raise the question of whether symptoms of psychological disorder vary as a function of variations in risk factors and trauma type. For example, do different risk factors function to (1) increase the probability of developing PTSD (Yehuda, 1999a), (2) increase the probability, depending on interactions with the type of trauma experienced, of different *types* of PTSD, or (3) determine the differential likelihood of different disorders (e.g., see Marshall et al., 2000; McEwen, 2000; Pelcovitz et al., 1996; Putnam, 1997, 2000), depending on the particular risk factors involved in a given case, regardless of the severity or type of stressful event?

Accurate assessment of what ails a given client assists the therapist in choosing a brief treatment approach that best suits the presenting needs and symptoms of the client, and also allows for informed determination of treatment effectiveness. For example, treatment of depression will have some similarities and some major differences relative to treatment of PTSD. Similarly, treatment of Complex PTSD (i.e., the associated features to PTSD) will differ in substantial ways from the treatment of simple PTSD.

For clients who suffer from PTSD and associated features, a treatment plan that involves treating the client in "brief treatment blocks" may be most suitable for stabilization and treatment of the complex symptoms. With such clients, phase-oriented treatment approaches are strongly recommended (e.g., see Chu, 1998; Herman, 1992). Such clients require safety and stabilization prior to confronting traumatic memories. Linehan's Dialectical Behavioral Therapy (DBT) skills training modules, provided to patients in "brief treatment blocks" with sufficient time between blocks to practice and reinforce the skills on their own, have therapeutic value for beginning phases of treatment. Some preliminary treatment outcome data (Prisman, Dietrich, & Shercliffe, 2000) on an intensive, time-limited treatment program using DBT principles showed that, of the 21 patients who were followed over four time periods (baseline and three follow-up periods), all showed reductions of symptoms on a variety of outcome measures, including the Crime-Related PTSD scale. With reductions in their symptoms and improvements in their coping and functioning, these clients are better equipped to engage in trauma work at a later period of time (i.e., during a later "brief treatment block").

According to Brett (1996) and Davidson and Foa (1991b), the DSM-IV Task Force was faced with the decision of whether to classify PTSD as an anxiety disorder, a dissociative disorder, or a stress disorder. The final decision, based only partially on empirical evidence, was to classify PTSD as an anxiety disorder. Some of the more substantive reasons for including PTSD as an anxiety disorder were the fact that PTSD involves symptoms of fear and avoidance; PTSD has similarities with panic disorder in terms of symptoms and patterns of autonomic arousal, response to yohimbine challenge, and corticotrophin-releasing factor; and many clients with simple PTSD respond to treatments that were originally developed for the treatment of anxiety (Davidson & Foa, 1991b). Davidson and Foa (1991b) opined that the empirical data favor PTSD as an anxiety disorder.

According to Brett (1996), arguments against classifying PTSD as an anxiety disorder in favor of classifying it as a stress disorder include the unanswered question of whether the arousal in PTSD is simply anxiety and whether it has the same physiological pathway as other anxiety disorders; the arousal and numbing phases of PTSD have similarities to processes of mourning and bereavement; and PTSD appears distinct from other anxiety disorders in terms of memory components (e.g., traumatic amnesia). PTSD also has similarities with dissociative disorders (Brett, 1996).

Brett (1996) argues that classification of PTSD as an anxiety disorder can narrow options in the following ways: Viewing PTSD as one syndrome can prevent study of other forms or variations of PTSD (p. 124); the diagnosis is restricted to essential features, with the concomitant risk of focusing treatment at only those essential features and failure to consider and treat the associated features to PTSD; and looking at PTSD at only one point in time may result in failure to notice and study fluctuations and variations of the disorder over time. Different treatment approaches may be required for different symptoms and at different points in time as the symptoms of the disorder fluctuate and vary. For example, child sexual abuse survivors may be relatively symptom-free until later normative events (e.g., they have a child of their own) trigger their earlier traumas. Thus, clinicians should remain aware that previously traumatized individuals can become symptomatic during or following normative life events (e.g., delayed PTSD).

Moreover, empirical studies that have looked at the risk factors for PTSD may not have sufficiently taken into account other important variables (such as type of trauma experienced) or the potential confounding effects of third variables. For example, studies may confound symptoms from other DSM constructs with symptoms of PTSD, such as through the failure to assess and rule out differential diagnoses. Thus, when looking at the effectiveness of one's treatment for a given disorder, it is important to correctly assess the problem from the start.

TREATMENT TARGETS

Simple PTSD

To the extent that core post-traumatic symptoms are learned responses to overwhelming events, exposure and desensitization/habituation and cognitive restructuring appear sufficient for symptom management. As noted by Briere (in press), desensitization of traumatic distress requires exposure to the trauma stimuli, activation of the conditioned emotional and cognitive response to the trauma, inclusion of disparate information, and cognitive-emotional reprocessing. It is not clear that complete amelioration of the symptoms will result (e.g., Bouton, 1994).

Briere (in press) holds that the intrusive and avoidant symptoms of PTSD represent natural healing processes in response to trauma. That is, he posits that intrusions reflect how the individual is attempting to process the traumatic experience, whereas avoidance is a natural attempt at titrating intense distress. In short, he views intrusions and avoidance as a natural, innate form of systematic desensitization.

Counter-conditioning techniques appear to effectively reduce post-traumatic symptoms of intrusions and hyperarousal. This is borne out by empirical evidence (Rothbaum et al., 2000). Techniques that have clients experientially return to their original traumas through various routes of guided, gradated exposure (e.g., titrated imaginal exposure), while simultaneously introducing information that is discrepant from the original trauma (e.g., the safety of the therapeutic setting; a relaxation response through muscle relaxation or laughter), assists clients in tolerating the affective distress from the trauma and thus facilitates their habituation to it.

It is less clear as to whether desensitization is key with regard to helping clients overcome their initial avoidance of traumatic memories (e.g., see van der Kolk, McFarlane, & van der Hart, 1996). There is some evidence (Brom, Kleber, & Defares, 1989) that dynamic psychotherapy is helpful for mastering avoidance, after which desensitization and cognitive restructuring can occur. Conversely, body-oriented approaches (Ogden & Minton, in press) can teach clients to feel safer in their bodies and to defend themselves against unwanted intrusions (Ogden & Minton, 2001). This sense of somatic safety can function to reduce tendencies toward subsequent avoidance. Somatic safety can also function as disparate information when the client is exposed to fearful stimuli. If clients engage in a high degree of avoidance when exposed to traumatic memories, desensitization will be precluded because the emotional and cognitive responses to the traumatic memory will be immediately shut down or will not be activated at all. With dissociative clients, avoidance is likely associated with a different dissociative system, that is, the system that has not integrated the traumatic memory. Thus, it seems that there may be parallel reactivity of two dissociative systems in such situations, which makes treatment more complex.

Chronic and Complex PTSD/Associated Features

Active ingredients involved in effective trauma treatments might become more complex as a function of the presence, nature, number, and role of various risk factors for a given client, as well as the type, severity, and numbers of traumatic events experienced. Moreover, if empirical evidence further supports the notion of PTSD as a stress disorder with particular physiological indices (e.g., cortisol irregularities) (Yehuda, 1999b), as well as the possibility that there are different types of PTSD and variations in course of the disorder over time, then other treatment ingredients are conceivably important. For example, there is some evidence to the effect that prolonged stress and/or trauma leads to hippocampal atrophy and thus impairs memory (e.g., see McEwen, 2000). As such, for clients who have memory impairments or who evidence other neurological disruptions, interventions may need to be modified to take into account cognitive processing deficits, and pharmacotherapy may be an important treatment component.

Thus, it is hypothesized that in more complex cases, treatment targets, and hence active ingredients, might depend on the nature of the event, the presence and severity of the particular risk factors in a given situation, and the particular form that the resultant symptoms take. Clearly, some of the risk factors (e.g., genetics, family history of disorder, gender,[6] intelligence, biological alterations, and temperament) are not amenable to treatment, or are less amenable to treatment than others. Treatment outcome may thus depend, in part, on the presence of these risk factors.

Some of the other identified risk factors appear to be more amenable to treatment. For example, certain pre-morbid or co-morbid disorders (e.g., substance abuse disorders) can be targets of treatment prior to desensitization of the trauma. When the risk factors consist of (presumed) temperamental factors (e.g., hyper-reactivity to stress) or associated features, safety and stabilization will be the initial focus of treatment, such as through skills training (Linehan, 1993), identification of feeling states (van der Kolk, McFarlane, & van der Hart, 1996), pharmacotherapy,[7] working with and desensitizing transference material (Briere, in press), and so forth.

To the extent that disruptions in early attachments lead to non-conscious and dysfunctional schemata of self, others, and relationships, and to the degree that they also constitute a risk factor for PTSD, the therapeutic relationship becomes a source of distress (through transference) that also requires desensitization. This may be particularly important when working with clients whose symptoms and schemata result in significant interpersonal disruptions (see Briere, in press, for a thorough discussion of this concept). Fostering the therapeutic alliance may be particularly challenging.

As noted by van der Kolk, McFarlane, and van der Hart (1996), treatment targets may need to vary at different stages of the client's life and at different phases of chronic PTSD, and may also need to vary as a function of the predominant symptoms that are currently expressed by the client.

SUMMARY AND CONCLUSIONS

In summary, it has been argued that exposure, desensitization, and cognitive-emotional processing are active mechanisms of therapeutic change for symptoms of PTSD. It is also argued that exposure, desensitization, and processing are key mechanisms for particularly chronic and complicated forms of PTSD and associated features; however, additional mechanisms of change are likely required for complete and successful treatment in the latter. Finally, for individuals who are severely traumatized and incapacitated by their symptoms, teaching symptom management skills in combination with medication might be the most that can be done, until current techniques are refined, further developed, and subjected to continual study.

To the degree that risk factors function to determine both the development of PTSD and recovery from trauma, it is plausible that targeting risk factors (when possible) may help both in the treatment of PTSD and in preventing recurrences of PTSD over time. This hypothesis is in need of clinical and empirical study.

Studies that have looked at risk factors for PTSD vary in terms of instrumentation, sampling methods, types of traumas studied, and other research design factors. These variations have led to different studies reporting some conflicting results. Moreover, most studies use retrospective or cross-sectional designs rather than prospective designs. As such, knowledge of etiological factors, interactions, and pathways is not conclusive at this point in time. In my view, it has not been ruled out that particularly severe traumas per se can result in PTSD in the absence of risk factors.

One of the limitations of this treatment conceptualization is that it presumes that treatment should target etiological factors; however, there is no a priori reason to believe that treatment effectiveness requires targeting of etiological factors. It may be that exposure, desensitization, and processing are effective components for the treatment of PTSD, regardless of the exact causal nature of the symptoms.

Another limitation is that this view does not take into account the synergistic effects of etiological/risk factors, nor does it take into account the synergistic effects of various treatment ingredients. It is possible that various combinations of treatment components (e.g., therapist warmth, empathy, safety, structure, exposure, relaxation, cognitive restructuring, inclusion of body-focused techniques, and mastery experiences) combine in a manner such that the synergistic effects are particularly efficacious in terms of treatment outcome. The chapters of these volumes provide the reader many diverse and interesting practical applications with which to potentially assist traumatized clients.

Ideas for Clinical and Empirical Study

What follows are suggestions for those who wish to subject their experimental treatment approaches to systematic clinical (case) study, followed by a few brief suggestions for empirical study in relation to the roles of various etiological pathways and variables.

Clinical Study

As noted by van der Kolk, McFarlane, and van der Hart (1996), results from the Koach project (Solomon, Bleich, Shoham, Nardi, & Kotler, 1992) show that subjective impressions of treatment success (i.e., anecdotal reports) are not always borne out by objective data. As such, when clients appear to improve, objective ratings of their symptoms may fail to substantiate those impressions, and some clinicians may wish to conduct case study analyses of their treatment approaches. When case studies meet specific criteria, they offer information that can approximate the information that is obtained by experimental research (Kazdin, 1998).

Kazdin places case study criteria into two broad categories. The first refers to characteristics of the case, and the second refers to threats to internal validity. Documenting characteristics of the case functions to provide information that is important for ruling out threats to internal validity (internal validity refers to the evidence that observed treatment effects are actually due to the treatment, and not to other factors).

Characteristics of the case include

1. *The type of data that are obtained* (e.g., self-report indices, physiological measurements, etc., as opposed to anecdotal reports). According to Kazdin (1998), "anecdotal reports are usually not sufficient to conclude that changes really occurred in client behavior" (p. 406), and "scientific inferences are difficult if not impossible to draw from anecdotal information" (p. 406).

2. *The frequency with which measurements are taken.* Taking several measurements over the course of treatment and follow-up assists in controlling for statistical regression to the mean (which can lead to inaccurate findings of treatment effectiveness) and other testing artifacts that can confound results.

3. *Stability and course of the disorder.* Stability and course of the disorder will influence the interpretation of the observed treatment effects. For example, if a given treatment procedure results in changes during the acute phases of PTSD, it is not clear whether the changes are due to the treatment, or simply to natural healing (e.g., Briere, in press). However, with chronic PTSD, changes in symptoms that occur immediately following the treatment and are maintained over follow-up periods suggests that the treatment is what led to the changes.

4. *Whether observed effects are immediate and marked.* When effects are immediate (occur in close proximity to the interventions) and marked (result in considerable changes in the severity of symptoms), it is more likely that the changes are due to the treatment intervention. As such, third variables can be more easily ruled out as causal factors.

5. *The use of multiple, diverse cases.* The more cases that show change following treatment, the less likely it is that extraneous factors are what is leading to the observed changes.

All of the above information is useful in terms of providing evidence for internal validity. Threats to internal validity include historical and maturation effects, testing effects, instrumentation (i.e., using different assessment measures at different times can distort results), and statistical regression to the mean, which cannot be easily ruled out with simple pre–post measurements. Thus, for given clients, the clinician might wish to obtain informed consent to include the client in case study analyses and administer the same measures of PTSD and associated features to each client before treatment begins, immediately after treatment ends, and at several pre-determined follow-up times. In addition, the clinician should keep detailed records that document the nature and type of the trauma(s), the stability and course of PTSD and associated features for each client, whether observed changes are immediate and marked, and demographic data for each client (e.g., age, sex, and so forth). It is also recommended that clinicians document the risk factors present. (See Appendix B for a sample Case Study form.)

Empirical Study

It is recommended that further study on etiological factors in PTSD take into consideration the following:

1. When assessing for PTSD, take steps to consider and rule out differential diagnoses.
2. Utilize large sample sizes to allow comparisons of effects of different types of traumatic stressor events and their interactions with risk factors.
3. Consider creative ways in which to measure the stimulus properties of the traumatic stressor event (e.g., severity of injury) when doing retrospective studies.
4. Utilize research design and statistical analyses to assess the effects of proposed mediating and moderating variables.
5. Identify physiological markers (e.g., cortisol) (Yehuda, 1999b) that might differentiate PTSD from other disorders.

For those interested in the topic of empirical studies, see Yehuda (1999a) for further issues and ideas in studying risk factors in PTSD.

In closing, these volumes provide the reader with several diverse and interesting treatment applications for use with traumatized clients. Some of these approaches (e.g., cognitive-behavioral therapy and EMDR) have strong evidence for their treatment efficacy with PTSD. The evidence for other of the approaches consists largely of case study data. It is my view that the professional community would be at an advantage if it were more fully exposed to the findings observed with case studies (e.g., Ogden & Minton, 2001). To this end, systematic analysis of clinical case material (e.g., Kazdin, 1998), written up and published in professional journals, would assist in this endeavor.

APPENDIX A: RISK FACTORS CHECKLIST

Client Identification: _____

❑ Extended duration of trauma(s):

_____

_____

_____

❑ Significant life threat:

_____

_____

_____

❑ Severe injury:

_____

_____

_____

❑ Loss of life and/or property:

_____

_____

_____

❑ Close proximity to the event:

_____

_____

_____

❑ Prior history of other DSM disorders:

_____

_____

_____

❑ Family members who have PTSD:

_____

_____

_____

❑ Family members who have a mood disorder:

_____

_____

_____

❑ Family members who have an anxiety disorder:

_____

_____

_____

❑ Prior traumas:

_____

_____

_____

❑ Peritraumatic dissociation:

_____

_____

_____

❑ Physiological stress reactions (if known):

_____

_____

_____

❑ Neurocognitive sequelae (e.g., memory impairments):

_____

_____

_____

❑ Personality factors:

_____

_____

_____

❑ History of child maltreatment/neglect:

_____

_____

_____

_____

_____

Total Number of Risk Factors (out of 15): _____

A higher number of risk factors suggests that treatment may be more complex and may require specialized interventions, such as stabilization or skills training prior to processing of traumatic memories. Treatment may require interventions aimed at specific risk factors in addition to treatment of the trauma symptoms per se.

APPENDIX B: CASE STUDY FORM

Date: _____

Client Identification: _____

Age at treatment start date: _____

Sex: _____

SES: _____

Race: _____

Marital Status: _____

Type and duration of treatment(s) given:

_____

_____

_____

Type and nature of trauma(s) (e.g., single-event trauma, chronic trauma, multiple single-event traumas):

_____

_____

_____

Presence and nature of risk factors (see Appendix A):

_____

_____

_____

Diagnosis:

_____

_____

Length of time with PTSD at intake: _____

Course of PTSD over time: _____

Associated features:

_____

_____

Pre-treatment measures given, including dates and scores (it is important to use the same measurement instruments at pre-treatment, post-treatment, and follow-up periods):

_____

_____

_____

_____

Post-treatment measures given, including dates and scores:

_____

_____

_____

_____

_____

Follow-up measures given, including dates and scores:

_____

_____

_____

_____

_____

Notes (including factors that may affect internal validity, such as clinical observations of whether any changes are immediate and marked, and so forth):

_____

_____

_____

_____

_____

NOTES

The author would like to acknowledge and thank Ellert Nijenhuis, Charles Figley, and Anne Winter for their helpful comments and feedback on this chapter.

1. Note that "cognitive" does not refer *only* to thoughts or beliefs.

2. Genetic risk factors may find their active expression in partial response to environmental triggers (McEwen, 2000).

3. See McFarlane (1999) for an interesting discussion on possible etiological pathways in terms of interactions between properties of the stressor event (severity of threat and/or severity of injury) and the reaction during the event (e.g., peritraumatic dissociation, acute psychological symptoms, and/or acute biological symptoms).

4. One difficulty includes the retrospective rating of the stimulus properties by respondents, which may be affected by (a) the current level of symptoms, such that ratings are magnified (Yehuda, 1999a), or (b) by avoidance or suppression, such that they are minimized (Briere, 1997).

5. For example, there are several commonalities between symptoms of PTSD and symptoms of depression.

6. Gender may not constitute a direct risk factor, but may function to increase the risk of exposure to certain traumatic events, such as rape (Kessler et al., 1999).

7. SSRIs have been found to be very effective in the treatment of PTSD (Friedman, Davidson, Mellman, & Southwick, 2000).

REFERENCES

American Psychiatric Association. (2000). *Diagnostic and statistical manual of mental disorders* (DSM-IV-TR) (4th ed., text rev.). Washington, DC: American Psychiatric Association.

Bouton, M. E. (1994). Context, ambiguity, and classical conditioning. *Current Directions in Psychological Science*, 3, 49–53.

Bouton, M. E., & Schwartzentruber, D. (1991). Sources of relapse after extinction in Pavlovian and instrumental learning. *Clinical Psychology Review*, 11, 123–140.

Brett, E. A. (1996). The classification of posttraumatic stress disorder. In B. A. van der Kolk, A. C. McFarlane, & L. Weisaeth (Eds.), *Traumatic stress: The effects of overwhelming experience on mind, body, and society* (pp. 117–128). New York: Guilford Press.

Briere, J. (1997a). *Therapy for adults molested as children*. New York: Springer-Verlag.

Briere, J. (1997b). *Psychological assessment of adult posttraumatic states*. Washington, DC: American Psychological Association.

Briere, J. (in press). Treating adult survivors of severe childhood abuse and neglect: Further development of an integrative model. In J.E.B. Myers, L. Berliner, J. Briere, C. T. Hendrix, C. Jenny, & T. Reid (Eds.), *The APSAC handbook on child maltreatment* (2nd ed.). Newbury Park, CA: Sage Publications.

Brom, D., Kleber, R. J., & Defares, P. B. (1989). Brief psychotherapy for posttraumatic stress disorders. *Journal of Consulting and Clinical Psychology*, 57(5), 607–612.

Burstein, A. (1985). Post-traumatic stress disorder. *Journal of Clinical Psychiatry*, 46, 554–556.

Chu, J. A. (1998). *Rebuilding shattered lives: The responsible treatment of complex post-traumatic and dissociative disorders*. New York: John Wiley & Sons.

Davidson, J.R.T., & Foa, E. B. (1991a). Diagnostic issues in posttraumatic stress disorder: Considerations for the DSM-IV. *Journal of Abnormal Psychology*, 100(3), 346–355.

Davidson, J.R.T., & Foa, E. B. (1991b). Refining criteria for Posttraumatic Stress Disorder. *Hospital and Community Psychiatry*, 42(3), 259–261.

Dietrich, A. M. (2000). As the pendulum swings: The etiology of PTSD, complex PTSD, and revictimization. *Traumatology* [online], 6(1). http://www.fsu.edu/~trauma/v6i1a4.html.

Dietrich, A. M., Baranowsky, A., Devich-Navarro, M., Gentry, E. J., Harris, C. J., & Figley, C. R. (2000). A review of alternative approaches to the treatment of posttraumatic sequelae. *Traumatology* [online], 6(4). http://www.fsu.edu/~trauma/v6i4a2.html.

Dietrich, A. M., & van der Kolk, B. A. (in preparation). PTSD, somatization, self-harm, abuse type, and retraumatization of adults abused as children. Manuscript in preparation.

Foa, E. B., Keane, T. M., & Friedman, M. J. (Eds.). (2000). *Effective treatments for PTSD*. New York: Guilford Press.

Foa, E. B., & Kozak, M. J. (1986). Emotional processing of fear: Exposure to corrective information. *Psychological Bulletin*, 99, 20–35.

Friedman, M. J., Davidson, J. T., Mellman, T. A., & Southwick, S. M. (2000). Pharmacotherapy. In E. B. Foa, T. M. Keane, & M. J. Friedman (Eds.), *Effective treatments for PTSD* (pp. 84–105). New York: Guilford Press.

Glaser, D. (2000). Child abuse and neglect and the brain—A review. *Journal of Child Psychology and Psychiatry*, 41(1), 97–116.

Harvey, P. D., & Yehuda, R. (1999). Strategies to study risk for the development of PTSD. In R. Yehuda (Ed.), *Risk factors for posttraumatic stress disorder* (pp. 1–22). Washington, DC: American Psychiatric Press.

Helzer, J. E., Robins, L., & McEvoy, L. (1987). Post-traumatic stress disorder in the general population. *New England Journal of Medicine*, 317, 1640–1634.

Herman, J. L. (1992). *Trauma and recovery*. New York: Basic Books.

Ito, Y., Teicher, M. H., Glod, C. A., Ackerman, E. (1998). Preliminary evidence for aberrant cortical development in abused children: A quantitative EEG study. *The Journal of Neuropsychiatry and Clinical Neurosciences*, 10, 298–307.

Ito, Y., Teicher, M. H., Glod, C. A., Harper, D., Magnus, E., & Gelbard, H. A. (1993). Increased prevalence of electrophysiological abnormalities in children with psychological, physical, and sexual abuse. *Journal of neuropsychiatry and clinical neurosciences*, 5, 401–408.

Kazdin, A. E. (1998). Drawing valid inferences from case studies. In A. E. Kazdin (Ed.), *Methodological issues and strategies in clinical research* (2nd ed., pp. 403–417). Washington, DC: American Psychological Association.

Kessler, R. C., Sonnega, A., Bromet, E., Hughes, M., Nelson, C. B., & Breslau, N. (1999). Epidemiological risk factors for trauma and PTSD. In R. Yehuda (Ed.), *Risk factors for posttraumatic stress disorder* (pp. 23–60). Washington, DC: American Psychiatric Press.

Kilpatrick, D. G., & Best, C. L. (1984). Some cautionary remarks in treating sexual abuse victims with implosion. *Behavior Therapy*, 15, 421–423.

Lazarus, R. S. (1990). Theory-based stress measurement. *Psychological Inquiry*, 1 (3), 3–13.

Lazarus, R. S. (1993). Coping theory and research: Past, present, and future. *Psychosomatic Medicine*, 55, 234–247.

Linehan, M. M. (1993). *Skills training manual for treating of borderline personality disorder*. New York: Guilford Press.

Litz, B. T., Blake, D. D., Gerardi, R. D., & Keane, T. M. (1990). Decision-making guidelines for the use of direct therapeutic exposure in the treatment of posttraumatic stress disorder. *The Behavior Therapist*, 13, 91–93.

Marshall, R. D., Schneier, F. R., Lin, S., Simpson, H. B., Vermes, D., & Liebowitz, M. (2000). Childhood trauma and dissociative symptoms in Panic Disorder. *American Journal of Psychiatry*, 157, 451–453.

McEwen, B. S. (2000). Allostasis and allostatic load: Implications for neuropsychopharmacology. *Neuropsychopharmacology*, 22(2), 108–124

McFarlane, A. C. (1999). Risk factors for the acute biological and psychological response to trauma. In R. Yehuda (Ed.), *Risk factors for posttraumatic stress disorder* (pp. 163–190). Washington, DC: American Psychiatric Press.

McFarlane, A. C., & de Girolamo, G. (1996). The nature of traumatic stressors and the epidemiology of posttraumatic reactions. In B. A. van der Kolk, A. C. McFarlane, & L. Weisaeth (Eds.), *Traumatic stress: The effects of over-*

whelming experience on mind, body, and society (pp. 129–154). New York: Guilford Press.

Nijenhuis, E.R.S., van der Hart, O., & Kruger, K. (submitted). *The psychometric charactersitics of the Traumatic Experiences Checklist (TEC)*. Unpublished manuscript.

Nijenhuis, E.R.S., van der Hart, O., & Steele, K. (in press). Strukturale dissoziation der persönlichkeit: Über ihre traumatischen wurzeln und die phobischen mechanismen die sie in gang halten [Structural dissociation of the personality: Traumatic origins, phobic maintenance]. In A. Hofmann, L. Reddemann, & U. Gast (Eds.), *Behandlung dissoziativer störungen [Treatment of dissociative disorders]*. Stuttgart: Thieme Verlag.

Ogawa, J. R., Sroufe, L. A., Weinfield, N. S., Carlson, E. A., & Egeland, B. (1997). Development and the fragmented self: Longitudinal study of dissociative symptomatology in a nonclinical sample. *Development and Psychopathology*, 9, 855–879.

Ogden, P., & Minton, K. (2001, March). *Movement and action in the transformation of trauma: The role of somatic experience, purposeful action, and theater in the treatment of trauma*. Workshop at the Psychological Trauma: Maturational Processes and Therapeutic Interventions Conference, Boston, MA.

Orr, S. P., & Pitman, R. K. (1999). Neurocognitive risk factors for PTSD. In R. Yehuda (Ed.), *Risk factors for posttraumatic stress disorder* (pp. 125–142). Washington, DC: American Psychiatric Press.

Pelcovitz, D., van der Kolk, B. A., Roth, S., Mandel, F., Kaplan, S., & Resick, P. (1996). Development of a criteria set and a structured interview for disorders of extreme stress (SIDES). *Journal of Traumatic Stress*, 10(1), 3–16.

Pitman, R. K., Altman, B., Greenwald, E., Longpre, R. E., Macklin, M. L., Poire, R. E., & Steketee, G. S. (1991). Psychiatric complications during flooding therapy for posttraumatic stress disorder. *Journal of Clinical Psychiatry*, 52, 17–20.

Pitman, R. K., Orr, S. P., Altman, B., & Longpre, R. E. (1996). Emotional processing and outcome of imaginal flooding therapy in Vietnam veterans with chronic posttraumatic stress disorder. *Comprehensive Psychiatry*, 37(6), 409–418.

Prisman, D., Dietrich, A. M., & Shercliffe, R. (2000, November). *Treatment outcome for severe personality disorders*. Presentation at the annual meeting of the International Society of Traumatic Stress Studies, San Antonio, Texas. Chaired by Greg Passey, M.D.

Putnam, F. (1997). *Dissociation in children and adolescents. A developmental perspective*. New York: Guilford Press

Putnam, F. (2000, March). *Developmental pathways following sexual abuse in girls*. Presentation at the conference on Psychological Trauma: Maturational Processes and Therapeutic Interventions, Boston, MA.

Putnam, F. W., Carlson, E. B., Ross, C. A., Anderson, G., Clark, P., Torem, M., Bowman, E. S., Coons, P., Chu, J. A., Dill, D. L., Loewenstein, R. J., & Braun, B. G. (1996). Patterns of dissociation in clinical and nonclinical samples. *Journal of Nervous and Mental Disease*, 184, 673–679.

Putnam, F. W., & Trickett, P. K. (1997). Psychobiological effects of sexual abuse:

A longitudinal study. *Annals of the New York Academy of Sciences*, 821, 150–159.

Rothbaum, B. O., Meadows, E. A., Resick, P., & Foy, D. W. (2000). Cognitive behavioral therapy. In E. B. Foa, T. M. Keane, & M. J. Friedman (Eds.), *Effective treatments for PTSD* (pp. 60–83). New York: Guilford Press.

Schnurr, P. P., & Vielhauer, J. J. (1999). Resonality as a risk factor for PTSD. In R. Yehuda (Ed.), *Risk factors for posttraumatic stress disorder* (pp. 191–222). Washington, DC: American Psychiatric Press.

Scott, M. J., & Stradling, S. G. (1997). Client compliance with exposure treatments for posttraumatic stress disorder. *Journal of Traumatic Stress*, 10, 523–526.

Shalev, A. Y. (1996). Stress versus traumatic stress: From acute homeostatic reactions to chronic psychopathology. In B. A. van der Kolk, A. C. McFarlane, & L. Weisaeth (Eds.), *Traumatic stress: The effects of overwhelming experience on mind, body, and society* (pp. 77–101). New York: Guilford Press.

Shalev, A. Y. (1999). Psychophysiological expression of risk factors for PTSD. In R. Yehuda (Ed.), *Risk factors for posttraumatic stress disorder* (pp. 143–162). Washington, DC: American Psychiatric Press.

Shalev, A. Y., Bonne, O., & Eth, S. (1996). Treatment of posttraumatic stress disorder: A review. *Psychosomatic Medicine*, 58, 165–182.

Solomon, R. L., & Corbit, J. D. (1974). An opponent-process theory of motivation. I. Temporal dynamics of affect. *Psychological Review*, 81(2), 119–145.

Solomon, Z., Bleich, A., Shoham, S., Nardi, C., & Kotler, M. (1992). The Koach project for the treatment of combat related PTSD: Rationale, aims and methodology. *Journal of Traumatic Stress*, 5, 175–194.

Steele, K., van der Hart, O., & Nijenhuis, E.R.S. (2001). Phase-oriented treatment of dissociative disorders: Overcoming trauma-related phobias. Allgemeine behandlungsstrategien komplexer dissoziativer störungen [General treatment strategies for complex dissociative disorders]. In S. O. Hoffman & A. Eckhart-Henn (Eds.), *Dissoziative störungen des bewusstseins [Dissociative disorders of consciousness]*. Stuttgart: Schattauer Verlag.

Teicher, M. H., Glod, C. A., Surrey, I., Swett, C. (1993). Early childhood abuse and limbic system ratings in adult psychiatric outpatients. *Journal of Neuropsychiatry and Clinical Neurosciences*, 5, 301–306.

True, W. R., & Lyons, M. J. (1999). Genetic risk factors for PTSD: A twin study. In R. Yehuda (Ed.), *Risk factors for posttraumatic stress disorder* (pp. 61–78). Washington, DC: American Psychiatric Press.

True, W. R., Rice, J., Eisen, S. A., Heath, A. C., Goldberg, J., Lyons, M. J., & Nowak, J. (1993). A twin study of genetic and environmental contributions to liability for posttraumatic stress symptoms. *Archives of General Psychiatry*, 50, 257–264.

van der Kolk, B. A., McFarlane, A. C., & van der Hart, O. (1996). A general approach to treatment of posttraumatic stress disorder. In B. A. van der Kolk, A. C. McFarlane, & L. Weisaeth (Eds.), *Traumatic stress: The effects of overwhelming experience on mind, body, and society* (pp. 417–440). New York: Guilford Press.

van der Kolk, B. A., McFarlane, A. C., & Weisaeth, L. (Eds.). (1996). *Traumatic stress: The effects of overwhelming experience on mind, body, and society*. New York: Guilford Press.

Vaughan, K., & Tarrier, N. (1992). The use of image habituation training with posttraumatic stress disorders. *British Journal of Psychiatry*, 161, 658–664.

Watson, C. G., Tuorila, J., Detra, E., Gearhart, L. P., & Wiclkiewicz, R. M. (1995). Effects of a Vietnam War Memorial Pilgrimage on veterans with posttraumatic stress disorder. *Journal of Nervous and Mental Disease*, 183(5), 315–319.

Wilson, S. N., van der Kolk, B., Burbridge, J., Fisler, R., & Kradin, R. (1999). Phenotype of blood lymphocytes in PTSD suggests chronic immune activation. *Psychosomatics*, 40(3), 222–225.

Yehuda, R. (1999a). *Risk factors for posttraumatic stress disorder*. Washington, DC: American Psychiatric Press.

Yehuda, R. (1999b). Parental PTSD as a risk factor for PTSD. In R. Yehuda (Ed.), *Risk factors for posttraumatic stress disorder* (pp. 93–123). Washington, DC: American Psychiatric Press.

Yehuda, R. (2001, March). Developmental risk factors for PTSD: Role of parental PTSD, childhood trauma and neuroendocrine responses. Presentation at the Psychological Trauma Conference, Boston, MA.

Part II

Generic Treatments

Chapter 4

Behavioral/Cognitive Approaches to Post-traumatic Stress: Theory-Driven, Empirically Based Therapy

Lizabeth Roemer, Nicole T. Harrington, and David S. Riggs

Our goal in this chapter is to provide an overview of our behavioral/cognitive approach to the treatment of trauma-related psychological difficulties. We intend for readers to first read Chapter 2 in this volume, on behavioral/cognitive theories of post-traumatic stress, because those theories provide the conceptual basis for the therapeutic approach we outline here.

Often, clinicians who have not been trained in the methods of behavior therapy have the misconception that behavior therapists are unfeeling and mechanistic in their application of "techniques" (as opposed to therapy) to individuals viewed as subjects in an experiment, rather than clients in need of help. These feelings are particularly notable among clinicians treating the psychological sequelae of traumatic stress, where behavioral techniques are often characterized as re-traumatizing the client rather than providing the empathic and safe environment needed for healing. We believe this is an inaccurate characterization and that it is our responsibility as behavior therapists to better describe the behavioral approach to therapy and the rich theoretical and empirical tradition on which it is based.

As we noted in Chapter 2, the central tasks of behavior therapy are to carefully assess the circumstances surrounding any given behavior, hypothesize the function(s) of this behavior, derive interventions based on this functional evaluation, continually assess the effects of these interventions, and revise one's conceptualization and intervention strategies accordingly. Each element is guided by empirically supported theory as well as by existing treatment outcome research.

Treatment outcome research in the area of trauma (Foa, Rothbaum, Riggs, & Murdock, 1991; Keane, Fairbank, Caddell, & Zimering, 1989) has focused primarily on alleviation of post-traumatic stress disorder (PTSD; American Psychiatric Association, 1980). However, basic behavioral principles and empirically based treatments from other areas of psychopathology can be used to understand and treat the range of traumatic sequelae that often impact trauma survivors. Treatments focused on PTSD symptoms can be augmented with interventions adapted from extant theories and treatments of co-morbid disorders (e.g., substance abuse: Marlatt & Vandenbos, 1998; depression: Beck, Rush, Shaw, & Emery, 1979; Lewinsohn, 1975; eating disorders: Garner & Garfinkel, 1997; Leitenberg & Rosen, 1988; other anxiety disorders: Borkovec & Roemer, 1994; Craske & Barlow, 1993; Riggs & Foa, 1993), as well as interventions aimed at associated features of post-traumatic adjustment, such as emotional dysregulation (e.g., Linehan, 1993a, 1993b), interpersonal difficulties (e.g., Cordova & Jacobson, 1993; Linehan, 1993a, 1993b;), and dissociative symptomatology (Wagner & Linehan, 1998).

We do not have sufficient space here to comprehensively describe behavioral/cognitive treatment for trauma survivors. Instead, we will do our best to capture the spirit of this model of therapy, show how it stems from behavioral theory, provide guidelines for implementing behavioral techniques along with clinical examples,[1] and provide references for those interested in learning more. In particular, we recommend Goldfried and Davison's (1994) *Clinical Behavior Therapy* for general information regarding behavioral approaches; and Foa and Rothbaum's (1998) *Treating the Trauma of Rape: Cognitive-Behavioral Therapy for PTSD*, along with Follette, Ruzek, and Abueg's (1998) edited volume, *Cognitive-Behavioral Therapies for Trauma*, for specific guidelines regarding behavioral treatment for trauma survivors. Our approach to treating post-traumatic stress is adopted from both cognitive-behavioral treatments for post-traumatic stress disorder (e.g., Foa & Rothbaum, 1998; Keane, Girardi, Quinn, & Litz, 1992; Levis, 1980; Resick & Schnicke, 1993), and from cognitive and behavioral approaches to treating other psychological difficulties that often characterize trauma survivors (e.g., anxiety disorders: Barlow, 1993; Borkovec & Roemer, 1994; depression: Beck et al., 1979; emotional dysregulation and interpersonal difficulties: Linehan, 1993a, 1993b; dissociation: Wagner & Linehan, 1998). As such, this approach incorporates a number of elements common to behavioral and cognitive-behavioral therapies, including psychoeducation, monitoring, exposure to feared stimuli, cognitive restructuring, training to remedy skills deficits, and relapse prevention.

For clarity, we have divided this chapter into the initial phase of treatment (including assessment, monitoring, psychoeducation, and establishing a therapeutic relationship), and then separate sections for exposure-based, cognitive, and skills-training interventions as well as relapse prevention. However, it is important to note that these are somewhat arbitrary distinctions. The elements crucial to the initial phase of treatment remain essential throughout therapy and constitute active intervention, in our view. Similarly, the "interventions" overlap and interact both with one another and with the elements of psychoeducation, assessment, and monitoring.

INITIAL PHASE OF TREATMENT

The primary goals of the initial phase of treatment are establishing a therapeutic relationship, establishing safety, assessment of strengths and weaknesses, formulating a behavioral conceptualization, and sharing with the client the formulation and plan for treatment. We emphasize the psychoeducational component of treatment throughout these early sessions so that clients come to understand their responses and the rationale behind the intervention strategies we propose. Throughout this and later phases of treatment, we emphasize the collaborative nature of the therapeutic relationship. We see the therapist as the expert in anxiety, behavioral principles, and the aftereffects of trauma, but maintain that the client is the expert in his or her own experience and history and is best able to recognize how the general principles we present relate (or do not relate) to his or her specific experience. Collaboration between the two ensures optimal results from treatment.

Assessment

A comprehensive evaluation at the outset of therapy is invaluable in order to provide the information necessary to make informed clinical decisions and prioritize treatment goals. Keane and colleagues have detailed the importance of a comprehensive multimodal assessment of PTSD (Keane, Newman, & Orsillo, 1997; Keane, Wolfe, & Taylor, 1987; Litz, Penk, Gerardi, & Keane, 1992); the reader should explore these resources for further details. In addition to assessing PTSD symptomatology, the therapist should evaluate social and occupational functioning, co-morbid conditions, and any potentially destructive behaviors. It is important to ascertain a client's strengths as well as weaknesses—these will guide the choice of interventions and will help alleviate the demoralization commonly experienced by clients. Once the therapist has developed initial hypotheses regarding the patient's identified problems and has specified a point of intervention, specific cognitive-behavioral techniques can be introduced.

Another important component of assessment is history-taking. The client is given an opportunity to describe his or her life before the traumatic event(s), to describe the events themselves, and then to describe how he or she has adjusted since. This provides a narrative that helps both the client and the therapist understand the client's experience and the historical factors relevant to his or her current difficulties. This understanding helps validate the client's experience and increase his or her understanding of seemingly incomprehensible responses. Also, the therapist learns the meaning the client places on events in his or her life, which has implications for how current events are perceived and interpreted. Further, disclosure of the traumatic event(s) strengthens the therapeutic relationship and shows the client that he or she can trust the therapist with the strong emotions that accompany disclosure. Such disclosure also constitutes a first step in emotionally processing these events and reducing associated distress and shame.

For example, an adult survivor of childhood sexual abuse may report that she is unable to assert her needs in interpersonal relationships. During the course of the interview, she may recall that the feelings of powerlessness and lack of self-confidence she frequently experiences in her current relationships date back to the abuse she experienced during adolescence. When asked to describe herself prior to the abuse, she may recall, for the first time in years, her previous sense of herself as competent and capable. This process of developing a complete narrative not only provides a context for her current behavior, it also brings to mind alternative, positive response options in her repertoire that she has not been using recently.

While historical information is useful for validation and hypothesizing about etiological factors, assessment of current maintaining factors is crucial for generating interventions. In addition to formal assessments such as structured interviews (with the client and significant others) and self-report instruments, behaviorists utilize a host of monitoring and observational strategies to gather information about the situations, thoughts, feelings, and consequences that impact various target behaviors. These may include formal behavioral observations (e.g., viewing a client interacting with a spouse), observation of the client's behavior during sessions with the therapist (an essential component of behavioral treatment), self-monitoring between sessions, and use of SUDS ratings (subjective units of distress reported on a 100-point scale ranging from not at all distressing to extremely distressing) to track levels of distress across situations as well as within and across sessions.

For the survivor of childhood sexual abuse described above, it would not be sufficient to establish that current feelings of powerlessness and low self-esteem were related to early traumatic experiences. We would want to assess the current antecedents and consequences of the client's unassertive behavior and feelings of powerlessness. So we might start by asking her to identify thoughts, feelings, sensations, and behaviors associated with her experience of interpersonal powerlessness. Then we might ask her to describe the most recent situation in which she felt this way, noting the cues preceding and consequences following this experience. We would also teach the client to monitor the circumstances surrounding this experience of powerlessness outside of session and we would collaboratively monitor her feelings of powerlessness within session. This analysis would help us determine the cues that trigger this experience and the function of the behaviors associated with it (i.e., the consequences that may serve to reinforce the behaviors), both of which provide important information for treatment. For instance, we may discover that when she feels powerless she experiences heightened anxiety and tends to respond by acquiescing to whomever she is interacting with. These individuals tend to respond positively to this behavior, so it is immediately reinforced. However, in the long run, this pattern serves to maintain her feelings of powerlessness because situations are so rarely resolved as she would like. Awareness of the immediate versus delayed consequences of her behavior will help her alter this pattern of responding despite the natural contingencies that maintain it (i.e., people's positive reactions to her non-assertiveness).

Overall, the primary goal of initial assessment is to determine the factors that contribute to problem behavior so that interventions can be planned. Relevant questions include: In what situations does this behavior occur? What thoughts/feelings typically precede this behavior? What consequences follow this behavior? What does the client tell him or herself about this behavior? What kinds of rules does this client seem to follow? What underlying beliefs are evident? In other words, the behavior therapist is exploring each aspect of behavioral theory introduced in Chapter 2 of this volume. Once an initial formulation has been established (collaboratively with the client), decisions regarding intervention are made. A comprehensive assessment allows a behavior therapist to predict how an intervention in one area will affect other areas. For instance, if substance abuse is conceptualized as negatively reinforced by the distress it alleviates, one can predict an increase in distress when substance use is curtailed. Therefore, concurrent skills training in distress tolerance might be indicated.

Initial assessment does not result in a static conceptualization. With each subsequent intervention, assessment continues in order to determine its efficacy and to evaluate the accuracy of the conceptualization. The principles of hypothesis-testing apply in clinical work as well as in research; any theory needs to be refutable and the good clinician will be willing to consider alternative hypotheses if his or her predictions are not borne out.

Psychoeducation

An essential component of successful behavioral/cognitive therapy is helping a client understand responses that he or she has found puzzling, unreasonable, and frightening. Often, it is important to highlight the function of emotional responses, and how this function can be derailed through a variety of learning experiences. The fight-or-flight function of anxiety not only provides an excellent, easily explained example, but it also helps highlight the multiple components of anxiety (cognitive, physiological, behavioral) that clients will be asked to monitor (described below). The therapist can use this example to illustrate how the three components may interact to maintain and escalate maladaptive, anxious reactions. Having clients imagine a frightening situation and notice the bodily changes that accompany this image, even though they are fully aware they are not currently in danger (e.g., heart rate increases, sweaty palms), provides a vivid example of how thoughts and perceptions influence bodily responses. The circularity of this response system should be highlighted, so the client understands how these bodily responses confirm the perception of danger, escalating the cycle of anxiety. Similar explanations can be provided for a host of emotional responses, setting the stage for reconceptualizing the client's presenting "problem" as examples of how his or her adaptation has gone awry.

As part of educating our clients, we provide information about post-traumatic stress disorder, as well as other common difficulties associated with traumatic exposure. We have found that, even as part of research protocols, participants often spontaneously report that they have found learning about the 17 symptoms of PTSD extremely helpful; that it has enabled them to put their disparate, distressing experiences into a context. Normalizing a client's experience can be extremely therapeutic. We similarly provide information about the behavioral conceptualization of these difficulties and provide a rationale for any proposed interventions. For instance, we commonly explain classical conditioning and draw a graph of how fear diminishes over repeated presentations so that clients can understand the theory behind exposure-based treatments. It is particularly important to explain the consequences of avoidance, as much of treatment will focus on reducing avoidance in order to minimize its negative aftereffects. Explaining these principles to the client helps the client generalize what he or she learns in therapy and use the same principles to guide behavior even after therapy has ended.[2]

One component that distinguishes behavior therapy from dynamic approaches is the emphasis on the therapist communicating the conceptualization of the client's difficulties to the client. In addition to sharing with the client a general model of post-traumatic stress, the therapist offers his or her ideas regarding the function of various problematic behaviors, and communicates observations regarding the salient antecedent, organismic, and consequent variables relevant to target behaviors. Also, hypotheses are presented regarding relevant historical factors in order to validate the client and decrease self-blame. Client feedback is elicited and consensus is reached regarding case conceptualization. In this way, a working alliance is established and intervention proceeds based on an agreement between therapist and client. That is not to say that disagreements may not occur; in fact, in an honest, healthy therapeutic relationship they are inevitable. The successful behavior therapist will be able to listen to (and genuinely consider) the client's perspective, clearly communicate his or her own, and negotiate an agreement regarding a course to pursue. In addition, the therapist and client should agree on further assessments to conduct and a period after which to renegotiate and reconsider the treatment plan. For instance, a client may be reluctant to proceed with exposure therapy, despite the therapist's belief that it is essential. Given that avoidance of emotional distress is common, this reluctance might be conceptualized as emotional avoidance. However, the therapist may negotiate with the client to proceed with a more gradual course of exposure or a different form of exposure. In this way, the client's comfort with the procedure is increased, and he or she is able to experience some of the positive effects of this approach, which is likely to increase motivation.

Monitoring

A crucial aspect of behavioral/cognitive approaches to psychological difficulties is the monitoring of stimuli, responses, and consequences relevant to the presenting problem. The focus on monitoring reflects the behavioral emphasis on individual experience. By monitoring responses in a range of situations, the therapist and client are able to explore the function of each response in each given situation and therefore derive appropriate interventions. Continued monitoring allows for the assessment of the impact of a given intervention, and information obtained through monitoring is used to reconceptualize and establish new interventions in the absence of significant behavioral change.

Monitoring serves several other important functions. It serves to increase a client's awareness of his or her ways of responding. Many problematic responses happen largely outside of the client's awareness, making it difficult to alter behaviors. When an individual is able to detect early cues of a particular cycle (e.g., "When I start tapping my fingers, I know I am beginning to feel anxious"), he or she can implement coping responses before escalation and success is more likely. Similarly, if avoidance is a significant problem for an individual, early detection of the urge to avoid will help the person stay in the feared situation until anxiety and distress subside. Combined with education, this awareness may also help diminish a client's feelings of being "irrational" or "crazy" by providing a context for understanding seemingly unreasonable responses. For instance, one Korean War veteran felt he was heartless and unfeeling because he didn't experience any positive emotions when reunited with his high school buddies. However, monitoring of his responses in that situation revealed that he experienced a tightness in his stomach, and he recalled thoughts of "bracing" himself for a loss. This apparently happy reunion was a cue that reminded him of his friends who had died in Korea. His response to this memory was to "shut down" and experience nothing except a pain in his stomach.

Monitoring also serves a crucial function in maintaining the client's safety. Initial assessment will highlight any of the client's potentially destructive behaviors. These behaviors are continuously monitored throughout the course of therapy. The therapist should pay particular attention to any threats to safety during the more intensive periods of therapy. Again, detecting early cues that might elicit unsafe or self-injurious behavior will help the client effectively implement new coping strategies.

Monitoring can be conducted in a variety of ways (see Beck et al., 1979; Goldfried & Davison, 1994, for more details). Standard cognitive-behavioral protocols usually include some type of daily record sheet in which clients are asked to note their anxiety, depression, or other target response levels at several points in the day (e.g., morning, noon, dinnertime, before bed) and record various details about emotion-eliciting situations (e.g., situational cues, thoughts, emotions, responses, outcomes). During the course of therapy, this monitoring can be expanded to include identification of distorted thought patterns, alternative ways of viewing the situation, and other forms of coping responses. Time is spent reviewing monitoring sheets in session and helping the client problem-solve difficulties that emerge in completing monitoring assignments. Methods of monitoring should be altered in order to increase clients' success in completing the task; a more simplified form may be used or monitoring may be initially done through in-session recall with the help of the therapist, if a client is having trouble doing it on his or her own. As with all behavioral techniques, it is important to minimize failure experiences and maximize success; this will increase clients' expectancies of therapeutic success and their own sense of self-efficacy, both of which correlate with behavior change (Bandura, 1977; Goldstein, 1962).

Monitoring is particularly useful in session. In-session monitoring of subtle changes in the client's affect and calling attention to those changes will help the client recognize a number of external and internal cues for various emotional responses. It will be easier for a client to recognize conditioned emotional responses and subtle forms of avoidance when a therapist can notice them in the moment and share this observation. Gradually, this responsibility should be shifted to the client. Any observation made by the therapist must be framed as a hypothesis. The therapist should be extremely careful to avoid taking the role of the all-seeing expert. Instead, the therapist can appropriately present as someone who is outside of the client's subjective experience and therefore able to describe some contingencies that may be more difficult for the client to perceive. The client remains the expert in his or her own experience and evaluates the accuracy of any observations made by the therapist.

Monitoring can also be done through imaginal exercises. A client may relate a particularly distressing experience but be unaware why she or he felt distressed in this situation. The therapist can have the client imagine him or herself back in that situation and ask him or her to attend to a variety of somatic, situational, emotional, cognitive, and behavioral cues in order to fully recall the situation. This focused attention will help elucidate the salient stimuli and contingencies associated with the experience of distress. Also, although such an exercise will initially elicit some distress, it will aid in emotionally processing the event and lead to a decrease in distress if it is continued for a sufficient period of time (Foa & Kozak, 1986).

SPECIFIC INTERVENTION STRATEGIES

Assessment, psychoeducation, and monitoring, as described above, are essential to any behavioral treatment and are incorporated in most empirically supported cognitive-behavioral treatments for PTSD (e.g., Foa & Rothbaum, 1998; Keane et al., 1992). However, their individual contribution to treatment outcome has yet to be explored. In contrast, the interventions that follow have been designated as active ingredients in the treatment of PTSD and studies have supported their efficacy. These interventions also have demonstrated efficacy with other presenting problems (e.g., exposure and cognitive restructuring for eating disorders; exposure for anxiety disorders; cognitive restructuring for depression) and so can be used for co-morbid disorders as well.

Exposure-Based Methods

Extensive research has established exposure to feared stimuli as a critical feature of treatment of anxiety disorders (e.g., Craske & Barlow, 1993; Lindemann, 1989; Riggs & Foa, 1993). Similarly, direct therapeutic exposure (DTE; repeated imaginal rehearsal of traumatic events) has emerged as the PTSD treatment with the strongest empirical support (Foa & Meadows, 1997; Keane, 1998). The basic principle behind exposure is that prolonged exposure to conditioned feared stimuli without the occurrence of the unconditioned stimuli will lead to fear reduction and a decrease in threatening associations. Exposure is accomplished by accessing the fear network (presenting stimulus, response, and meaning cues, eliciting an initial fear response) and maintaining exposure so that fear can diminish and new, non-threatening meanings can be incorporated (Foa & Kozak, 1986). Because avoidance interferes with the process of fear reduction and with emotional processing in general, careful attention must be paid to any form of avoidance, and the client must be encouraged to approach any feared or distressing material.

The emphasis on exposure and encouraged non-avoidance is central to our treatment approach with trauma survivors and is why we consider behavioral principles fundamental to our work. Much of our therapy involves providing learning experiences in which clients confront feared material and discover that feared outcomes do not follow: They are not re-traumatized, they do not "fall apart," their therapist does not leave them, they do not start crying and never stop. Direct learning experiences such as these lead to the most powerful forms of behavioral change. Simply rationally determining that an event or a memory is not dangerous or a feared outcome is not likely is often insufficient. We have all had the experience of *knowing* that something isn't dangerous but still *feeling* that it is. This distinction can be highlighted and discussed, but the most effective way of counteracting it is to experience both the feared situation (even imaginally) and the lack of negative outcome. Because of the way our cognitive biases (schemas) guide our observations, it is important to direct a client's attention toward both the threatening cues and the non-threatening outcome in any given exposure, so that new learning can take place and danger schemas can be altered.

Direct Therapeutic Exposure

The tradition of exposure-based treatment for anxiety disorders led to the development of direct therapeutic exposure (DTE) for the treatment of PTSD. Techniques of DTE were developed based on the principles of anxiety reduction that have evolved from a long history of laboratory research. These studies indicated that prolonged, focused exposure associated with initial arousal and subsequent within-session and between-session habituation yields the most beneficial outcomes in treating phobic anxiety (see Foa & Kozak, 1986, for a review of this literature).

In the most common forms of direct therapeutic exposure for PTSD, flooding or prolonged exposure, the client is asked to imaginally relive the traumatic event, with all of the associated stimulus, response, and meaning elements. This is done repeatedly, in the safe context of therapy, until the arousal and distress associated with the memory decrease. Although this therapy is associated with an initial increase in distress, studies demonstrate a significant decrease in post-traumatic symptomatology and trauma-related arousal following repeated imaginal exposure (e.g., Foa et al., 1991; Keane et al., 1989). In fact, a recent process analysis of therapeutic change revealed that rape survivors who displayed high levels of emotional response or "engagement" during initial imagery along with habituation (decreased fear ratings across sessions) had the highest positive response rates to prolonged exposure (Jaycox, Foa, & Morral, 1998).

Typically, in direct therapeutic exposure, the client first describes the event in as much detail as possible. For the retelling, the client is encouraged to close his or her eyes, while the therapist asks questions that focus and enhance the image. For example: "Where are you standing?" "What do you see? Smell? Hear? Taste?" "What do you feel in your body?" "What are you saying to yourself?" "What happened next?" The therapist pays particular attention to any cues of distress or avoidance in order to target the most traumatic portions of the memory. The therapist gently redirects the client toward the components that seem most emotionally evocative, in order to ensure complete processing. This procedure is done repeatedly with SUDS ratings preceding and following each trial, until reported distress decreases. It is important to leave sufficient time at the end of the session to process the experience, regulate distress, and assess safety. For this reason, it may be necessary to schedule sessions lasting longer than 45 minutes. With certain clients we will plan exposure sessions to last 90 or even 120 minutes in order to allow time for distress to reduce and processing to occur.

In conducting imaginal exposure, it is important to remain cognizant of the underlying principles and guide intervention accordingly. Clients should be encouraged to approach threatening, distressing material sufficiently, abstain from subtle forms of avoidance (e.g., distraction, engaging in neutralizing thoughts), and maintain exposure until some relief is experienced. Clients need to experience a sufficiently strong emotional response so the full memory network (with details of stimulus, response, and meaning) is activated and new information (for instance, safety cues) is incorporated. An initial lack of emotional responding is often an indication that the client is engaging in some form of emotional avoidance; this avoidance needs to be eliminated. On the other hand, it is important not to elicit such a pronounced emotional response that the client dissociates or engages in other dangerous forms of avoidance (substance use, self-injury). Initial training in distress tolerance skills (e.g., Linehan, 1993b) can be helpful in teaching the client to tolerate concomitant emotions so that new learning can occur. Collaboration with the client in maximizing therapeutic exposure but minimizing risk (e.g., suicidal ideation, substance abuse, dissociation) is imperative. The therapist and the client should carefully monitor any potential risky behaviors throughout the course of exposure-based treatment and maintain specific contracts to ensure the client's safety. The therapist needs to maintain a careful balance between ensuring that exposure is tolerable, but not colluding in the client's avoidance of distress and traumatic memories. This is particularly crucial because therapists are human, and therefore likely to have their own tendency to avoid traumatic material and intense emotions.

If the client has experienced multiple traumatic events, each is given a SUDS level and a hierarchy is created from least to most distressing. The client and therapist then choose an event to begin exposure with (typically one that is at least moderately distressing). The client is often encouraged to select an event that is being frequently re-experienced. Repeated exposure of the initial memory is continued until habituation occurs. At that point, the clinician and client work to identify another memory that continues to elicit distress and begin imaginal exposure with that memory. Imaginal exposure with one memory often leads to reduced distress associated with other memories.

In selecting target events, the therapist should be guided by behavioral theory: Distress must be significant enough to access the memory structure but not so high as to result in avoidance and interfere with incorporation of new information. Assessment of this balance is an ongoing process and therapists must work flexibly and thoughtfully with fear hierarchies. It may turn out the target initially chosen is not the most appropriate one. For instance, a female veteran had experienced several sexual assaults as well as a combat-related trauma. After developing a fear hierarchy, it was determined that exposure would begin with one of the sexual assault experiences, which was rated as moderately distressing. However, the initial imaginal exposure was not sufficiently distressing, and no avoidance could be detected, so the client was encouraged to move up the hierarchy to a more distressing event. The processing of the latter event was followed by improvement in symptoms related to both events.

Although direct therapeutic exposure is an emotionally evocative therapeutic technique, in our experience, clients ultimately welcome the invitation to face the memories that have plagued them. Although they are reluctant to remember, or to share, the traumas they have endured, they are well aware that their avoidance is ineffective and they are able to understand the rationale behind direct therapeutic exposure. A collaborative stance in which client and therapist agree to work together to overcome the client's avoidance facilitates the efficacy of direct therapeutic exposure and avoids the risk of the client feeling re-traumatized. The therapist acts as a gentle, caring, but insistent guide, helping the client to accomplish his or her stated goal of reducing the distress associated with memories. For a more detailed guide in this type of treatment, the reader is referred to Foa and Rothbaum (1998).

Although the efficacy of prolonged imaginal exposure in the treatment of PTSD has been demonstrated, comparison and dismantling studies (such as those conducted with the other anxiety disorders) have yet to be conducted with trauma survivors. Thus, there remains more to learn about the optimal form of direct therapeutic exposure for this population. Although fear is clearly an important component of post-traumatic reactions, other emotions are also implicated, so we cannot be certain that findings from the fear literature generalize. Resick (Resick & Schnicke, 1993) has included an alternate form of exposure as one component in her Cognitive Processing Therapy (CPT): Clients are asked to write about their traumatic event repeatedly, and encouraged to fully experience all of the concomitant emotions. Direct comparisons of imaginal and writing forms of exposure have yet to be conducted. In the absence of sufficient data, it is advisable to rely on theory and existing evidence from the other anxiety disorders in formulating exposure-based interventions for trauma. Also, research has indicated that images are more emotionally evocative than words (Vrana,

Cuthbert, & Lang, 1986), further supporting the use of imaginal exposure to facilitate emotional processing (Foa & Kozak, 1986).

Adding an In Vivo Element to Exposure

Although imaginal exposure provides an excellent means for clients to confront the feared memories of their trauma, exposure to objects or real-life situations is often helpful or even necessary to fully address clients' fears. Behavior therapists flexibly and creatively construct a host of imaginal and in vivo exercises in order to help clients face the range of experiences they have come to fear. Again, treatment rests on a well-developed case conceptualization. Exposure exercises are constructed by identifying central conditioned stimuli and preventing habitual forms of avoidance. Straightforward in vivo exercises are often indicated: Clients may develop a hierarchy of avoided situations and begin approaching them and remaining in them until their fear subsides. In vivo exposure exercises may focus on situations that are perceived as dangerous (e.g., standing in a crowded room) or stimuli that elicit memories of the specific trauma (e.g., watching TV documentaries about rape survivors). The exposure exercises may be incorporated as homework, or conducted during sessions with therapist assistance. Following are several examples of ways we have used the principle of exposure and incorporated in vivo elements in our treatment of trauma survivors.

Some variations involve minor alterations of the procedure described above. For example, in vivo and imaginal exposure techniques may be combined. One female combat veteran who experienced a nighttime firefight was encouraged to turn the lights out during the imaginal exposure exercise in order to enhance the intensity of the emotional response. For another survivor, imaginal exposure exercises took place in an isolated clinic stairwell, as she had been assaulted in a similar location. These combinations of imaginal and in vivo exposure both intensify the emotional responding during exposure and increase generalization of new learning to salient cues.

Sometimes a client will present with marked avoidance of concrete trauma-related cues that can be incorporated into in vivo exposure. For example, a combat veteran was encouraged to bring to session a large unopened box of war memorabilia. Initially, these items were too distressing to view during session, so several sessions were spent with the box in the middle of the room, until the client was ready to approach the material. Several sessions were spent reviewing each item, discussing its meaning and importance and making decisions regarding what to do with each item. In this way, the client not only approached previously avoided physical objects, but also reconnected with long-avoided memories. After these recollections were sufficiently processed, the client was able to physically and emotionally achieve closure through disposition of the items.

In vivo exposure can also involve exposure to previously avoided interpersonal relationships. In one case, a woman engaged in imaginal exposure to several sexual assault experiences. While many of her symptoms improved, this client continued to experience high levels of shame and interpersonal avoidance. This was addressed by constructing a series of opportunities for her to disclose the experiences she considered shameful to individuals other than the therapist (other clinic staff). In order to fully access this emotional network, a hierarchy was constructed whereby initial planned disclosures were met with empathic responses, whereas later disclosures were met with more judgmental responses. The therapist worked closely with the client to help her prepare for each exposure, so that when she met with the judgmental responses she was able to dismiss them and maintain her own positive self-regard. Following this intervention, the client reported a sustained improvement in interpersonal relationships and reduction in feelings of shame.

In addition to these types of explicit exposure exercises, the principles of exposure guide the behavior therapist's moment-to-moment interactions with the client. Attention is paid to subtle cues of avoidance, and the client is gently guided to face distressing feelings, memories, thoughts, and situations. As always, the case conceptualization serves as a backdrop that helps the therapist determine where to focus attention and facilitates detection of important in-session behaviors. Again, these observations and subsequent interventions are conveyed to the client, so that although the terms "exposure" and "habituation" may not be used, the concepts are conveyed. For instance, in the course of therapy with a male combat veteran, it became clear that avoidance of any degree of interpersonal intimacy was a crucial factor in the client's difficulties. Emotional disclosure within the therapeutic relationship was thus construed as an essential form of exposure, habitual avoidance was noted when it occurred, and the client was encouraged to stay with the feelings of intimacy and trust as they arose, along with the terror that accompanied them. Gradually, the client was able to tolerate higher levels of intimacy both within the therapeutic relationship and in outside relationships as well.

Cognitive Components

Behavioral/cognitive therapy for trauma-related difficulties incorporates consideration of cognitive elements of adjustment. As discussed above, associative networks include cognitive elements that may be easily activated, so that a survivor perceives the world as dangerous, him or herself as somehow inherently flawed, others as untrustworthy, and so on (Foa & Riggs, 1994). Direct therapeutic exposure, and other exposure exercises such as those described above, directly challenge traumagenic schemas so that in many cases other forms of cognitive therapy may not be needed. For example, a male client did imaginal exposure with an extremely distressing memory in which he was attacked from behind in an alley. He struggled with his assailant, and eventually strangled him. For the first five repetitions of this scene, the client was extremely focused on the sensations in his hands as he strangled the man. However, during the sixth session, this client spontaneously reported that he was aware of the feeling of the man's hands around his neck, and his own inability to breathe. Following termination of the image, this man exclaimed, "He would have killed me. I had to kill him." The therapist had not addressed these issues cognitively yet; this new realization emerged from the repeated emotional processing of the event. Following this session, the client reported a dramatic decrease in nightmares and intrusions, as well as a decrease in feelings of shame and guilt.

In the example above, the client came to accept the event and his actions by emotionally processing it. We feel that acceptance of traumatic memories is often a crucial element in the treatment of trauma survivors (see Hayes, Jacobson, Follette, & Dougher, 1994, for a broader discussion of the role of acceptance in psychotherapy). While this acceptance may spontaneously emerge during the course of direct therapeutic exposure, it may also need to be more directly addressed. For example, the therapist might help the client frame his or her behavior (or lack thereof) in light of the absence of viable alternatives.

Often, cognitive techniques are used as an adjunct to exposure-based treatments. However, Resick and Schnicke (1993) outline an approach for treating rape survivors in which cognitive therapy serves as the primary intervention. This approach, labeled Cognitive Processing Therapy (CPT), adapts Beck et al.'s (1979) cognitive therapy for depression to address rape-related schemas (McCann & Pearlman, 1990). As noted above, this treatment also incorporates an exposure element in which clients write about their traumatic experience repeatedly, and are encouraged to focus on the emotions evoked. This treatment (CPT) led to significant symptomatic improvement in rape survivors with PTSD compared to a wait-list control group (Resick & Schnicke, 1992). A recent study found that cognitive restructuring alone was also beneficial in the treatment of PTSD, leading to comparable improvement to direct therapeutic exposure (DTE) alone, and greater improvement than relaxation alone (Marks, Lovell, Noshirvani, Livanou, & Thrasher, 1998).

Cognitive therapy can be conducted formally by monitoring thoughts, identifying distorted thought styles, challenging beliefs, and conducting behavioral experiments to explore new hypotheses (see Beck et al., 1979). Beck recommends teaching the client to act as a scientist and treat his or her thoughts as hypotheses rather than facts. This spirit can be communicated more informally as well. We often introduce the notion of alternative perspectives or multiple ways of viewing a given situation (one can give an example of how several people witnessing a given event may construe it differently) and then simply encourage clients to question their interpreta-

tions and to explore alternative ways of viewing circumstances. The ultimate goal is cognitive flexibility. It is extremely important in this work not
to convey that the client's views are somehow wrong or irrational. Rather,
we choose to take a stance that many possible interpretations have merit,
but it is worthwhile to explore a variety of options and actually test out
different predictions. Further, we encourage clients to examine the way
their schemas have been shaped by their traumatic experience and how this
may bias their interpretation of current events.

Skills Training

A final component of many behavioral/cognitive approaches to treatment
is skills training. In the PTSD literature, this component has focused primarily on control of anxiety in the form of cognitive restructuring as described above, and relaxation training. Treatment packages such as stress
inoculation training that incorporate anxiety-reduction skills training as
well as self-monitoring components have been shown to be more effective
than wait-list controls in treating rape survivors with PTSD (Foa et al.,
1991). Clients can be taught a number of different methods of relaxation
(diaphragmatic breathing, progressive muscle relaxation, applied relaxation, meditation) and taught to implement these relaxation techniques in
response to cues of anxious responding. However, it is important that relaxation not begin to serve an avoidant function. Trauma survivors have
often come to fear their own emotional responses and to construe anxiety
as inherently dangerous. Learning to relax may help counter the lack of
control clients feel over their responses, but it can also interfere with learning that in fact anxiety isn't dangerous and can be tolerated. It is important
to attend to these distinctions; ideally, clients would learn to master their
experience of anxiety, so they can tolerate it in some moments and lessen
it in others.

Cognitive restructuring and various forms of self-talk can also be taught
as coping skills to use in stressful situations. Linehan's (1993b) skills training manual for borderline personality disorder (BPD) contains several distress tolerance skills that may be applicable to this population (but have
yet to be empirically tested).

Skills training that extends beyond the target of anxiety may be similarly
beneficial in this population. As noted in Chapter 2 trauma survivors often
exhibit deficits in emotion regulation and interpersonal functioning. Those
individuals who were raised in traumatic or invalidating environments may
never have learned to recognize, communicate, or regulate their emotional
states and would therefore benefit from emotion skills training. Similarly,
those who never had sufficient models of healthy interpersonal relationships
may benefit from social skills training. Linehan (1993b) has outlined a
series of emotion regulation skills and interpersonal (communication) skills

in her treatment of BPD that may serve as beneficial interventions for trauma survivors. A treatment package that included these skills training components (along with individual cognitive-behavioral therapy) was associated with improvements in interpersonal functioning among women with borderline personality disorder (Linehan, Tutek, Heard, & Armstrong, 1994). A study is currently underway (M. Cloitre, Principal Investigator) exploring the efficacy of a treatment package that combines Foa's prolonged exposure and Linehan's interpersonal and emotion regulation skills training in the treatment of adult female child sexual assault survivors. Preliminary findings reveal improvements in PTSD symptomatology as well as in alexithymia, dissociation, and anger regulation compared to a wait-list control group (Cloitre, 1998). Integration of skills training approaches into exposure-based treatment may be a promising avenue for future research, particularly with more chronic traumatized individuals among whom emotional and interpersonal skills deficits may be more common (Cloitre, Scarvalone, & Difede, 1997).

LATER STAGES OF TREATMENT, RELAPSE PREVENTION, AND TERMINATION

As we discussed earlier, behavioral/cognitive therapy involves a constant process of assessment, conceptualization, intervention, reassessment, reconceptualization, and continued intervention. As presenting problems diminish and new, more desirable patterns of behavior develop, it is important to monitor these changes, both so that the client becomes aware of the progress he or she is making, and so that discontinuation of therapy can be considered. In the course of behavioral change, new difficulties may become evident, and therapy may need to be altered accordingly. For instance, social skills deficits were not initially apparent in a veteran with chronic PTSD who experienced such marked interpersonal avoidance that he rarely left his basement. However, following successful processing of his combat experiences and training in stress management skills, he began to desire social interaction, but found that he did not know what to say to people or how to interpret what they said. Therapy focused on interpersonal skills training using psychoeducation, modeling, problem solving, and provision of feedback on in-session interpersonal behavior. In this instance, ongoing assessment prevented premature termination and helped determine additional targets of treatment.

The final phase of treatment also incorporates the principles of relapse prevention outlined in Marlatt and Gordon's model for alcohol abuse treatment (Marlatt & Gordon, 1985). Given that therapy involves helping clients learn new behavioral patterns, we expect that old, habitual patterns of responding may reemerge in the future, particularly during times of stress. Numerous laboratory studies provide evidence that extinction (re-

mission of learned responses) does not involve the unlearning of an association, but rather new learning of a second association, so that in some
contexts the old associations will reemerge (e.g., Bouton, 1994). We prepare clients for the reemergence of such behaviors and encourage them to
recognize less desirable ways of responding and to use what they've learned
in therapy. We believe that an important aspect of recovery is developing
a perspective that allows one to take the challenges that will arise in the
future and cope with them successfully, rather than viewing them as evidence that one isn't really "better" and is still "damaged" in some way.
Marlatt and Gordon (1985) convey this by relabeling apparent "relapses"
in drinking behavior as "lapses" that provide an opportunity to learn more
about antecedents and consequences for this behavior, resulting in more
successful coping in the future.

Once therapeutic gains have been made, both the client and the therapist
need to begin evaluating the continued need for treatment. Often the decision to end therapy is obvious—clients are no longer experiencing the
interpersonal, emotional and behavioral difficulties that caused them to
seek treatment, the skills they have learned have become habitual, and they
have a more flexible, adaptive view of themselves and the world. Other
times, particularly in cases of chronic developmental trauma histories, although substantial gains have been made, some difficulties still linger. However, a break from therapy may help a client increase his/her sense of
self-efficacy so that termination, or at least temporary suspension of therapy, is advisable. We feel it is important to encourage clients to try newly
acquired coping skills on their own. We have found that often clients come
to feel that they are only doing well because they are in therapy and need
to challenge this assumption by demonstrating that they can maintain gains
independent of therapy. When working with trauma survivors it is also
important to address the reality that therapy cannot accomplish what may
be most desirable—that the trauma never happened. Although memories
can be processed, skills can be learned, and new, adaptive belief systems
can be developed, the reality of their history cannot be undone and often
therapy needs to incorporate grieving for all they have lost.

Termination is best accomplished as therapy is—collaboratively, with the
therapist expressing his or her faith in the client's ability to cope. The
ending of the therapeutic relationship may serve as a cue for interpersonally
related, conditioned emotional responses, such as fears of abandonment
and rejection. Throughout the termination process, attention should be
paid to these responses and they should be understood in the context of
other issues addressed in therapy. The ending of the therapeutic relationship
may also provide a first opportunity for a trauma survivor to say good-bye
and grieve the end of a relationship in a healthy, meaningful way. Clients
are encouraged to recontact the therapist as needed. We have found that
an effective way to assure maintenance of therapeutic gains is to remain

available for brief booster sessions, so that if a time of significant stress arises, a client can return for one or two sessions to reestablish the coping abilities that they gained in therapy.

We have attempted to capture here both the empirical rigor and the clinical sensitivity that we feel characterizes a behavioral approach to the treatment of post-traumatic stress. We have a great deal left to learn from basic research and clinical trials about the relevant mechanisms of emotional processing and therapeutic change among the diverse clinical presentations of trauma survivors. However, behavioral approaches validated in the treatment of other presenting problems, coupled with those developed particularly for the treatment of trauma, provide a firm empirical and clinical basis on which to construct our individualized treatment plans and formulate future research studies.

NOTES

Preparation of this chapter was supported in part by National Institute of Mental Health Grant MH59044 to the first author. We wish to thank Carolyn Pepper and Amy Wagner for their helpful comments on an earlier draft of this manuscript.

1. In order to protect the confidentiality of our clients, we provide very little identifying information for cases and have altered this information in several places. We kept crucial clinical information intact, however.

2. We have found that clients with a broad range of intellectual abilities are able to understand this material when it is presented clearly.

REFERENCES

American Psychiatric Association. (1980). *Diagnostic and statistical manual of mental disorders* (3rd ed.). Washington, DC: American Psychiatric Association.

Bandura, A. (1977). Self-efficacy: Toward a unifying theory of behavioral change. *Psychological Review*, 84, 191–215.

Barlow, D. H. (Ed.). (1993). *Clinical handbook of psychological disorders: A step-by-step treatment manual* (2nd ed.). New York: Plenum.

Beck, A. T., Rush, A. J., Shaw, B. F., & Emery, G. (1979). *Cognitive therapy of depression.* New York: Guilford Press.

Borkovec, T. D., & Roemer, L. (1994). Generalized anxiety disorder. In R. T. Ammerman & M. Hersen (Eds.), *Handbook of prescriptive treatments for adults* (pp. 261–281). New York: Plenum.

Bouton, M. E. (1994). Context, ambiguity and classical conditioning. *Current Directions in Psychological Science*, 3, 49–53.

Cloitre, M. (1998). Sexual revictimization: Risk factors and prevention. In V. M. Follette, J. I. Ruzek, & F. R. Abueg (Eds.), *Cognitive-behavioral therapies for trauma* (pp. 278–304). New York: Guilford Press.

Cloitre, M., Scarvalone, P., & Difede, J. A. (1997). Posttraumatic stress disorder, self- and interpersonal dysfunction among sexually retraumatized women. *Journal of Traumatic Stress*, 10, 437–452.

Cordova, J. V., & Jacobson, N. S. (1993). Couple distress. In D. H. Barlow (Ed.), *Clinical handbook of psychological disorders: A step-by-step treatment manual* (2nd ed., pp. 481–512). New York: Plenum.

Craske, M. G., & Barlow, D. H. (1993). Panic disorder and agoraphobia. In D. H. Barlow (Ed.), *Clinical handbook of psychological disorders: A step-by-step treatment manual* (2nd ed., pp. 1–47). New York: Plenum.

Foa, E., & Riggs, D. (1994). Posttraumatic stress disorder and rape. In R. S. Pynoos (Ed.), *Posttraumatic stress disorder: A clinical review* (pp. 133–163). Lutherville, MD: Sidran Press.

Foa, E. B., & Kozak, M. J. (1986). Emotional processing of fear: Exposure to corrective information. *Psychological Bulletin*, 99, 20–35.

Foa, E. B., & Meadows, E. A. (1997). Psychosocial treatments for posttraumatic stress disorder: A critical review. *Annual Review of Psychology*, 48, 449–480.

Foa, E. B., & Rothbaum, B. O. (1998). *Treating the trauma of rape: Cognitive-behavioral therapy for PTSD*. New York: Guilford Press.

Foa, E. B., Rothbaum, B. O., Riggs, D. S., & Murdock, T. (1991). Treatment of post-traumatic stress disorder in rape victims: A comparison between cognitive-behavioral procedures and counseling. *Journal of Consulting and Clinical Psychology*, 59, 715–723.

Follette, V. M., Ruzek, J. I., &. Abueg, F. R. (Eds.). (1998). *Cognitive-behavioral therapies for trauma*. New York: Guilford Press.

Garner, D. M., & Garfinkel, D. E. (Eds.). (1997) *Handbook of treatment of eating disorders* (2nd ed.). New York: Guilford Press.

Goldfried, M. R., & Davison, G. C. (1994). *Clinical behavior therapy* (2nd ed.). New York: John Wiley & Sons.

Goldstein, A. P. (1962). *Therapist-patient expectancies in psychotherapy*. New York: Pergamon.

Hayes, S. C., Jacobson, N. S., Follette, V. M., & Dougher, M. J. (Eds.). (1994). *Acceptance and change: Content and context in psychotherapy*. Reno, NV: Context Press.

Hope, D. A., & Heimberg, R. G. (1993). Social phobia and social anxiety. In D. H. Barlow (Ed.), *Clinical handbook of psychological disorders: A step-by-step treatment manual* (2nd ed., pp. 99–136). New York: Plenum.

Jaycox, L. H., Foa, E. B., & Morral, A. R. (1998). Influence of emotional engagement and habituation on exposure therapy for PTSD. *Journal of Consulting and Clinical Psychology*, 66, 185–192.

Keane, T. M. (1998). Psychological and behavioral treatments for post-traumatic stress disorder. In P. E. Nathan & J. M. Gorman (Eds.), *A guide to treatments that work* (pp. 398–409). New York: Oxford University Press.

Keane, T. M., Fairbank, J. A., Caddell, J. M., & Zimering, R. T. (1989). Implosive (flooding) therapy reduces symptoms of PTSD in Vietnam combat veterans. *Behavior Therapy*, 20, 245–260.

Keane, T. M., Gerardi, R., Quinn, S., & Litz, B. T. (1992). Behavioral treatment of post-traumatic stress disorder. In S. M. Turner, K. S. Calhoun, & H. E.

Adams (Eds.), *Handbook of clinical behavior therapy* (2nd ed., pp. 87–98). New York: John Wiley & Sons.

Keane, T. M., Newman, E., & Orsillo, S. M. (1997). Assessment of war-zone related PTSD. In J. P. Wilson & T. M. Keane (Eds.), *Assessing psychological trauma and PTSD: A handbook for practitioners* (pp. 267–290). New York: Guilford Press.

Keane, T. M., Wolfe, J., & Taylor, K. L. (1987). Post-traumatic stress disorder: Evidence for diagnostic validity and methods of psychological assessment. *Journal of Clinical Psychology, 43,* 32–43.

Leitenberg, H., & Rosen, J. C. (1988) Cognitive-behavioral treatment of bulimia nervosa. In M. Hersen & R. M. Eisler (Eds.), *Progress in behavior modification* (Vol. 23, pp. 11–35). Newbury Park, CA: Sage Publications.

Levis, D. J. (1980). Implementing the technique of implosive therapy. In A. Goldstein & E. B. Foa (Eds.), *Handbook of behavioral interventions* (pp. 92–151). New York: John Wiley & Sons.

Lewinsohn, P. M. (1975). The behavioral study and treatment of depression. In M. Herson, R. M. Eisler, & P. M. Miller (Eds.), *Progress in behavior modification* (Vol. 1, pp. 19–64). New York: Academic Press.

Lindemann, C. (Ed.). (1989). *Handbook of phobia therapy.* Northvale, NJ: Jason Aronson.

Linehan, M. (1993a). *Cognitive behavioral treatment of borderline personality disorder.* New York: Guilford Press.

Linehan, M. (1993b). *Skills training manual for cognitive behavioral treatment of borderline personality disorder.* New York: Guilford Press.

Linehan, M. M., Tutek, D. A., Heard, H. L., & Armstrong, H. A. (1994). Interpersonal outcome of cognitive behavioral treatment for chronically suicidal borderline patients. *American Journal of Psychiatry, 151,* 1771–1776.

Litz, B. T., Penk, W. E., Gerardi, R., & Keane, T. M. (1992). Behavioral assessment of PTSD. In P. Saigh (Ed.), *Post-traumatic stress disorder: A behavioral approach to assessment and treatment* (pp. 50–84). Boston: Allyn & Bacon.

Marks, I., Lovell, K., Noshirvani, H., Livanou, M., & Thrasher, S. (1998). Treatment of posttraumatic stress disorder by exposure and/or cognitive restructuring: A controlled study. *Archives of General Psychiatry, 55,* 317–325.

Marlatt, G. A., & Gordon, J. R. (1985). *Relapse prevention: Maintenance strategies in the treatment of addictive behavior.* New York: Guilford Press.

Marlatt, G. A., & Vandenbos, G. R. (Eds.). (1998). *Addictive behaviors: Readings on etiology, prevention and treatment.* Washington, DC: American Psychological Association.

McCann, I. L., & Pearlman, L. A. (1990). *Psychological trauma and the adult survivor: Theory, therapy, and transformation.* New York: Brunner/Mazel.

Resick, P. A., & Schnicke, M. K. (1992). Cognitive processing therapy for sexual assault victims. *Journal of Consulting and Clinical Psychology, 60,* 748–756.

Resick, P. A., & Schnicke, M. K. (1993). *Cognitive processing therapy for rape victims: A treatment manual.* Newbury Park, CA: Sage Publications.

Riggs, D. S., & Foa, E. B. (1993). Obsessive compulsive disorder. In D. H. Barlow (Ed.), *Clinical handbook of psychological disorders: A step-by-step treatment manual* (2nd ed., pp. 189–239). New York: Plenum.

Vrana, S. R., Cuthbert, B. N., & Lang, P. J. (1986). Fear imagery and text processing. *Psychophysiology, 23,* 247–253.

Wagner, A. W., & Linehan, M. M. (1998). Dissociative behavior. In V. M. Follette, J. I. Ruzek, & F. R. Abueg (Eds.), *Cognitive-behavioral therapies for trauma* (pp. 191–225). New York: Guilford Press.

Chapter 5

The Use of Narrative Therapy with Couples Affected by Anxiety Disorders

Neil C. Headman

OVERVIEW OF THE PRESENTING PROBLEM

Although anxiety affects most people to some degree, there are those for whom it is extremely problematic. Those who have been severely traumatized experience some of the most distressing effects of anxiety and are often labeled as being mentally ill and having an anxiety disorder. The Fourth Edition of the *Diagnostic and Statistical Manual of Mental Disorders* (DSM-IV) published by the American Psychiatric Association (1994) specifies 12 varieties of so-called anxiety disorders. One of the most common among these is panic disorder, which is estimated to affect as much as 5% of the general population at one time or another. The "essential feature" of this disorder is "the presence of recurrent, unexpected panic attacks followed by at least 1 month of persistent concern about having another panic attack, worry about the possible implications or consequences of the panic attacks, or a significant behavioral change related to the attacks" (p. 397).

Approximately one-third to one-half of those diagnosed with panic disorder are also said to have agoraphobia. Its "essential feature" is "anxiety about being in places or situations from which escape might be difficult (or embarrassing) or in which help may not be available in the event of having an unexpected or situationally predisposed Panic Attack or panic-like symptoms" (p. 396). Summarized from these notions, people diagnosed as having panic disorder with agoraphobia are so afraid of having a panic attack in a public place that they avoid leaving home whenever possible. Unfortunately, not only do these individuals experience the restrictive effects of intense fear, but too often they become marginalized by society as being mentally ill.

In reviewing the literature on anxiety disorders, Craske and Zoellner (1995) found empirical support suggesting that anxiety disorders develop under stressful or traumatic life circumstances. As such a circumstance, separation from or loss of a spouse is a potential precursor of panic and agoraphobia. Other studies suggested that anxiety operates more as a cause than effect of marital distress. Whatever one's view about the causal processes involved, it is clear that anxiety not only adversely affects individuals but it affects their interpersonal relationships.

TRADITIONAL TREATMENT APPROACHES

Originally, panic attacks were viewed as some sort of free-floating anxiety and were treated with relaxation training and cognitive restructuring. Such treatment often gave way to the use of pharmacotherapy. In the 1970s there was a movement toward more specific, exposure-based treatments of anxiety and fears. In reviewing the literature on these treatments, Emmelkamp (1994) found a significant amount of research indicating their effectiveness. However, exposure-based treatments were potentially problematic in that they were used to treat individuals in isolation from their interpersonal contexts.

Soon researchers began comparing exposure-based treatments to a variety of cognitive approaches, based on the premise that "anxiety symptoms result from dysfunctional cognitive processes" (Morretti, Feldman, & Shaw, 1990, p. 224). Evidence suggested that the exposure-based treatments were more effective overall than several, more recent cognitive approaches (i.e., rational-emotive therapy, paradoxical intention, and self-instructional training).

More recently, there has been a move toward the use of more comprehensive cognitive-behavioral approaches for treating anxiety (Craske & Barlow, 1993). These often include elements such as cognitive restructuring, breathing retraining, relaxation, and exposure. The findings of early research on these methods are encouraging, but insufficient for conclusions about effectiveness.

Most approaches to anxiety disorders have been cognitive, behavioral, and/or pharmacological and have dealt only with the individual client, as opposed to involving his or her interpersonal context (Craske & Zoellner, 1995). A common thread running through these approaches is their implication that something about the client needs to be changed; that he is somehow pathological until treated. Patterson and Van Meir (1996) argue that such a view is in conflict with the tenets of family therapy. In addition to potentially alienating their clients, family therapists taking an individualistic-psychopathological stance are likely to experience inconsistencies in the language, etiology assumptions, diagnoses, and treatment perspectives of their approach. When working with anxiety-troubled individuals in intimate relationships, an approach more in harmony with the objectives of family therapy, one involving important others in the client's life, should be used.

Narrative therapy offers a unique approach for assisting individuals, couples, and families who are experiencing the devastating effects of problems such as anxiety. Narrative therapy has been used successfully to free individuals, and their relationships, from the unwanted effects of such problems as anorexia/bulimia (Epston, Morris, & Maisel, 1995), dissociative disorder (Gallant, Brownlee, & Vodde, 1995), affective disorder (Focht & Beardslee, 1996), and obsessive-compulsive disorder (White, 1986). It has the potential as an effective means for assisting people who experience the limiting effects of fear and anxiety.

NARRATIVE THERAPY

Unlike many traditional therapies, narrative therapy is not held up as a "treatment" cure but as a therapeutic relationship, wherein therapist and client work together to create more beneficial and preferred ways of knowing and being. Narrative therapy is also distinct in that it draws on "postmodern" theoretical writings, concerned with the possibilities and implications of language. Michael White, recognized as the originator of narrative therapy, was highly influenced by the writings of Foucault and Goffman, who criticized the dehumanizing processes of institutions. David Epston, also known as a pioneer in narrative therapy, first introduced White to the narrative metaphor. This, along with numerous conversations between Michael White, Cheryl White, and David Epston (White & Epston, 1990), spawned the development of narrative therapy.

Narrative therapy is designed to assist clients in freeing themselves from the demeaning and constrictive discourses prevalent in culture/society and in realizing new and preferred ways of being. The narrative therapist works with the client to create new meanings from his or her past, present, and future experiences. Self-defeating and disempowering meanings are changed to those which will be more beneficial and empowering for the client.

The narrative therapist takes a collaborative, listening position toward the client and utilizes respectful curiosity and optimism to begin exploring for the client's more heroic aspects. The therapist avoids labeling and assumption-making while working to deconstruct externally imposed, restrictive labels the client has been "recruited" into accepting. One of the most fundamental tasks of narrative therapy is to externalize the problem from the person. Too often clients are recruited into believing that *they* are the problem and end up constructing "problem-saturated stories" of themselves and their relationships. Narrative therapists work to minimize the

power of these stories and work with clients to co-author more empowering, satisfying, and fulfilling life stories. Similar to other family therapies, narrative therapy promotes respectful views of clients and takes into
consideration the contexts and interactions that influence human behavior. However, it is unique in that it also accounts for the socially constructed meanings and discourses that affect clients. Western cultures
frequently discuss problems as being flaws or pathologies of the individual. As a result many social institutions established to help people end up
compounding their problems through the processes of marginalization
and shame. Contrarily, narrative therapy treats clients as unique individuals, who are separate from their problems, and who are the experts on
their own lives.

BASIC ASSUMPTIONS

Narrative therapy is built on a number of basic assumptions, many of
which originate in the postmodern, constructivist, and social constructionist
schools of thought. Narrative therapy assumes that:

Experience Is Ambiguous; Meaning Created

Since human beings have no way of being fully objective, human "knowledge" relies heavily on individual experiences and perceptions. Even if it
were possible for two people to have an identical experience, they would
undoubtedly attach their own unique meanings to it. It is the meanings
individuals create about experience that they carry with them. Human beings work to create meaning and meaning systems that help explain their
lived experiences. It is, therefore, more important to learn about individuals' meanings than about their behaviors.

People Act Out of Their Stories (Narratives)

People's stories about themselves are strong determinants of their future
actions, experiences, and interpretations. These stories influence the way
people view themselves and the world around them; thus, "To a man with
a hammer, everything looks like a nail." A change in narrative is required
for a significant change in behavior.

Dominant Narratives Often Limit Individual Experience

Our life experiences are embedded in a context of strong societal norms.
These socially constructed norms often limit the scope of individuals' lived
experiences and perceived opportunities. Dismantling dominant discourses
can make room for new life possibilities.

Narratives Can Be Changed

Because life experience is so rich and extensive, not all aspects of a person's life are able to be integrated into his or her life-narrative; information is selectively highlighted and/or downplayed according to its fit with the individual's dominant self and life discourses. By selecting different information to be emphasized or minimized, new alternative stories are possible. In working with clients to create new, more preferred meanings about past, present, and future experiences, they can experience dramatic life change.

Change in Narrative Is Necessary for Significant Behavior Change

In order for clients to make significant change, they need to identify, and separate themselves from, the problem-saturated stories and disempowering cultural themes they have internalized. The narrative therapist assists the client in this process by joining with him or her in liberating and empowering conversations.

The "narrative metaphor proposes that persons live their lives by stories—that these stories are shaping of life and that they have real, not imagined, effects—that these stories provide the structures of life" (White, 1993, p. 36). People have life stories, or narratives, which they develop over time, that represent the whole or part of their lived experience. These created entities serve as structures for the meaning of future life events and as screens for what is seen/not seen; accepted/not accepted. Meanings, coherent with the individual's dominant narrative, are extracted from experience and included as reinforcers of that narrative.

Narrative therapy makes no judgment of what is normal or abnormal. Such judgments would assume the possibility of an objective knowledge of reality, and narrative therapists do not assume that they have the corner on reality. Similarly, no particular course of family development is seen as being more appropriate than others, for this would necessitate viewing the family or family members as problematic. Narrative therapy posits that the client/family is not the problem—the problem is the problem.

Narrative therapy argues for the elimination of all general categories of problems, such as those found in the DSM-IV. Problems are viewed as results of individuals being induced by their culture into self-defeating views of themselves and those around them. Narrative therapists seek to free their clients from the restrictive discourses operating in their lives so as to open up new possibilities and ways of being.

ASSESSMENT AND TREATMENT PROCEDURES

In general, narrative therapy involves (1) recasting client problems as afflictions (externalization), focusing on the effects of problems rather than on the causes; (2) finding exceptions (unique outcomes) in the client's problem-saturated story, when he or she experienced partial triumphs over the affliction and took effective action; (3) opening space for alternative stories and life possibilities; and (4) recruitment of support for the client's new preferred meanings and ways of living.

During sessions the therapist listens closely for demeaning labels or self-views that the client has applied to him or herself. When such constructs are discovered, the narrative therapist works to deconstruct them by exploring their origin and by eliciting the clients' preferences regarding the associated meanings. This process is effective for helping clients regain their voice and sense of self-determination; they are then better prepared to consider options and opportunities previously unavailable to them.

Rather than searching for the pathology in the client's world, the narrative therapist engages the client in conversations aimed at discovering and promoting preferred meanings and ways of living. Most of the therapist's activity during sessions involves the use of curiosity-guided questions. A variety of questions are used to assist clients in the process of deconstructing old, restrictive, ways of viewing themselves and their world and constructing new ones. The following are some examples of questions that might be used by narrative therapists:

- *Questions used to deconstruct externally imposed labels and meanings experienced as problematic by the client.*

  "When you use the term 'co-dependent,' what do you mean?"

- *Questions used for discovering exceptions to the problem-saturated stories clients have been telling themselves and those around them.*

  "Have there been times when conflict could have hurt your relationships, but didn't?"

- *Questions used for discovering clients' meanings and preferred ways of thinking and being.*

  "Is that how you prefer things to be, or would you rather have them some other way?"

- *Questions used to assist clients in integrating their new, preferred meanings and ways of living into the past, present, and future of their life-narratives.*

  "Is this a new way of doing things or have you done things like this before?"
  "How do you predict this change will affect your relationships with your friends?"

- *Questions that provide clients with the opportunity to create new, preferred views of self and others that are more productive and enhancing.*

  "What does that experience tell you about your relationship?"

- *Questions used to extend the story into the future and to support/reinforce those positive changes selected by the client as being important.*

"Now that you have taken charge of this aspect of your life, what do you predict for the future?"

These questions can be used to help clients free themselves from old, restrictive, and undesirable ways of viewing and living in the world. Almost immediately after the use of externalizing questions, many clients exhibit an alleviation of anxiety and seem be more free to discuss their interactions with the problem. Externalized problems can then be used as tools for unifying couples and families who previously viewed each other as the problem source.

Finally, once clients have discovered more preferred meanings and ways of knowing about the world and themselves, the therapist assists them in finding audiences (friends, family members, churches, etc.) that will be supportive of their new self-narrative.

Evidence of Effectiveness

Little empirical data is available on the effectiveness of narrative therapy. In fact, the theory behind the therapy calls into question scientific methodologies and their supposed utility for uncovering "truth." From this perspective the sciences are socially constructed technologies for constructing socially acceptable meanings of the world.

In spite of the narrative view of science, some have used scientific approaches to evaluate the effectiveness and operational processes of narrative therapy. Besa (1994), for example, used Single-System Research Designs to evaluate narrative family therapy's effectiveness at reducing parent–child conflicts. Six families were treated and, when compared to baseline rates, five of them demonstrated an 88–98% decrease in conflict. Aside from Besa's study, a textual analysis investigation by Kogan and Gale (1997), and case examples used by various authors for technique illustration, no empirical attempts at evaluating the effectiveness of narrative therapy were found in the literature.

CASE ILLUSTRATION

Janet and Robert originally came into therapy for problems they were experiencing with their daughter and her husband. Robert had a desire to improve his marital relationship with Janet and they decided to come into therapy. Janet presented herself as having a number of "mental illnesses," the primary one being "agoraphobia." She reported experiencing panic attacks when out in public.

After Janet reports having agoraphobia, the therapist seeks to understand how the couple bypassed their difficulties in order to attend the session.

Janet: I have agoraphobia anyway, so I'm very isolated.

Therapist: So, this was kind of a bold move on your part to come in here today. Is that . . .

Janet: I didn't want to. I wanted to go to bed. I've been sleeping in a lot lately, but I came. Robert was disappointed that I said, "I really want to go to bed; I don't want to come." So, I got dressed and came.

Therapist: So it was your view that he was disappointed that got you to come today?

Janet: Yeah, and that he wanted to make an effort to keep us together, I think?

Robert: Of course I want to keep us together.

Therapist: Did you mean . . .

Janet: That's why I came.

Therapist: You think that Robert's desire to keep your marriage together is what got you to come in today?

Janet: Right.

Therapist: Okay so, does that mean you still feel a little unclear exactly why you decided to not go to bed but to go ahead and make the bold move of coming out here?

Janet: I know that I need help and I had considered before trying to pick out some sort of therapy again just to . . . I'm on medication from my psychiatrist, but I only see him for medication. And I do know that it can help me deal with stress. I also know that sometimes it's not a good time to deal with it. I need some of my coping mechanisms right now, healthy or not.

Therapist: Anti-anxiety medication?

Janet: I have major depression and I'm on Welbutrin, Xanax, and I was on Prozac and Adaval. I have spells of narcolepsy, spells of excessive sleepiness. And that's not going to change, I know that.

Therapist: It sounds like fear has had a lot to do with the problems of your life. Is that right?

Janet: Oh yeah.

Therapist: I'm wondering how it is coming into your relationship and I wonder the kinds of things that fear keeps you from doing that you want to do or gets you to do that you don't want to do.

Janet: My life revolves around it, honestly. I don't like not driving. I can drive, but a panic attack is a hard thing to have in the middle of traffic.

Therapist: So driving is one thing that you like.

Janet: I don't know that I like it, but it would get me from point A to point B. I was going back to school and I'm sure Robert would let me go with him again. I would ride to school with him, but I've been out the last couple of semesters.

Therapist: So school is something that you've wanted to do.

Janet: I'd like to finish my degree, yeah.

Therapist: But for now fear has kind of gotten in there and stopped you from doing it?

Janet later discusses her past and present tendencies toward suicidal ideations. She reported that her love for her children and the potential for being hospitalized currently keep her from attempting suicide. Next the therapist discusses suicidal ideations as something Mental Illness gets her to participate in and begins a conversation about unique outcomes, ways, and times that Janet has been able to minimize the effects of Mental Illness on her life.

Therapist: So, Mental Illness has got you to the point of considering suicide?
Janet: Oh yeah.
Therapist: It sounds like it's so strong and so destructive to you that you get to points where you feel like, "I don't want to fight the battle against Mental Illness"?
Janet: Yeah, and I used to . . . it sounds so strange . . . cut myself or hurt myself just to get a little relief; and somehow that brings a relief. Now I just stay on the computer probably twenty hours a day when I'm not in my bed twenty hours a day.
Therapist: So, somehow you've found a way to keep it from at least getting in your mind?
Janet: Yeah, I either sleep or go to the computer.
Therapist: So you have some tools that you've been using to hold Mental Illness off from getting the complete best of you?
Janet: Exactly, and I can't do this (marital therapy). Robert has a very strong personality and in my own way I am strong, although I feel I'm perceived weak . . . you know, mental illness, depression. .
Robert: She's not weak. She has a strong personality.

The therapist then works on challenging the socially constructed meanings the client has accepted which serve to limit her, how she views herself, and how she experiences the world around her.

Therapist: Would it sound right to say that Mental Illness has been attacking you your whole life?
Janet: Attacking. I feel like it's sort of inbred. It's part of me. No, I don't feel it attacks me . . . it's just me.
Therapist: So, it's got you believing that you are the Mental Illness?
Janet: Yeah. I am.
Therapist: So, right now, you believe that you are the Mental Illness?
Janet: Yeah, I'm on disability. I mean . . . I hate it.

Co-therapist: I wonder when you first started thinking you were the Mental Illness. When did that come about?

Janet: I don't really know. I've had some problems since I can remember, but the worst breakdown was when my second child died and I had some really odd symptoms with that depression and I never could really spring back . . . I never came back from that. I just kind of went away . . . I did go away.

Labels have been socially constructed for behaviors or ways of being that are outside the norm. Janet had some reactions to severe traumas that, though natural for her, fell into a category of mental illness. From then on she began to see herself and to be seen by others as a mentally ill person.

Next the therapist explores with the client some alternative and preferred ways of being for the client. As she is provided the opportunity to discuss other aspects of her life that are more empowering, the potential for new self-views and stories is present.

Therapist: So, say that somehow you started to get some advantage in this battle against Mental Illness and were able to free up some resources so that you could fight the battle with one hand. What would you like to do with the other hand?

Janet: I did go to school and I painted.

Therapist: So there are some things that you would like to do. Tell me, would there be any difference in the way you would approach your relationship with Robert?

Janet: Most definitely. There are some things that need to be dealt with.

The emerging story of the client as a person, apart from the mental illness which affects her, begins to emerge and the therapist begins to assist the client in re-storying her life experiences.

Therapist: I keep getting this picture in my mind of Mental Illness being like a dam that you are holding back.

Janet: That's a good description.

Therapist: It sounds like you've almost decided that you can't really turn and face other issues right now because you have to hold the dam back.

Janet: That helps clarify for me, the way you put it. I have a lot of guilt for not being more involved with Melissa (daughter) and Robert. I have a lot of guilt every day.

Therapist: So how do you think others have, perhaps, misinterpreted your battle against Mental Illness? or have they?

Janet: Yeah. I'm lazy, selfish, and don't accomplish anything, most of which is true, except I'm really not a lazy person, when I'm not really hit by narcolepsy.

Therapist: It sounds like guilt plays a role here.

Janet: It's got a lot to do with it.

SUMMARY

When clients come in for therapy, they are ready to talk about and deal with their problems. They often view their problems as being part of themselves; they view themselves or their family members as the problem. As illustrated in the case example, narrative therapy is a useful approach for externalizing the problem from the client and his or her relationship(s); decreasing interpersonal conflict and eliminating the need for blame; counteracting problem-induced, self-defeating beliefs clients have about themselves and their relationships; opening the way for mutual respect and communication between partners and family members and uniting them against the problem; freeing individuals, couples, and families from limiting cultural discourses; and opening space for clients to construct new self-knowledges and ways of interaction. Even with severe problems such as anxiety, a therapist using the narrative approach can facilitate near-immediate alleviation of anxiety and fear by engaging clients in liberating, empowering conversations.

REFERENCES

American Psychiatric Association. (1994). *Diagnostic and statistical manual of mental disorders* (DSM-IV) (4th ed.). Washington, DC: American Psychiatric Association.

Besa, D. (1994). Evaluating narrative family therapy using single-system research designs. *Research on Social Work Practice*, 4(3), 309–325.

Craske, M. G., & Barlow, D. H. (1993). Panic disorder and agoraphobia. In D. H. Barlow (Ed.), *Clinical handbook of psychological disorders: A step-by-step treatment manual* (pp. 1–47). New York: Guilford Press.

Craske, M. G., & Zoellner, L. A. (1995). Anxiety disorders: The role of marital therapy. In N. S. Jacobson & A. S. Gurman (Eds.), *Clinical handbook of couple therapy* (pp. 394–410). New York: Guilford Press.

Emmelkamp, P.M.G. (1994). Behavior therapy with adults. In A. E. Bergin & S. L. Garfield (Eds.), *Handbook of psychotherapy and behavior change* (4th ed., pp. 379–427). New York: John Wiley & Sons.

Epston, D., Morris, F., & Maisel, R. (1995). A narrative approach to so-called anorexia/bulimia. In K. Weingarten (Ed.), *Cultural resistance: Challenging beliefs about men, women, and therapy* (pp. 69–96). New York: Haworth Press.

Focht, L., & Beardslee, W. R. (1996). "Speech after long silence": The use of narrative therapy in a preventive intervention for children of parents with affective disorder. *Family Process*, 35, 407–422.

Gallant, J. P., Brownlee, K., & Vodde, R. (1995). "Not with me you don't": A story of narrative practice and dissociative disorder. *Contemporary Family Therapy*, 17(1), 143–157.

Kogan, S. M., & Gale, J. E. (1997). Decentering therapy: Textual analysis of a narrative therapy session. *Family Process*, 36, 101–126.

Morretti, M. M., Feldman, L. A., & Shaw, B. F. (1990). Cognitive therapy: Current issues in theory and practice. In R. A. Wells & V. J. Giannetti (Eds.), *Handbook of the brief psychotherapies* (pp. 217–237). New York: Plenum Press.

Nichols, M. P., & Schwartz, R. C. (1998). *Family therapy: Concepts and methods* (4th ed.). Needham Heights, MA: Allyn and Bacon.

Patterson, J. E., & Van Meir, E. (1996). Using patient narratives to teach psychopathology. *Journal of Marital and Family Therapy*, 22(1), 59–68.

White, M. (1986). Negative explanation, restraint, and double description: A template for family therapy. *Family Process*, 25(2), 169–184.

White, M. (1993). Deconstruction and therapy. In S. Gilligan & R. Price (Eds.), *Therapeutic conversations* (pp. 22–61). New York: W. W. Norton & Co.

White, M., & Epston, D. (1990). *Narrative means to therapeutic ends*. New York: W. W. Norton & Co.

Chapter 6

Using Thought Field Therapy to Help Survivors of Destructive Cults

Monica Pignotti

Survivors of destructive cults report a number of symptoms resulting from the aftereffects of traumatic experiences of physical, sexual, emotional, mental, and spiritual abuse, which include: depression, anxiety, panic attacks, flashbacks, nightmares, guilt, self-blame, anger, shame, humiliation, and a variety of other distressing emotions. Current treatment approaches focus on educating the person about the cult experience and giving the survivor coping strategies for dealing with the emotional distress, which can last up to 24 months or longer after the person leaves the cult. Callahan Techniques Thought Field Therapy (TFT) is a revolutionary treatment for psychological problems, discovered by Roger Callahan, Ph.D., that is capable of rapidly eliminating the symptoms of trauma, often within minutes. Unlike many treatments for trauma, TFT does not require painful reliving of traumatic experiences and offers real help for the emotional distress commonly experienced by the cult survivor.

OVERVIEW OF THE PRESENTING PROBLEM

The cult-related tragedies of Heaven's Gate, the Branch Davidians, the Solar Temple and the sarin gas attacks in the Tokyo subways have made it clear that cults are as much of a phenomenon today as they were in the 1970s. Cult expert Dr. Margaret Singer (1995) estimates that,

depending on how one defines a cult, there are anywhere from three thousand to five thousand cults in the United States alone. Over the past two decades as many as twenty million people have been involved . . . not only are cult members affected but millions more family members and loved ones worry and wonder, sometimes for years, about what has happened to their relatives or friends. (p. 5)

It is very likely that at some point in their careers, mental health professionals, especially those who specialize in dealing with the aftereffects of trauma, will work with cult members, former cult members, or their families.

Definition of a Destructive Cult

Cults are best defined in terms of their deeds rather than their creeds. As former director of the International Cult Education Program, Marcia Rudin (1994) puts it, "Beliefs are not the issue. Cults spring from all ideologies" (p. 65). Not all cults are destructive in nature. Some are relatively benign and harmless. In the context of this chapter, however, it is destructive cults and their aftereffects that are being defined and discussed.

To formulate a precise definition of a destructive cult, Chambers, Langone, Dole, and Grice (1994) determined by factor analysis that the following four factors clustered together with regards to the cult experience: (1) compliance; (2) exploitation; (3) mind control; and (4) anxious dependency. From these factors they formed the empirical definition that "Cults are groups that often exploit members psychologically and/or financially by making members comply with leadership's demands through certain types of psychological manipulation, popularly called mind control, and through the inculcation of a deep-seated, anxious dependency on the group and its leader" (pp. 105–106).

Aftereffects of Cults

From the above definition, one can see that having been a member of a destructive cult can produce severe aftereffects in those who leave them. Paul Martin, Ph.D., director of Wellspring, a residential facility for the treatment of ex-cult members in Ohio, points out that "The ex-cultist has been traumatized, deceived, conned, used, and often emotionally, physically, sexually and mentally abused while serving the group and/or the leader. Like other trauma victims (for example, of criminal acts, war atrocities, rape and serious illness), former cultists often re-experience the painful memories of their group involvement" (p. 208).

For the purposes of this chapter, I am going to confine my discussion to people who have suffered from cult abuse as an adult. The effects on children who have been abused in cults, including satanic and ritual abuse, are a whole separate phenomenon and topic that would deserve its own chapter to do it justice. Such people have, however, been helped with TFT.

Conway and Siegelman (1995) compare the experience of ex-cult members to Vietnam veterans. In a survey of 400 former cult members from 48 different cults, they found the following most commonly reported symptoms: depression (75%); loneliness (68%); anger (68%); disorientation (66%); humiliation/embarrassment (59%); guilt feelings (59%); nightmares (48%); suicidal/self-destructive tendencies (35%). In a later study, done by Michael Langone (1992), of 308 former cult members, over three-quarters of the respondents rated their cult experience as either harmful or very harmful and respondents reported much the same post-cult symptoms as in the earlier study.

Symptoms reported by clinicians who have extensive experience working with ex-cult members include: depression, panic attacks, fears, phobias or anxiety, nightmares and flashbacks, loneliness, guilt, shame, or embarrassment; grief and loss; and feelings of anger and/or betrayal (Goldberg, 1993; Goldberg & Goldberg, 1982; Hassan, 1988, 2000; Martin, 1993; Singer, 1979, 1995; Tobias & Lalich, 1994).

Physical, sexual, emotional, and mental abuse is also common in cults (Martin, 1993). At one recovery conference for former cult members, 40% of the women in attendance chose to attend a workshop for women sexually abused in cults (Tobias & Lalich, 1994).

TRADITIONAL TREATMENT APPROACHES

Therapy with former cult members needs to be twofold; it needs to be psychoeducational, and it must deal with the emotional aftereffects (Goldberg, 1993). An educational component is necessary so ex-cult members can learn about cults and mind control and come to an understanding of how they were manipulated into a cult that they would not have otherwise chosen to become involved in (Hassan, 1988, 2000; Singer, 1995; Tobias & Lalich, 1994). It is necessary for individuals who have been in cults to become aware of the beliefs they acquired while in the cult and sort out what they now choose to believe in after having left the cult. This aspect of the recovery process is adequately addressed in treatment approaches currently being used by professionals who specialize in cults. Increased awareness and understanding, however, usually do not do anything to relieve the emotional distress experienced by the cult survivor.

According to Margaret Singer, ex-cult members must "face psychological and emotional stirrings that can cause intense agonies for awhile" (1995, p. 301). Singer points out to ex-members that these symptoms most often do go away with time and estimates the recovery process to be between 6 and 24 months, although some may take longer. Treatment, for Singer, consists of ex-cult members learning to label what they are experiencing, so they can better understand what is happening, and are better equipped to cope with the psychological distress they experience, which she believes is inevitable.

Tobias and Lalich (1994) suggest cognitive behavioral techniques to deal with triggers of the cult. In this way, the ex-cult member can learn to cope with the symptoms, but this does not eliminate the symptoms themselves. Hassan (1988) suggests using a technique similar to Neuro-Linguistic Programming's Visual-Kinesthetic Dissociation (VKD) and Change History, where the cult involvement can be redone in the individual's mind, with the resources that are currently available to that person. This process brings about increased feelings of empowerment for the individual that were not present in the original situation where victimization by the cult occurred. Hassan (2000) also reports success with using an educational as well as a cognitive-behavioral approach to undo phobias that have been installed by the cult. Colleagues of mine have reported using EMDR with ex-cult members, and while they report some success, EMDR can frequently produce painful abreactions of the traumatic experience during treatment.

William and Lorna Goldberg (1982), who have run a support group for ex-cult members for more than 22 years, have found that support from peers in the group who have gone through similar experiences can be very beneficial to the ex-cult member, and helps to provide an education about how cults operate. People who attend such groups learn that their experience was not unique and find others who have experienced what they have, which helps them to feel less ashamed and alone and enables them to identify patterns that bring about further insight into their experiences.

While ex-members report getting a certain amount of relief from these treatment approaches, there is nothing in the literature of current treatments being used that can give the person full emotional relief from the pain suffered from the trauma of cult involvement. This author has been a part of several Internet discussion groups where former cult members have reported that they have not found relief from their suffering, in spite of having tried every type of therapy currently available.

The treatment being discussed in this chapter, Thought Field Therapy (TFT), can give people suffering from the aftereffects of trauma relief that, in my own experience, no other treatment method has been able to provide. No treatment can give the person back the years he or she lost to the cult or undo the reality of the cult experience. However, TFT can bring the person immediate relief from the many symptoms of psychological distress that ex-cult members suffer from, and will help that person get on with living the rest of his or her life.

OVERVIEW OF TFT

Brief Description

Thought Field Therapy, also known as Callahan Techniques, is a treatment developed by psychologist Dr. Roger Callahan that can offer a person rapid relief from a variety of psychological problems, including the after-effects of trauma and sequelae. The person being treated is asked to stimulate energy meridian points on the body in a specific sequence (determined by a procedure that will be elaborated on in the sections following) that diagnoses the problem at its root cause. In essence, TFT diagnosis provides a code which, when applied to the psychological problem to which the person is attuned, will eliminate the disturbance at its root.

TFT is fast, painless, and produces immediate results. Unlike many of the traditional treatments for trauma, which require exposure and abreaction, there is no painful reliving of the traumatic event with TFT. The person only needs to think about the trauma and then stimulate the energy meridian points on his or her body, as directed by a therapist trained in TFT procedures.

History

Roger Callahan is a psychologist who has been working with clients since 1950. He was a pioneer in cognitive-behavioral approaches and hypnosis when these treatments were new and controversial. Throughout his long career, he has been continuously looking for better ways to help his clients with their psychological problems.

In the late 1970s, a psychiatrist colleague of his showed him a muscle-testing technique that he had learned from chiropractors, known as Applied Kinesiology (Walther, 1988). Dr. Callahan was fascinated with the phenomenon that his arm, while initially strong when pushed on, could go weak if he was thinking about something emotionally distressing. At the time, he was not sure how this applied to his field, but he took a 100-hour course in Applied Kinesiology. He also began learning about the energy meridian points on the body that are used in acupuncture.

In 1980, he was working with Mary, a woman in her forties who had a severe, lifelong phobia of water (Callahan, 1997a). Her fear was so bad that she was able to take only sponge baths, was terrified every time it rained, and regularly had terrible nightmares of water coming to get her. He had tried every treatment he knew, in his large repertoire of treatment approaches, to help her with this phobia. After a year and a half, there was only a very small amount of progress. Mary was able to sit at the edge of his swimming pool, but was still so terrified that she was unable to look at the water.

Mary had commented that whenever she thought about water, she got a terrible feeling in the pit of her stomach. Using his knowledge of energy meridian points and Applied Kinesiology, he tested the energy meridian point connected with her stomach and found that it was off-balance. Not expecting much to happen, he asked her to tap under her eye, which is the end point to the stomach meridian. Immediately after doing so, Mary said,

"It's gone." When Dr. Callahan asked her what was gone, she said, "That terrible feeling I get in the pit of my stomach every time I think of water is gone." She then went running out of his office toward his swimming pool. Fearing that Mary might jump in the pool, not knowing how to swim, he called after her, "Mary, look out!", to which she responded, "Don't worry, Dr. Callahan. I know I can't swim." This showed that even though this treatment had completely eliminated her phobia of water, it did not eliminate her common sense.

Later that night, there was a big storm and Mary put her phobia to the ultimate test by going to the beach, which had previously terrified her, even on a nice day. She was completely free of her fear of water and remains so to this day, which has been confirmed by a videotaped interview (Callahan, 1997b).

After curing Mary of her phobia, Dr. Callahan began trying this form of diagnosis and treatment on all of his clients. Much to his surprise, he found that the treatment not only worked on phobias; it worked equally well on traumatic experience, where the person had good reason to be upset. The first person he treated for trauma was a young woman who, 10 years earlier, had been held in her apartment for five days by a gang of men and repeatedly gang-raped, while they threatened to kill her young child. Needless to say, this experience was so traumatic for her that 10 years later she was still having nightmares about it and unable to date men. After a very brief treatment, where she was asked to tap at the beginning of her eyebrow near the bridge of her nose, her trauma was completely eliminated. She was able to date men and her nightmares completely vanished.

Over the years, through his causal diagnostic procedure, Dr. Callahan made additions and refinements to his procedures. In working with hundreds of clients with the same conditions, he found, through causal diagnosis, sequences that worked 70 to 90% of the time in the average client population, which became known as the TFT Algorithms. Those who do not respond to the algorithms can usually be successfully treated with sequences determined by individualized TFT Diagnosis by a therapist trained in such procedures, as can psychological problems that do not fall into any of the algorithm categories.

In the 1990s, Dr. Callahan began doing training certification programs in TFT diagnosis for therapists and other health professionals. As of the year 2000, there are more than 500 therapists from all over the world trained in TFT diagnosis, thousands trained in the TFT Algorithms, and 20 therapists trained in the voice technology. Roger Callahan has trained therapists from England, Sweden, The Netherlands, France, Spain, Italy, Canada, Greece, Germany, Australia, Brazil, Denmark, Switzerland, Bolivia, Mexico, and Japan. The treatments now have official recognition as an approved medical treatment in Alberta, Canada (College of Physicians and Surgeons), and are officially recognized in Nevada as an approved medical homeopathic treatment.

BASIC ASSUMPTIONS AND MAJOR THEORETIC PRINCIPLES OF TFT

What Is a Thought Field?

A "field" is a term that comes from physics, defined as "an invisible non-material structure in space which has an effect upon matter" (Callahan & Callahan, 1996, p. 117). We cannot see the field itself, but we can see the effects that it has. For instance, we cannot see a magnetic field, but we can see the effect it has on iron filings when they are drawn up by a magnet. We cannot see a gravitational field, but we can observe the effects of dropping a solid object and watching it fall to the ground.

The biologist Rupert Sheldrake (1981, 1988) introduced the concept of morphic resonance, which is a theory that explains how information not contained in DNA can be passed down through successive generations via morphogenetic fields. According to TFT theory, information in thought fields can also be passed down through the generations. For instance, all land-based chordates are born with a fear of heights. For our ancestors, a fear of heights was necessary for survival and in modern times, we have inherited this fear, not through our genes but through the transmission of information contained within such fields. This is somewhat analogous to Jung's notion of the collective unconscious. Thus, the person who has a fear of heights, for instance, is not necessarily experiencing his own trauma of falling, but could be experiencing the collective trauma of his ancestors who have fallen in the past (Callahan and Callahan, 1996, p. 121).

Perturbations

According to TFT theory, the perturbation is the root cause of all emotional distress. Callahan (1996, p. 121) defines a perturbation (p) in the following manner:

A p is a subtle but clearly isolable aspect of a thought field which is responsible for triggering all negative emotions. No p, no negative emotion. The p is the generating structure which determines the chemical, hormonal, nervous system, cognitive and brain activity commonly associated with, and an intrinsic and necessary part (but not the fundamental cause) of the negative emotions.

From this definition, there are a several important principles relevant to perturbations.

Perturbations as Active Information

The perturbation contains *active information*, a term coined by physicist David Bohm. In *The Undivided Universe*, Bohm and Hiley (1993) elaborate on what he means when he uses the word "information":

What is crucial here is that we are calling attention to the literal meaning of the word, i.e., to in-form, which is actively to put form into something or to imbue something with form. . . . The basic idea of active information is that a form having very little energy enters into and directs a much greater energy. The activity of the latter in this way is given a form similar to that of the smaller energy. (p. 35)

Perturbations as the Root Cause

TFT theory is revolutionary, as it overturns all of the commonly held and currently accepted theories held by psychologists. According to TFT theory, brain chemistry is not the primary cause of emotional distress. Negative emotions start with the perturbation, which in turn affects the body's bioenergy system, which then affects brain chemistry. According to Callahan, theories that attribute psychological problems to brain chemistry are completely in the wrong ballpark (Callahan & Callahan, 2000). The basis for this claim is that with TFT, emotional distress can be completely eliminated by addressing energy meridian points on the body in specified sequences. The treatment does not directly do anything to the brain, but nevertheless it eliminates the problem.

Perturbations Are Isolable

In relation to the thought field that contains them, perturbations are isolable. This means that when perturbations are eliminated, the rest of the information relevant to the problem remains intact, as in the case of Mary, where her phobia of water was eliminated, yet she still remembered that she could not swim. The pain of a trauma can be eliminated, while the memory of the experience remains intact. Contrary to what is believed in conventional psychotherapy, it is not the memory that is the problem, but rather the perturbation that is the source of the emotional charge.

Isomorphism

An isomorphism is a one-to-one relationship between two distinctly different sets of objects. In TFT, a one-to-one relationship exists between specific energy meridian points on the body and perturbations. For every perturbation, there is a correct corresponding energy meridian point on the body that needs to be addressed (Callahan & Callahan, 1996).

Tuning the Thought Field

In order for a TFT treatment to be effective, the individual being treated must be attuned to the thought field, which means that the person needs to be directed to think about the problem being treated. This differs from other forms of treatment, such as that given by a doctor or dentist, where the patient does not need to be thinking of anything in particular for the treatment to work. In the case of infants, young children, or developmentally disabled adults, who are unable to direct their attention to the problem, they can be successfully treated if they are in the situation pertaining to the problem being treated.

Causal Diagnosis

Now that we know that perturbations contained in thought fields are the root cause of emotional distress and that they correspond to energy meridian points on the body, the next question that needs to be addressed is, how do we know what points need to be treated and in which sequence? There are 14 potential treatment points in TFT that, mathematically, have the potential for 87 billion possible combinations of treatment points. If we just guessed at which points needed to be treated through random trial and error, it would take over 100,000 years to hit on a correct combination and sequence of treatment points, if we worked continuously with no breaks.

Fortunately, there is a solution to this; we are able to determine which points need to be treated and in what sequence by a method called *causal diagnosis*. Because TFT's method of diagnosis reveals perturbations, which are the root cause of the psychological disturbance, it is called *causal* diagnosis, which is radically different from the nosological diagnosis done from sets of symptoms listed in the DSM-IV. According to Roger Callahan:

Causal diagnosis means our diagnostic procedure reveals the fundamental constituents of psychological problems. We call these constituents perturbations. TFT diagnosis is a process of revealing the specific perturbations in the precise order in which they occur. It is the revelation of this order, or encoding of perturbations, which reveals the exact treatments to do leading to our unusually high success. (Callahan & Callahan, 1996, Acknowledgments)

The TFT causal diagnostic procedure was developed by Roger Callahan over a period of years, culminating in the development of the state-of-the-art causal diagnosis of the Voice Technology. The causal diagnostic procedure consists of: Having the client tune the thought field by thinking about the problem, testing for psychological reversal, and diagnosing which treatment points are needed and in what sequence, either through the Voice

Technology or through a muscle-testing procedure. The muscle-testing procedure comes from the field of Applied Kinesiology, developed by chiropractor George Goodheart. Dr. Callahan does not, however, recall ever seeing anyone in Applied Kinesiology use a muscle-testing procedure to diagnose sequences of acupuncture points in a correct order to diagnose and treat psychological problems. Furthermore, he states that he never saw anyone cured of a psychological problem before discovering TFT (Callahan, 1998d). Callahan has stated that without the discoveries of George Goodheart, he (Callahan) could not have made the further discoveries that led to his system of TFT causal diagnosis. However, he also points out that without his own subsequent discoveries unique to TFT (i.e., perturbations as the root cause of psychological problems, tuning the thought field, psychological reversal, the 9-gamut sequence, explained in more detail below), we would not have the current system of causal diagnosis of psychological problems that makes the very high rate of success regularly obtained with TFT possible (Callahan, 1998d).

The diagnosed sequence of treatment points, in TFT, is crucial to the success of the treatment. The causal diagnostic procedure provides the TFT practitioner with a code that, much like a combination lock, must be followed in the exact sequence revealed by diagnosis in order to produce the desired result of eliminating the perturbation(s) and thus, the emotional distress. Just as one cannot expect to open a combination lock using the correct numbers and the wrong sequence, the energy meridian points of TFT need to be stimulated in their proper sequence. Like combination locks, some treatment sequences are very simple, requiring only one or two points, whereas others require a series of intricate combinations to get results (Callahan, 1995–1998).

Definition of TFT

The following formal definition of TFT has been derived from the above principles:

TFT is a treatment for psychological disturbances which provides a code, that when applied to a psychological problem an individual is attuned to, will eliminate perturbations in the thought field, the fundamental cause of all negative emotions. This code is elicited through TFT's causal diagnostic procedure through which the TFT algorithms were developed. (Callahan, 1998)

Levels of TFT

There are three levels of TFT treatments: algorithms, diagnosis, and Voice Technology.

Algorithms represent the simplest TFT procedures. The algorithms are recipes of treatment sequences that have been predetermined by Roger Callahan through the use of causal diagnosis. By working with hundreds of people who had the same problem (for instance, a trauma), it was discovered that there were sequences that worked on approximately 70 to 90% of the people treated in the average client population. There are algorithms for phobias, trauma, anxiety/panic attacks, addictive urges, grief/loss, love pain, compulsions, OCD, pain, depression, jet lag, anger, guilt, shame, and embarrassment. Because the treatment sequence is already known through previous causal diagnoses, the therapist does not need to learn the skills of diagnosis. The TFT algorithms can be easily learned by therapists in a two-day training program and used as a self-help method by lay people. Children can even learn to do algorithms on one another.

TFT Diagnosis is the next level of training, where the person learns to do causal diagnosis and the therapy localization procedure. Diagnosis will provide individualized treatments by giving precise sequences of meridian points to be stimulated. People who do not respond to algorithms will usually respond to the TFT diagnostic procedure, which has about a 95% success rate. Diagnosis can also be used for psychological problems that do not fall into any of the categories of the algorithms. Those trained in diagnosis readily see the importance of sequence, when a person who did not respond to the sequence of an algorithm responds to an individually diagnosed sequence.

The current training program for diagnosis is in three parts (Callahan, 1998): Step A is a home study course consisting of a manual, videotapes, and audiotapes that explain the procedure. After 30 days of practice with the Step A materials, the trainee is then eligible to take Step B, which is an in-person, three-day seminar given through Callahan Techniques, Ltd., where more advanced aspects of TFT theory and testing for energy toxins and sensitivities are learned. After completion of Step B, the next is Step C, which consists of six months of supervision with Roger Callahan, where he uses the Voice Technology to help the trainee's clients who did not respond to diagnosis. After completion of Step C, the person is then eligible to take an examination that qualifies him or her to teach Callahan-approved algorithm seminars and to use the title TFTdx.

TFT Voice Technology™ (VT) has the highest rate of success of all forms of TFT and is the most rapid form of treatment. The VT can help people who do not respond to algorithms or diagnosis. This is the treatment that Dr. Callahan uses to treat the most difficult cases. The VT, which is done over the telephone, reveals perturbations that are contained in a person's voice and those trained in the VT can diagnose a precise sequence of treatment points. VT represents the gold standard of TFT and a therapist trained in this technology can treat clients from all over the world.

Psychological Reversal

The phenomenon of psychological reversal (PR) was discovered by Dr. Callahan in 1979. At the time he was treating people who were finding it impossible to lose weight. He found that when he muscle-tested them on the statement "I want to lose weight," their arms went weak and when he tested them on the statement "I want to gain weight," their arms became strong. Later, after making his discovery of TFT treatment, he found that PR was a literal reversal of the body's energy flow and that this could be treated and quickly corrected by tapping on the side of the hand, which is the end point to the small intestine meridian. After doing this, he found that a treatment that was previously ineffective would now work. Making this discovery doubled his success rate for TFT procedures. The effects of PR and its treatment can be readily seen, by anyone who knows algorithms, by doing an algorithm that did not work on a person, doing the PR treatment, and observing that the treatment that was once ineffective is suddenly effective after correcting for PR.

Mini-PR is a block to the treatment that occurs when the person's distress level has gone down from the starting point, but has not gone down all the way and thus, part of the problem still remains. When Mini-PR is successfully corrected, and the treatment is repeated, this will lead to complete elimination of the psychological distress being treated.

The SUD Scale

Roger Callahan has stated that "there is no substitute for the client's report" (Callahan & Callahan, 1996). Traditional behavior theory does not acknowledge the existence of consciousness and thus measures success in therapy only through changes in behavior, dismissing the client's "subjective" report as invalid. Thus, such therapy is considered a success if clients show a change in behavior, even if they still report feeling emotional distress. Although changes in objective measures have been reported with TFT, according to Roger Callahan: "as much as I like objective measures, there is not and cannot ever be a substitute for the subjective report of how an individual feels." (Callahan, 1998a, p. 4).

The Subjective Units of Distress Scale (SUD), originally developed by Wolpe (1969), provides a precise way to measure change in the client's self-reported emotional state. An important part of the TFT protocol is to have the client think about the problem and then report how upset he or she feels on a scale of 1 to 10, where a 10 represents the most upset possible and a 1 represents no trace of emotional upset. The therapist writes down the beginning SUD and after proceeding with the treatment, asks the client to rate his or her upset again on the SUD scale. The goal of TFT treatment is complete elimination of all subjective units of distress, which is a SUD of 1.

The Apex Problem

The term "apex" comes from Arthur Koestler (1967), who describes those moments when a human being is able to function at his or her peak, or apex. Thus, the apex problem represents a problem in optimum functioning. In TFT we use this term to describe a phenomenon we see quite often, where the client recognizes that his emotional distress is completely eliminated, but attributes this to something other than the treatment. The person, unable to recognize that TFT eliminated his problem, makes up an irrational reason for the change. Some common statements clients make that indicate the presence of the apex problem include:

- "This treatment distracted me."
- "This must be a placebo effect." (often said by clients who are very skeptical and have no belief whatsoever in the procedure)
- "I'm finding it hard to come up with a SUD." (when the client previously had no trouble giving a very high SUD)
- "The treatment must have repressed my feelings."
- "I'm not able to think about the problem."

Sometimes the person even forgets he ever had the problem. For this reason it is advisable for the therapist to write down the beginning SUD or, with the client's permission, taperecord the session. It also might be useful to explain the apex problem to the client, although this is not always effective.

Some people have asked me why it is important for the client to recognize the apex problem. After all, the client got better, and isn't that all that counts? My response to this is that it is, indeed, important for a client who has been helped by a procedure to recognize the source of the help. After all, very few clients suffer from only one problem. If the client does not recognize that TFT was responsible for the alleviation of his problem, he will not use it to treat other problems, and if the problem recurs, he will not return and thus will be deprived of further help.

METHODS OF ADDRESSING ENERGY MERIDIAN POINTS

Commonly, people who have not grasped the basics of TFT have referred to it as "tapping therapy." According to Roger Callahan, the method of addressing the energy meridian points is trivial and "tapping is not the essence of TFT" (Callahan, 1998b). There are a variety of ways in which meridian and other points on the body can be addressed, including: needles, electrical stimulation, finger pressure or massage, tapping, non-piercing needles, moxibustion (burning herbs on a point), and acu-aids (small steel balls placed on a point) (Walther, 1988), lasers, and electroacupuncture (Callahan, 1998d). Callahan experimented with stimulating points with acu-aids and, while he did get results, they were not superior to any other method of stimulation used (Callahan, 1998b). Callahan states that he

settled on tapping because it made theoretical sense to me since I felt we were directly putting energy into a meridian, however, I would like to emphasize that all of the various procedures mentioned work. The key to successful treatment, I also emphasize, is not the manner of stimulation but rather the order and specific meridians which through causal diagnosis are found to be pertinent for an individual with a particular problem. (Callahan, 1998b)

RECURRENCES AND THE ROLE OF TOXINS

One of the most common questions I and others who teach TFT have been asked by skeptical new therapists being trained in TFT, following a successful treatment that has eliminated all traces of the client's upset is, "How long will this last?" Callahan and Callahan (1996) point out that

Although I treated patients for over three decades prior to my discoveries, I never once heard the question "How long will it last?" Since the discovery of TFT, I have heard this question thousands of times. Whether intended or not, it is a supreme compliment to ask this question. It implicitly acknowledges that something of significance has happened and wonders about the duration. (p. 30)

Recognizing that we now have a treatment that will, in the case of many clients for the first time, eliminate all subjective units of distress, the next issue becomes tracking the results. In order to accomplish this, the client is instructed to call immediately if the problem does return. In recent years, Callahan (in press-b) has discovered the important role that energy toxins play in the return of problems. An energy toxin is any substance the client comes into contact with that undoes the effects of the treatment. Callahan stated that "From experience we now know that an energy toxin is, by far, the most likely reason for the return of a successfully treated problem" (Callahan, 1996b). More recently, after experience with even more people, he has amended this statement to say that the reason for the return of a successfully treated problem is "almost always a toxin" (Callahan, 1998c).

Although the role of toxins in the return of a problem is Callahan's unique discovery, the role of toxins in psychological problems has been recognized by others, including Travis, McLean, and Ribar (1990). Dr. Doris Rapp (1978, 1991), a pediatric allergist, has clearly shown the role that ingested toxins play in hyperactive children. One of the leading clinical ecologists, Dr. Theron Randolph (1989), has pointed out that sensitivities to various commonly eaten foods and other substances can affect a person physically and/or mentally. Some mental symptoms he attributes to such sensitivities are: impaired thinking ability, mental exhaustion, depression, mania, anxiety, and hyperactivity.

Callahan first discovered the role of toxins when he noticed that clients had a return of their problem after smoking cigarettes (Callahan & Callahan, 1996). Later he discovered that normally healthy foods such as wheat, corn, eggs, milk, and others can also act as energy toxins and are actually more common culprits in anxiety disorders than caffeine (Callahan, 1995c). More recently, experiments using Heart Rate Variability tests after exposure to a toxin have shown the harmful impact of toxins on the autonomic nervous system (Callahan, in press-b).

Energy toxins can be tested for by a therapist trained in TFT Diagnosis or Voice Technology. Once a toxin is identified, the client is asked to stay completely away from the substance until he or she has been symptom-free for at least two months, to stabilize the results of the treatment. However, clients should not be tested for toxins unless there is a problem with a treatment holding. Since most treatments do hold, it is not necessary in these cases to ask the client to make such changes in his or her diet (Callahan, 1995c). However, because of the adverse effect such toxins have been shown to have on Heart Rate Variability (Callahan, in press-b), which has been linked to all-cause mortality, a person who has a toxin identified might wish to consider staying away from the substance for reasons other than the return of a psychological problem.

EMPIRICAL EVIDENCE OF TFT'S EFFECTIVENESS

Due to the strange appearance of these techniques, professionals sometimes mistakenly assume that this approach is "unscientific" or "mystical," when nothing could be further from the truth. TFT is said to be "on line with reality" (Callahan and Callahan, 1996) because its laws can be easily tested by any individual that uses TFT and thus, each person can conduct firsthand experiments and immediately see the predicted results.

It is a common assumption in our profession that the only valid evidence for efficacy of a particular therapy is experimental, designed studies with control groups, which have been held forth as the gold standard for scientific proof. The readily observable and obvious results of the efficacy of TFT strongly challenge this assumption. Traditional therapies, if they produce any improvement at all, only yield small improvements over long periods of time. For this reason, sophisticated statistical tests must be performed to determine if the difference between the treatment and an untreated control group is significant. However, many people forget the fact that there is a major difference between statistical significance and what is clinically meaningful. If you get a large enough sample, even the slightest difference can be statistically significant, although in clinical terms the results are virtually meaningless. For instance, if a study on treatment for phobias is done and a client's SUD level drops from a 10 to a 9.75, this might, with a large enough sample, produce a statistically significant result. To the person who suffers from a psychological problem, however, this means very little in terms of the degree of suffering that is alleviated. Thus, the study, although statistically significant, is meaningless clinically.

Helmut Kiene (Kiene & von Schon-Angerer, 1998), founder of the Institute for Applied Epistemology and Medical Methodology in Freiburg, Germany, challenges the current assumptions that the experimental placebo, double-blind, control group study is the ultimate proof for the efficacy of a therapy. Kiene examines, discusses, and challenges the basic epistemological elements of the conventionally accepted, randomized trials, and states that "Along with this technology, however, a dogma was born. This dogma states that there is no valid causality assessment other than randomized trials. . . . Causality assessment in single cases is deemed impossible. However, as will be argued below, this dogma is incorrect" (p. 43).

Kiene then goes on to describe a new, alternative model of causality assessment that he calls "figural correspondence" or the "figural experiment," where one can observe the entire gestalt of a process within one treatment application. Kiene writes that photography is an excellent example of this: "Taking a Polaroid picture for the first time and comparing it with the original, one can be certain right away—because of the figural correspondence—that photography is a causal process" (Kiene & von Schon-Angerer, 1995, p. 114).

The same can be said for the laws of TFT. When we do TFT we can observe the gestalt of the process and thus assess causality from single observations. We establish and observe that a person has a particular psychological problem. We can readily observe that a particular person gets upset whenever he or she thinks about a particular psychological problem, to which he or she typically gives a high SUD rating. We do diagnosis and apply a specific TFT sequence (or do a previously diagnosed algorithm) and observe that the person is no longer upset when thinking about the problem. In the case of a phobia of heights, for instance, we observe just prior to treatment that the person exhibited tremendous upset when faced with the prospect of climbing a simple stepladder. After the treatment the person is then easily able to climb the ladder without a trace of upset. We perceive the entire gestalt and thus can say with certainty that the treatment was the cause of the result.

By these standards, evidence for TFT is abundant in the many case studies and publicly demonstrated results. Numerous case reports in the journal

The Thought Field (1995–1998) show that the results of TFT can be easily replicated by therapists trained in the method, who follow the procedures. For instance, psychologist Jenny Edwards (1998), who treated traumatized victims of the recent bombing of the U.S. embassy in Nairobi, reports that she eliminated all traces of their intense trauma and their physical pain with the use of the appropriate algorithms. Another therapist (Sakai, 1998) reports in this same issue on her successful treatment of 20 cases in a psychiatric setting using TFT Diagnosis. These patients had a variety of symptoms, including depression, Bipolar II, PTSD, addictive urges, anxiety, phobias, and headaches, all of which responded favorably to TFT diagnostic procedures.

In addition to the case histories, there are a growing number of studies that are showing the efficacy of TFT. A recent study done at a major HMO (Sakai et al., 2001) reported 1,578 applications of TFT. Statistically significant changes in the SUD at the .001 level were reported for a wide variety of conditions including anxiety, adjustment disorder, depression, alcohol abuse, anger, bereavement, chronic pain, fatigue, maladaptive health behavior, obsessive-compulsive disorder, obsessive compulsive personality disorder, panic disorder without agoraphobia, parent–child stress, partner relational stress, post-traumatic stress disorder, relationship stress, social phobia, specific phobia, trichotillomania, and work stress.

Another recently published study (Johnson et al., 2001) was done on 105 survivors of trauma in Kosovo. Of these, 103 reported complete relief from their symptoms and in the follow-up done an average of five months later, every person that was contacted reported that the effects of the treatment had been sustained.

A study using the TFT Voice Technology on individuals with phobias and anxiety being treated on call-in radio shows, initially done by Callahan in 1985–1986 (Callahan, 1987) was replicated 10 years later by Glen Leonoff (1995). Each therapist treated 68 individuals with a 97% success rate in both cases. Although this study had no control group, it is important to remember that the purpose of a control group is to determine if the response was due to a placebo effect and there are no studies where a placebo was reported to have a 97% success rate.

A preliminary report of ongoing clinical research being conducted by VT-trained therapist Stephen Daniel (1998), had similar results with a larger sample. Dr. Daniel treated 214 therapists with the VT by telephone; they attended algorithm trainings and had problems that did not respond to the usually effective algorithms. The average pre-treatment SUD was 7.74 and the average post-treatment SUD was 1.11, with 1 meaning complete elimination of all distress. Based on follow-up phone calls, Daniel reports that "the response was overwhelmingly positive. Most reported maintaining the gains; a small number noticed the role of toxins in reactivating the symptoms (as predicted in CTTFT)" (p. 3). Daniel's study is further replication of the 97% success rate in the Callahan and Leonoff studies.

Ian Graham (1998), a therapist from the United Kingdom trained at the diagnostic level, has done a clinical study where he reports a success rate of 94% in treating 177 individuals over a six-month period. Eleven individuals did not respond to the treatments in this study. The pre-treatment average SUD was 8.29 and the post-treatment average SUD 2.17.

In the four clinical studies done by Callahan (1987), Leonoff (1995), Daniel (1998), and Graham (1998), a total of 527 individuals were included in the collective sample and the success rate was, as predicted, well above 90%, and in the case of VT, 97% or greater.

A controlled study on acrophobia, which was presented at the 1998 American Psychological Association conference, was conducted by Carbonell (1995). The study was done with 49 college students who had a fear of heights. Prior to treatment, subjects were asked to give a Subjective Units of Distress (SUD) rating on how anxious they felt just thinking about a situation in which they they were confronted with heights, where 0 represented no fear at all and 10 represented the most fear possible. Subjects were then randomly assigned to receive a real TFT Algorithm treatment, or a "placebo" TFT treatment where they were asked to tap on places that were not treatment points. The subjects did not know which group they were assigned to. All subjects were treated for psychological reversal and then treated either with a real TFT Algorithm or a placebo algorithm. The subjects were then all post-tested by an experimenter who did not know who had received the real algorithms. The post-test consisted of asking the subjects to climb the ladder and to give a post-treatment SUD. Both groups showed some improvement, probably due to the fact that both groups had been treated for psychological reversal, which could have provided some benefit even for the placebo control group. Nevertheless, there was a statistically significant difference between the group treated with the real algorithm and the group given the placebo algorithm.

In 1990, Joel Wade did his doctoral dissertation on the effects that the TFT treatment for phobias had on a person's self-concept (Wade, 1997). Wade's study had 28 subjects in the group that received TFT and 25 in the control group that received no treatment. Subjects in both groups were given two questionnaires measuring self-concept: the Tennessee Self Concept Scale (TSCS), and the Self Concept Evaluation of Location Form (SELF); they were also asked to rate the intensity of their phobia on a 10-point SUD scale. Subjects in the experimental group were then treated with the phobia algorithm. Sixteen subjects from the experimental group reported a drop in SUDS of 4 or more points, while by contrast, only four subjects in the control group reported a drop in SUDS of 2 or more points. Three months after the treatment, all subjects were post-tested with the same self-concept scales. The results were that there was significant change on the self-acceptance scale of the TSCS, and on the self-esteem and self-incongruence (how I see myself versus how I would like to be) scales of the SELF.

Recently, in addition to the client's self-reported SUD, we have attained results with an objective outcome measure for TFT, known as Heart Rate Variability (HRV) (Malik & Camm, 1995). The results of TFT using HRV were first measured by Dr. Fuller Royal. HRV provides information about the operation of a person's autonomic nervous system, has been shown to have stability over time, and is known not to respond to placebo (Kleiger et al., 1991). Having learned only the TFT phobia algorithm, Dr. Royal pre-tested his patients with HRV, did the algorithm, and then did a post-test with the HRV immediately afterward. Where the pre-test showed abnormalities in the autonomic nervous systems of the patients, after the algorithm, the post-tests showed that the measurements of the autonomic system became normal. Graphs of these results are featured on a videotape, available through Callahan Techniques (1997c).

Since Dr. Royal's experimentation, a number of TFT practitioners have been using HRV as an outcome measure in their clinical practice. Pre- and post-TFT treatment HRVs have shown changes after a brief TFT treatment that usually took only minutes to do, which, as far as we have been able to determine, are unprecedented (Callahan, 2001a, 2001b; Pignotti & Steinberg, 2001).

Another impressive change in a patient was reported by Dr. Roopa Chari (1998), concerning a 26-year-old female diagnosed with a pituitary tumor, whom Dr. Chari treated using TFT Diagnosis for anxiety and depression, as well as testing for and eliminating toxins. The patient, because of the tumor, had elevated levels of the hormone prolactin. After the TFT treatments, the patient requested a second test for prolactin levels, six weeks after her previous test, because she reported feeling very well. The neurosurgeon who had conducted the tests had told her it was too soon to retest and that he expected it to take eight months for her prolactin levels to go down even 8–10 points. However, at the patient's insistence, the test was redone and showed that her prolactin level had dropped 36 points. Such reports of robust changes in physical problems indicate that further clinical reports and research in this area would be of great value and interest.

SPECIFIC ASSESSMENT AND TREATMENT PROCEDURES

Algorithms

TFT Algorithms are therapeutic recipes that contain specific sequences of treatment points, which have been previously determined, through TFT's Causal Diagnostic procedure, to work on 70 to 90% of people in the average client population who have a particular problem. Assessment would consist of determining what algorithm to use. It is not necessary for the client to talk about the problem; all that is necessary is knowing the category the problem falls into (i.e., trauma, phobia, addictive urge, depression, etc.).

Introducing the Client to TFT

In introducing TFT to clients, it is helpful to show them a videotape such as *Introduction to TFT* (Callahan, 1997b), which explains some of the basic principles and shows people with a variety of psychological problems who have been helped by TFT. Unless the client is interested, a lengthy explanation of the theory is not necessary. It is interesting to notice that clients will respond in the predicted way to the laws of TFT, even when they have no expectations about what occurs. For instance, when a client who does not initially respond to a treatment is given the treatment for psychological reversal and the treatments repeated, the client will now respond, even though he or she knew nothing about the phenomenon.

How to Do the Tapping

It is recommended that the client do the tapping, unless he or she has a disability that prevents it, in which case, with the client's permission, it can be done by the therapist or a caregiver. Having the client do the tapping eliminates the necessity of the therapist touching the client, which can be problematic, especially for clients who have histories of severe abuse. Furthermore, having the client do the treatment is more empowering, although it will work equally well if someone else needs to do it for a particular client who is unable to tap. The client should be instructed to tap hard enough to put energy into the system, but not nearly hard enough to hurt.

The Architecture of TFT

Each treatment has a specific structure, which consists of:

1. *The Majors*, which is the initial sequence of treatment points. For instance, for the trauma algorithm, the majors consist of the following treatment points: eyebrow, under the eye, under the arm, collarbone.
2. *The 9-Gamut Sequence*. This treatment was discovered by Roger Callahan to further lower the SUD, after the initial sequence of majors is done. The 9-gamut consists of 9 treatments, presented in detail in the instructions. While tapping the gamut spot, the client is asked to perform a series of 6 eye movements and then hum, count, and hum again, which is believed to activate the left and right brain (Callahan and Callahan, 1996). While some people will experience a com-

plete elimination of the problem in just doing the majors, most people need the 9-gamut sequence to further lower the SUD.

3. *The Majors.* After the 9-gamut sequence, the initial majors sequence is repeated. For instance, if the sequence was eyebrow, under eye, under arm, collarbone, this would be repeated at this time.

This therapy sequence of majors—9 gamut treatments—majors is known as a holon (Callahan and Callahan, 1996). While many people will respond to one holon, others might require individualized diagnosis of treatment sequences, which can consist of more than one holon.

Treatment Affirmations

In earlier versions of TFT, affirmations were done with some of the treatments. For instance, while doing the PR treatment, the client was asked to say the words, "I accept myself, even though I have this problem." Since 1996, however, Roger Callahan has eliminated these affirmations (Callahan, 1997d) because he found that they were not necessary in order for the treatments to be effective, and they sometimes created an apex problem of the client falsely attributing the efficacy of the treatments to the affirmations.

Important: What to Do if a Treatment Does Not Work

If at any time in these procedures you get stuck, do not continue to repeat a treatment that is not working, as this will only serve to frustrate both you and your client. Furthermore, having a severely traumatized client continue to focus on a trauma while doing an ineffective treatment can produce adverse reactions for the client. Remember that TFT has no adverse reactions when done properly, and part of the proper procedure means not continuing to repeat a treatment that is not working. The treatment given in this chapter is an algorithm for trauma. If it does not work, there are further corrections a person trained in an approved TFT Algorithm training has learned. If that fails, TFT Causal Diagnosis is available by therapists who have been trained at the TFT Diagnostic and/or the Voice Technology level, who can easily remedy the situation in a high percentage of cases. Referrals can be obtained by calling Callahan Techniques at 760–564–1008 or going to the Website at http://www.tftrx.com.

Treatment Steps for the Trauma Algorithm

Here are the steps for the TFT Algorithm for trauma, as this would be the most common algorithm to use for the presenting problem being discussed in this chapter:

1. *Tuning the Thought Field and Getting the SUD.* Ask the client to think about the upsetting event and rate the degree of upset he or she feels *right at this*

moment (not how the persons thinks he or she might feel in the future or has felt in the past) while thinking about it on a scale of 1 to 10, where 1 means that the person is free of all traces of the upset, and 10 is the most upset the person could possibly be. A scale of 0–10 may also be used, as long as you clarify with the client whether a 1 or a 0 represents complete elimination of the upset. Remember that it is not necessary to make the client any more upset than he or she already is, since this treatment does not require a person to painfully relive the traumatic experience.

It is helpful to write down the SUD the client gives you, so if there is an apex problem later and the client denies previous upset, you can refer back to this.

2. Ask the client, using two fingers, to tap five times on the beginning of the eyebrow above the bridge of the nose.

3. Tap five times under the eye about an inch below the bottom of the eyeball, at the bottom center of the bony orbit, high on the cheek.

4. Tap under the arm five times. This point is about four inches directly below the armpit, even with the nipple on a male or the center of the bra on a female.

5. Have the client find the next point, called the collarbone point, in the following manner. Take two fingers of either hand and run them down the center of the throat to the top of the center collar bonenotch, which is about even with where a man would tie his tie. From this point, go straight down one inch and then go to the right one inch. Tap this point five times.

6. You have now completed the initial majors sequence. At this point, ask the client to rate the degree of upset he or she feels *right at this moment* on a scale of 1 to 10. If the initial SUD was 7 or higher and there is a drop of at least 2 points, proceed to Step 7. If the initial SUD was less than 7 and there is a drop of at least 1 point, proceed to Step 7. If there was a drop of 1 point (in an initial SUD of 7 or higher) or less, do the correction for psychological reversal, by asking the client to tap the outside edge of the hand about midway between the wrist and the base of the little finger. This spot is at the point of impact if one were to do a karate chop. After the PR treatment, always remember to *repeat the majors sequence* and recheck the SUD. If the SUD is now lower, proceed to Step 7.

   If there is still no change, STOP. You will need to consult with a therapist who has more training in these procedures. The Level 1 and 2 algorithm train-ings have further corrections that can be done, and if these fail, a therapist trained in TFT Diagnosis or Voice Technology can diagnose a different treat-ment sequence for the client.

7. Now do the 9-gamut treatments. To locate the gamut spot on the back of the hand, make a fist with one hand. This causes the large knuckles to stand out on the back of the hand. Place the index finger of your other hand in the valley between the little finger and ring finger knuckles. Move index finger about one inch back toward the wrist. This point is called the gamut point. Tap this point continuously while going through each of the nine procedures described below:

    a. Eyes open.

    b. Eyes closed.

    c. Open eyes and point them down and to the left.

    d. Point eyes down and to the right.

    e. Whirl eyes in a circle in one direction.

    f. Whirl eyes in a circle in the opposite direction.

    g. Hum a few bars of any tune (more than one note)

    h. Count aloud from one to five.

    i. Hum the tune again.

Remember to remind the client to keep tapping the gamut spot while doing all nine steps. If your client has a disability that prevents him or her from doing any of the eye movements (for example, blindness), you can have the person imagine doing the eye movements while tapping the gamut spot. If you are in a public place and unable to hum and count aloud, you can imagine humming and counting and this usually works.

8. You are now going to have the client repeat Steps 2–5: Tap the eyebrow point (Step 2); then tap under the eye (Step 3); tap under the arm (Step 4), and tap the collarbone point (Step 5).

9. Now ask the client to once again rate the degree of upset, again on a scale of 1 to 10. Remember that when rating the upset, the client should rate it according to how he or she is feeling *right at this moment*, not how the person thinks he or she might feel in the future. At this point you will notice one of three things:

    a. The upset will be at a 1 (completely eliminated) or a 2 (just a slight trace of it left). In this case, end the treatment by doing the floor-to-ceiling eye roll. To do this, ask the client to tap the gamut spot (the same spot described in the 9-gamut sequence) and while holding the head rather level, place the eyes down so he or she is looking at the floor and then slowly and steadily (taking about 6–7 seconds) roll them up toward the ceiling. This treatment will typically bring a 2 to a 1, or stabilize the 1, leaving the person completely free of upset.

    b. If the number with which the client rates the upset has dropped at least two points, but is not down to a 2 or lower, repeat the treatment (Steps 1–9).

    c. If there is a change of only 1 point (if rated upset at a 7 or higher) or no change, do the treatment for mini-psychological reversal (mPR). Tap the outside edge of the hand about midway between the wrist and the base of the little finger. This treatment point is the same one that was used for PR. The only difference is that the client has reported some drop in the SUD, so the PR is said to be a Mini-PR. After you have done this treatment, repeat Steps 1–9.

10. As long as the degree of upset continues to drop two points from a rating of 7 or above or one point from a rating of below 7, continue to repeat the treatment. If at any point the number the client gives you is unchanged (for instance, you dropped on the first round from a 7 to a 4, but when you re-

peated the treatment, you stayed at a 4), do the treatment of the karate chop spot, described in Step 9 for Mini-PR and then repeat the treatment (Steps 1–9).

Trauma with Anger

If the upset contains anger add on the following two treatment points to the treatment sequence outlined above.

1. Tap the inside lower corner (the side facing your thumb) at the bed of the nail on your little finger.
2. Tap the collarbone point (see Step 5 for description).

Putting this together with the original treatment, your treatment sequence for trauma with anger will be the original sequence: eyebrow, under the eye, under the arm, collarbone, little finger, collarbone, 9-gamut sequence, eyebrow, under the eye, under the arm, collarbone, *plus the added points*: little finger, collarbone.

Trauma with Guilt

If the upset contains guilt, add on these two treatment points:

1. Tap the inside lower corner (the side facing your thumb) at the bed of the nail on your index finger.
2. Tap the collarbone point (see Step 5 for description).

Putting this together with the original treatment, your treatment sequence for trauma with guilt will be the original sequence: eyebrow, under the eye, under the arm, collarbone, index finger, collarbone, 9-gamut sequence, eyebrow, under the eye, under the arm, collarbone, *plus the added points*: index finger, collarbone.

Trauma with Anger and Guilt

If the upset contains both anger and guilt, add on both of these treatments. In this case, your treatment would consist of the following points: the original sequence: eyebrow, under the eye, under the arm, collarbone, little finger, collarbone, index finger, collarbone, 9-gamut sequence, eyebrow, under the eye, under the arm, collarbone, *plus the added points*: little finger, collarbone, index finger, collarbone.

Complex Trauma

Sometimes you will find that you have eliminated the upset that you were working on, but another related upset will come to mind. This is because when we treat one layer of an upsetting experience, especially if it is complex, another layer might come up. If another upset comes to mind, you can easily take care of it by repeating this treatment while thinking about that upset. At times, earlier upsetting experiences similar to the one you were treating might come to mind, which you can then treat. Sometimes different emotions will come up. For instance, the first time you do the treatment, the person might feel upset and sad; after the sadness is eliminated, the person might feel anger and need to repeat the treatment for the anger, remembering to add on the extra treatment points designed to treat anger. If this happens, keep doing the treatment on each layer of the upsetting experience, until you have dealt with them all and the person reports being completely free of all upset.

Inertial Delay

In rare cases, there can be a delayed response to the treatment. This can occur anywhere from a few minutes after doing the treatment to, in very rare cases, a few days later. Keep in mind, however, that this type of delay is unusual and what we usually see are immediate, dramatic changes.

APPLICATION OF THE TREATMENT APPROACH TO PEOPLE SUFFERING FROM THE AFTEREFFECTS OF CULT INVOLVEMENT

The negative cult experience is essentially a trauma, and the typical survivor of a destructive cult presents with the symptoms associated with such trauma. As mentioned in the earlier literature review, these symptoms can include: depression, panic attacks, fears, phobias or anxiety, nightmares and flashbacks, guilt, shame or embarrassment, grief and loss, and feelings of anger and/or betrayal. I have personally seen all of the above symptoms and more in my practice working with people who have been in cults.

TFT has algorithms for all the above symptoms (Callahan & Trubo, in press), the most common of which is the trauma algorithm. Since there is an identifiable trauma, if algorithms are being used, I would usually recommend doing the trauma algorithm first, unless there is an overriding symptom, such as depression, that would indicate a different algorithm. If symptoms such as anger and/or guilt are present, then it is best to do the complex trauma algorithm with anger and guilt. Remember that the trauma algorithm will give the person help, not only for the trauma itself but for sequelae such as nightmares and flashbacks which will also disappear when the treatment is successful.

Former cult members will often have triggers that they encounter, which bring back the cult experience and can induce a dissociative state cult experts call floating (Hassan, 1988; Singer with Lalich, 1995) or trigger intense anxiety. For example, one former cult member I worked with experienced anxiety every time she saw certain numbers and colors that held special significance for her in the cult, making it very difficult for her to function in life. These triggers can be dealt with by doing either the anxiety or trauma algorithm, or if that fails, using TFT Diagnosis or VT to identify an individualized treatment sequence.

It is also important to realize that in many cases, a person who has been in a cult has often suffered from years of prolonged abuse and trauma, so there is almost certainly going to be more than one issue to treat. Therefore, it might be necessary to treat each traumatic event that is bothering the client separately, while treating current symptoms the person is experiencing, such as anger, anxiety, and guilt.

Sometimes a person will present with one issue and, after that is treated, will become aware of another issue that the person had not been previously aware of, because of the overwhelming presence of the first issue (Callahan & Callahan, 1996). For instance, someone in a cult might initially present with feelings of guilt, confusion, or loss of the group. When these feelings have been resolved and the person is feeling stronger, it is common for the person to then begin to get very angry at the group and its leaders (Goldberg & Goldberg, 1982). As the person moves through various stages of recovery, symptoms can be treated with the appropriate algorithm. A person trained in TFT Diagnosis or Voice Technology can simply get the person to think about the issue, give it a SUD rating, and diagnose a treatment sequence, without having to be concerned about which algorithm to use, since the treatment sequences are individualized according to what is diagnosed.

One of the greatest challenges I have encountered in working with this population is that some former cult members tend to equate anything that is new, unusual, and different with the cult they were in, since cults also fit that description and often purport to have "innovative" treatments for problems that no one else can solve. Consequently, former cult members can tend to be very distrustful of a truly innovative treatment such as TFT, saying that it reminds them of the cult they were in. Ironically, due to the nature of their trauma, they are resisting the very treatment that can help them to eliminate the aftereffects of their trauma and thus learn to trust. When I introduce such a person to TFT and he or she reacts with distrust and resists doing it, I have found that a very low-key approach is best, rather than in any way pushing or even attempting to subtly persuade the person to do it. I let clients know what is available, the results people have had, and that I respect their wishes and will not bring the subject up with them again, however, if they ever change their minds, I ask them to let me know. Because of the replicable success of TFT, I am confident that this method will eventually become more accepted by mainstream psychology and thus in the future, this issue will not be a problem.

CASE ILLUSTRATION

Although I am currently trained in the Voice Technology, for the purposes of this presentation, I have chosen to focus on one of the first clients I worked with using algorithms, since this is the level of TFT the reader is most likely to know and be able to utilize. However, it is important to recognize the levels of TFT that have been described earlier and realize that if the algorithms do not work or hold up over time, further help is available with a practitioner trained in these higher levels, and one should not give up.

Jane is a 30-year-old woman who had been a member of an Eastern guru cult for 10 years, from age 18 to 28. The cult, while very abusive to its members, discouraged them from the expression of any emotions and critical thoughts, which they learned to suppress through the misuse of chanting and meditation, as well as sleep and nutritional deprivation.

I spent approximately the first 20 minutes of the session taking a history, getting some basic information about her experience and what some of her issues were. After 10 years of involvement, Jane had left the group on her own when she learned of abuse that went on in the group that was so shocking to her, it overrode her previous programming enough for her to leave. Because she had not received counseling initially, she spent the first year away from the group in a state of confusion, which is typical of people who leave cults. After about a year, she was fortunate enough to make contact with a support group of former cult members and through that was able to attend a conference on cults, where she began to learn about the techniques that cults use to control people.

While she found this education to be very helpful in identifying what she had experienced, after two years away from the group, she was still having feelings of intense anger and subsequent guilt about her anger. After years of repressing feelings that the cult had taught her were bad, her anger was coming out uncontrollably in situations that were greatly interfering with her life. She had, in the past year, been fired from three different jobs because of this loss of control and would afterwards feel great regret and remorse about losing control. It was also interfering with her relationship with her new boyfriend. She had tried several forms of traditional talk therapy, as well as relaxation techniques and hypnosis for this problem, but had not been helped.

To help her understand what we were going to do, I had her view the *Introduction to TFT* videotape prior to the session. Since she had previously been interested in and tried various forms of alternative treatments, she was open to TFT, although she was skeptical about whether or not it could help her with her problem, since other treatments had failed.

Since anger was obviously Jane's major presenting issue at this time, we treated that first. We knew that she had trauma connected with this anger, so the algorithm I chose was the trauma algorithm with anger. To get her to *tune the thought field*, I asked her to think about a situation that would make her angry and to tell me how angry she felt *right at that moment* thinking about the situation. She immediately told me she was at a 9. I then instructed her to tap 5 times on each treatment point of the trauma with anger algorithm: eyebrow, under the eye, under the arm, collarbone, little finger, collarbone, index finger, collarbone, and asked her for a SUD, which was down 3 points to a 6. At the time, we were still using affirmations with the anger treatment and at this time she commented that it was like hypnosis. This was an indication to me that she was developing an apex problem, so I asked her if the hypnosis she had had previously had given her any relief from her anger, and she acknowledged that it had not, and saw my point.

Because the initial majors sequence had dropped her SUD 3 points, we proceeded to the 9-gamut treatments and a repetition of the majors sequence, which dropped her SUD to a 3. Because her SUD was continuing to drop, I repeated the entire treatment. However, after repetition of the treatment, her SUD was still at a 3, so I did the correction for Mini-PR, by asking her to tap on the side of her hand. Remember that Mini-PR occurs when the SUD has dropped to a certain level, but remains there, rather than going completely down to a 1. The main principle to keep in mind here is that whenever there is no change in the SUD, a reversal correction needs to be done and treatment repeated. If that fails, a more highly trained practitioner of TFT needs to be consulted. After the Mini-PR treatment, we repeated the entire algorithm, at the end of which she reported her SUD to be at a 1 and said she felt a great release of a feeling that had been with her for several years. I asked her if she had ever been able to think of this situation without getting angry and she stated she had not, prior to the treatment. Making the client aware of this is often helpful in preventing an apex problem for the client who thinks the treatment is just a temporary distraction. We then did the floor-to-ceiling eye roll to stabilize the treatment.

Although completely free of the anger, Jane was still aware of some guilt around this issue. She had been taught in her cult that getting angry or displaying any negative emotion was wrong and felt guilty anytime this occurred. On an intellectual level, she knew that emotions were not good or bad, but she nevertheless still felt guilty. We then went through the treatment for trauma with guilt, in a manner similar to the above description, and got her down to a 1, where she reported she was free of all traces of this guilt.

At the end of our session, I told her that it was very likely that this would take care of the issues we had worked on, but if even a trace of the feelings were to recur, she was to call me immediately and we could take care of it. The length of the entire session was 40 minutes, although the actual time for each treatment was approximately 5 minutes. The rest of the time was spent in her initially telling me about her experience, taking a history, finding out what issues she wished to address, and my giving her information about CT-TFT™ to explain the procedures.

About two weeks later, Jane called me to tell me that she felt great. She had been in a situation involving her boss at her new job that would have previously provoked an angry outburst, and she was able to remain calm in the face of it and be appropriately assertive in the situation. I reminded her that if she has any problem in the future or any other issues she would like to work on, she is always welcome to call.

Now that I do the Voice Technology, my clients can call me anytime they are experiencing a problem rather than having to wait for a weekly session. I can give them an individualized treatment sequence over the telephone, which will offer them immediate help. Through VT, I have been able to help people who have not been responsive to the usually effective algorithms or diagnosis. If the successfully treated problem returns, this is also easy to deal with, by testing with the VT for toxins. A person trained at the Diagnosis level can also test for toxins, but must see the client in person in order to do so. Once identified, having the person stay away from that substance for at least two months will stabilize the results of the treatment if the person has problems with recurrences.

SUMMARY AND CONCLUSION

I hope that the reader can now see why TFT has been called a revolutionary treatment in the field of psychotherapy. This chapter has dealt specifically with the issue of cults, but we are routinely able to help people with a variety of psychological problems including PTSD from any type of trauma, phobias, anxiety disorder, obsessive-compulsive disorder, depression, addictive urges, and a wide variety of other problems.

In conclusion, I would like to add that I do not expect anyone reading this to take my word for it. I realize that many therapies that have made big claims have come and gone. What sets TFT apart from the rest of these treatments, however, is that TFT is a treatment that therapists can take into their offices and replicate the very specific predictions made by TFT for themselves. I urge the reader to try the algorithm given in this chapter, to observe the laws of TFT at work for yourself, and thus experience the tremendous sense of fulfillment that those of us trained in these procedures get when we recognize that we have truly helped someone who has not previously been able to get help from any other source. We truly owe Dr. Roger Callahan a tremendous debt of gratitude for his remarkable discoveries which, for the first time in the history of psychology, have made help of this caliber possible.

REFERENCES

Bohm, D. & Hiley, B. J. (1993). *The undivided universe*. London: Routledge.

Callahan, J. (1998). Restructuring of TFT Basic Diagnostic Training. *The Thought Field*, 4(1), 1–2.

Callahan, R. (1987). Successful treatment of phobias and anxiety by telephone and radio. *Collected Papers of ICAK*, Winter.

Callahan, R., with Perry, P. (1991). *Why do I eat when I'm not hungry?* New York: Doubleday.

Callahan, R. (1995a). A TFT algorithm for the treatment of trauma. *Traumatology* [online], 1(1). http://www.fsu.edu/~trauma/callahan.html.

Callahan, R. (1995b). The apex problem. Unpublished paper.

Callahan, R (1995c). The psychological effects of toxins. Unpublished paper.

Callahan, R. (1995–1998). TFT diagnostic certification trainings, TFT Training Center, La Quinta, CA.

Callahan, R. (1996b). The proper testing of energy toxins. Unpublished paper.

Callahan, R. (1997a). Thought Field Therapy: The case of Mary. *Traumatology* [online], 3(1). http://www.fsu.edu/~trauma/T039.html.

Callahan, R. (1997b). Videotape: *Introduction to TFT*, TFT Training Center, Indian Wells, CA.

Callahan, R. (1997c). Videotape: *TFT and HRV*, TFT Training Center, Indian Wells, CA.

Callahan, R. (1997d). Response to Hooke's review of TFT. *Traumatology* [online], 3(2). http://www.fsu.edu/~trauma/v3i2art4.html.

Callahan, R. (1998a). On the irreplaceable importance of clients' subjective reports. *The Thought Field*, 4(3), 3–5.

Callahan, R. (1998b). On tapping and setting the record straight. Unpublished paper.

Callahan, R. (1998c). Callahan Techniques™ TFT Diagnostic Training, August 21–23, San Diego, CA.

Callahan, R. (1998d). Personal communication.

Callahan, R. (2001a). The impact of thought field therapy on heart rate variability. *Journal of Clinical Psychology*, 57(10), 1153–1170.

Callahan, R. (2001b). Raising and lowering of heart rate variability: Some clinical findings of thought field therapy. *Journal of Clinical Psychology*, 57(10), 1175–1186.

Callahan, R., & Callahan, J. (1996). *Thought Field Therapy and Trauma*, TFT Training Center, Indian Wells, CA.

Callahan, R., & Callahan, J. (2000). *Stop the nightmares of trauma*. Chapel Hill, NC: Professional Press.

Callahan, R., & Trubo, M. (2001). *Tapping the healer within*. New York: Contemporary.

Carbonell, J. (1995). An experimental study of TFT and acrophobia. *The Thought Field*, 2(3), 1, 6.

Chambers, W., Langone, M., Dole, A., & Grice, J. (1994). The group psychological abuse scale: A measure of the varieties of cultic abuse. *Cultic Studies Journal*, 2(1), 88–117.

Chari, R. (1998). CT-TFT in a medical setting. *The Thought Field*, 4(2), 1–2.

Conway, F., & Siegelman, J. (1982). Information disease: Have cults created a new mental illness? *Science Digest*, January.

Conway, F., & Siegelman, J. (1995). *Snapping: America's epidemic of sudden personality change* (2nd ed.). New York: Stillpoint Press.

Daniel, S. (1998). A preliminary report: Ongoing clinical research with Callahan Techniques™ Thought Field Therapy Voice Technology. *The Thought Field*, 4(3), 3.

Edwards, J. (1998). The right place at the right time: Nairobi embassy bombing. *The Thought Field*, 4(3), 1–2.

Goldberg, L. (1993). Guidelines for therapists. In M. Langone (Ed.), *Recovery from cults: Help for victims of psychological and spiritual abuse* (pp. 232–250). New York: W. W. Norton.

Goldberg, L., & Goldberg, W. (1982). Group work with former cultists. *Social Work*, March, 165–169.

Graham, Ian. (1998). An introduction to thought field therapy. Unpublished manuscript.

Hassan, S. (1988). *Combating cult mind control*. Rochester, VT: Park Street Press.

Hassan, S. (2000). *Releasing the bonds: Empowering people to think for themselves*. Boston: Freedom of Mind Press.

Johnson, C., Mustafe, S., Sejdijaj, X., Odell, R., & Dabishevci, K. (2001). Thought field therapy—soothing the bad moments of Kosovo. *Journal of Clinical Psychology*, 57(10), 1237–1240.

Kiene, H., & von Schon-Angerer, T. (1998). Single-case causality assessment as a basis for clinical judgment. *Alternative Therapies*, 4(1), 41–47.

Kleiger, R., Bigger, J., Bosner, M., Chunk, M., Cook, J., Rolnitzky, L., Steinman, R., & Fleiss, J. (1991). Stability over time of variables measuring heart rate variability in normal subjects. *Am J Cardiol*, 68, 626–630.

Koestler, A. (1967). *The ghost in the machine*. London:Arkana.

Langone, MD. (1992). Psychological abuse. *Cultic Studies Journal*, 9(2), 206–218.

Leonoff, G. (1995). Successful treatment of phobias and anxiety by telephone and radio: A preliminary report on a replication of Callahan's 1987 study. *The Thought Field*, 1(2), 1, 6.

Malik, M., & Camm, J. (Eds.). (1995). *Heart rate variability*. Armonk, NY: Futura Publishing. *The Thought Field* Newsletter (1995–1998 issues), TFT Training Center, La Quinta, CA.

Martin, P. (1993). Post-cult recovery: Assessment and rehabilitation. In M. Langone (Ed.), *Recovery from cults: Help for victims of psychological and spiritual abuse*. (pp. 203–231). New York: W. W. Norton.

Pignotti, M. & Steinberg, M. (2001). Heart rate variability as an outcome measure for thought field therapy in clinical practice. *Journal of Clinical Psychology*, 57(10), 1193–1206.

Randolph, T., with Moss, R. (1989). *An Alternative approach to allergies: New field of clinical ecology unravels the environmental causes of mental and physical ills* (rev. ed.). New York: Harper and Row.

Rapp, D. (1978). Does diet affect hyperactivity? *Journal of Learning Disabilities*, 11(6), 383–389.

Rapp, D. (1991) *Is this your child?* New York: William Morrow.

Rudin, M. (1994). Into the mainstream: The new world of cults. *Gauntlet*, 2, 65–67.

Sakai, C. (1998). CT-TFTDX cases in a psychiatric setting. *The Thought Field*, 4(3), 5–7.

Sakai, C., Paperny, D., Mathews, M., Tanida, G., Boyd, G., Simons, A., Yamamoto, C., Mau, C., & Nutter, L. (2001). Thought field therapy clinical applications: utilization in an HMO in behavioral medicine and behavioral health sciences. *Journal of Clinical Psychology*, 57(10), 1215–1227.

Sheldrake, R. (1981). *A new science of life*. Los Angeles: J. B. Tarcher.

Sheldrake, R. (1988). *The presence of the past*. New York: Times Books.

Singer, M. (1979). Coming out of the cults. *Psychology Today*, January, 72–82.

Singer, M., with Lalich, J. (1995). *Cults in our midst*. San Francisco: Jossey-Bass.

Singer, M., & Ofshe, R. (1990). Thought reform programs and the production of psychiatric casualties. *Psychiatric Annals*, 20(4), 183–193.

Tobias, M., & Lalich, J. (1994). *Captive hearts, captive minds: Freedom and recovery from cults and abusive relationships*. Alameda, CA: Hunter House.

Travis, C., McLean, B., & Ribar, C. (Eds.). (1990). *Environmental toxins: Psychological, behavioral, and sociocultural aspects, 1973–1989*. Washington, DC: American Psychological Association, PsychINFO 5.

Wade, J. (1997). TFT and self-concept. *The Thought Field*, 2(4), 6.

Walther, D. (1988). *Applied kinesiology: Synopsis*. Pueblo, CO: Systems DC.

Wolpe, J. (1969). *The practice of behavior therapy*. New York: Pergamon Press.

Chapter 7

Sensorimotor Approach to Processing Traumatic Memory

Pat Ogden and Kekuni Minton

For most traumatologists, a sensorimotor approach to helping traumatized people recover from their traumatic experiences requires adopting a new paradigm. In contrast to most prevailing methods rooted in traditional psychotherapy concepts and theories, this new paradigm suggests that the unassimilated sensorimotor reactions to trauma may provide an important key to helping clients. These sensorimotor reactions consist of sequential physical and sensory patterns involving autonomic nervous system arousal and orienting/defensive responses that seek to resolve to a point of rest and satisfaction in the body. During a traumatic event such a satisfactory resolution of responses might be accomplished by successfully fighting or fleeing. However, for the majority of traumatized clients, this does not occur. Traumatized individuals are plagued by the return of dissociated, incomplete, or ineffective sensorimotor reactions in such forms as intrusive images, sounds, smells, body sensations, physical pain, constriction, numbing, and the inability to modulate arousal.

These unresolved sensorimotor reactions condition emotional and cognitive processing, often disrupting the traumatized person's ability to think clearly or to glean accurate information from emotional states (van der Kolk, 1996). Conversely, cognitive beliefs and emotional states condition somatic processing. For instance, a belief such as "I am helpless" may interrupt sensorimotor processes of active physical defense; an emotion such as fear may cause sensorimotor processes such as arousal to escalate. Most psychotherapeutic approaches favor emotional and cognitive processing over body processing, and it has been shown that such approaches can greatly relieve trauma symptoms. However, since somatic symptoms are significant in traumatization (McFarlane, 1996, p. 172), the efficacy of trauma treatment may be increased by the addition of interventions that facilitate sensorimotor processing. We propose that sensorimotor processing interventions can help regulate and facilitate emotional and cognitive processing, and we find that confronting somatic issues by directly addressing sensorimotor processing can be useful in restoring normal healthy functioning for victims of trauma, regardless of the nature of the trauma's origin. However, we also find that sensorimotor processing alone is insufficient; the integration of all three levels of processing—sensorimotor, emotional, and cognitive—is essential for recovery to occur.

In this chapter we will discuss Sensorimotor Psychotherapy, a comprehensive method that utilizes the body as a primary entry point in trauma treatment, but one which integrates cognitive and emotional processing as well. We will emphasize sensorimotor processing, which entails mindfully tracking (following in detail) the sequential physical movements and sensations associated with unassimilated sensorimotor reactions, such as motor impulses, muscular tension, trembling, and various other micromovements, and changes in posture, breathing, and heart rate. These body sensations are similar to Gendlin's (1978) "felt sense" in that they are physical feelings, but while the felt sense includes emotional and cognitive components, the sensations we refer to are purely physical. Clients are taught to distinguish between physical sensations and trauma-based emotions through cultivating awareness of sensations as they fluctuate in texture, quality, and intensity until the sensations themselves have stabilized, and clients are able to experience these sensations as distinct from emotions.

Sensorimotor processing is similar to Peter Levine's (1997) "Somatic Experiencing" in the tracking of physical sensation, but it differs in intent. For Levine, tracking physical sensation is an end in itself; his approach does not specifically include therapeutic maps to address cognitive or emotional processing. Similar to "Somatic Experiencing," Sensorimotor Psychotherapy encourages sensorimotor processing when necessary to regulate sensorimotor reactions, often the case in shock and non-relational trauma; but sensorimotor processing is most often used as a prelude to holistic processing on all three levels (cognitive, emotional, and sensorimotor). For example, a traumatized client's affective and cognitive information processing may be "driven" by an underlying, dysregulated arousal, causing emotions to escalate and thoughts to revolve around and around in cycles. When the client learns to self-regulate her arousal through sensorimotor processing, she may be able to more accurately distinguish between cognitive and affective reactions that are merely symptomatic of such dysregulated arousal and those cognitive-emotional contents that are genuine issues that need to be worked through. As this occurs, the approach of Sensorimotor Psychotherapy might shift from sensorimotor processing alone to include cognitive and emotional processing, and to address relational and transferential dynamics as well. Sensorimotor Psychotherapy's use of the therapeutic interaction to work through relational issues and promote self-regulation can be very effective in the resolution of relational trauma. Thus, Sensorimotor Psychotherapy lends itself to the treatment of relational trauma as well as shock and non-relational trauma.

Before discussing Sensorimotor Psychotherapy more fully, we will first address the question of how experience is processed on cognitive, emotional, and sensorimotor levels, and the effects of unresolved sensorimotor reactions on all levels of information processing. Ken Wilber's (1996) notion of hierarchical information processing describes the evolutionary and functional hierarchy among these three levels of organizing experience— cognitive, emotional, and sensorimotor—a hierarchy that reflects the evolutionary development of the human brain.

While functionally the three levels of information processing are mutually dependent and intertwined (Damasio, 1999; LeDoux, 1996; Schore, 1994), clinically we find that it is important for the therapist to observe the client's processing of information on each of these three related but distinct levels of experience; differentiate which level of processing will most successfully support integration of traumatic experience in any moment of therapy; and apply specific techniques that facilitate processing at that particular level. Such an approach ultimately fosters "holistic" processing, where all three levels will operate synergistically.

These three levels interact and affect each other simultaneously, functioning as a cohesive whole, with the degree of integration of each level of processing affecting the efficacy of other levels, as described by Fisher and Murray (1991):

The brain functions as an integrated whole, but is comprised of systems that are hierarchically organized. The "higher-level" integrative functions evolved from and are dependent on the integrity of "lower-level" structures and on sensorimotor experience. Higher (cortical) centers of the brain are viewed as those that are responsible for abstraction, perception, reasoning, language, and learning. Sensory integration, and intersensory association, in contrast, occur mainly within lower (subcortical) centers. Lower parts of the brain are conceptualized as developing and maturing before higher-level structures; development and optimal functioning of higher-level structures are thought to be dependent, in part, on the development and optimal functioning of lower-level structures. (p. 16)

Sensorimotor processing is in many ways foundational to the others and includes the features of a simpler, more primitive form of information processing than do its more evolved counterparts. With its seat in the lower, older brain structures, sensorimotor processing relies on a relatively higher number of fixed sequences of steps in the way it does its work. Some of these fixed sequences are well-known, such as the startle reflex and the fight, flight, or freeze response. The simplest sequences are involuntary reflexes (e.g., the knee-jerk reaction) which are the most rigidly fixed and determined. More complex are the motor patterns that we learn at young ages, which then become automatic, such as walking and running. In the more highly evolved emotional and cognitive realms, we find fewer and fewer fixed sequences of steps in processing, and more complexity and variability of response. Thus, sensorimotor processing is more directly associated with overall body processing—the fixed action patterns seen in active defenses, changes in breathing and muscular tonicity, autonomic nervous system activation, and so forth.

The nature of this hierarchy is such that the higher levels of processing often influence and direct the lower levels. We can decide (cognitive function) to ignore the sensation of hunger and not act on it, even while the physiological processes associated with hunger, such as the secretion of saliva and contraction of stomach muscles, continue. In cognitive theory, this is called "top-down processing" (LeDoux, 1996, p. 272), indicating that the upper level of processing (cognitive) can and often does override, steer, or interrupt the lower levels, elaborating on or interfering with emotional and sensorimotor processing.

Adult activity is often based on top-down processing. Schore (1994) notes that, in adults, "higher cortical areas" act as a "control center," and that the orbital cortex hierarchically dominates subcortical limbic activity (p. 139). A person might think about what to accomplish for the day, outline plans, and then structure time to meet particular goals. While carrying these plans through, one may override feelings of fatigue, hunger, or physical discomfort. It is as though we hover just above our somatic and sensory experience, knowing it is there, but not allowing it to be the primary determinant of our actions.

In contrast, the activities of very young children are often dominated by sensorimotor (Piaget, 1952) and emotional systems (Schore, 1994); in other words, by bottom-up processes. Tactile and kinesthetic sensations guide early attachment behavior as well as help regulate the infant's behavior and physiology (Schore, in press-a). Infants and very small children explore the world through these systems, building the neural networks that are the foundation for later cognitive development (Hannaford, 1995; Piaget, 1952). Hard-wired to be governed by somatic and emotional states, infants respond automatically to sensorimotor and affective cues and are unregulated by cognition or cortical control (Schore, 1994). The infant is a "subcortical creature . . . [who] lacks the means for modulation of behavior which is made possible by the development of cortical control" (Diamond, Balvin, & Diamond, 1963, p. 305). Similarly, traumatized people frequently experience themselves as being at the mercy of their sensations, physical reactions, and emotions, having lost the capacity to regulate these functions.

In summary, bottom-up and top-down processing represent two general directions of information processing. Top-down processing is initiated by the cortex, and often involves cognition. This higher level observes, monitors, regulates, and often directs the lower levels; at the same time, the effective functioning of the higher level is partly dependent on the effective functioning of the lower levels. Bottom-up processing, on the other hand, is initiated at the sensorimotor and emotional realms. These lower levels of processing are more fundamental, in terms of evolution, development, and function: These capacities are found in earlier species and are already intact within earlier stages of human life. They precede thought and form a foundation for the higher modes of processing.

The interplay between top-down and bottom-up processing holds significant implications for the occurrence and treatment of trauma. Psychotherapy has traditionally harnessed top-down techniques to manage disruptive bottom-up processes, through the voluntary and conscious sublimation of sensorimotor and emotional processing. This is achieved through activity, behavioral discharge, cognitive override, or distraction. When sensorimotor experience is disturbing or overwhelming, conscious top-down regulation can allow a person to pace herself, modulating the degree of arousal or disorganization in the system, as evidenced by the following example:

Harriet . . . had a problem and had found a way to begin to control it. When a hallucination began, she would try to picture her library at home. She would look at the imaginary shelves and start to count the books, focusing on each one as best she could as she counted. Soon, her hallucination would stop . . . she was imposing top-down control, which quashed the bottom-up hallucination signal. She was purposefully lighting up her cortex so that it drowned out her lower brain, snapping her out of her episode just as cognition wakes us up out of a dream. (Hobson, 1994, p. 174)

While the above technique is an effective way to manage hallucinations and provide significant relief, and thus can be an important first step in therapy, it may not address the entire problem. It engages cognition, but ignores sensorimotor processes. Such top-down processing alone may manage sensorimotor reactions, but may not effectuate their full assimilation. For instance, a client may learn to mitigate arousal by convincing herself that the world is now safe, but the underlying tendency for arousal to escalate to overwhelming degrees may not have been fully resolved. The traumatic experience and arousal from the sensorimotor and emotional levels may be redirected through top-down management, but the processing, digestion, and assimilation of sensorimotor reactions to the trauma may not have occurred.

In much the same way that a client who comes to therapy with unresolved grief must identify and experience the grief (emotional processing), a client who exhibits unresolved sensorimotor reactions must identify and experience these reactions *physically* (sensorimotor processing). Additionally, the client's awareness and processing of sensorimotor reactions on the sensorimotor level will exert a positive influence on emotional and cognitive processing, since, as we have seen, optimal functioning of the higher levels is somewhat dependent on the adequate functioning of the lower levels. Sensorimotor processing is often a precursor to holistic processing—the synergistic functioning of cognitive, emotional, and sensorimotor levels of processing.

In Sensorimotor Psychotherapy, top-down direction is harnessed to *support* rather than *manage* sensorimotor processing. The client is asked to mindfully track (a top-down, cognitive process) the sequence of physical sensations and impulses (sensorimotor process) as they progress through the body, and to temporarily disregard emotions and thoughts that arise, until the bodily sensations and impulses resolve to a point of rest and stabilization in the body. The client learns to observe and follow the unassimilated sensorimotor reactions (primarily, arousal and defensive reactions) that were activated at the time of the trauma. Bottom-up processing, left on its own, does not resolve trauma, but if the client is directed to employ the cognitive function of tracking and articulating sensorimotor experience while voluntarily inhibiting awareness of emotions, content, and interpretive thinking, sensorimotor experience can be assimilated. Furthermore, it is crucial that the cognitive direction is engaged to help clients learn self-regulation.

To harness such top-down cognitive direction, a specific kind of therapeutic relationship is imperative. Similar to a mother's interaction with her infant, the therapist must serve as an "auxiliary cortex" (Diamond et al., 1963) for clients, through observing and articulating their sensorimotor experience until they are able to notice, describe, and track these experiences themselves. Such relational communication is a process of "interactive psychobiological regulation," which resembles a mother's attunement to and interaction with her infant's physiological and emotional states (Schore, 1994). Schore writes that the therapist must act as an "affect regulator of the patient's dysregulated states to provide a growth-facilitating environment for the patient's immature affect regulating structures" (Schore, in press-b, p. 17).

In defining self-regulation, Schore (in press-b) differentiates between interactive and non-interactive forms, describing self-regulation as both "interactive regulation in interconnected contexts via a two-person psychology," and "autoregulation in autonomous contexts via a one-person psychology" (pp. 13–14). When self-regulation is fully developed, clients can observe, articulate, and eventually integrate sensorimotor reactions on their own as well as utilize relationships to self-regulate. Without what Schore calls the "adaptive capacity to shift between these dual regulatory modes" (p. 14), the sensorimotor reactions of arousal and defensive responses are subject to becoming either hyperactive or hypoactive, as we shall see in the following section, leaving traumatized persons at the mercy of their bodies.

PHYSICAL DEFENSIVE RESPONSES

Threat calls forth both psychological and physical defenses, the objectives of which are to evaluate and reduce stress and maximize the chances for survival (Nijenhuis & van der Hart, 1999). For the purpose of this chapter, we will focus on physical defenses, rather than psychological defenses (such as projection, reaction formation, displacement, rationalization, or minimization), acknowledging that both types may be responses to traumatic situations. Physical defenses are examples of the relatively fixed action patterns mentioned in the previous section, the effective functioning of which upper levels of processing depend on for their efficacy.

Physical defenses may precede cognitive and emotional reactions in acute traumatic situations. Hobson writes:

Bottom-up processing takes precedence in times of emergency, when it is advantageous to short-circuit the cortex and activate a motor-pattern generated directly from the brain stem. If we suddenly see a car careening toward us, we instantly turn our car away; we react automatically, and only later (even if it is only a split second later) do we realize there is danger and feel afraid. (1994, p. 139)

However, during a more prolonged trauma, voluntary physical defensive impulses that are mediated through the cognitive level—such as thoughts of striking out or reaching for the phone—might also come into play.

Physical defenses may be active or passive (Levine, 1997; Nijenhuis and van der Hart, 1999). Active defenses manifest through a wide variety of physical impulses and movements, depending on the nature of the threat, and vary in intensity of activity. They include fight/flight and a multitude of other possible reactions such as engaging the righting reflexes to regain balance, turning away from a falling branch, lifting an arm to avoid a blow, slamming on the brakes to prevent an accident, twisting out of the grip of an assailant, and so on. Additionally, the orienting response (scanning and adjusting to the environment) is heightened and all of the organism's attention is focused on the threat. The senses become hypersensitive, to better smell, hear, see, and taste the danger (Levine, 1997; Van Olst, 1972) in preparation for further assessment and response (Hobson, 1994).

In the animal kingdom, active defensive responses turn to passive freezing when active responses are likely to threaten survival (Nijenhuis and van der Hart, 1999). For humans as well, when active defenses are impossible or ill-advised, they may be replaced by passive defenses such as submission, automatic obedience, and freezing (Nijenhuis & van der Hart, 1999). Nijenhuis and van der Hart (1999) write:

applying problem-solving coping (attempted flight, fight or assertiveness) would be inevitably frustrating and nonproductive for a child being physically or sexually abused or witnessing violence. In some situations, active motor defense may actually increase danger and therefore be less adaptive than passive, mental ways of coping. (p. 50)

Furthermore, passive defenses may be the best option when active ones are ineffective, as when a victim is unable to outrun an assailant.

While Levine (1997) claims that hyperarousal and active defenses precede passive defense and immobility, both Nijenhuis (e.g., Nijenhuis, Vanderlinden, & Spinhoven, 1998) and Porges (1995, 1997) note that frozen states are not always preceded by active defenses or arousal. In some cases, such as those mentioned above, an individual might automatically engage passive defenses without first attempting active defense. Also, passive defenses alone are employed in infancy, long before capabilities for fight/flight.

In passive defense, the ordinarily active-orienting response, which includes effective use of the senses, scanning mechanisms, and evaluation capacities, may become dull and ineffective. The cognitive function of problem-solving may become severely diminished and confused, which may lead to a general dulling of cognition or "psychic numbing" (Solomon, Laror, & McFarlane, 1996, p. 106), a numbing of sensation, and the slowing of muscular/skeletal responses (Levine, 1997). Muscles may be extremely tense but immobilized, or flaccid. Clients may report that in this state, they find moving difficult, and they may even feel paralyzed.

Frequently, the complete execution of effective physical defensive movements does not take place during the trauma itself. As we have seen, a victim may instantaneously freeze rather than act, a driver may not have time to execute the impulse to turn the car to avoid impact, or a person may be overpowered when attempting to fight off an assailant. Over time, such interrupted or ineffective physical defensive movement sequences contribute to trauma symptoms. Herman (1992) observes:

When neither resistance nor escape is possible, the human system of self-defense becomes overwhelmed and disorganized. Each component of the ordinary response to danger, having lost its utility, tends to persist in an altered and exaggerated state long after the actual danger is over. (p. 34)

Traumatized people may exhibit a propensity for either hyperactive or passive defense, or an alternation between the two. When defenses become hyperactive, they manifest as habitual defensiveness, aggression against self or others, hyperalertness, hypervigilance, excessive motoric activity and un-

Figure 7.1
The Modulation Model: Optimum Arousal Zone

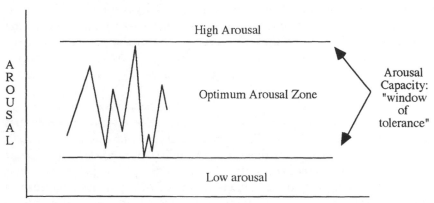

controllable bouts of rage, and so on. Habitual passive defenses may manifest as chronic patterns of submission, helplessness, inability to set boundaries, feelings of inadequacy, automatic obedience, and repetition of the victim role. The person may appear lifeless and non-expressive, and may fail to defend against or orient toward danger, or even attempt to get help.

Interrupted or ineffective physical defensive movements can disrupt the overall capacity for sensorimotor processing, similar to the way a repeated suppression of a particular emotion disrupts the overall capacity for emotional processing. Unsuccessful patterns of sensorimotor responses may become habitual, negatively affecting the normal and healthy interplay between top-down and bottom-up processing, and thus contribute to trauma symptoms.

THE MODULATION MODEL

Poor tolerance for arousal is characteristic of traumatized individuals (van der Kolk, 1987). The top and bottom lines of Figure 7.1 depict the limits of a person's optimum degree of arousal, which Wilbarger and Wilbarger (1997) call the "optimal arousal zone." When arousal remains within this zone, a person can contain and experience (not dissociate from) the affects, sensations, sense perceptions, and thoughts that occur within this zone, and can process information effectively. In this zone, modulation can occur spontaneously and naturally. This optimum zone is similar to Siegel's "window of tolerance," within which "various intensities of emotional arousal can be processed without disrupting the functioning of the system" (1999, p. 253).

During trauma, arousal initially tends to rise beyond the upper limits of the optimal zone, which alerts the person to possible threat (van der Kolk, van der Hart, & Marmar, 1996). In successful and vigorous fight or flight, this hyperarousal is utilized through physical activity (Levine, 1997) in serving the purpose of defending and restoring balance to the organism. In the ideal resolution of the arousal, the level returns to the parameters of the optimum zone. However, this return to baseline does not always occur, which contributes significantly to the problems with hyperarousal that are characteristic of the traumatized person.

In relation to energy dissipation following hyperarousal, Levine (1997) writes that trauma symptoms "stem from the frozen residue of energy that has not been resolved and discharged" and the individual exposed to trauma must "discharge all the energy mobilized to negotiate that threat or [the person] will become a victim" (pp. 19–20). Although we agree that discharge of energy may be an element in trauma therapy, just as expression of emotion also may be an element of trauma therapy, we disagree with the discharge model. We believe that trauma symptoms stem from unassimilated reactions on all three levels of information processing, and that these reactions must be integrated through restoring the balance and synergy between top-down and bottom-up processing. Rather than to "complete the freezing response" by discharging energy (Levine, 1997, p. 111), our immediate intention is to teach the client to modulate sensorimotor processes, which sometimes means stimulating arousal if the client is hypoaroused.

Hyperarousal involves "excessive sympathetic branch activity [which] can lead to increased energy-consuming processes, manifested as increases in heart rate and respiration and as a 'pounding' sensation in the head" (Siegel, 1999, p. 254). Over the long term, such hyperarousal may disrupt cognitive and affective processing as the individual becomes overwhelmed and disorganized by the accelerated pace and amplitude of thoughts and emotions, which may be accompanied by intrusive memories. As van der Kolk, van der Hart, and Marmar (1996) state, "This hyperarousal creates a vicious cycle: state-dependent memory retrieval causes increased access to traumatic memories and involuntary intrusions of the trauma, which lead in turn to even more arousal" (p. 305). Such state-dependent memories may increase clients' tendency to "interpret current stimuli as reminders of the trauma" (p. 305), perpetuating the pattern of hyperarousal. Van der Kolk points out that high arousal is easily triggered in traumatized persons, causing them to "be unable to trust their bodily sensations to warn them against impending threat, and cease to alert them to take appropriate action" (p. 421), thereby disrupting effective defensive responses.

At the opposite end of the Modulation Model, "excessive parasympathetic branch activity leads to increased energy conserving processes, manifested as decreases in heart rate and respiration and as a sense of 'numbness' and 'shutting down' within the mind" (Siegel, 1999, p. 254).

Figure 7.2
The Modulation Model: The Bi-phasic Response to Trauma

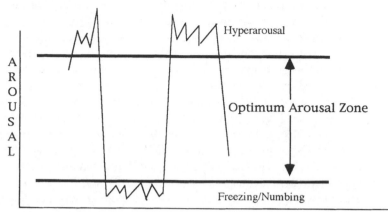

Such hypo-arousal can manifest as numbing, a dulling of inner body sensation, slowing of muscular/skeletal response, and diminished muscular tone, especially in the face (Porges, 1995). Here cognitive and emotional processing are also disrupted, not by hyperarousal as above, but by hypo-arousal.

Both hyperarousal and hypo-arousal often lead to dissociation. In hyperarousal, dissociation may occur because the intensity and accelerated pace of sensations and emotions overwhelm cognitive processing so that the person cannot stay present with current experience. In hypo-arousal, dissociation may manifest as reduced capacity to sense or feel even significant events, an inability to accurately evaluate dangerous situations or think clearly, and a lack of motivation. The body, or a part of the body, may become numb, and the victim may experience a sense of "leaving" the body. Additional long-term and debilitating symptoms might include "emotional constriction, social isolation, retreat from family obligations, anhedonia and a sense of estrangement" (van der Kolk, 1987, p. 3) along with "depression . . . and a lack of motivation, as psychosomatic reactions, or as dissociative states" (van der Kolk, McFarlane, & van der Hart, 1996, p. 422). As we can see, these symptoms are reminiscent of passive defenses, in which a person does not actively defend against danger.

The traumatized individual may reside primarily either above or below the parameters of the optimum arousal zone, or swing uncontrollably between these two states (van der Kolk, 1987, p. 2). This bi-phasic alternation between hyperarousal and numbing or freezing (p. 3)—the top and bottom segments of the modulation model in Figure 7.2—may become the new norm in the aftermath of trauma.

When a person's arousal is outside the optimum zone at either end of

the spectrum, upper levels of processing will be disabled, and holistic processing will be replaced by bottom-up reflexive action. As Siegel (1999)
notes, internal states outside the "window of tolerance" are "characterized
by either excessive rigidity or randomness. These states are inflexible or
chaotic, and as such are not adaptive to the internal or external environment" (p. 255). Siegel goes on to say, "In states of mind beyond the window of tolerance, the prefrontally mediated capacity [cognitive processing]
for response flexibility is temporarily shut down. The 'higher mode' of
integrative [cognitive] processing has been replaced by a 'lower mode' of
reflexive [sensorimotor] responding" (bracketed text added; pp. 254–255).

Stephen Porges's (1995, 1997) work, which elucidates a hierarchical relationship among the levels of the autonomic nervous system, has important implications for the regulation of both arousal and defensive responses.
He concludes that hypo-arousal (described above) is due to a specific
branch of the parasympathetic nervous system, the "dorsal vagal complex,"
which causes the organism to conserve energy by drastically slowing heart
and breath rates. The other branch of the parasympathetic nervous systems,
the "ventral vagal complex," which Porges calls the "Social Engagement
System," is the "smart" vagal because it regulates both the dorsal vagal
and sympathetic systems. This "smart" system is much more flexible than
the other two more primitive levels of the autonomic nervous system,
which, if unregulated, tend to the extremes of hyperarousal or hypo-
arousal. The Social Engagement System gives humans immense flexibility
of response to the environment (1995, 1997). For example, during social
engagement, interaction and conversation can rapidly shift from strong affect and animation one moment, to calm listening and reflection the next.
This "smart" branch of the parasympathetic nervous system regulates the
sympathetic and "freeze" (dorsal vagal parasympathetic) responses to
trauma and allows human beings to fine-tune their arousal to the needs of
the situation. This sophisticated "braking" mechanism of the Social Engagement System facilitates the regulation of overall arousal and is akin to
Schore's "interactive psychobiological regulation."

In effective modulation, the Social Engagement System regulates the more
extreme behavior of the autonomic nervous system. Under the stress of
trauma, an individual may at first attempt to use the Social Engagement
System to modulate, but, if ineffective, social engagement/interactive regulation will tend to shut down. As this occurs, the person has a compromised capacity to use relationships for regulation and instead reverts to the
more primitive sensorimotor and emotional systems. The healthy functioning of cognitive direction is diminished. As we shall see below, in Sensorimotor Psychotherapy the Social Engagement System is activated as the
therapist–client interaction effectively serves to regulate and modulate
arousal. After the therapist fulfills this role (in other words, becomes an
"auxiliary cortex" for the client), the client can learn the autoregulation

capacities of observing and tracking sensorimotor reactions. That is, the therapist's ability to interactively regulate the client's dysregulated arousal creates an environment in which the client can begin to access his own ability to regulate arousal (Schore, in press-b), independent of relational interaction. Through this process, the client is helped to move from frozen states and/or hyperarousal to full participation with the Social Engagement System.

SENSORIMOTOR PSYCHOTHERAPY: ESSENTIALS AND CASE DISCUSSION

Essentials of Sensorimotor Psychotherapy are (1) regulating affective and sensorimotor states through the therapeutic relationship and (2) teaching the client to self-regulate by mindfully contacting, tracking, and articulating sensorimotor processes independently. We believe that the former promotes the reinstatement and development of the client's Social Engagement System through interactive regulation, while the latter promotes an independent assimilation of sensorimotor reactions. The former is a prerequisite for the latter. As Schore observes, the therapist's "interactive regulation of the patient's state enables him or her to begin to verbally label the affective [and sensorimotor] experience" (bracketed text added; Schore, in press-b, p. 20). Interactive regulation provides the conditions under which the client can safely contact, describe, and eventually regulate inner experience.

The therapist must cultivate in the client an acute awareness of inner-body sensations, first, via the therapeutic interaction as the therapist observes and contacts sensorimotor states, and second, as the client herself notices these inner-body sensations without prompting by the therapist. Inner-body sensations are the myriad of physical feelings that are continually created within the body through biochemical changes and the movement of muscles, ligaments, organs, fluids, breath, and so on. These bodily feelings are of a distinctly physical character, such as clamminess, tightness, numbness, and electric, tingling, and vibrating sensations, and of course many others. However, when clients are asked to describe sensations, they frequently do so with words such as "panic" or "terror," which refer to emotional states rather than to sensation itself. When this occurs, clients are asked to describe how they experience the emotion physically: For example, panic may be felt in the body as rapid heart beat, trembling, and shallow breathing. Anger might be experienced as tension in the jaw, an impulse to strike out accompanied by a sense of heaviness and immobility in the arms. Similarly, a belief about oneself, such as "I'm bad" might be experienced as collapse through the spine, a ducking of the head, and tension in the buttocks.

Through cultivating such awareness and ability for verbal description, clients learn to distinguish and describe the various and often subtle qualities of sensation. Developing a precise sensation vocabulary helps clients expand their perception and processing of physical feelings in much the same way that familiarity with a variety of words that describe emotion aids in the perception and processing of emotions.

As clients describe traumatic experiences or symptoms, the therapist observes their arousal level, tracking for either hyperarousal or hypo-arousal. The therapist's task is to "hold" the client's arousal at the optimal limits of the Modulation Model, accessing enough traumatic material to process but not so much that clients become too dissociated for processing to occur. When arousal reaches either the upper or lower limit, clients are asked to temporarily disregard their feelings and thoughts and instead follow the development of physical sensations and movements in detail until these sensations settle and the movements complete themselves. In this way, the therapist acts as an auxiliary cortex, interactively modulating clients' levels of arousal, keeping them from going too far outside the optimum arousal zone, where it becomes difficult or impossible to process information without dissociating. At the same time, clients develop their capacity to self-regulate as they learn to limit the amount of information they must process at any given moment, which develops the capacity for self-regulation independent of their relationship with the therapist and prevents their being overwhelmed with an overload of information coming from within.

When a client describing a past trauma experiences panic, the therapist asks her to disregard the memory content and just sense the panic as bodily sensation. When the client then reports a trembling in her hands and a rapid heart rate, the therapist instructs her to track these sensations as they change or "sequence." As Levine notes, "Once you become aware of them, internal sensations almost always transform into something else" (Levine, 1997, p. 82). The trembling changes from affecting only the hands to involving the arms, which begin to shake quite strongly, then gradually quiet and soften; the heart rate also eventually returns to baseline. Only when this sensorimotor experience has settled is additional content described and emotional and cognitive processing included.

The therapist must learn to observe in precise detail the moment-by-moment organization of sensorimotor experience in the client, focusing on both subtle changes (such as skin color change, dilation of the nostrils or pupils, slight tension or trembling) and more obvious changes (collapse through the spine, turn in the neck, a push with an arm, or any other gross muscular movement). These sensorimotor experiences usually remain unnoticed by the client until the therapist points them out through a simple "contact" statement such as, "Seems like your arm is tensing," or "Your hand is changing into a fist," or "There's a slight trembling in your left leg." Any therapist is familiar with noticing and contacting emotional states ("You seem afraid") to facilitate clients' awareness and processing of emotions; the procedure is similar for sensorimotor reactions.

Mindfulness is the key to clients becoming more and more acutely aware of internal sensorimotor reactions and in increasing their capacity for self-regulation. Mindfulness is a state of consciousness in which one's awareness is directed toward here-and-now internal experience, with the intention of simply observing rather than changing this experience. Therefore, we can say that mindfulness engages the cognitive faculties of the client in support of sensorimotor processing, rather than allowing bottom-up trauma-related processes to escalate and take control of information processing. To teach mindfulness, the therapist asks questions that require mindfulness to answer, such as, "What do you feel in your body? Where exactly do you experience tension? What sensation do you feel in your legs right now? What happens in the rest of your body when your hand makes a fist?" Questions such as these force the client to come out of a dissociated state and future- or past-centered ideation and experience the present moment through the body. Such questions also encourage the client to step back from being embedded in the traumatic experience and to report from the standpoint of an observing ego, an ego that "has" an experience in the body rather than "is" that bodily experience.

For traumatized individuals, fully experiencing sensations may be disconcerting or even frightening, as intense physical experience may evoke feelings of being out of control or being weak and helpless. On the other hand, traumatized individuals are often dissociated from body sensation, experiencing the body as numb or anesthetized. Our view is that *failed active defensive responses* along with the inability to modulate arousal can be sources of such distressing bodily experiences, and that this distress can be at least somewhat alleviated by helping clients experience the somatic sequence of an active defensive response. Subsequently, clients may access sensation without dissociating or feeling uncomfortable.

To illustrate the above points, we will describe three sessions with Mary, a middle-aged, successful businesswoman who suffered both relational and shock trauma from being raped repeatedly by her uncle from age four to age ten. Although she suffered from panic attacks, depression, and what she described as having "no boundaries," she had no clear memory of the trauma until a recent altercation with an authority figure triggered flashbacks accompanied by insomnia and disturbing physical symptoms, such as hyperarousal, uncontrollable shaking, unprecedented vaginal bleeding, and a bout of immobility that lasted for over an hour. Mary reported that during the abuse she had tried to fight her uncle at first, but eventually she submitted and "watched from the ceiling."

As Mary recounted her history, she spoke rapidly with few pauses that would provide opportunity for verbal interaction with the therapist. Her Social Engagement System was markedly diminished; it was almost as though she were talking to herself, unable to utilize the relationship to interactively regulate her arousal. Mary appeared increasingly isolated and alone as she spoke. At times she experienced panic and hyperarousal, and she repeatedly spoke in judgment of herself for having allowed the abuse: "Why did I ever change clothes in front of him? Why didn't I tell my mother what was happening?" She also condemned herself for her inability to defend against the abuse, interpreting her dissociation and freezing as a personal weakness, a common response among trauma survivors (Nijenhuis & van der Hart, 1999, p. 54).

This first session with Mary illustrates an important point: The initial stage of therapy usually entails the therapist helping the client to begin to regulate arousal. This is accomplished at first through the interactive regulation within the therapeutic relationship, which sets the conditions under which the client can learn self-regulation. Obviously, a healthy relational rapport between client and therapist must be present for interactive regulation to occur. In Mary's case, the therapist facilitated interactive regulation through tracking changes and movements in her body, making contact statements, demonstrating an ability to understand Mary's distress, and tolerating the description of her traumatic experience without withdrawing or becoming hyperaroused himself. Gradually, Mary began to soften slightly in her body, slow her speech, and engage in reciprocal interaction with the therapist.

It was difficult at first for Mary to be mindful of her bodily sensations because when she tried to do so, the hyperarousal, shaking, panic, and terror became overwhelming. Similar to Levine's notion of "exchanging . . . an active response for one of helplessness" (Levine, 1997, p. 110), the therapist knew that if Mary could fully experience a physical defensive sequence, these symptoms might lessen. To accomplish this, he asked Mary if she would be willing to experiment by pushing with her hands against a pillow that he held, and to notice what happened in her body. Mary consented and as she performed this action, she first experienced nausea and increased fear, not uncommon when first working with activating a defensive sequence that has failed in the past. The therapist then asked Mary to temporarily disregard all memory and simply focus on her body to find a way to push that felt comfortable. Mary's sense of control was increased as she was encouraged to guide this physical exploration by telling the therapist how much pressure to use in resisting with the pillow, what position to be in, and so on. As Mary began to experience the active physical defense, the therapist tracked her body and made contact statements such as, "The strength of the pushing is increasing," and "You seem to be settling down," and so on. Mary was also instructed to be mindful of the details of her sensations: "What's happening in your body as you push? What do you feel in your back and spine?"

Mary eventually experienced a full sequence of active defensive response: lifting the arms, pushing tentatively at first with just her arms, then increasing the pressure and involving the muscles of her back, pelvis, and legs. The therapist continued to evoke mindfulness of sensation, and Mary began to experience the physical pleasure of pushing, reporting, "This feels good!" Because many traumatized clients are anhedonic (unable to feel physical pleasure), experiencing and savoring pleasurable sensations can increase their overall capacity for experiencing pleasure and also can change their relationship with the body, which heretofore may have felt like "the enemy," the source of disconcerting sensations and physical pain. When the defensive sequence had been thoroughly explored and completed, Mary was calmer and able to be mindful of sensations without becoming hyperaroused—in other words, she was now situated within the optimum arousal zone of the Modulation Model.

The intention in Sensorimotor Psychotherapy is to work at the edge of the Modulation Model, accessing enough of the traumatic material to work with, but not so much that the client becomes overwhelmed and dissociated. To serve this end, as Mary returned to describing the trauma (her decision, not the therapist's), she was instructed to stay mindful of her body sensations. As she described her abusive experience her jaw began to tighten, her right shoulder and arm began to constrict, and her breath became labored—all possible signs of defensive responses emerging spontaneously. After making contact statements with these physical observations by saying, "Your jaw and arm seem to be tightening up and your breathing is changing," the therapist directed Mary to be mindful of her bodily sensations: "Let's take a few moments to sense what's happening in your body before we go on with the content." Mary described the tension and stated that her head seemed to want to turn to the left, at which point she remembered a wall being on her left during the childhood abuse. Instead of interpreting her statements, or returning to the content of the memory, the therapist directed her to "allow that turning in your neck and notice what happens next."

At this point, Mary was no longer describing the past but was attentive only to present bodily experience. As she was mindful of her head and neck turning to the left, she was also aware of physical impulses that seemed involuntary, as if they were happening "by themselves." Her body seemed to take on a life of its own as she was encouraged to be mindful of her sensations and movements. Mary reported that "my hand wants to become a fist" and the therapist encouraged her to "feel the impulse and allow that to happen" without doing it voluntarily. While the previous pushing motion against the pillow was entirely voluntary, Mary's hand now slowly began to curl into a fist spontaneously.

Mary reported that her arm wanted to "hit out." The defensive movement sequence was now emerging without conscious top-down direction from either the client or the therapist. The therapist said, "Feel that impulse to hit out and just notice what happens next in your body." Mary was encouraged to simply track and allow the involuntary micromovements and gestures, rather than "do" them voluntarily. Sensorimotor processing was occurring spontaneously through mindful attention to body sensation and impulses, and by harnessing cognitive direction in suspending content and emotion to support the body's processing.

As the therapist directed Mary to track her sensations and involuntary movements, and as her right hand formed a fist, her forearm also tightened, and her arm slowly rose off her lap without conscious intention on her part. Mary stated that she was starting to feel panicky, and the therapist asked her to just experience the physical elements of the panic (which Mary reported as increased heart rate and constriction) rather than the emotion. This was an important directive to separate trauma-based emotions from sensation so that sensorimotor processing could occur without interference from emotional or cognitive processes, and without overloading Mary with more information than she could effectively handle. Gradually, Mary's head and body turned back toward the center, and her right arm progressed through a slow rising and hitting motion accompanied by shaking. (Inwardly, this experience of shaking is similar to shudders passing through the body when one is cold.) After several minutes of sensorimotor processing during which both Mary and the therapist followed the slow and unintended progression of movements, Mary's arm finally came to rest in her lap. Mary continued to shudder, and she was instructed to "stay with the shudders and sensations as long as you are comfortable doing so."

All the while, Mary was encouraged to trust her body by allowing the movements to occur without trying to direct them or change them in any way, and she was also encouraged to stop at any moment if she felt too much discomfort to go on. Since physical constriction from the gradual "exposure" to the traumatic memory can be extremely intense before it begins to unwind and soften, clients need the therapist's help in following the sensorimotor process. They are also encouraged to self-regulate—to stop if ever it becomes too intense.

Eventually, the shudders ceased, and Mary said she felt relief and a sensation of tingling throughout her body. The therapist instructed her to savor her bodily feeling and sense of relief, and to describe these physically in detail. Reporting a softening in her musculature, a slowed heart rate, and a good feeling of heaviness throughout her body, Mary stated that she felt peaceful for the first time in weeks. In speaking about the abuse, Mary was less judgmental of herself, saying she was angry that her mother had turned a blind eye to her uncle's behavior, and that no four-year-old girl should have to worry about changing clothes in front of a relative. While she had not worked directly with her self-judgments, beliefs, or emotions associated with the traumatic experience, working with sensorimotor processing had a positive effect on both her emotional and thinking processes. Toward the end of this session, the therapist helped Mary address emotional and cognitive processing. Mary gave full expression to her sadness and arrived at new meanings while she also became more fully conscious of her sensorimotor reactions. Mary experienced a new integration and reorganization of the physical, emotional, and cognitive levels of her experience as these three levels were addressed simultaneously.

At her next session, Mary reported that her sleep pattern had returned to normal, and she was much calmer in general. Her panic attacks had nearly ceased, and she wanted to continue to explore her childhood trauma, more confident in her ability to do so with an expectation of personal mastery. Mary was increasingly able to interact with the therapist, which was demonstrated by her asking questions, engaging in more dialogue in contrast to her original monologue, and in her using the relationship with the therapist to soothe herself. In subsequent sessions, Mary further developed her ability to actively defend herself and to set boundaries, which expanded her capacity to engage in interactive regulation; for the ability to actively defend and set boundaries increases one's safety in relationship. Mary was increasingly able to process emotional and cognitive elements of the trauma and to address relational issues with the therapist, while frequently returning to sensorimotor processing when physical impulses and sensations emerged, or when she again felt hyperaroused or dissociated.

Eventually, Mary experienced a therapy session in which she confronted the memory of the moment she first dissociated and "watched from the ceiling to what he [her uncle] was doing to another little girl," while another part of her submitted to the abuse. However, she now had developed the skill of tracking her body sensations, and she felt more confidence in being able to get through these experiences. Mary writes:

At the time of this session I had recently been experiencing what seemed like a new wave of earlier memories that had brought an increase both in the level of physical activation and in emotional terror and despair. This time though, it felt like I knew I could get through this, I'd been here before and knew there was a process and steps that led to a better, more whole experience.

In this session, Mary was again instructed by the therapist to be mindful of her body, and as she remembered the trauma, she became aware of the physical reactions she had experienced as a child. She experienced the physical components of submitting and dissociating from her body (numbness, muscle flaccidity, feeling paralyzed) *along with the impulse to fight back* (tension in her jaw and arms). Awareness of sensation became the unifying force in resolving this "dissociative split," as Mary realized: "This disintegration is not real . . . I'm two bodies in the same body, doing two different things." As Mary experienced this split somatically and processed the physical components of it (such as the impulse to fight her uncle), she was able to experience the grief associated with the abuse without dissociating from her body. More able to process cognitively, her negative beliefs about herself eventually were replaced by a sense of accomplishment of having been able to defend herself through dissociation and submission, acknowledging that these passive defenses had been effective in her particular situation, and realizing that active defenses at that time would probably have made her trauma worse. At one point in the session, Mary proudly says, "There's nothing wrong with me—look what I did!" referring to her dissociation as a way to survive unbearable abuse.

Shortly after this session, Mary's therapy terminated. Six months later, she writes:

I am aware that there has been a lasting and profound change in both my body (the way I hold it) and my sense of integration and ability to stay present with fearful situations, memories and sensations that would previously have been so overwhelming that they would be suppressed . . .

I also feel emotionally integrated in a new way. It's as though the part of me that had been the victim of . . . abuse is not alone any more but has other stronger, more whole and resistant parts mixed up with it. I no longer so desperately need the contact [with the therapist] to go into the memories. It's as though I can be there for myself.

CONCLUSION

Sensorimotor Psychotherapy was developed entirely from clinical practice, and although there has been no formal empirical research at this time, there are many anecdotal reports from both clients and therapists that attest to the efficacy of the method. Professionals who have learned Sensorimotor Psychotherapy report that it often reduces PTSD symptoms such as nightmares, panic attacks, aggressive outbursts, and hyperarousal, and that the ability to track body sensation helps clients experience present reality rather than reacting as if the trauma were still occurring. Such reductions of distressing bodily-based symptoms and increased capacity for both tracking body sensation and interactive self-regulation appears to help clients become increasingly able to work with other elements of trauma, such as attachment, meaning-making, and dissociative patterns that were previously overshadowed by bodily states and the inability to utilize interactive self-regulation.

Sensorimotor Psychotherapy provides clients with tools to deal with disturbing bodily reactions, and they frequently report feeling increasingly safe as they begin to learn how to limit the amount of information they must process at any given moment by focusing attention on sensation. Clients also report that their feeling of safety is enhanced when they experience the potential to physically protect and defend themselves. It should be noted that clients who experience hyperactive defenses in the form of uncontrollable rage may also increase their feeling of safety by learning to sense the physical precursors to full-blown aggressive outbursts, and at that moment begin to engage mindfulness. This intervention increases self-regulation and prevents the escalation of arousal to the point of discharge through aggression or other undesirable behavior.

On the other hand, therapists using Sensorimotor Psychotherapy report that some clients are not so available for, or interested in, body processing as was Mary. Such clients must slowly and painstakingly learn to experience sensation and be open to the potential value of doing so. They must gradually learn from their own somatic experience that paying full attention to body sensation and movements can be safe and even pleasurable. Additionally, severely disorganized or dissociated individuals may be unable to be mindful of sensation without becoming further disorganized or dissociated. It must be realized that accessing too much sensation too quickly, particularly before clients are able to observe their experience and put aside content and emotional states, may be counterproductive and may in fact increase dissociation and exacerbate PTSD symptoms. Therefore, therapists must proceed appropriately according to each client's pace and ability to integrate. Nevertheless, an occasional client may remain unable or unwilling to work with sensorimotor processing, finding body sensations too overwhelming and distressing, or otherwise finding a somatic approach uninteresting or unappealing. In such cases, sensorimotor processing is contraindicated and the therapist must use other techniques.

Although we have focused almost exclusively on sensorimotor processing in this chapter, the full spectrum of Sensorimotor Psychotherapy integrates sensorimotor processing with emotional and cognitive processing. During therapeutic sessions, the therapist must evaluate moment by moment which level of processing to address that will produce the most positive overall effect. Emotional or cognitive processing is often called for, and in fact can have a positive effect on further sensorimotor processing.

It should also be noted that while this chapter has emphasized sensorimotor processing, numerous other therapeutic maps and body-inclusive techniques exist in the overall approach developed by the authors and their colleagues, which deal in different ways with relational dynamics, psycho/structural patterns, and dissociation. Above all, it is important to stress that the ultimate and overriding goal of Sensorimotor Psychotherapy is to foster holistic processing by integrating the three levels of our being: cognitive, emotional, and sensorimotor.

REFERENCES

Damasio, A. (1999). *The feeling of what happens*. New York: Harcourt, Brace.
Diamond, S., Balvin, R., & Diamond, F. (1963). *Inhibition and choice*. New York: Harper and Row.
Fisher, A. G., & Murray, E. A. (1991). Introduction to sensory integration theory.

In A. Fisher, E. Murray, & A. Bundy (Eds.), *Sensory integration: Theory and practice* (pp. 3–26). Philadelphia: Davis.

Gendlin, E. (1978). *Focusing.* New York: Bantam Books.

Hannaford, C. (1995). *Smart moves: Why learning is not all in your head.* Arlington, VA: Great Ocean Publishers.

Herman, J. (1992). *Trauma and recovery.* New York: Basic Books.

Hobson. J. A. (1994). *The chemistry of conscious states.* New York: Back Bay Books.

LeDoux, J. (1996). *The emotional brain.* New York: Simon and Schuster.

Levine, P. (1997). *Waking the tiger: Healing trauma.* Berkeley, CA: North Atlantic Books.

MacLean, P. D. (1985). Brain evolution relating to family, play, and the separation call. *Archives of General Psychiatry,* 42, 405–417.

McFarlane, A. C. (1996). Resilience, vulnerability, and the course of posttraumatic reactions. In B. van der Kolk, A. C. McFarlane, & L. Weisaeth (Eds.), *Traumatic stress: The effects of overwhelming experience on mind, body, and society* (pp. 155–181). New York: Guilford Press.

Nijenhuis, E.R.S., & van der Hart, O. (1999). Forgetting and re-experiencing trauma: From anesthesia to pain. In J. Goodwin & R. Attias (Eds.), *Splintered reflections: Images of the body in trauma* (pp. 39–66). New York: Basic Books.

Nijenhuis, E.R.S., Vanderlinden, J., & Spinhoven, P. (1998). Animal defensive reactions as a model for trauma-induced dissociative reactions. *Journal of Traumatic Stress,* 11(2), 243–260.

Piaget, J. (1952). *The origins of intelligence in children.* New York: International Universities Press.

Porges, S. (1995). Orienting in a defensive world: Mammalian modifications of our evolutionary heritage. A polyvagal theory. *Psychophysiology,* 32, 301–318.

Porges, S. (1997). Emotion: An evolutionary by-product of the neural regulation of the autonomic nervous system. The integrative neurobiology of affiliation. *Annals of the New York Academy of Sciences,* 807, 62–77.

Schore, A. (1994). *Affect regulation and the origin of the self: The neurobiology of emotional development.* Hillsdale, NJ: Erlbaum.

Schore, A. (in press-a). The effects of a secure attachment relationship on right brain development, affect regulation, and infant mental health. *Infant Mental Health Journal.*

Schore, A. (in press-b). The right brain as the neurobiological substratum of Freud's dynamic unconscious. In D. Scharff & J. Scharff (Eds.), *Freud at the millenium: The evolution and application of psychoanalysis.* New York: The Other Press.

Siegel, D. (1999). *The developing mind: Toward a neurobiology of interpersonal experience.* New York: Guilford Press.

Solomon, Z., Laror, N., & McFarlane, A. C. (1996). Acute posttraumatic reactions in soldiers and civilians. In B. van der Kolk, A. C. McFarlane, & L. Weisaeth (Eds.), *Traumatic stress: The effects of overwhelming experience on mind, body, and society* (pp. 102–116). New York: Guilford Press.

van der Kolk, B. A. (1987). *Psychological trauma.* Washington, DC: American Psychiatric Press.

van der Kolk, B. A. (1996). The body keeps the score: Approaches to the psycho-biology of posttraumatic stress disorder. In B. van der Kolk, A. C. Mc-Farlane, & L. Weisaeth (Eds.), *Traumatic stress: The effects of overwhelming experience on mind, body, and society* (pp. 214–241). New York: Guilford Press.

van der Kolk, B. A., & Fisler, R. (1995). The psychological processing of traumatic memories: Review and experimental confirmation. *Journal of Traumatic Stress, 8,* 505–525.

van der Kolk, B. A., McFarlane, A. C., & van der Hart, O. (1996). A general approach to treatment of posttraumatic stress disorder. In B. van der Kolk, A. C. McFarlane, & L. Weisaeth (Eds.), *Traumatic stress: The effects of overwhelming experience on mind, body, and society* (pp. 417–440). New York: Guilford Press.

van der Kolk, B. A., van der Hart, O., & Marmar, C. (1996). Dissociation and information processing in posttraumatic stress disorder. In B. van der Kolk, A. C. McFarlane, & L. Weisaeth (Eds.), *Traumatic stress: The effects of overwhelming experience on mind, body, and society* (pp. 303–322). New York: Guilford Press.

Van Olst, E. H. (1972). *The orienting reflex.* The Hague, Netherlands: Mouton.

Wilbarger, P., & Wilbarger, J. (1997). *Sensory defensiveness and related social/emotional and neurological problems.* Van Nuys, CA: Wilbarger. (May be obtained from Avanti Education Program, 14547 Titus St., Suite 109, Van Nuys, CA, 91402).

Wilber, K. (1996). *A brief history of everything.* Boston: Shambhala.

Chapter 8

Eye Movement Desensitization and Reprocessing in the Treatment of Post-traumatic Stress Disorder

Louise Maxfield

Since Eye Movement Desensitization and Reprocessing (EMDR) was introduced 12 years ago (Shapiro, 1989a, 1989b) it has become the most researched treatment for post-traumatic stress disorder (PTSD) and its efficacy has been widely recognized. EMDR is a comprehensive treatment protocol in which the client attends to emotionally disturbing material in short sequential doses while simultaneously focusing on an external stimulus (therapist-directed eye movements, hand-tapping, auditory tones). This chapter provides an overview of the development of EMDR and Shapiro's (2001) Adaptive Information Processing model, which hypothesizes that EMDR works by forging new links between elements of traumatic memories and adaptive information contained in other memory networks. The empirical evidence is examined, with summaries of 12 controlled studies: Civilian participants demonstrated a 70 to 90% decrease in PTSD diagnosis after three to four EMDR sessions, and combat veterans a 78% decrease in PTSD diagnosis after 12 sessions. A concise explanation of the eight phases of EMDR treatment process is augmented with multiple client vignettes. Finally, a case illustration provides a detailed description of the application of EMDR in the treatment of PTSD.

OVERVIEW OF THE PRESENTING PROBLEM

Trauma is an experience of intense horror, or complete terror, or overwhelming helplessness (American Psychiatric Association, 1994). It is sudden and unexpected, and is perceived by the individual as non-normative and as exceeding his or her ability to cope. It is catastrophic, destructive, and disruptive and can change the course and direction of a person's life.

Although most people move on toward health, reorienting values and goals, there are others for whom trauma creates lasting psychological and biological changes, resulting in post-traumatic stress disorder (PTSD).

Exposure to traumatic events is a common experience, with community surveys reporting rates of exposure from 62 to 69% (Breslau, Davis, Andreski, Peterson, & Schultz, 1997; Kessler, Sonnega, Bromet, Hughes, & Nelson, 1995; Resnick, Kilpatrick, Dansky, Saunders, & Best, 1993). Approximately 20% of those exposed will develop PTSD. It appears that post-traumatic stress may often be underidentified and undertreated (Van Etten & Taylor, 1998). There are many other persons with subsyndromal levels of PTSD, who are so distressed by the trauma that their function is impaired (Maes et al., 1998).

TRADITIONAL TREATMENT APPROACHES

The National Comorbidity Survey found that persons with PTSD who received treatment recovered more rapidly than those without treatment, and that remission was most rapid within the first year (Kessler et al., 1995). After six years, however, treatment effects were minimal and almost 40% of both groups still met the diagnostic criteria for PTSD. This percentage was unchanged at 10 years post trauma. The fact that 40% of persons treated for PTSD were unable to find relief demonstrates the need for different and more effective treatments.

Cognitive-Behavioral Therapy (CBT) is the psychological treatment most commonly used in the treatment of PTSD, and research has demonstrated its effectiveness (see Chapter 4, this volume). CBT often includes a "flooding" or "directed exposure" procedure that requires a concentrated, chronological focus on the original trauma and elicits high levels of affective distress. Clients can find it difficult to endure the intense emotional arousal. CBT usually requires 12 to 16 sessions with daily homework assignments.

This chapter examines Eye Movement Desensitization and Reprocessing (EMDR). EMDR is a relatively new treatment that appears to be as effective as CBT and that may require less time and be less painful for clients. Researchers using both techniques remark that EMDR, with its alternating dosed exposure and client-directed focus, seems to be better tolerated and preferred over exposure therapy by both clients and therapists (Boudewyns, Stwertka, Hyer, Albrecht, & Sperr, 1993; Pitman et al., 1996). In a treatment process study comparing EMDR to exposure, Rogers et al. (1999) found that although clients rated both treatments equally, EMDR resulted in a rapid decrease in Subjective Units of Distress (SUD), whereas in the exposure group there was no decrease in SUD levels. This difference may contribute to the observation that EMDR is the more comfortable treatment.

In a meta-analysis that compared the efficacy of treatments for PTSD,

Van Etten and Taylor (1998) analyzed 61 treatment outcome trials from 39 studies of chronic PTSD. The treatments included pharmacotherapies, psychological therapies (behavior therapy, EMDR, relaxation training, hypnotherapy, and dynamic therapy), and control conditions (pill-placebo, wait-list controls, supportive psychotherapies, and non-saccade EMDR control). Although serotonin specific reuptake inhibitors (SSRIs) were effective, they were not well-tolerated: The high drop-out rate (36%) suggests that SSRIs may not be a treatment of choice for PTSD. Psychological therapies were more effective than drug therapies, and of these, CBT and EMDR were most effective. They showed generally equivalent effects on measures of PTSD, anxiety, and depression. The EMDR studies had significantly fewer treatment sessions than those using behavior therapy (4.6 versus 14.8 sessions) and EMDR took significantly less time (3.7 versus 10.1 weeks). It appears that EMDR may be equivalent in effectiveness to CBT and that it may be more efficient, producing more rapid recovery.

In 1995, the Clinical Psychology Division of the American Psychological Association initiated a project to determine the degree to which therapeutic methods were supported by solid empirical evidence. Using these criteria, independent reviewers (Chambless et al., 1998) placed EMDR, exposure therapy, and stress inoculation therapy on a list of "probably efficacious treatments"; no other therapies were judged to be empirically supported by controlled research for any PTSD population. In 2000, after the examination of additional published controlled studies, the Practice Guidelines of the International Society for Traumatic Stress Studies designated CBT and EMDR as efficacious for PTSD (Chemtob, Tolin, van der Kolk, & Pitman, 2000; Rothbaum, Meadows, Resick, & Foy, 2000).

OVERVIEW OF EMDR

Brief Description

Described by originator Francine Shapiro as "a model, set of principles, procedures and protocols that together represent a new approach to psychotherapy" (1994a, p. 155), EMDR is said to facilitate the accessing and processing of traumatic memories and to bring these to an adaptive resolution, indicated by desensitization of emotional distress, reformulation of associated cognitions, and relief of accompanying physiological arousal. EMDR is a therapeutic process in which the client attends to emotionally disturbing material in short, sequential doses while simultaneously focusing on an external stimulus. Therapist-directed eye movements are the most common dual attention stimulus, but a variety of other stimuli, including hand-tapping and auditory tones, are often used (Shapiro, 1991, 1994b, 1995). This dual (external/internal) attention is combined with frequent brief periods of focusing on new associations as they arise, in a highly structured and client-directed process.

Shapiro (1995, 2001) maintains that EMDR, with its brief exposures to associated material, dual attention stimuli, and therapeutic protocol, is a distinctly different form of therapy, activating internal processes that move the individual toward healing. According to Hyer and Brandsma (1997) and Fensterheim (1996), EMDR is a complex multi-component, multi-staged process, blending many elements of other effective therapies into a comprehensive treatment protocol. It includes many features of CBT, including cognitive restructuring, anxiety desensitization, breathing, and exposure. EMDR also integrates elements of many other effective therapies such as psychodynamic, body-focused, person-centered, and interactional therapies (Bohart, in press; Brown, in press; Fensterheim, 1996; Lazarus & Lazarus, in press; Manfield, 1998; Wachtel, in press). Additionally, it possesses a number of non-specific therapeutic components, including therapeutic rapport, client empowerment, and expectations of positive outcome.

By far, the most unusual element of EMDR is the eye movement component. Primary research that studied eye movements in relation to thinking processes, dreaming, brain function, perception, and memory (e.g., Andrade, Kavanagh, & Baddeley, 1997; Antrobus, 1973; Antrobus & Singer, 1964; Christman & Garvey, 2000; Drake, 1987; Stickgold, 1998, 2002), has provided indications that the clinical use of eye movements could be beneficial (see Shapiro 2001, 2002; Shapiro & Maxfield, in press). There have also been dismantling EMDR studies in which eye movements were removed or modified to examine their effects (e.g., Montgomery & Allyon, 1994; Renfrey & Spates, 1996; Wilson, Silver, Covi, & Foster, 1996). Although these studies indicated that eye movements may contribute to clinical treatment outcome, the aggregate results are inconclusive because of the poor methodology typically used in these studies. While ongoing research is attempting to answer this question, it should be recognized that, as of yet, no psychotherapy, including CBT, has definitively identified or measured its active mechanisms (e.g., Jacobson et al., 1996; Marks, Lovell, Noshirvani, Livanou, & Thrasher, 1998).

History

Francine Shapiro was a 38-year-old Ph.D. psychology student when she made the "chance observation" (Shapiro, 1995, p. 2) that resulted in the creation of EMDR. While walking in the park in May 1987, she noticed that the emotional distress connected to some old memories disappeared when she moved her eyes rapidly from side to side (Shapiro & Silk Forrest, 1997). Experimenting with friends and colleagues, she developed a procedure to facilitate eye movements and to expedite the processing of distress. She then administered this treatment to about 70 persons and standardized a procedure that was consistently successful. Since Shapiro's primary goal was to reduce anxiety, and since she was, at this time, a behaviorist, she called her technique Eye Movement Desensitization (EMD).

Shapiro conducted a case study, and a controlled study for her doctoral thesis, which resulted in two published papers (Shapiro, 1989a, 1989b). The subjects were 22 individuals who were very disturbed by various traumas that had occurred an average of 23 years previously, and who had received an average of 6 years of unsuccessful treatment. Subjects were randomly assigned to one session of EMD or a modified flooding procedure (EMD without eye movement). The response of the EMD group was significantly superior to controls on SUD ratings and behavioral indicators. Results were independently corroborated at one-and three-month follow-ups, and replicated with EMD treatment of the controls. These findings were limited by the lack of standardized assessments and the multiple roles played by Shapiro. Such unprecedented treatment success generated both enthusiastic interest (e.g., Wolpe, in a footnote to Shapiro, 1989b) and critical skepticism (e.g., Acierno, Hersen, Van Hasselt, Tremont, & Mueser, 1994).

While working as a Research Fellow at the Mental Research Institute in Palo Alto, California, Shapiro observed that EMD appeared to result not only in desensitization, but also in the cognitive restructuring of memories and personal attributions. EMD became EMDR, renamed to capture the concept of Reprocessing (Shapiro, 1991). This conceptual development was accompanied by the development and refining of method protocols and procedures, and the formulation of Shapiro's theory of Adaptive Information Processing (Shapiro, 1995, 2001).

By 1991, an EMDR National Training Schedule was established, with training restricted to licensed clinicians. Training was controlled to ensure that all persons practicing EMDR received identical training, and were following the same protocols. When Shapiro published her book in 1995, the restriction on training was lifted. Presently, more than 40,000 therapists worldwide have received EMDR training (Shapiro, 2001) and there are reports of more than one million individuals having been treated with EMDR (EMDRIA, 2000). Twelve years after its inception, with the publication of over 100 case studies and 30 controlled studies, EMDR is becoming a recognized, established treatment (see Allen, Keller, & Console, 1999; Chemtob et al., 2000; Maxfield, 1999; Shapiro, 1995, 2001; Shepherd, Stein, & Milne, 2000). This recognition has been driven by research findings substantiating its apparent efficacy in the treatment of PTSD (Feske, 1998; Hembree & Foa, 2000; Lipke, 1999; Maxfield & Hyer, 2002; Shalev, Foa, Keane, & Friedman, 2000; Spector & Read, 1999).

The Adaptive Information Processing Model

Shapiro (Shapiro, 2001; Shapiro & Maxfield, in press) has adopted the term "Adaptive Information Processing" (AIP) model to describe her theoretical model of information processing, and to distinguish this conceptual model from the treatment itself which is understood to be an "Accelerated Information Processing" treatment. Humans are assumed to have an inherent information processing system that is physiologically geared and neurologically balanced to process information to a state of mental health. Information is conceptualized as being stored in a system of memory networks, which are viewed as neurobiological structures containing related memories, thoughts, images, emotions, and sensations. During normal adaptive processing, connections are made to appropriate associations, emotional distress is relieved, experiences are used constructively, and learning takes place.

Pathology is thought to occur when information acquired at the time of a traumatic event is inadequately processed, and then is dysfunctionally stored with its sensory content in a state-specific form. It is held in an excitatory condition and may be more readily stimulated and triggered than other associations; the distressing intrusive reexperiencing symptoms of PTSD are a prime example. Recollecting the event appears to elicit the same negative self-attributions, affect, and physical sensations as those experienced at the time of the event.

The AIP model (Shapiro, 1995, 2001) postulates that adaptive resolution is achieved by activating the brain's own information processing system, with its "inherent self-healing processes." Adaptive reprocessing is understood to take place on a neurophysiological level. When the dysfunctional memory network links up with more adaptive information, insight and integration are achieved. Desensitization and cognitive restructuring are considered by-products of this process. Adaptive reprocessing results in the elimination of maladaptive negative emotion, and in some kind of positive resolution. It may even include a positive schematic shift. For example, a person no longer sees himself as a victim, and instead claims his resiliency and strength.

EMDR is an Accelerated Information Processing treatment. It works directly with all the perceptual components of memory (cognitive, affective, somatic) to forge new associative links with more adaptive material. It is structured to rapidly and effectively access the dysfunctionally stored information and to directly mobilize the information processing system. A number of treatment elements (e.g., eye movements, free association, brief exposures) are specifically formulated to enhance information processing.

EMPIRICAL EVIDENCE OF THE EFFECTIVENESS OF EMDR

The level of evidence for EMDR is based upon 12 controlled studies that investigated the efficacy of EMDR treatment of participants with PTSD. The seven civilian studies, with one exception, all found EMDR to be efficacious in the treatment of PTSD: EMDR was equivalent to cognitive-behavioral therapy, and superior to other control conditions. Four of the five studies with combat veterans addressed only one or two memories in this multiply traumatized population, and their findings were equivocal. The one combat veteran study that administered a longer course of treatment provides preliminary evidence that EMDR may be efficacious with that population. EMDR is a rapid treatment and appears to be well tolerated by clients, with effects being maintained at follow-up. Dismantling studies that examined the use of eye movements or other treatment components are not discussed here (e.g., Pitman et al., 1996) because their focus was on determining the mechanism of action rather than on assessing treatment efficacy.

EMDR with Civilian PTSD

EMDR was compared to wait-list conditions by Wilson, Becker, and Tinker (1995; 1997) and Rothbaum (1997). Participants in the Rothbaum study were 18 adult female rape victims with PTSD who were randomly assigned to either a wait-list control group or three treatment sessions of EMDR. Results showed significantly greater improvement for the EMDR subjects, with scores on standardized measures moving to within normal range. At post-treatment, 90% of the EMDR subjects no longer met PTSD criteria. In the Wilson et al. study, participants were 80 civilian trauma survivors, 46% of whom had PTSD. Those subjects receiving EMDR treatment showed significantly greater improvement than the wait-list group. Scores on standardized measures moved to within normal range. After three-month follow-up, treatment was provided to the wait-list group, with results replicating the original findings. At 15-month follow-up (Wilson et al., 1997), 84% of those originally diagnosed with PTSD no longer met PTSD criteria. The wait-list design is limited: No comparison is made to other treatments, and it does not control for non-specific factors such as therapeutic alliance, expectations, or placebo effects.

Two studies with civilian PTSD subjects compared EMDR to other treatments for which there is no established evidence of efficacy with PTSD. In an outpatient HMO, Marcus, Marquis, and Sakai (1997) randomly assigned 67 individuals to EMDR or to "Standard Kaiser Care" (SKC). SKC consisted of cognitive, psychodynamic, or behavioral therapies. Participants received an unlimited number of 50-minute treatment sessions. EMDR produced significantly lower scores than SKC for PTSD, depression, and anxiety symptoms. After three sessions, 50% of the EMDR participants no longer met the criteria for PTSD, compared to 20% of the SKC group. At post-treatment, 77% of the EMDR group no longer met criteria for PTSD compared to 50% of the SKC group. Even though the wide variety of treatments used in the control group accurately represents standard care in an HMO setting, there is no specific knowledge of their effectiveness for PTSD treatment; this limits the conclusions that can be drawn.

Scheck, Schaeffer, and Gillette (1998) compared EMDR to an active listening (AL) control with a group of 60 traumatized young women, 77% of whom were diagnosed with PTSD, and who were engaging in high-risk behavior such as sexual promiscuity, runaway behavior, or substance abuse. The women received two 90-minute treatment sessions, and had a homework assignment of journal writing. Both AL and EMDR resulted in significant reductions on all measures. The effects of EMDR were significantly greater than that of AL on all measures except a self-concept scale. Treatment gains were maintained at three-month follow-up for both groups. The results indicate that EMDR is superior to a condition that controls for some of the non-specific effects of treatment such as attention, therapeutic rapport, and active listening.

EMDR has been compared to CBT for civilian PTSD in three studies. Vaughan et al. (1994) found relative equivalency for EMDR and CBT exposure and relaxation therapies. Thirty-six participants received three to five treatment sessions. All treatments led to significant decreases in depression and PTSD symptoms for subjects in the treatment groups compared to those on the wait-list. A comparison between treatment groups found a significantly greater reduction at post-treatment for the EMDR group on PTSD intrusive symptoms, and at follow-up for the relaxation group on self-reports of depression. At follow-up, 70% of the PTSD subjects no longer met PTSD diagnostic criteria. Lee, Gavriel, Richards, Drummond, and Greenwald (in press) randomly assigned 24 PTSD civilian subjects to EMDR or to Stress Inoculation Training with Prolonged Exposure (SITPE). Participants received seven 60-minute treatment sessions. Both EMDR and SITPE were found to be highly effective, with significant decreases on PTSD measures. EMDR was more effective on intrusion scales. At follow-up, 83% of the EMDR subjects and 75% of the SITPE subjects no longer met PTSD criteria. EMDR may be more efficient by not requiring homework assignments.

Devilly & Spence (1999) provided 23 civilian PTSD subjects with eight sessions of either EMDR or a CBT treatment package combining elements of CBT, Stress Inoculation Training, and Prolonged Exposure. This "Trauma Treatment Protocol" (TTP) was developed by Devilly. Both EMDR and TTP were significantly effective on all measures and TTP was significantly more effective than EMDR on combined PTSD measures. At three-month follow-up, 58% of the TTP subjects no longer met PTSD criteria, compared to only 18% of the EMDR group. Although Vaughan et al. (1994) and Lee et al. (in press) found EMDR and CBT exposure therapies to be relatively equivalent, this was not the finding of Devilly and Spence (1999), who had uncharacteristically poor results with EMDR. When considering the wide variation in outcome of these three studies, methodological rigor should be considered. It appears that differences in outcome are related to differences in methodology, and that low ratings of methodological rigor predict low treatment effect sizes (Maxfield & Hyer, 2002).

EMDR with Combat Veterans with PTSD

Five controlled studies have examined the efficacy of EMDR with combat veterans. This research area has suffered from poor methodology. In four studies (Boudewyns et al., 1993; Boudewyns & Hyer, 1996; Devilly, Spence, & Rapee, 1998; Jensen, 1994), the participants were receiving adjunctive concurrent treatments, confounding the effect of the experimental conditions, and making it impossible to determine unique effects. Also, subjects in these four studies were provided with only two or three treatment sessions, or addressed only one or two of multiple traumatic memories. Other methodological limitations include poor treatment fidelity and lack of blind independent assessors. Although some changes in diagnostic status were found (Boudewyns & Hyer, 1996; Devilly et al., 1998), because of the methodological limitations, these four studies provide no clear evidence of the effectiveness of EMDR with combat PTSD.

In the fifth study, Carlson, Chemtob, Rusnak, Hedlund, and Muraoka (1998) provided 35 Vietnam combat veterans with an adequate course of treatment (12 sessions). EMDR was compared to wait-list and to biofeedback relaxation, and resulted in significantly lower scores on measures of PTSD and self-reported symptoms. Both treatment groups and the wait-list control showed significant improvement on physiological measures, with no differences between groups, and with the decrease in physiological arousal maintained at three-month follow-up. At nine-month follow-up, 78% of the EMDR subjects no longer met diagnostic criteria for PTSD.

ASSESSMENT AND TREATMENT: THE EIGHT PHASES OF EMDR

EMDR consists of eight phases, each considered essential for effective application (Shapiro, 1995, 2001; Shapiro & Silk Forrest, 1997). EMDR utilizes a direct holistic approach, with attention to ongoing affective and physiological changes throughout the session. Clinical evidence indicates that application of the full protocol may be essential for optimal outcome, and that truncating the procedure by eliminating various procedural elements can result in poorer outcomes. Shapiro (1999) and her colleagues reviewed EMDR phobia outcome studies and determined that those using fewer than half of the required elements had poorer outcomes than those which used more than half of the protocol elements.

Patient History and Treatment Planning

During the first phase, the therapist takes a full history, assesses the client's suitability for EMDR, and develops a treatment plan. The therapist evaluates aspects such as diagnosis, co-morbidity, existing support system, suicidality, life stability, presence of current stressors, physical health, and substance use. Although the obtaining of a full history is a procedure followed in most psychotherapies, in EMDR it has additional theoretical importance. It is understood that earlier traumas may underlie current presenting symptoms, and that the processing of related memory networks will activate such prior incidents. Therefore, an effort is made to identify these, so that both client and therapist are aware of the material that may be accessed during processing.

"Trina" was the first person to arrive on the scene after a car had crashed on a deserted road and rolled into a river. She rescued those passengers who were still alive. Afterwards, she blamed herself for the deaths of the non-surviving passengers. While processing this with EMDR, she realized how closely this related to the drowning death of a younger sibling when she was five years old. Her parents had accused her of being responsible for the tragedy. This earlier incident had fueled her emotional response to the current event. (Note: Trina's story and subsequent clinical vignettes are based on actual clients, with names and minor details changed to protect confidentiality).

The therapist also wants to ensure that the client can tolerate the intense affect that can arise during EMDR sessions. EMDR activates the memory network and clients can feel like they are reexperiencing the physical, emotional, and cognitive elements of the trauma. For example, during the Vietnam War, "Sam" had been viciously attacked and his arm almost severed with a knife. During the EMDR process, he felt severe pain in his arm. Additionally, the processing of material can continue after the session is over, with other memories and emotions surfacing. The therapist must ensure that the client can handle the despair, anger, fear, or other emotions associated with the memory before stimulating the memory network. Therefore, client assessment must include an evaluation of the client's ability to self-soothe, regulate affect, and relax. If the client lacks such skills, these resources are enhanced in Phase Two, before beginning the processing of the event.

Preparation

Preparation for EMDR includes education about the EMDR process and ensuring that the client has adequate impulse control and affect management skills. For clients without deficits in these areas, this phase of treatment is often brief, and EMDR is typically used to enhance "safe place" visualization. This involves adding eye movements, according to certain interactive clinical guidelines, while the client imagines a past memory or fantasy that evokes a feeling of safety. Client reports indicate that EMDR amplifies the sensory content and somatic experience of the visualization.

For clients with deficits in these areas, brief treatment is not recommended, and this phase of treatment may be extensive. Therapists can use a form of EMDR to assist in the development of resources and strengths, and to establish client safety and stabilization (Korn & Leeds, in press). This resource enhancement work combines relaxation, imagery, and EMDR to assist the client in developing new skills and strengths.

Assessment

In the third phase, the client and therapist select which specific memory to target, and the client identifies the most distressing visual image connected to that event. The therapist helps him to identify the current negative belief about himself that is related to the target memory. Negative cognitions are beliefs such as "I'm powerless," or "I am worthless." Next, the client develops a potential positive cognition, which expresses a desired sense of empowerment and agency, such as "I'm competent," or "I have value as a person." He rates the accuracy of this positive belief on the Validity of Cognition Scale (VOC), where 1 represents "completely false" and 7 represents "completely true."

The articulation of the cognitions can take substantial work, and may constitute a "significant piece of cognitive therapy" (Allen & Lewis, 1996, p. 246). The development of these positive and negative cognitions serves to identify the irrationality of the negative belief attached to the traumatic memory. These cognitions tend to cognitively anchor each end of the EMDR process (Boudewyns & Hyer, 1996). For example, "John," a man abused by his mother, chose for his target image a mental picture of his mother's angry face, and the belief "I'm unlovable." Combining those two elements elicited powerful emotions, and the recognition of how deeply his sense of self had been rooted in early experiences with his mother.

The client next identifies the emotions that are elicited when the visual image is combined with the negative belief. He rates the level of distress on the Subjective Unit of Disturbance (SUD) scale, where 0 is "calm" and 10 is "the worst possible distress" and identifies and locates the body sensations accompanying the emotions. The therapist's simple acceptance of the client's low VOC and high SUD scores indicates to the client that there are no expectations, and shows an acceptance of the client in his present state.

Desensitization

During the fourth phase, the client focuses on the visual image, the identified negative belief, and body sensations, while experiencing eye movements in sequential dosed exposures. The client holds all these elements in mind while simultaneously moving his eyes from side to side for 15 or more seconds, following the therapist's fingers as they move across the visual field. Alternative dual attention stimuli such as hand-tapping or auditory tones can replace the eye movements (Shapiro, 1991, 1994b, 1995). After the set of eye movements the client is told to take a deep breath, and then is asked what material was elicited in the process. Generally, this material (image, thought, sensation, or emotion) then becomes the target of the next set of eye movements. This cycle of alternating focused exposure and client feedback is repeated many times and is accompanied by shifts in affect, physiological states, and cognitive insights (e.g., Vaughan et al., 1994). If the processing stalls, specialized interventions are worded and timed in a specific manner to facilitate processing. The SUD level is usually not reassessed until emotional, physical, and cognitive resolution is apparent. A SUD rating of 0 or 1 generally indicates completion of this phase.

It is during this phase that the client is exposed to the traumatic material, with exposure occurring in brief segments. Because EMDR uses a nondirective free association method, clients may spend very little time exposed to the details of the presenting trauma. Instead they may move sequentially through related material. When "Margie" started processing the emotional distress related to physical assaults by her ex-husband, she found that her focus shifted to childhood experiences of harsh parental criticism. When she had resolved the pain related to parental rejection, the distress related to abuse by the ex-husband resolved rapidly.

Installation of Positive Cognition

In the fifth phase, the therapist invites the client to pair the previously identified, or an emergent, positive self-statement with the original traumatic image, using eye movements. The therapist encourages the client to continue until strong confidence in the positive cognition is apparent, and a VOC of 6 or 7 is achieved. This phase allows for the expression and consolidation of the client's cognitive insights. For many clients it involves a profound shift in self-concept, integrating self-acceptance with new, positive and realistic perceptions of the self. When "John" (the man abused as a child) paired his positive belief "I deserve love" with the targeted image of his mother's face, he noticed that the image no longer had any power, and that he could make this statement with great confidence.

Body Scan

In Phase Six, the clinician asks the client, while thinking of the image and the positive cognition, to notice if there is any tension or unusual sensation in his body. Because emotional distress is also often experienced physiologically, processing is not considered complete until the client can bring the traumatic memory into consciousness without feeling any body tension. Any sensations found in the body scan are targeted with more eye movements; this continues until the tension is relieved. Sometimes such body sensations are linked to aspects of the memory network that have not yet been processed. For example, "Melinda" had apparently finished processing the trauma of a rape. When the therapist asked her to scan her body for any discomfort, she reported that her wrists hurt. This sensation was then targeted, and Melinda remembered how the rapist had gripped her wrists, holding her hands above her head, and how powerless she felt. After this aspect of the rape was targeted, the pain in her wrists disappeared and Melinda felt free and able to reclaim her own power.

Closure

In Phase Seven, the therapist assesses that the material has been adequately worked through, and if not, assists the client with self-calming interventions. These are the skills and techniques that have been developed and strengthened in Phase Two. Clients are also asked to keep a journal to note any material that emerges after the session. During the week after the session in which she processed memories of the rape, "Melinda" began thinking about her parents' refusal to believe that this has happened to her. This new material became a treatment target in a subsequent session.

Reevaluation

Reevaluation takes place at the beginning of every subsequent EMDR session. The therapist checks with the client to assure that the treatment gains have been maintained, via SUD, VOC, and body self-report measures. These reevaluations assist the therapist in continuing to direct the treatment to achieve maximum benefit for the client. The goal of EMDR therapy is to produce the most substantial treatment effects possible in the shortest period of time, while simultaneously maintaining client function and preventing emotional overload. Therefore thorough, ongoing evaluation of reprocessing, stability, behavioral change, and integration within the larger social system is essential.

The eight phases of treatment may be completed in a few sessions or over a period of months, depending on the needs of the client and/or the seriousness of the pathology. "Melinda" required only three treatment sessions to eliminate the PTSD that followed a rape, whereas "John" required more extensive therapy to deal with child abuse issues. For most persons, EMDR appears to accelerate treatment and to result in thorough and complete processing. "Susan" sought EMDR treatment after 10 years of various therapies (CBT, group, feminist, art therapy, etc.) had failed to resolve PTSD resulting from extensive childhood physical, emotional, and sexual abuse. Susan had been unemployed for 12 years following the onset of PTSD; her relationships with husband and children were compromised by her daily rages, and she dissociated frequently. After 10 weeks of EMDR, Susan no longer met diagnostic criteria for PTSD; her rages were eliminated, and her dissociation was markedly reduced. Susan continued in treatment for about a year. Her life was transformed on multiple levels. In addition to mental and emotional change and growth, Susan improved her relationships with husband and children, reconciled with her parents, developed a social life, and found employment in a highly satisfying position.

APPLICATION OF EMDR TO PTSD AND TRAUMA-RELATED DISORDERS

EMDR is formulated to expedite the accessing and processing of traumatic memories, by forging new links between the memory and adaptive information contained in other memory networks. EMDR takes a three-pronged approach to ensure that all past, present, and future aspects of the clinical picture are thoroughly addressed. In addition to targeting the traumatic events, the current conditions that elicit distress are processed to eliminate sensitivity, and a template for appropriate future action is incorporated to enhance positive behaviors and skill acquisition.

Although EMDR has recognized efficacy only in the treatment of PTSD, published case reports indicate that it can be successfully used to treat other trauma-related disorders, such as phobias. For example, "Angela" almost died when she was trapped in a crevice while mountain climbing. Subsequently, she developed a phobia about being in any enclosed space. This phobia became disabling and prevented her from sitting in restaurants or traveling on airplanes. When EMDR was used to target the near-death experience, her phobia was eliminated and she was able to resume her active and adventuresome lifestyle. Future research is needed to evaluate such applications of EMDR.

CASE ILLUSTRATION

Session 1

"Frank" was a 45-year-old man who had been in a severe car accident 18 months earlier. He had collided at high speed with three horses on a rural highway. The horses were dismembered, and lay on the road screaming, while he sat waiting for help, with a broken arm and leg and multiple lacerations. Although Frank recovered adequately from his physical injuries, he was immobilized by his PTSD. He could not sleep for more than 90 minutes before horrific nightmares replayed the accident. He avoided driving a vehicle because this was accompanied by severe anxiety. Frank had withdrawn from all his previous activities and never saw any of his friends. His attempts to return to work since the accident had been unsuccessful. Now his wife "Joan" had delivered an ultimatum, "Get help and get better, or get out!" She was determined to leave with their three children if he did not improve. Frank sobbed throughout the session as he explained what brought him to the therapist's office. He felt like he had lost everything: his emotional stability, his health, his ability to work, and now, his family.

The therapist and Frank briefly reviewed his life history, and determined that there were no earlier severe traumas. Although it was apparent that Frank's current sadness and fears were primarily related to the possible loss of his wife and children, Frank and the therapist decided to start by targeting the accident, because the accident was the precipitating event.

Session 2

The therapist asked Frank to identify the most disturbing visual image or scene connected with the accident. Frank said that the moment of impact was the most distressing and stated that this visual image was exceptionally clear and vivid. As he talked about it, his eyes filled with tears, and he gripped the arms of the chair.

"I can still see the horses caught in my headlights, and then an instant later, crashing into the windshield and smashing over the roof of my car!"

A discussion about the beliefs associated with this image revealed that Frank felt completely powerless. He had been helpless to prevent the accident, and this sense of impotence had continued. When he combined the statement "I am a capable person" with thoughts of the accident, the statement did not feel true, and he gave it a VOC of 2. Next, the therapist asked Frank to look at the image of the accident, to say "I'm powerless," and to notice his feelings. He reported that he felt "helpless and sick, like crying." He gave this a SUD rating of 10, and mentioned feeling tightness in his chest and stomach.

Processing started with the therapist asking Frank to look at the image, to think the words "I'm powerless," and to notice the sensations in his body, while he followed her fingers with his eyes. After the first set of eye movements (EMs), she told Frank to take a deep breath and to let his mind go blank, and then to just notice what came up for him. Frank said, "I see the horses standing there, frozen." The therapist then said, "Go with that," and started another set of EMs. After this next set, he reported, "I can see the light shining in their eyes." The therapist responded, "Just go with that," and did another set of EMs. Frank continued to process the most distressing elements of the incident, including the arrival of the police, and his mixed feelings of guilt and relief when they put the horses down.

At the session's end, the therapist asked Frank to think of the original target and to report a SUD rating. He reported a low SUD rating, and the positive belief "I am a capable person" was installed, with a VOC of 7.

Session 3

When Frank arrived a week later for the following session, he reported that he had not had one graphic or gory nightmare since the EMDR. He related that he was happy and relieved. He had been out visiting his old friends, for the first time since the accident, and had been very talkative and social. In reviewing his journal and the material that had emerged over the week, Frank said, "Although I feel so much better, I still feel very frustrated; I can't do anything; Joan is still upset; I'm still not back at work."

This session targeted an image of Frank waiting for help to arrive, sitting beside the deserted highway, listening to the horses cry. As processing progressed, Frank realized that his primary emotion at the time of the accident had been anger. "I just realized—when I saw that I couldn't avoid hitting those horses, I was furious. And you know, I've been angry ever since; I don't think that I ever stopped being angry!"

He recognized how this anger had affected his relationship with Joan. Processing resulted in a dissipation of the anger and a feeling of calm acceptance at the end of the session. The positive belief installed was "I'm okay now," with a VOC of 7.

Session 4

Frank reported that the PTSD symptoms were almost entirely eliminated, he had arranged to return to work and the marital situation was much improved. However, at times he would feel overwhelmed with sadness. For this session, the targeted image was the "blood everywhere," the beliefs were "I can't protect myself" and "It's okay to be vulnerable," and the emotion was sadness. During the collision, Frank had thought that he was going to die. As he processed this with EMDR he remembered feeling great grief about dying and never seeing his wife and children again. As Frank worked through this, he recognized that his feelings of vulnerability during the accident were similar to those that he now felt about his current life situation. A future template was targeted, in which Frank imagined feeling both vulnerable and confident. At session's end, Frank experienced no distress connected to the accident. He expressed a strong commitment to his family and a calm readiness to cope with life's uncertainties.

Three-Month Follow-Up

After the first session of EMDR, Frank never had another nightmare about the accident. At three-month follow-up, he was back at work and doing well, and the marital relationship was stronger and more enjoyable than it had been prior to the accident. Frank continued to be free from PTSD symptoms and the driving phobia was completely gone.

Six-Year Follow-Up

Frank is now the supervisor at work, with multiple responsibilities that he performs well. No further symptoms of PTSD have ever surfaced. Frank and Joan continue to enjoy a rich and satisfying life.

SUMMARY

EMDR appears to facilitate the accessing of disturbing memories, and to activate the information processing system. During EMDR the client focuses on an external stimulus while simultaneously attending, in brief sequential doses, to emotionally disturbing material that is elicited through free association. These treatment elements (e.g., eye movements, free association, brief exposures) are specifically formulated to enhance information processing and are embedded in a comprehensive, eight-stage protocol. The protocol seeks to ensure that all past, present, and future aspects of the clinical picture are thoroughly addressed.

The AIP model posits a physiologically based information processing system that has a tendency to move toward health by processing information to a state of adaptive resolution. It is hypothesized that EMDR works by forging new links between the traumatic memory and adaptive information contained in other memory networks. Complete reprocessing is evident in the desensitization of triggers, elimination of emotional distress, elicitation of insight, reformulation of associated beliefs, relief of accompanying physiological arousal, and acquisition of desired behaviors.

Currently, EMDR has been found efficacious in the treatment of PTSD. Civilian participants have shown a 70 to 90% decrease in PTSD diagnosis and a substantial improvement in reported symptoms after three or four EMDR sessions. The only combat veteran study that provided a full course of treatment revealed EMDR to be efficacious with a 78% decrease in PTSD diagnosis after 12 sessions.

REFERENCES

Acierno, R., Hersen, M., Van Hasselt, V., Tremont, G., & Mueser, K. T. (1994). Review of the validation and dissemination of eye-movement desensitization and reprocessing: A scientific and ethical dilemma. *Clinical Psychology Review*, 14, 287–299.

Allen, J. G., Keller, M. W., & Console, D. (1999). *Program manual: EMDR: A closer look.* New York: Guilford Press.

Allen, J. G., & Lewis, L. (1996). A conceptual framework for treating traumatic memories and its application to EMDR. *Bulletin of the Menninger Clinic*, 60(2), 238–263.

American Psychiatric Association. (1994). *Diagnostic and statistical manual of mental disorders* (DSM-IV) (4th ed.). Washington, DC: Author.

Andrade, J., Kavanagh, D., & Baddeley, A. (1997). Eye-movements and visual imagery: A working memory approach to the treatment of post-traumatic stress disorder. *British Journal of Clinical Psychology*, 36, 209–223.

Antrobus, J. S. (1973). Eye movements and non-visual cognitive tasks. In V. Zikmund (Ed.), *The oculomotor system and brain functions* (pp. 354–368). London: Butterworths.

Antrobus, J. S., & Singer, J. L. (1964). Eye movements accompanying daydreaming, visual imagery, and thought suppression. *Journal of Abnormal and Social Psychology*, 69, 244–252.

Armstrong, M. S., & Vaughan, K. (1996). An orienting response model of eye movement desensitization. *Journal of Behavior Therapy and Experimental Psychiatry*, 27, 21–32.

Bohart, A. C. (in press). EMDR and experiential psychotherapy. In F. Shapiro (Ed.), *EMDR as an integrative psychotherapy approach.* Washington, DC: American Psychological Association Press.

Boudewyns, P. A., & Hyer, L. A. (1996). Eye movement desensitization and reprocessing (EMDR) as treatment for post-traumatic stress disorder (PTSD). *Clinical Psychology and Psychotherapy*, 3, 185–195.

Boudewyns, P. A., Stwertka, S. A., Hyer, L. A., Albrecht, J. W., & Sperr, E. V. (1993). Eye movement desensitization and reprocessing: A pilot study. *Behavior Therapist*, 16, 30–33.

Breslau, N., Davis, G. C., Andreski, P., Peterson, E. L., & Schultz, L. R. (1997). Sex differences in posttraumatic stress disorder. *Archives of General Psychiatry*, 54, 1044–1048.

Brown, L. S. (in press). Feminist therapy and EMDR: A practice meets a theory. In F. Shapiro (Ed.), *EMDR as an integrative psychotherapy approach.* Washington, DC: American Psychological Association Press.

Carlson, J. G., Chemtob, C. M., Rusnak, K., Hedlund, N. L., & Muraoka, M. Y.

(1998). Eye movement desensitization and reprocessing for combat-related posttraumatic stress disorder. *Journal of Traumatic Stress*, 11, 3–24.

Chambless, D. L., Baker, M. J., Baucom, D. H., Beutler, L. E., Calhoun, K. S., Crits-Christoph, P., Daiuto, A., DeRubeis, R., Detweiler, J., Haaga, D.A.F., Bennett Johnson, S., McCurry, S., Mueser, K. T., Pope, K. S., Sanderson, W. C., Shoham, V., Stickle, T., Williams, D. A., & Woody, S. R. (1998). Update on empirically validated therapies. *The Clinical Psychologist*, 51, 3–16.

Chemtob, C. M., Tolin, D. F., van der Kolk, B. A., & Pitman, R. K. (2000). Eye movement desensitization and reprocessing. In E. A. Foa, T. M. Keane, & M. J. Friedman (Eds.), *Effective treatments for PTSD: Practice guidelines from the International Society for Traumatic Stress Studies* (pp. 139–155, 333–335). New York: Guilford Press.

Christman, S., & Garvey, K. (2000). *Episodic versus semantic memory: Eye movements and cortical activation.* Poster presented at the 41st Annual Meeting of the Psychonomic Society, New Orleans, November.

Devilly, G. J., & Spence, S. H. (1999). The relative efficacy and treatment distress of EMDR and a cognitive behavioral trauma treatment protocol in the amelioration of post traumatic stress disorder. *Journal of Anxiety Disorders*, 13, 131–157.

Devilly, G. J., Spence, S. H., & Rapee, R. M. (1998). Statistical and reliable change with eye movement desensitization and reprocessing: Treating trauma with a veteran population. *Behavior Therapy*, 29, 435–455.

Drake, R. A. (1987). Effects of gaze manipulation on aesthetic judgments: Hemisphere priming of affect. *Acta Psychologica*, 65 (North Holland), 91–99.

EMDRIA. (2000). *EMDR International Association.* www.emdria.org.

Fensterheim, H. (1996). Eye movement desensitization and reprocessing with complex personality patterns: An integrative therapy. *Journal of Psychotherapy Integration*, 6, 27–38.

Feske, U. (1998) Eye movement desensitization and reprocessing treatment for posttraumatic stress disorder. *Clinical Psychology: Science and Practice*, 5, 171–181.

Hembree, E. A., & Foa, E. B. (2000). Posttraumatic stress disorder: Psychological factors and psychosocial interventions. *Journal of Clinical Psychiatry*, 61 (Suppl. 7), 33–39.

Hyer, L., & Brandsma, J. M. (1997). EMDR minus eye movements equals good psychotherapy. *Journal of Traumatic Stress*, 10, 515–522.

Jacobson, N. S., Dobson, K. S., Truax, P. A., Addis, M. E., Koerner, K., Gollan, J. K., Gortner, E., & Prince, S. E. (1996). A component analysis of cognitive-behavioral treatment for depression. *Journal of Consulting and Clinical Psychology*, 64, 295–304.

Jensen, J. A. (1994). An investigation of eye movement desensitization and reprocessing (EMD/R) as a treatment for post-traumatic stress disorder (PTSD) symptoms of Vietnam combat veterans. *Behavior Therapy*, 25, 311–326.

Kessler, R., Sonnega, A., Bromet, E., Hughes, M., & Nelson, C. B. (1995). Posttraumatic stress disorder in the National Comorbidity Survey. *Archives of General Psychiatry*, 52, 1048–1060.

Korn, D. L., & Leeds, A. M. (in press). Preliminary evidence of efficacy for EMDR resource development and installation in the stabilization phase of treatment of complex posttraumatic stress disorder. *Journal of Clinical Psychology.*

Lazarus, C. N., & Lazarus, A. A. (in press). EMDR: An elegantly concentrated multimodal procedure. In F. Shapiro (Ed.), *EMDR as an integrative psychotherapy approach.* Washington, DC: American Psychological Association Press.

Lee, C., Gavriel, H., Drummond, P., Richards, J., & Greenwald, R. (in press). Treatment of PTSD: Stress inoculation training compared to EMDR. *Journal of Clinical Psychology.*

Lipke, H. (1999). Comments on "thirty years of behavior therapy" . . . "and the promise of the application of scientific principles." *Behavior Therapist*, 22, 11–14.

Lohr, J. M., Tolin, D. F., & Lilienfeld, S. O. (1998). Efficacy of eye movement desensitization and reprocessing: Implications for behavior therapy. *Behavior Therapy*, 29, 123–156.

MacCulloch, M. J., & Feldman, P. (1996). Eye movement desensitization treatment utilizes the positive visceral element of the investigatory reflex to inhibit the memories of post-traumatic stress disorder: A theoretical analysis. *British Journal of Psychiatry*, 169, 571–579.

Maes, M., Delmeire, L., Schotte, C., Janca, A., Creten, T., Mylle, J., Struyf, A., Pison, G., & Rousseeuw, P. J. (1998). The two-factorial symptom structure of post-traumatic stress disorder: Depression-avoidance and arousal-anxiety. *Psychiatry Research*, 81, 195–210.

Manfield, P. (Ed.). (1998). *Extending EMDR.* New York: Norton.

Marcus, S. V., Marquis, P., & Sakai, C. (1997). Controlled study of treatment of PTSD using EMDR in an HMO setting. *Psychotherapy*, 34, 307–315.

Marks, I. M., Lovell, K., Noshirvani, H., Livanou, M., & Thrasher, S. (1998). Treatment of posttraumatic stress disorder by exposure and/or cognitive restructuring: A controlled study. *Archives of General Psychiatry*, 55, 317–325.

Maxfield, L. (1999). Eye movement desensitization and reprocessing: A review of the efficacy of EMDR in the treatment of PTSD. *Traumatology* [online], 5(4). http://www.fsu.edu/~trauma/a1v5i4.htm.

Maxfield, L., & Hyer, L. A. (2002). The relationship between efficacy and methodology in EMDR treatment of PTSD. *Journal of Clinical Psychology*, 58, 23–41.

Montgomery, R. W., & Ayllon, T. (1994). Eye movement desensitization across subjects: Subjective and physiological measures of treatment efficacy. *Journal of Behavior Therapy and Experimental Psychiatry*, 25, 217–230.

Pitman, R. K., Orr, S. P., Altman, B., Longpre, R. E., Poire, R. E., & Macklin, M. L. (1996). Emotional processing during eye movement desensitization and reprocessing therapy of Vietnam veterans with chronic posttraumatic stress disorder. *Comprehensive Psychiatry*, 37, 419–429.

Renfrey, G., & Spates, C. R. (1994). Eye movement desensitization and reprocessing: A partial dismantling procedure. *Journal of Behavior Therapy and Experimental Psychiatry*, 25, 231–239.

Resnick, H. S., Kilpatrick, D. G., Dansky, B. S., Saunders, B. E., & Best, C. L. (1993). Prevalence of civilian trauma and posttraumatic stress disorder in a representative national sample of women. *Journal of Consulting and Clinical Psychology*, 61, 984–991.

Rogers, S., Silver, S., Goss, J., Obenchain, J., Willis, A., & Whitney, R. (1999). A single session, controlled group study of flooding and eye movement desensitization and reprocessing in treating posttraumatic stress disorder among Vietnam War veterans: Preliminary data. *Journal of Anxiety Disorders*, 13, 119–130.

Rothbaum, B. O. (1997). A controlled study of eye movement desensitization and reprocessing in the treatment of posttraumatic stress disordered sexual assault victims. *Bulletin of the Menninger Clinic*, 61, 317–334.

Rothbaum, B. O., Meadows, E. A., Resick, P., & Foy, D. W. (2000). Cognitive-behavioral therapy. In E. A. Foa, T. M. Keane, & M. J. Friedman (Eds.), *Effective treatments for PTSD: Practice guidelines from the International Society for Traumatic Stress Studies* (pp. 60–83, 320–325). New York: Guilford Press.

Scheck, M. M., Schaeffer, J. A., & Gillette, C. S. (1998). Brief psychological intervention with traumatized young women: The efficacy of eye movement desensitization and reprocessing. *Journal of Traumatic Stress*, 11, 25–44.

Shalev, A. Y., Foa, E. A., Keane T. M., & Friedman, M. J. (2000). Integration and summary. In E. A. Foa, T. M. Keane, & M. J. Friedman (Eds.), *Effective treatments for PTSD: Practice guidelines from the International Society for Traumatic Stress Studies* (pp. 359–379). New York: Guilford Press.

Shapiro F. (1989a). Efficacy of the eye movement desensitization procedure: A new treatment for post-traumatic stress disorder. *Journal of Traumatic Stress*, 2, 199–223.

Shapiro F. (1989b). Eye movement desensitization: A new treatment for post-traumatic stress disorder. *Journal of Behavior Therapy and Experimental Psychiatry*, 20, 211–217.

Shapiro, F. (1991). Stray thoughts. *EMDR Network Newsletter*, 1–3.

Shapiro, F. (1994a). Alternative stimuli in the use of EMD(R). *Journal of Behavior Therapy and Experimental Psychiatry*, 25, 89.

Shapiro, F. (1994b). EMDR: In the eye of a paradigm shift. *Behavior Therapist*, 17, 153–156.

Shapiro, F. (1995). *Eye movement desensitization and reprocessing: Basic principles, protocols and procedures*. New York: Guilford Press.

Shapiro, F. (1999). EMDR and the anxiety disorders: Clinical and research implications of an integrated psychotherapy treatment. *Journal of Anxiety Disorders*, 13, 35–67.

Shapiro, F. (2001). *Eye movement desensitization and reprocessing: Basic principles, protocols and procedures* (2nd. ed.). New York: Guilford Press.

Shapiro, F. (2002). EMDR twelve years after its introduction: A review of past, present, and future directions. *Journal of Clinical Psychology*, 58, 1–22.

Shapiro, F., & Maxfield, L. (in press). A current evaluation of EMDR. *The Psychologist*.

Shapiro, F., & Silk Forrest, M. (1997). *EMDR: The breakthrough therapy for overcoming anxiety, stress, and trauma*. New York: Basic Books.

Shepherd, J., Stein, K., & Milne, R. (2000). Eye movement desensitization and reprocessing in the treatment of post-traumatic stress disorder: A review of an emerging therapy. *Psychological Medicine, 30,* 863–871.

Spector, J., & Read, J. (1999). The current status of eye movement desensitization and reprocessing (EMDR). *Clinical Psychology and Psychotherapy, 6,* 165–174.

Stickgold, R. (1998). Sleep: Off-line memory reprocessing. *Trends in Cognitive Science, 2,* 484–492.

Stickgold, R. (2002) Neurobiological concomitants of EMDR: Speculations and proposed research. *Journal of Clinical Psychology, 58,* 61–75.

van Etten, M. L., & Taylor, S. (1998). Comparative efficacy of treatments for post-traumatic stress disorder: A meta-analysis. *Clinical Psychology & Psychotherapy, 5,* 125–144.

Vaughan, K., Armstrong, M. S., Gold, R., O'Connor, N., Jenneke, W., & Tarrier, N. (1994). A trial of eye movement desensitization compared to image habituation training and applied muscle relaxation in post-traumatic stress disorder. *Journal of Behavior Therapy and Experimental Psychiatry, 25,* 283–291.

Wachtel, P. L. (in press). EMDR and psychoanalysis. In F. Shapiro (Ed.), *EMDR as an integrative psychotherapy approach.* Washington, DC: American Psychological Association Press.

Wilson, D., Silver, S. M., Covi, W., & Foster, S. (1996). Eye movement desensitization and reprocessing: Effectiveness and autonomic correlates. *Journal of Behavior Therapy and Experimental Psychiatry, 27,* 219–229.

Wilson, S. A., Becker, L. A., & Tinker, R. H. (1995). Eye movement desensitization and reprocessing (EMDR) treatment for psychologically traumatized individuals. *Journal of Consulting and Clinical Psychology, 63,* 928–937.

Wilson, S. A., Becker, L. A., & Tinker, R. H. (1997). 15-month follow-up of eye movement desensitization and reprocessing (EMDR) treatment for psychological trauma. *Journal of Consulting and Clinical Psychology, 65,* 1047–1056.

Part III

Trauma-Focused Treatments

Chapter 9

The Use of Multi-sensory Trauma Processing to Treat Post-traumatic Stress Disorder in Law Enforcement Officers

Nancy Davis

As American soldiers returned from the Vietnam War in the 1970s, it became apparent that violent combat situations had dramatically altered the functioning of many of these men and women (Figley, 1978). Mental health professionals who treated these soldiers were instrumental in creating the diagnosis of Post Traumatic Stress Disorder (PTSD) and having this diagnosis recognized in the 1980 *Diagnostic and Statistical Manual of Mental Disorders* (DSM-III) (American Psychiatric Association, 1980; van der Kolk et. al., 1991). Prior to the recognition of PTSD, traumatized soldiers were diagnosed as having "shell shock" or "combat fatigue," but the reasons for their symptoms had been little researched or understood (Spiller, 1990). Rather than understanding the role of trauma in creating PTSD, soldiers with "shell-shock" and "combat fatigue" were viewed as weak or as cowards (Pastorella, 1991; van der Kolk, McFarlane, & Weisaeth 1996a). PTSD was the first diagnosis in the DSM III based on external events experienced by an individual (Long, 1996).

As awareness of the impact of war experiences increased, mental health workers dealing with law enforcement officers began to understand that these professionals could also develop PTSD from job-related traumatic incidents (Everly & Lating, 1995). Additionally, research led to the recognition that a variety of traumatic incidents could result in symptoms of PTSD; for example, car accidents, rape, violent or sudden death of a loved one, life-threatening situations, child abuse, exposure to domestic violence, and natural disasters (Jimerson, 1987; Marcey, 1995; van der Kolk et al., 1996b).

Being a law enforcement officer carries with it inherent stressors including regular exposure to traumatic incidents (Sheehan, 1999). "Over 50,000 law enforcement officers are assaulted each year. One of every three officers assaulted is injured, and approximately 70 officers make the ultimate sacrifice in the performance of law enforcement service, losing their lives. Law enforcement is the third most dangerous profession" (Pinizzotto, Davis, & Miller, 1997).

In addition to the frequent danger they face, some categories of law enforcement officers are being exposed to traumatic incidents more frequently and for longer duration than their predecessors of 20 or more years ago. The formation of specialty units such as Special Weapons and Tactics (SWAT), Evidence Response Teams, Bomb Investigation Squads, Accident Reconstruction Teams, Hostage Negotiation Units, and Profiling Units expose officers assigned to such units on a concentrated basis to some of the most traumatic events in law enforcement. Moreover, advances in scientific analysis of evidence have necessitated more lengthy and painstaking evidence collection, thereby increasing the exposure of officers to traumatic scenes, such as those involving body recovery and identification. Compounding this situation, officers with such specialization or assignments generally do not experience the positive, even humorous, everyday incidents and encounters that are part of the job of patrol officers or general investigators. Stated another way, their jobs often lack the "balance" which is present in more general law enforcement duties and which is helpful in putting traumatic events in perspective (Davis, 1999).

In addition to traumatic incident exposure, law enforcement officers incur additional stress from physical and verbal threats and abuse, court leniency with criminals, unbalanced or negative press accounts of their activities, shift work, and the often unpredictable and "hurry up and wait" nature of court appearances (Delprino, O'Quin, & Kennedy, 1997; Reese & Hodinko, 1991). An added stressor is the constant awareness that citizens, the news media, and even their own Internal Affairs Office may later judge any action taken in the most life-threatening of circumstances to be faulty or illegal. Furthermore, criminals arrested or wounded, even in the act of committing a crime, are increasingly filing civil or criminal actions against officers.

Probably as a result of both job-related traumatic incidents and stressors, a law enforcement officer is more likely to die by his own hand than in violent encounters with criminals—and this trend is increasing. "Law enforcement officers are one and one-half times more likely to commit suicide than their predecessors only a decade ago," according to John Violanti, an expert in police suicide (Armstrong, 1998). The role that exposure to traumatic incidents plays in suicide is just beginning to be recognized, but recent research has revealed that for every suicide caused by clinical depression, 15 were the result of PTSD (Davidson, Hughes, Blazer, & George, 1991).

The "corporate culture" of law enforcement is an additional factor that can increase the impact of traumatic events on an officer. Officers are trained to ignore their own feelings and to deal with the public in a polite and non-aggressive fashion. In addition, the culture is viewed as "macho" with a very high representation of males in the profession (Kopel & Friedman, 1997). Research has supported that talking about feelings helps to reduce the impact of traumatic events; however, there is evidence that the differences in male and female brains cause men to generally have more difficulty in expressing their emotions (Amen, 1998; Gottman & Silver, 1999). Female officers, in trying to be successful and accepted in a traditionally male vocation, often hesitate to discuss their emotional responses with their fellow officers, lest they be regarded as "a typical woman" who cannot handle the job.

Officers who are having problems coping with the stress of the job frequently are reluctant to disclose this to fellow officers, fearing that their peers or superior officers will view this as a deficiency in their performance. When found "unfit for duty" officers are often placed on limited duty, aka "the rubber gun squad"; administrative leave, or they are dismissed or placed on disability. In addition, when placed on administrative leave as a result of emotional problems, officers routinely have their badges and weapons confiscated—a highly humiliating event. Furthermore, recent legal decisions in many jurisdictions allow defense attorneys access to the disciplinary/administrative action records of officers called to testify by the prosecution. Defense attorneys routinely use the knowledge gained from an officer's personnel file to challenge his or her reliability as a credible witness. These changes have increased the reluctance of officers to disclose to management that they are experiencing symptoms of depression, stress, and/or PTSD. Therefore, for a multitude of reasons, the law enforcement culture conditions officers to maintain an appearance of being strong and in control, while carefully concealing any emotional problems they may be experiencing.

Despite growing recognition of the impact of exposing law enforcement officers to multiple traumatic and stressful incidents, few departments are preparing their officers for this emotional impact (Linton, 1995). Most officers have little understanding of the way in which exposure to job-related traumatic incidents can result in PTSD, even though a number of researchers have found that between 7 and 35% of police officers suffer from symptoms of PTSD at any given time. (Carlier, Lambert, van Uchelen, & Gersons, 1998; Mann & Neece, 1990; Martin, McKean, & Veltkamp, 1986; Robinson, Sigmon, & Wilson, 1997). Law enforcement officers who have experienced severe childhood or adolescent trauma are more at risk to develop PTSD from job-related traumatic experiences because the early trauma creates a heightened biological reactivity to traumatic experiences (Johnson, Rosenheck, & Fontana, 1996; Long, 1996; van der Kolk, 1997a). Furthermore, it is now understood that the impact of exposure to traumatic events can be cumulative; acute symptoms of PTSD may not appear until exposure to many job-related traumatic situations ultimately compromises their ability to compensate.

TRADITIONAL TREATMENT APPROACHES

In 1968, Dr. Martin Reiser was hired by the Los Angeles Police Department; he was the first psychologist to deal specifically with problems that law enforcement officers were experiencing (Depue, 1979). Since that time, a growing number of departments have either hired psychologists and/or other mental health professionals or have contracted with outside agencies to provide mental health services. Employee assistance programs were initiated by a few departments as early as 1955, but the primary focus of these early mental health services was dealing with alcohol abuse by officers or the use of assessment techniques in hiring (Reese & Hodinko, 1991; Stratton, 1985).

The first crisis intervention training class designed specifically for law enforcement officers was taught by Special Agent Roger Depue at the FBI Academy in 1974. In 1976, Dr. Michael Roberts recognized the impact of a trauma specific to law enforcement, line-of-duty shootings, calling this "Post Shooting Trauma" (Pinizzotto et al., 1997; Solomon, 1996a). The following year (1977), John Minderman, an FBI agent in the Behavioral Science Unit of the FBI Academy, took the lead in putting together the first conference for police psychologists.

Many large departments and agencies now have mental health therapists, employee assistance counselors, and police chaplains who offer free assistance to law enforcement officers. These professionals generally handle a range of employee difficulties, in addition to symptoms created by job-related trauma. Generally, and not surprisingly, these professionals have employed the more traditional treatment techniques. Furthermore, even when help is available through the department, police officers do not typically seek the help of mental health professionals. One reason is that law enforcement officers must trust their peers to protect their lives; therefore, a fellow officer with a mental health problem may be regarded as a threat to the safety of other officers (Delprino et al., 1997; Harvey & Tidwell, 1997). Furthermore, PTSD symptoms cause officers to use "avoidance coping strategies" i.e., finding ways to both avoid thinking and talking about their traumatic experiences and to avoid seeking help for these symptoms caused by on-the-job trauma (Harvey & Tidwell, 1997).

Recognizing the reluctance of officers to seek help from private mental health therapists, Dr. Edward Donovan of the Boston Police Department initiated the first peer support program in 1977 (Depue, 1979). Many departments, particularly the larger ones, are currently using peer counselors to provide emotional support following a traumatic incident. Peer counselors are often more trusted by their fellow officers than a mental health professional, and they have, in a number of instances, had positive results (Ott, 2000; Robinson & Murdoch, 1998). The success of peer counseling may be the result of the social support other officers provide, as their training in providing mental health services is generally limited (Chamberlin, 2000; Hobfoll et al. 1991).

Stress management programs were instituted in the 1980s to lessen the impact of critical incidents that involved multiple officers. The initial focus of these programs was to work with officers individually, until Jeff Mitchell, an EMT fireman, developed the Critical Incident Stress Management protocol (CISM) in 1983. CISM includes education, on-scene support, Critical Incident Stress Debriefing (CISD), and individual crisis intervention services (Mitchell & Bray, 1990).

CISM is the form of mental health intervention most widely used in the law enforcement community. To date, it is estimated that 10,000 law enforcement officers and 12,000 mental health professionals have been trained in CISM worldwide (Mitchell, 1999).

CISD is used for law enforcement officers involved in a variety of critical incidents; for example, gathering evidence in major disasters, treating victims, removing bodies from accident or murder scenes, or being involved in events such as plane crashes, natural disasters, shooting incidents, or multiple injury accidents. One aspect of CISM which is widely used is debriefing. Debriefing does not occur until officers have completed their assignments, at which time they are seen in a group setting by a team of law enforcement officers and a mental health professional. Debriefing allows officers to share knowledge, recognize the typical symptoms that being involved in a critical incident might invoke, and gain a support group of peers (Mitchell & Everly, 1995).

Two studies have supported the effectiveness of debriefing when a comprehensive CISM program was in place. Mitchell and Everly (1997) reported a reduction in suicides in the Air Force, and Ott and Henry, (1995) documented a 90% reduction in costs related to stress-related illness for correctional officers at the Goulburn Correctional Center in Australia. Dr. Nancy Bohl (1991) found that providing officers a one- to two-hour debriefing provided within 48 hours of their involvement in a critical incident significantly reduced the occurrence of delayed symptoms. The majority of support for the effectiveness of debriefing comes from anecdotal evidence and clinical experience wherein officers report that being debriefed reduced their stress reactions (Solomon, 1996b). Carlier and his associates (1998), however, found professionals who had been debriefed shortly after a critical incident had an increase rather than a decrease in symptoms of PTSD several months after the incident. This debriefing was not based on the Mitchell model (Mitchell, 1999).

Large departments, in particular, seem to recognize the traumatic nature of a line-of-duty shooting. These departments require officers involved in these shootings to participate in a variety of mental health services. Twenty years ago, 95% of officers involved in a line-of-duty shooting would leave police work within five years. By 1984, however, large departments had reduced this rate to 3% by providing routine and mandatory interventions for the involved officers. In contrast, small departments which had not developed formalized programs or services, were losing two to three officers for every line-of-duty shooting (McMains, 1991). Officers who resigned from their law enforcement jobs included those directly involved in the shootings as well as others who had a variety of supporting roles in the incident.

Even large departments often appear unaware that the following events commonly and predictably induce symptoms of PTSD in law enforcement officers:

- Seeing a law enforcement officer killed, or viewing the body at the scene, especially a friend or partner. Trauma is often increased if the officer believed he or she should have protected the person who died, or if the dead officer was temporarily serving in place of the officer. Trauma is increased when an officer imagines him or herself as the dead officer, then visualizes the impact that their death would have on those they love.
- A reasonable belief that death or critical injury was imminent and certain.
- An officer accidentally kills or wounds a bystander, especially if the victim is a child.
- An officer fails to stop a perpetrator from injuring or killing someone after the initial encounter.
- Killing or wounding a child or teenager even if the life of the officer was threatened by the person injured or killed.
- Viewing the body of a child victim, particularly if the officer has children and even more so if the officer's child is the same age and sex of the victim, or if the child victim is similar in some other way to the officer's child, such as appearance, clothing, toys, or school. The impact of this experience is often increased if the body has deteriorated, if the child was tortured, and/or if the officer hears a graphic confession of the murderer, especially when pain was intentionally inflicted on the child.
- An officer is blamed or told he or she is responsible for the death of an innocent bystander, law enforcement officer, or a child victim by his or her department, family members of the victim, or the media. Guilt, such as feeling responsible for violence or death, whether irrational or based on fact, usually intensifies symptoms of PTSD. Events such as exchanging shifts with another officer who is killed while working the exchanged shift or responding to a call minutes after an officer is killed can intensify symptoms of PTSD when the officer blames him or herself for the event. ("It's my fault he or she is dead; I should not have taken sick leave," or "I should have been there sooner.")
- When a dead victim becomes personalized, rather than just an unknown body, through interaction with grieving family members or friends, or from information

gained in numerous ways from the scene, news reports, search warrants, and so on. Continued association with the pain of survivors through an investigation and trial (and often long after) also can personalize the dead victims.

- The terror of being caught in a violent riot. Trauma may be increased when children are present in the crowd and the officer cannot use deadly force to defend him or herself for fear of hurting the children.

- Particularly bloody or gruesome scenes. Horror of the crime and/or the suffering of the victims. Length of exposure to crime or accident scenes that involve decaying and dismembered bodies.

- Observing an event involving violence or murder, but not being able to intervene (e.g., "I watched him kill her. She was screaming for my help but there was nothing I could do.")

- Feeling responsible for someone's life (e.g., a crisis or hostage negotiator), attempting to resolve a potentially lethal situation, especially if the event drags on for hours. Symptoms may occur even when victims are rescued, because of stress hormones released during long negotiations.

- An undercover assignment in which the officer is constantly "on-guard" because of the likelihood of being hurt, killed, or discovered. This is particularly a problem if the officer grew up in a family where he or she had to always be "on-guard" against physical, emotional, or sexual abuse, because the undercover experience mirrors the fear of the childhood experience.

- When an "informant" or "asset" developed by an officer is murdered for providing information to law enforcement.

- When suspects who have been indicted, are being tried, or are incarcerated threaten the officer and /or the officer's family with violence and are deemed capable of carrying out these threats.

Many law enforcement managers have not been trained to recognize that the symptoms of PTSD often cause officers to have problems in planning, memory, concentration, appropriate expression of anger; and in excessive use of sick leave, tardiness, on-the-job accidents, and citizen complaints. Exposure to traumatic and stressful incidents may also lead to faulty decision making, disciplinary problems, substantially increased levels of alcoholism and divorce, as well as spouse and child abuse in law enforcement officers, compared to the general public (Gershon, 1999; Robinson et al., 1997). In defense of law enforcement management, research supporting the impact of exposure to a variety of traumatic events has just begun to appear in the professional literature in the past 10 to 15 years and has yet to be integrated into most training programs (Ochberg, 1993).

Although it might be assumed that an officer's family would be a substantial source of support, officers exposed to horror, death, child abuse, and the most vile of human behavior, rarely wish to share with their families the traumatizing incidents experienced on the job. Officers tend to remain silent about traumatic experiences because they do not want to traumatize their families and because they want their home to be a refuge from the difficult and often repulsive experiences of police work (Delprino et al., 1997). As a result, officers create a close-knit and exclusionary fraternity of those who have been through similar experiences, who understand what the job entails, and on whom their very life may depend in a critical situation. The countless hours that these officers spend together talking about life experiences while waiting for court, patrolling together as partners, and engaged in lengthy and often uneventful surveillance strengthens this bond.

ADAPTING THERAPEUTIC TECHNIQUES TO TREAT TRAUMATIZED LAW ENFORCEMENT OFFICERS

Because the law enforcement culture, as well as the symptoms of PTSD make officers resistant to mental health services, and because officers generally want quick results, Multi-sensory Trauma Processing (MTP), a short-term treatment, has been developed by the author to treat the performance-related dysfunction of these officers. MTP follows the model of short-term counseling offered by many law enforcement agencies, while merging and expanding many therapeutic models and treatments found effective in reducing or eliminating the debilitating symptoms of PTSD (Eller, 1999; Figley & Carbonell, 1995; Gallo, 1996a, 1996b). MTP has evolved through treating hundreds of officers traumatized by exposure to multiple critical incidents. These officers were drawn from a number of federal law enforcement agencies, the National Academy training program conducted at the FBI Academy (including officers from state and local departments, as well as officers from foreign countries), multi-agency task forces, and a variety of law enforcement agencies located in Virginia, Maryland, and the District of Columbia.

Multi-sensory Trauma Processing (MTP) is a short-term treatment technique designed to deal with many common problems that arise in more long-term therapeutic interventions. Eyemovement Desensitization and Reprocessing (EMDR) is a critical element of this therapy; however, it varies in several ways from the standard EMDR protocol used in research (Shapiro, 1995). Referring to it as MTP helps to distinguish the more global approach of this therapy from that of EMDR. Giving this therapy a new name in no way diminishes the importance that EMDR has had in the basic structure and development of MTP (Figley & Carbonell, 1995; Shapiro, 1995). MTP uses the alternating stimulation that is the foundation of EMDR; however, MTP simultaneously uses three alternating stimulations consisting of alternating sounds and tapping, as well as eye movement. Although it is unclear exactly how this alternating stimulation creates positive change, there are two credible theories which seek to explain its efficacy. One is that stress hormones released during exposure to a traumatic incident cause the memory of the incident to become "frozen" or unprocessed in the right brain, particularly the hippocampus (van der Kolk, 1995). This frozen memory apparently leads to the symptoms of PTSD. Alternating stimulation may enable both hemispheres of the brain to process the traumatic memory, moving it from being "stuck" to an appropriate memory of the past. Other theorists have noted the eye movement commonly used in EMDR is similar to the back-and-forth movement of eyes in REM sleep; one symptom of PTSD is disturbed REM sleep and a change in eye movement accompanying this type of sleep. By replicating what the brain does naturally in REM sleep, the natural ability of the brain to process a memory may be reactivated (Mellman, Kulick-Bell, Ashlock, & Nolan, 1995).

Neuro-Linguistic Programming (Bandler & Grinder, 1979; Klein, 1986), Gestalt Therapy (Yontef, 1993); Cognitive Therapy (Beck, 1995); Rational-Emotive Therapy (Ellis & Harper, 1974); and imagery based on Ericksonian principles (Haley, 1973; Hammond, 1990; Klein, 1986) are also components of MTP, added to increase the processing of a traumatic incident, to replace negative or traumatic images and belief systems with more positive ones, and to provide a way of altering the manner in which a past loss is experienced. MTP has been designed with the understanding that PTSD is a biologically based disorder, caused by the stress hormones released during exposure to trauma incidents and defined by previous experiences and belief systems (van der Kolk, 1997b). The foundation of MTP is Milton Erickson's belief that an individual has all the resources needed to effect a change (Haley, 1973), which is also the foundation of EMDR (Shapiro, 1995).

MTP, as does EMDR, moves a traumatic event from being "stuck" in the present to becoming a past memory. This leads to a reduction of symptoms. Officers experiencing symptoms related to trauma from ongoing incidents do not typically experience the same level of symptom reduction because it is not possible to move an ongoing experience into the past. However, these officers often benefit from MTP as it focuses on increasing problem-solving skills and confidence to deal with the ongoing traumatic incident.

In developing MTP to treat symptoms of law enforcement officers, numerous problems specific to this population were considered and solutions created:[1]

Problem One: When using the 50-minute treatment model typically used in therapy, the review of traumatic incidents that is necessary in the first session resulted in flashbacks and unpleasant reactions. These reactions and the symptoms of avoidance, typical of PTSD, often caused an officer to refuse to be seen for the second session where treatment could begin.

Solution: Extending the first (and often the only) session to as long as three to four hours helped to deal with this problem.

Problem Two: Issues of the security of sensitive or classified information or concerns about the confidentiality of their conversations keep officers from discussing a traumatic incident with a private practice therapist, a profession of which they are typically quite wary.

Solution: A mental health professional employed or under contract with a law enforcement agency may obtain a security clearance, and/or the authorization to hear topics that officers are ordered by their superiors or required by law not to discuss outside of the department. The academic credentials of a therapist rarely impress the men and women in law enforcement; these officers do respond, however, to demonstrated results (typically spread through word of mouth from fellow officers) and a detailed understanding of the system.

Problem Three: Law enforcement officers are reluctant to reveal details of their symptoms and the incidents that caused them, fearing this information may be made available to others in the department or the court system.

Solution: Although MTP requires that the mental health professional take detailed notes during the session of the past events that traumatized the officer, after confidentiality safeguards are discussed, an agreement can be made with the officer to destroy these notes as he or she leaves the session. However, an officer may want the records maintained for purposes such as Workman's Compensation claims. When treatment notes are destroyed, a list of symptoms is maintained for a short period to measure the success of treatment when the officer is recontacted in the days following the session.

Problem Four: Officers have little knowledge of the manner in which exposure to traumatic incidents can have an impact on their functioning.

Solution: Law enforcement officers typically have limited or no training in recognizing incidents that may be traumatizing, the typical symptoms of PTSD, or the cumulative impact that exposure to traumatic incidents commonly causes. Very few are aware of techniques recently developed to quickly reduce and often eliminate symptoms of job-related traumatic exposure (Figley & Carbonell, 1995; Scheck, Schaeffer, & Gillette, 1998; Shapiro & Solomon, 1996). *One reason for this lack of understanding is that writers in the field of police psychology usually fail to distinguish between job stress and job-related situations that are traumatizing.* If the difference between general job stress and trauma is not recognized, law enforcement officers who are traumatized may feel guilt and embarrassment for being unable to handle what they have come to believe is the normal stress of the job. Education of all officers in the department is, therefore, the first step in convincing officers to take advantage of treatment offered.

Officers generally respond to an explanation of the biological nature of PTSD, demonstrating how stress hormones change the way in which the brain and body function (Ochberg, 1991). Law enforcement officers are generally a difficult group to convince, so hard evidence such as slides contrasting a brain scan of a normal brain with the brain of someone in PTSD are helpful (Rauch et al., 1996). Avoiding psychological jargon is also important. Furthermore, educating officers to the impact of critical events commonly experienced in law enforcement is essential.

After teaching officers about the biological nature of PTSD, the symptoms of PTSD, and the types of situations which can most traumatize officers, techniques which may quickly and successfully reduce or eliminate symptoms of job related PTSD should be explained. The testimony of fellow officers (through video or audiotape, written accounts, or from other members of the group) appears to be the most useful technique for convincing officers to change their thinking about the impact of trauma and how to treat the resulting symptoms. Furthermore, officers are more likely to report symptoms to a mental health professional who is focused on using treatment to keep the officer on the job rather than as a basis for a fitness-for-duty evaluation (which can result in the officer being suspended from or losing his or her job). Consequently, for mental health services to be effective, officers must be able to clearly differentiate fitness-for-duty evaluations from the treatment of symptoms caused by job-related trauma. These two functions must be clearly separate and handled in independent offices by different mental health professionals.

Problem Five: Traumatic incidents, even those occurring while off-duty, or pre-employment, can impact on the officer's ability to do his or her job.

Solution: Educating officers to understand that personal traumas, even those of childhood, can have an impact on the traumatic experiences encountered on the job. Being the victim of physical, emotional, or sexual child abuse; the death of a parent or family members (especially when the loss was at a young age, the loss was sudden, or the death was from a long, debilitating illness); accidents; rape; violence; natural disasters; and war are among the most common personal events that have been found to have traumatic impact (Jimerson, 1987; Marcey, 1995; van der Kolk et al., 1996b).

Problem Six: Obtaining a complete history of traumatic incidents.

Solution: Because many officers have unconsciously minimized or failed to understand the impact of their past traumatic experiences on present functioning, the mental health professional must elicit and review the officer's traumatic experiences from childhood forward. This professional should record the exact words that the officer uses to describe an incident, especially the ones that reflect why the incident was so traumatizing or resulted in feelings of guilt, shame, or embarrassment. The questioning is divided into two phases, trauma occurring before and after age eighteen, with memory cues provided by the following questions:

Before age eighteen:

• Did anyone you love die or commit suicide—parents, siblings, friends, other?

• Did you have any serious surgery, accidents, diseases, or were you hospitalized?

• Was there a time when you were separated from your primary caretaker?

• Were you ever mugged, assaulted, bullied, or raped?

• Were you a witness to violence between your parents or caretakers?

• Did your parents degrade, humiliate, or say negative things to or about you?

• How were you punished? (Preferable to "Were you abused?" since many abuse victims do not recognize their punishment as abuse, believing it was deserved. The questioning in this area should progress in a direction from punishment to abuse. If it is clear that the officer was not punished in a manner other than an occasional spanking, the questioning in this area stops. If, however, answers to questions are affirmative, the questioning continues until all the ways in which the officer was abused are reviewed. The abuse questions end with, "What is the worst thing that (the abuser) did to you?"

• As a child or adolescent, what is the worst thing that ever happened to you?

After age eighteen:

• Have you ever thought you were going to die or that someone you loved or worked with was going to die quickly or violently?

• Are your parents living? If not, how did they die? (Many officers are traumatized by the death of parents, especially if death was slow and painful, because they have no control over the course of the disease and death.)

• Do you have any phobias or extreme fears?

• Have you experienced guilt or shame related to any of these experiences?

• Using the events that commonly traumatize law enforcement officers, listed previously, review each event by making it into a question. For example: "Have you ever seen a law enforcement officer killed, or viewed the body at the scene? If so, is there anything about this event that makes you feel guilty?"

• Did you serve in the Vietnam War (for officers older than 45 years of age)?

The interview segment of the treatment is very important, as it forms the foundation for the treatment that follows. This part of the session can last at least one to two hours. The mental health professional must have an extensive understanding of the impact of varying types of trauma on law enforcement officers in order to explore the impact of past experiences on present functioning.

Problem Seven: The impact of exposure to traumatic incidents is often cumulative, causing gradually increasing symptoms or a sudden onset of symptoms.

Solution: A number of traumatic incidents are treated with MTP in one lengthy session. Although many officers seeking treatment believe that their symptoms evolved from a single traumatic incident, it often becomes apparent that they have been exposed to numerous job-related traumas, and also have experienced traumatic incidents in their personal lives, all of which have been contributing to the PTSD.

Problem Eight: The symptoms of PTSD that impact job performance may be *linked* or interwoven among a number of traumatic incidents experienced by the officer. Discovering the links among traumas is critical in improving results (Perry, 1999).

Solution: It is important for the interviewer to discover links in the traumatic incidents, which make them similar by event (such as vehicle accidents or death of loved ones), or by theme or belief system. The officer often has little understanding that these traumas are linked, or how they are connected, and may make a statement which reveals the connection between an experience and his or her reactions without any conscious recognition of having done so. It is imperative, therefore, that the mental health professional be alert for these connections, carefully recording the words of the officer for use during the treatment phase. Belief systems which have common links include: "I'm all alone and no one cares for me"; "I have no control"; "It's all my fault"; "I should never make mistakes"; "I'm dead"; "I'm less than"; "I'm not safe."

EXAMPLES OF LINKED TRAUMATIC EXPERIENCES

Events Linked by Similarity in Theme

Officer Knight[2] casually mentioned his unpleasant reaction to the color red. Informed that this could be a blood phobia, he later asked for an appointment. An exploration of Officer Knight's past revealed the following linked traumas: (1) At five years of age, his father, who was pretending to box with him, violently punched him. (2) When his father demanded that they fight when he was 18, Officer Knight opened his arms, responding, "I don't want to fight you." At that point, his father punched him with such force that three teeth were broken. (3) As a young military officer, Officer Knight, a passenger in a jeep with his driver and bodyguard, fell asleep. Suddenly awakened by enemy fire, Officer Knight returned fire. A battle ensued in which Officer Knight was wounded and he killed three attacking enemy soldiers. His driver and bodyguard were killed by enemy fire. (4). After making an undercover drop, Officer Knight, feeling safe, walked away. Suddenly, a passing man stabbed him in the chest with such force that the knife handle broke off, leaving the blade in his chest. Officer Knight recalled being face-down on an operating table as blood squirted from his chest onto the doctor's white shoes (the basis for his blood phobia). (5) With no warning of problems in his marriage, Officer Knight's wife called him at work one day to say, "I'm leaving you." The theme of his traumas was, *"I didn't see it coming!"* MTP eliminated the blood phobia and the emotional response to the traumatic scenes. Using alternating stimulation, each scene was described in the officer's words, as the therapist added, "I didn't see it coming" to defuse this link.

Events Linked by Similarity of Event and Ensuing Fear

Officer Carl asked for treatment related to an event that had occurred almost 30 years ago, early in his career. His symptoms involved fear of crowds, panic when riding by certain neighborhoods, and intense PTSD symptoms when observing riots on the news. Officer Carl had been in a riot in the early 1970s (when police were often referred to as "pigs"). The rioters repeatedly assaulted him, threatened to kill him by sticking guns in his mouth, while they robbed and burned the neighborhood he was sent to protect. After repeatedly believing his death was imminent, Officer Carl was rescued by a community resident using a shotgun and guard dog. Treatment initially reduced the traumatic image and the panic that crowds elicited, but this panic would soon return. After several sessions where treatment focused on the riot, Officer Carl was asked if there was another event from his past that reminded him of the riot. He paused, then indicated that in his childhood his family would get together for holidays. Each time they would say "This time it's going to be different!" However, on each occasion after the adults began drinking, they would begin fighting violently. Officer Carl indicated, "I tried to intervene, but I couldn't stop them. I felt so helpless"—the link between the two traumas. When the links between these events became apparent, MTP was used to process both traumatic experiences, as well as the words and belief system that connected them. The vivid scenes from these past events and panic have not returned.

Problem Nine: Finding techniques that process the greatest number of traumatic incidents in the shortest amount of time.

Solution: The basic MTP process involves using two treating professionals, one often being a law enforcement officer who is a peer or Employee Assistance Program counselor; one lengthy initial session, sometimes followed by one or two short sessions (rather than many short ones); and EMDR-type bilateral stimulation. Using a law enforcement officer as a part of the treatment team reassures the officer being treated that the unique law enforcement culture will be understood; the peer support officer also helps to educate a treating therapist who has not been a law enforcement officer. In MTP, three separate stimulations (a combination of tapping of the shoulders, sounds, and tapping of the knees or eye movement) are used simultaneously while the officer focuses on traumatic incidents from his or her past (Shapiro, 1995; Yourell, 1996). Tapping, eye movement, and alternating sounds are used to alternately stimulate each side of the body. The shoulders are tapped alternately by one professional standing behind the seated officer, with hands held flat. Drum sounds,[3] which alternate from separated stereo speakers, allow the officer to hear the drums separately and sequentially. It has been noted that the alternating drum sounds and tapping also seem to help the therapist and peer support officer process the traumatic events disclosed by the officer, thus decreasing compassion fatigue (where the therapist becomes traumatized through hearing of someone else's trauma) in the treating professionals (Figley, 1995). If eye movement is used, the officer is asked to follow an object with his or her eyes from left to right. Alternate tapping of knees may be used in place of eye movement. Furthermore, if, at the beginning of the session, the officer becomes distraught during the interview phase, one of the treatment team taps his or her shoulders as he or she relates the details of what happened. This seems to process some of the trauma of the event and allow the officer to talk more freely about the incident.

Additional techniques may be integrated into the treatment session at this point, to deal with a variety of problems that arise. These techniques increase the processing of specific traumatic incidents, and are described in Problems Ten through Fourteen.

Problem Ten: The elicited memory of the trauma is fragmented or weak, because of the amnesia or fragmented memory common in traumatic incidents.

Solution: Using props to more vividly recreate the trauma or phobia helps to intensely elicit the emotions and sensory responses triggered by traumatic experiences, and in this way, to more completely eliminate them, a form of systematic desensitization (Frueh, De Arellano, & Turner, 1997). These "props" have been used successfully by the author in MTP:

- Blood from red meat.
- Pictures, video- or audiotapes, news broadcasts and articles on the traumatizing event.
- Sirens, light flashes, badges, sounds of explosions, gunfire.
- Police radio transmission of events, ringing telephone.
- Photographs of the items eliciting phobic responses, such as spiders.

Problem Eleven: A traumatic image or belief system that does not reduce in intensity or fade away as alternating stimulation is used.

Solution: When a traumatic image or belief stays vivid or changes little after three sets of MTP, the officer is asked to visualize one of the following to speed up the processing:

- The image or belief fading until it disappears like a scene at the end of a movie.
- The image or belief on a television screen followed by the scene fading or disappearing as the television set is turned off.

- A computer screen displaying the traumatic scene or faulty belief; followed by the negative image or belief being erased from the screen as the delete button is pressed.
- Officers may also be reluctant to let go of a traumatic image involving the death of someone they cared about, out of guilt or for fear of losing the last image of a loved one, loyal partner, or friend. When this occurs, this officer is reassured that MTP moves only the traumatic memory into the past while allowing positive memories to become stronger.

Problem Twelve: The feeling of fear and helplessness elicited when remembering an abusive or violent individual is so overwhelming that it interferes with the processing of the traumatic incident.

Solution: To reduce this fear and/or helplessness, the officer is asked to:

1. Close his or her eyes and visualize the person who terrorizes, dominates, or interferes with their appropriate functioning, standing in front of them.
2. When he or she sees this person clearly, to visually shrink this person to be very small.
3. Say everything that he or she needs to say to this person. (The mental health worker can add statements that the officer has failed to include, e.g., "I'm not afraid of you any more.")
4. Visually shrink this person, in their mind, until he or she totally disappears.
5. Move his or her mind to a place of safety and comfort. Alternating stimulation is used throughout this imagery, and for a minute or so after the officer visualizes a place of safety.

Problem Thirteen: The sudden or violent death of a friend or loved one causes the traumatic death scene to be stuck in the present memory, thus interfering with the processing of grief and leaving important things, such as "good-bye," unsaid.

Solution: The Gestalt "empty chair" technique (Self-Awareness, 2000) helps to relieve guilt and reestablish a broken connection with the individual who has died. If the death was sudden, this creates a way to say good-bye.

1. Ask if the officer believes that the family member, partner, or friend who died is in heaven (or another after-life aligned with his or her religious beliefs).
2. If the answer is "yes," the officer is asked to close his or her eyes and imagine the person who died in Heaven . . . happy, healthy, and without pain.
3. The officer is directed to talk to this person, in his or her mind, communicating whatever needs to be said and allowing the person to answer, if appropriate. The officer is reminded that he or she can take as much time as needed, and when the conversation seems complete, to nod his or her head, continuing to keep eyes closed.

4. The officer is then directed to visualize the love that this person feels for him or her, represented as a light in that person's heart, asking if he or she can see this. When the officer can see this light, he or she is asked to imagine that the light doubles in size and divides in two, so that the individual who has died keeps the same amount of love and the other half of the light (representative of the love the deceased person feels for this officer) drifts down and moves into the officer's heart.

5. The officer is reminded that the love the person who died feels for him or her will now always be available, as a light in their heart, and is asked if he or she can visualize this.

6. When the officer replies in the affirmative, he or she is asked to pick a positive scene from the past that he or she would most like to remember about the person who has died. When this scene is vivid, the positive memory seems to become stronger as alternating stimulation continues while the officer continues to keep his or her eyes closed.

Traumatic images which are frozen in the present memory, a symptom of PTSD, can interfere with the grief process (Marcey, 1996). This visual imagery technique helps move the traumatic scene of loss into the past, replaced with a more positive one, thus allowing grief to process in a natural way.

Problem Fourteen: Determining if traumatic incidents are processed.
Solution:

1. When a traumatic scene is reviewed during MTP, an emotional response of varying intensity is usually observable in the officer. Sets of MTP are repeated until this response is significantly reduced or eliminated. A set is the review of one to all traumatic incidents while alternating stimulation is used.

2. Visual imagery and/or sensory responses are also used. After each set of MTP, the officer is asked, "Close your eyes, take a deep breath in, let it go. What do you find?" The response reflects how the traumatic experience is processing. Common responses indicating the trauma is moving into past memory are:

   • "The room is getting dimmer."

   • "I can only see part of the scene."

   • "Most of the scene has been replaced by a light."

   • "I am driving away from the murder scene."

   • "I'm no longer there; I'm at the beach with my family."

   Responses may also be in symbolic form (e.g., "I see a bright light," "There is a clear glass ball.") When responses are symbolic, sets of MTP should continue until it is clear to the therapist that the last symbol the officer reports visualizing is a positive one.

3. When all traumatic memories have been reviewed using MTP, the officer is asked to again review each traumatic scene by closing his or her eyes. The officer is then asked to review each traumatic memory, comparing it to the way in which

it was previously experienced. If the response indicates that an event, or a specific part of an event, has not been completely processed, MTP is repeated on scenes that remain vivid. Changing the stimulation type should be tried, that is, from alternatingly tapping knees to eye movement or from eye movement to tapping of the knees. In many cases, traumatic reactions continue to process following the session; therefore treatment success may not be totally evident for several days.

4. Comparing pre-treatment and post-treatment symptoms during follow-up contact is one of the best ways to determine treatment success. For example, if the officer previously was averaging three hours of sleep a night and, following MTP, is sleeping eight hours nightly, there has been a reduction of symptoms (Ross, Ball, Sullivan, & Caroff, 1989). If appropriate, and with consent, consulting with spouses or friends is another way of measuring the effectiveness of the treatment. This can independently confirm the reduction of symptoms the officer reports.

5. Use of a "letting go" metaphor is an additional way of insuring that traumatic images, experiences, and cognitive distortions are processed. For example, the officer (with eyes closed) is asked to imagine placing all the negative and traumatic experiences reviewed during the session into a trailer behind his or her car. The mental health worker asks the officer to note how difficult the car is to steer with the heavy trailer load connected to the back. Then, the officer is asked to stop the car and unhook the trailer. Following this, the officer is asked to imagine getting back into the car, noticing, as the car pulls away, how the trailer becomes smaller and smaller until it disappears. He or she is then asked to notice just how easy the car is to drive now that the heavily loaded trailer has been left behind. At this point, the officer is guided to visualize a positive future scene, where trauma symptoms are gone. Alternating stimulation is used throughout this image and continues for a minute or two as the positive scene is described by the officer.

6. The officer is given a tape, called "Letting Go"[4] which includes progressive relaxation, visual imagery, and suggestions for "letting go" of traumatic symptoms and negative thought patterns, as well as messages for sleeping and healing (Jimerson, 1987). The officer is instructed to play the tape after going to bed, and advised that even if he or she falls asleep, his or her unconscious will still hear and learn from the messages. If the officer wakes up during the night, he or she is instructed to rewind the tape to the beginning, and play it again so that the tape soon becomes an anchor that helps induce sleep.

Problem Fifteen: Memories of traumatic experiences are sometimes disassociated to the point that an officer is unable to verbally recall or express them. Even when the scene is vividly experienced in flashbacks, the officer may be unable to find words to express what happened (i.e., the event is frozen in the right brain while the left brain, which controls language, shuts down) (Solomon, 1996b; van der Kolk. 1997a).

Solution: One solution is to use alternating stimulation while reviewing not only the aspects of the traumatic memory that the officer can recall, but all possible traumatic incidents common to officers who were involved in similar critical incidents. This review should reflect the facts and the officer's behavior during the incident. For example: An officer is trying to negotiate with a bank robber to give up when the robber shoots and kills a bank teller. The officer clearly remembers parts of the incident, but is unable to describe other segments. The therapist (who would need to understand all of the possible traumatic points of this type of situation) would ask the officer to close his or her eyes (while using three kinds of alternating stimulation) and go through the traumatic event.

Close your eyes and go through the scene as I describe it. You are on patrol. You get a radio call of a bank robbery in progress; you and your partner are the first officers on the scene. A man comes out of the bank dragging a screaming woman, who, you later find out, was a teller. He has a gun to her head, screaming obscenities and that he is going to kill her unless you allow him to escape. You call on the radio for hostage negotiators. You and your partner try to defuse the situation, but the perpetrator becomes more and more enraged. You are not sure if what you are saying to the perpetrator is the right thing to say and wish the negotiators would show up. Suddenly, he puts his gun to the sobbing woman's head and pulls the trigger. Remember the blood and what the gun did to her head. Remember the smells, perhaps of gunpowder, and anything else that symbolizes the scene. Go through anything that you heard . . . what the woman said before she was shot and the screams of spectators . . . any other sounds that are associated with this scene. Then go through what you saw . . . the face of the woman before she was murdered and as he shot her, other people at the scene, the vivid image of her being shot, the colors, the horror, the way your partner reacted. Then remember the perpetrator shooting at you, you and your partner returning the fire . . . the perpetrator being hit and falling. Experience everything you felt and said and smelled and tasted and thought as you ran up to the bodies of the victim and perpetrator. Perhaps you felt guilty or ashamed for not being able to keep the perpetrator from killing the teller. Then go through what happened as other officers arrived, and your lieutenant screamed at you, "Why didn't you just talk to him until the hostage negotiation team arrived?" Go through everything that was said to you following the shootings . . . the facial expressions of the other officers and spectators and family members. Then recall having your weapon taken away and the feelings that arose when that happened. See yourself driving back to the station and filling out reports. Hear other officers telling you how they would have reacted differently and how this made you feel both angry and guilty, questioning if you had done something wrong. Then see the picture of the incident on the front page of the paper the next day with your name as one of the shooters. [Alternating stimulation follows for a minute or two, as the therapist is silent.] Now imagine that whole scene fading away, going further and further into the past until it is no longer visible. The woman's death was not your fault, you were doing your job. You did not kill the teller; the bank robber killed her. Perhaps the perpetrator was using "suicide by cop"; you are refusing to allow this man to traumatize you by his actions. So let any thought that you had which blamed yourself for this murder, any guilt, shame, or belief that you were responsible fade away. You routinely risk your life for people you do not even know. You are not responsible for the evil people in the world. Let go of the scene, let go of anything you heard or smelled or saw or felt or thought. Let go of your lieutenant implying you were responsible for the teller's death, the comments of your fellow officers, the pictures in the paper and in your mind. Let all parts of this horrifying event move far, far into the past, keeping anything you learned from this incident, letting everything else go.

The alternating stimulation is continued for a couple of minutes at this point to allow the officer to process the event. This is followed by checking to see if the scene has been processed . . . "Close your eyes; what do you find?" At this point, the officer may have processed much of the incident; MTP is repeated to complete this processing. Some officers, at this point, begin to remember or verbalize other traumatic parts of this incident. If this happens, these are processed with alternating stimulation while the therapist goes through these new memories.

Problem Sixteen: Traumatic memories, which can not be expressed verbally, are often experienced in the body as illness, body sensations (such as pain), or as emotions. (van der Kolk et al., 1996a).

Solution: During the initial interview, the therapist checks for physical symptoms that may be the body's way of expressing the stress or unresolved nature of the traumatic experience. Then, after processing the traumatic incidents and while continuing alternating stimulation, the officer is instructed to "let go" of any illness or pain that his or her body is experiencing because of any past traumatic experience, and to "let go" of any ways in which his or her body is using physical illness or pain as a way of empathizing with or trying to save victims. The therapist can do this by:

1. Asking the officer to visualize the illness, pain, or destructive reactions having a size, color, shape leaving his or her body, shrinking, and disappearing.
2. Having the officer visualize standing under a waterfall that washes away anything taken into the body destructively or any illness or pain related to their traumatic experiences.
3. Imaging illness or pain being vacuumed out of the body.

The officer is then asked to visualize something positive replacing the spaces in his or her body left empty by letting go of the pain or illness—perhaps a light or positive feeling.

EXAMPLE OF BOTH JOB-RELATED PROBLEMS AND PHYSICAL PROBLEMS CAUSED BY LINKED TRAUMAS

Officer Joy indicated that she had many physical problems related to an accident in which she was driving her patrol car during rush-hour traffic. Having come to a stop behind an 18-wheeler, she was rear-ended by another 18-wheeler traveling in excess of 60 miles an hour. Officer Joy was a firearms instructor and admitted that the pain from her accident continued to be so intense that she could no longer fire her weapon. The pain also prevented her from exercising. The greatest pain was located in her neck and back, resulting in an inability to raise her arm to the position required to fire her weapon.

After first being referred to a medical doctor, the question arose as to whether some of the physical problems might be symptoms of the traumatic experience. Officer Joy agreed to MTP, having successfully experienced this procedure to eliminate the trauma resulting from a line-of-duty shooting.

Officer Joy had the following linked traumas:

1. Her grandparents and aunt were killed in a head-on collision when she was young; her father took pictures of the accident scene and funeral and showed these pictures to her several times in her childhood.

2. At age 15, Officer Joy was a passenger in a car driven by a 16-year-old friend which was rear-ended by an 18-wheeler; the only part of the car that remained intact after the accident were the front seats on which she and her friend sat.

3. At age 16, Officer Joy was driving home from school one day with friends. She passed a car with two male students. Taking this as a challenge, the boys passed her car on a hill and were struck head-on by a truck; one young man died.

4. Two younger friends of Officer Joy rear-ended a flatbed truck and were decapitated.

5. A college sorority sister was killed in an accident in which she was thrown from a car and run over by an 18-wheeler.

When asked to describe the most recent accident, she replied: "I was stopped in rush-hour traffic when I looked in the rear-view mirror and saw the grill of the truck coming toward me. I braced my shoulders. The truck hit me and then I realized that the driver had not hit his brakes and the truck was going to hit me again. I visualized myself being decapitated, just like my friend. I screamed 'No' as my friend had in the accident when I was fifteen. It sounded like gunfire when the truck hit me again."

The link between the accidents and trucks is obvious. MTP was used on all traumas, with special focus on her last accident. Suggestions were given to let go of the pain and trauma that she had stored in her body. Her statement, "It sounded like gunfire when the truck hit me again," was repeated numerous times while reviewing her last accident, as a way of processing this thought and its links to her belief at the time that she was going to die and her present difficulty firing her weapon. After this session, Officer Joy's pain decreased significantly and she began to exercise. A week later, MTP was used with the officer at an indoor range. First, a peer officer fired his weapon, while the mental health worker tapped the shoulders of Officer Joy again repeating the words in which she had described the accident (i.e., "It sounded like gunfire when the truck hit me again.") While continuing to tap her shoulders, the mental health worker switched to positive statements such as "You are a great firearms instructor. Let go of the sound of the truck accident. Your ability to teach officers how to shoot well has probably saved many lives." When she no longer reacted to the sound of the peer officer shooting, Officer Joy fired her weapon while the mental health worker tapped her shoulders. Officer Joy reported that two days after this session, she shot a 98 (out of 100). The pain that remains is a localized neck pain for which she will continue to seek medical advice.

Problem Seventeen: Following exposure to a traumatic incident, law enforcement officers may develop difficulty in firing or even carrying their service weapon.

Solution: Education of officers as to reactions that commonly occur during a line-of-duty shooting and other life-threatening or violent encounters. Typical responses occurring in life-threatening encounters include tunnel vision, hearing distortions (lack of awareness of gun fire, noises, or voices), experiencing the events in slow motion, distortions in movement of perpetrators, and an inability to correctly recall the number of shots fired from his or her weapon. Memory blanks are also common. Officers who understand these common reactions have less difficulty with guilt or second guessing their own judgment of responses.

Line-of-duty shootings, shooting deaths of fellow officers, or suicide of friends or family members by use of a firearm may also have an impact on an officer's ability to use his or her weapon. These experiences may create panic at the thought of having to shoot and/or refusal to even carry a weapon. The startle reaction common in PTSD also can interfere with an officer's shooting accuracy, causing problems in training and requalifying with a service weapon (Shalev, Brandes, Freedman, Orr, & Pitmann, 2000). When a problem in using his or her weapon occurs, after a session to process traumatic incidents, the officer is taken to a shooting range for MTP. This treatment must be done in complete privacy, while following the steps described with Officer Joy: A peer officer fires his or her weapon while the mental health worker taps the shoulders of the officer to eliminate negative responses to sound, sight, or smell. Then the officer fires his or her weapon while his or her shoulders are tapped and while the therapist repeats positive statements. MTP is continued until the officer can shoot independently and without interference from the distracting triggers related to PTSD. Because traumatic experiences may continue to process for several days following MTP, accuracy and skill in shooting often continue to improve.

Problem Eighteen: Following a traumatic incident, the perceived need to have reacted perfectly leads to guilt, cognitive distortions, and/or negative or pessimistic thinking. This interferes with healthy behavioral and emotional responses.

Solution: Cognitive therapy is used throughout the session to alter destructive belief systems and to change or substitute new beliefs that are more realistic and/or optimistic. During the treatment, as each traumatic scene is reviewed, the therapist first repeats the negative beliefs or self-statements that have arisen from the traumatic incidents. As the scenes are processed, the therapist substitutes positive statements that counteract the negative cognitions. For example: "It's my fault the suspect died. If I were smart enough, I could have talked him into giving up" (negative cognition). Followed by: "I am a good hostage negotiator. My negotiating skills saved the victim. The suspect is responsible for his own death. I can let this go" (positive cognition). Additionally, positive cognitions can help the officer "reframe" the traumatic scene, that is, "I learned that I can survive." "I learned to pay attention to the passenger in a car when I am arresting the driver." These statements are repeated to the officer as the traumatic scene is reviewed by the mental health worker and while using alternating stimulation.

When reviewing a traumatic scene for which the officer is experiencing guilt, it is important that the therapist emphasize the officer's on-scene actions that demonstrated effective planning, training, and problem solving. For example: After shooting and killing a perpetrator, an officer begins to feel guilty and second-guess himself, especially after the newspaper and the man's wife accuse him of murder. During the review of the event, the therapist notes all of the steps the officer took to attempt to end the incident in a non-violent manner and inserts these steps as the incident is being reviewed, using alternating stimulation. For example: "You arrive at the scene after the 911 operator repeatedly contacts you, warning that shots are being fired and screams are heard from this location. You and your partner jump out of your patrol cars, duck behind other cars parked in the yard and listen, your first technique to assess the situation. You and John run to both sides of the porch and knock loudly on the wall, demanding that whoever is in the trailer come out to talk . . . your second technique to defuse the situation. Numerous shots are fired from inside. You ask your partner if he has tear gas . . . the third technique you consider to defuse the incident. You killed him only after everything else did not work and he ran toward you aiming a shotgun at your head. You had tried 10 different techniques to defuse this situation; you used your training and experience as a law enforcement officer in an attempt to convince the perpetrator to give up, but he refused. If you had not shot him, he probably would have killed you and his wife. You did what you had to do. You risked your own life trying to convince him to give up. It could have ended differently, if he had given up. He is responsible for the way this incident ended. A police officer is often exposed to traumatic situations and the worst of human behavior, but you did your job and you can let this go."

Problem Nineteen: The symptoms of PTSD interfere with planning for and creating a mental picture of positive change in the future.

Solution: Positive projections of the future and new learning is practiced (future-pacing; Klein, 1986) at the end of the session by having the officer see him or herself both on the job and in his or her personal life being successful and returning to healthy functioning.

REVIEW OF USING MULTI-SENSORY TRAUMA PROCESSING WITH LAW ENFORCEMENT OFFICERS

1. Review symptoms typical of PTSD with the officer to determine the extent and severity of his or her reactions, and obtain a baseline of symptoms from which to review the success of the treatment at a later time. Educate the officer about PTSD during this phase, with emphasis on the biological basis for PTSD and the cumulative nature of the impact of traumatic experiences.

2. Explain techniques that will be used; obtain written permission to treat traumatic symptoms.

3. Elicit and review the officer's traumatic experiences from childhood forward; give examples and ask questions. Look for and record links between traumas.

4. When review of the traumatic events seems complete and the links are clear, the second phase of treatment begins, using two professionals, and three alternating stimulations.

5. Agree with the officer that the alternating stimulation used in MTP is an unusual therapeutic technique; then talk about the current understanding of the ways in which alternating stimulation helps to process traumatic memories. Explain the reactions that may occur during stimulation, that the mind processes the event during the stimulation and the officer need only be present and cooperative during the process for it to occur.

6. Begin with the oldest traumatic incident. Use MTP with each traumatic event from the officer's life, one at a time, until the emotional response to the event has significantly decreased or is eliminated. While tapping the shoulders, using alternating drum sounds and either eye movement or knee tapping, the first trauma is described from beginning to end, using the officer's words, including what he or she has repeated as a cognitive distortion after the event (i.e., "What is wrong with me, I'm a hostage negotiator and the victim lived; why am I having these flashbacks?"). Use props to more vividly re-create the trauma or phobia, if appropriate.

7. The degree of emotional reaction to reexperiencing the traumatic event is one guide as to how many sets of MTP this summary requires. Visual imagery and/or sensory response are also used to determine traumatic scene reduction.

8. If the officer continues to experience the traumatic scene with little change, visual imagery or a form of NLP is inserted to speed up the processing of the event. If traumatic grief is present, imagery is used to reduce

reaction. If fear is interfering with the processing, imagery is used to reduce the reaction.

9. During the review of each traumatic scene, the therapist first repeats the negative cognitions that the officer has associated with the traumatic incidents. As the scenes are processed, the therapist substitutes positive statements to counteract the negative cognitions.

10. Using visual imagery, and while continuing the alternating stimulation, the officer is instructed to let go of his or her body's expression of traumatic exposure through pain or illness.

11. The traumatic scenes are reviewed to determine if they have been processed.

12. The alternating stimulation continues as the therapist presents a metaphor for letting go of all traumatic images and experiences.

13. The officer is asked to image a scene in the future where he or she is functioning effectively and is happy.

14. When all traumatic images seem to have been processed, the reactions that may occur following the session are explained a second time.

15. The officer is given a visual imagery and relaxation tape, called "Letting Go."

16. The officer is reminded that traumatic events can continue to process for several days, and this may result in emotions or scenes bubbling to the surface as they are released. Furthermore, officers with numerous traumatic experiences often find that traumatic scenes of lesser impact, which have not been recalled for years, might surface as those with the most impact are processed. Instructions are given to call if there is a question or problem.

17. The officer is contacted one to three days later to check on functioning, using the baseline symptoms as a comparison, especially sleep patterns. Another check is made after two to three weeks. One or two further sessions may be required if additional traumatic incidents are recalled or symptoms persist. Officers with experiences, symptoms or physical reactions that are of concern to the therapist are encouraged to seek the help of outside professionals.

CASE HISTORY EXAMPLE

Officer John Day presented with the following symptoms, described by his wife:

His face lost feeling. He stopped laughing. His breathing changed; when he was driving sometimes it kind of bubbled when he breathed out, or he would breathe in a very shallow way.

His speech was choppy; he would say three words and pause, three more words and pause. He stopped playing with the kids. He became intolerant, focused and single-minded. We had shared picking up our son from private school, but I got so I didn't call him to pick him up because he seemed "put off." Our kids just responded like he was dead. I told them that their daddy had been through something that had hurt his heart so much that it had changed him.

He had a lot of trouble sleeping. The first month he had a lot of nightmares; since then he has yelled out and was frantic in bed about once a month and he jerked in his sleep, especially in his legs. If I tried to wake him up to stop the nightmare or bumped him in his sleep, he was instantly and loudly awake. If he fell asleep on the floor, I could not wake him up gradually . . . he startled awake. His stomach was really bad for months; he said it just ached. He gained 20–30 pounds, even though I couldn't see that he ate any more than he used to. Since this happened, he would say, "You're not listening to me—I just told you that." But he hadn't just told me that. I think he must have been thinking the words in his head, and thought he said them to me, but he didn't. If I wanted him to listen to me, I had to make direct eye contact with him to make sure he was listening, or he wouldn't hear me. He was in his own world.

Before this happened, we related as adults . . . we listened to each other, and respected each other and helped each other. My first marriage had been to a very controlling man and we had agreed that John would not try to control me, tell me what to do, and we would be a team of two adults. After it happened, he wanted things his way. He started treating me like a child and tried to control me. He started wanting me to do things like he wanted them done. He even started telling me what to do when I had problems at work. I thought, "Oh no, he's acting just like my first husband." Sex decreased in frequency and became mechanical.

If something bothered him, he left. He would go in the next room or out in the backyard, or leave in the car. Before this happened, he never wanted to be away from home. After it happened, he did not want to be around groups of people he knew; we would be the last to arrive at a party and the first to leave. He stopped talking and going out with his friends from the job. The only friend he would talk to was a friend whose son had died. He would sit in the dark for hours and smoke. One day he came home and just picked me up and put me outside. He never got violent and he was slow at expressing anger, but he just couldn't stand to be with me. I called his Chief to tell him what happened; the Chief told me that he hadn't noticed that there was anything wrong with my husband.

He lost patience. He couldn't tolerate standing in line, being stuck in traffic, doing the normal things that make a family run, like paying bills. We had shared the duties, but I had to take over all of them. He thought most things weren't important enough for him to participate in. It was as if this event was so important that nothing else could compare, so he didn't want to hear the normal every day problems of the children and me.

When driving, he was more rigid, forceful and impatient. He drove faster and the safety zone between him and the car in front of him disappeared. One time he was driving and a tunnel was ahead. I could tell he was having a flashback and I didn't think he was going to make it through. He did it, but I could tell he was scared.

Officer Day described a life-changing incident that had occurred three years before the interview. Two professional divers were hired to clean out an irrigation system pipe filled with dark, black water; the pipe was a half mile long, 30 feet tall, and went as deep as a 10-story building under the ground. When the divers did not come out of the pipe at the expected time, police and fire and rescue divers responded. Two divers from the fire service then entered the pipe to attempt to rescue the professional divers, but also did not come out. Although convinced that he would also die, Officer Day and a fellow police diver entered the irrigation system and located the bodies of the dead rescue workers. His partner became disoriented and panicked. Officer Day pulled the body of one rescue worker to the surface, believing his partner was retrieving the other body. However, still panicked, she had held on to the leg of the rescue worker as he pulled him out. At the point of total exhaustion, and believing he would die, Officer Day went back in the pipe for the body of the second rescue worker. As he pulled the body to the surface, family members of the professional divers hysterically demanded that Officer Day retrieve the bodies of their loved ones. Too exhausted to dive again, Officer Day left and returned to his office. As he sat at his desk, the Fire Chief called and blamed him for the death of the rescue workers. The Fire Chief later apologized. Lawsuits and endless publicity followed.

Officer Day indicated that since this incident,

I have only been able to sleep two to three hours a night. I have earphones so I can watch television while my wife sleeps. Whenever I turn on the shower, it reminds me of everything in the event. I hate how it makes me feel. It colors everything I do and say and feel and think. My mind is always racing and on a thousand things; I am hearing someone's voice, but I am thinking about all kinds of other things. I look but I do not see. I get paranoid. I keep wondering what everyone is thinking about me. I can't concentrate or read. I'm not interested in anything. I am very shut down. I know the trial is coming up and I am going to have to go through this again. I dread it.

After Officer Day explained the incident, his symptoms, and thoughts, MTP was explained to him and he gave permission to be treated.

Alternating shoulder tapping, alternating drum sounds, and tapping of Officer Day's knees was used simultaneously. He was instructed to close his eyes and allow himself to review the scene as his description of what had happened was repeated to him. He was told that during the stimulation, his brain would process the event in a natural way. The therapist reviewed the entire scene using the same words or phrases in which he had described his trauma. Suggestions to bring up the sights, smells, feelings, body sensations, and what he heard during the event were given, so that the trauma would be reexperienced in the most vivid manner possible.

Officer Day had negative beliefs related to the incident, typical of officers involved in line-of-duty traumatic events, (i.e., "I could have done more" and "I should have stopped the rescue workers from diving").

These were repeated during the alternating stimulation. After reviewing the traumatic incident from beginning to end, Officer Day was asked, "Close your eyes, take a deep breath, let it go. . . . What do you find?" He reported that the scene was less vivid. The process was repeated two additional times, again reviewing the traumatic event in his words. Following the reading of the entire event, scenes which had been the most traumatic were presented, one at a time, while eye movement was used in combination with alternating sounds and alternating shoulder tapping. These scenes included the rescue workers entering the pipe, the feeling that he was going to die, viewing the bodies of the rescue workers inside the pipe, the panic of his partner, seeing his partner hanging onto the leg of the diver's body, family members of the professional divers demanding he dive again, and the Fire Chief blaming him for the rescue workers' deaths.

Following this step, when asked, "What do you find?", Officer Day recalled his response to a news report of the accident and the funeral of the rescue workers. Alternating stimulation was used on these scenes until they were processed. As alternating stimulation continued, positive cognitions were given by the therapist, such as, "You are a good officer; you have helped many people in your role as a law enforcement officer. Sometimes tragic events happen that cannot be predicted; tragedy is a part of the job of a police officer. It is important that you let this experience go so that you can continue to help others and do your job." Directives to let go of any guilt or responsibility for this event were given. He was also directed to let go of any pain or illness that his body was experiencing related to this trauma. Asked "What do you find?" Officer Day saw himself at home with his children. (Moving to a positive scene generally indicates that the traumatic scene has been processed.)

Officer Day was then asked to review the traumatic scene in his mind from beginning to end and indicate how he was experiencing it compared to the way he experienced it at the beginning of the session. He indicated that the scene had faded and seemed to have lost its power.

Officer Day was contacted several times during the week following the treatment to review how he was functioning. He reported a great relief of his symptoms and that he was sleeping six hours a night, rather than two. Because the primary trauma Officer Day had experienced was so powerful and overwhelming, other traumas in his past had not been reviewed during the first session.

In his second session, Officer Day reported two additional job-related traumatic experiences: (1) car accidents with child victims; (2) a diving incident where he had to retrieve the body of another diver who had gone through a turbine and been torn into pieces.

Alternating stimulation was used while reviewing each of these traumatic events. Because the diving incident involving the four deaths had been so life-altering, it was reviewed again several times, while using alternating stimulation. Officer Day had brought with him newspaper articles about the incident. He was asked to look at these and remember how he reacted to them while alternating stimulation was used. Asked about phobias resulting from these events, Officer Day reported that his National Academy class was required to dive into the pool, fully clothed. He had done this, but with a great deal of fear. In addition, he reported that although the fear experienced in the shower had decreased, showers continued to bother him. Officer Day also reported that he did not think he could ever dive again. Alternating stimulation was used while the experience of diving into the pool was reviewed, as well as taking showers, and diving. A visual image metaphor followed in which Officer Day imagined placing all of his traumatic experiences in a trunk, (including fear, guilt, shame, and all negative things he had repeated to himself concerning these events). He was instructed to imagine leaving the trunk and the trauma of his experiences behind, as he walked away. Officer Day was then asked to visualize himself in the future, at a lake where he was swimming and diving with his kids. Alternating stimulation stopped; he was asked, "Tell me what you find." He reported that he saw himself swimming and diving with his children, indicating the traumatic events had processed.

Several days later, Officer Day reported he was completely free of symptoms. His wife, who had come to visit him at the FBI Academy, was asked if she had noticed any changes in her husband. She indicated:

The smile is back on his face; he's laughing. We're talking about things like we used to. It's like the old husband is back, but deeper. His breathing is calmer and his speech isn't choppy any more. He has been listening to me and paying attention. I noticed that he did not get too close to cars or drive as fast. He didn't jump in his sleep and he woke up slowly. He slept well the whole night. We talked and talked and talked. I noticed on the way from the airport, I was reading the map and he was treating me like an adult. In the past three years, he would have been telling me what to do. He let me read the map myself, without his advice.

Officer Day later reported, with a smile, that the weekend with his wife had been "better than my honeymoon." He was sleeping eight hours a night, laughing, and telling jokes. He also had taken it on himself to describe his traumatic event, his treatment, and the change that he had experienced to other officers in his National Academy training class.

NOTES

The author acknowledges the significant contributions of Supervisory Special Agent Steve Spruill, Employee Assistance Program Manager at the FBI Academy,

Quantico, VA. SSA Spruill has teamed with the author as a peer support counselor in treating hundreds of law enforcement officers with MTP. SSA Spruill has not only educated the author as to the particular issues and perceptions of law enforcement officers, but also contributed ideas and techniques that improved MTP. He also provided editorial advice in describing MTP. SSA Spruill is entering graduate school to be trained as a therapist.

1. The effectiveness of MTP will be researched through field studies and brain scans.

2. Case examples were used with permission of law enforcement officers involved; names were changed to protect privacy.

3. "Biolateral" is available from Belmore, NY, (516) 785–0460.

4. "Letting Go" was created by the author, and is available from Therapeutic Stories, (703) 978–4321.

REFERENCES

Amen, Daniel G. (1998). *Change your brain, change your life*. New York: Times Books.

American Psychiatric Association. (1980). *Diagnostic and statistical manual of mental disorders* (DSM-III) (3rd ed.). Washington, DC: Author.

American Psychiatric Association. (1994). *Diagnostic and statistical manual of mental disorders* (DSM-IV) (4th ed.). Washington, DC: Author.

Armstrong, David. (1998). Police suicides rely on tools of guns, alcohol. *The Boston Globe Archives*. Wysiwyg://39/http://newslibrary.krmediastream.com/cgi-bin/document/bg_auth.

Bandler, R., & Grinder, J. (1979). *Frogs into princes: Neuro-Linguistic Programming*. Moab, UT: Real People Press.

Beck, J. (1995). *Cognitive therapy: Basics and beyond*. New York: Guilford Press.

Bohl, Nancy. (1991). The effectiveness of brief psychological interventions in police officers after critical incidents. In James T. Reese, James M. Horn, & Christine Dunning (Eds.), *Critical incidents in policing*. Washington, DC; Federal Bureau of Investigation.

Carlier, Ingrid V. E., Lamberts, Regina D., & Gersons, Berthold P. R. (1997). Risk factors for post-traumatic stress symptomatology in police officers: A prospective analysis. *Journal of Nervous & Mental Disease*, 185(8), 498–506.

Carlier, Ingrid V. E., Lamberts, Regina D., van Uchelen, Annephine J., & Gersons, Berthold P. R. (1998). Disaster-related post-traumatic stress in police officers: A field study of the impact of debriefing. *Stress Medicine*, 14(3), 143–148.

Chamberlin, Jamie. (2000). Cops trust cops, even one with a Ph.D. *Monitor on Psychology*, 31(1), 74–76.

Davidson, J., Hughes, D., Blazer, D., & George, L. (1991). Posttraumatic stress disorder in the community: An epidemiologic study. *Psychological Medicine*, 21, 713–721.

Davis, Joseph. (1999). Personal communication.

Delprino, Robert P., O'Quin, Karen, & Kennedy, Cheryl. (1997). *Identification of work and family services for law enforcement personnel*. National Institute of Justice. Police research and education project.

Denny, Nathan R. (1995). An orienting reflex/external inhibition model of EMDR and thought field therapy. *Traumatology* [online], 1(1). http://www.fsu.edu/~trauma/denny.html.

Depue, Roger L. (1979). Turning inward: The police officer counselor. *Law Enforcement Bulletin*, February. Federal Bureau of Investigation.

Eller, L. S. (1999). Guided imagery interventions for symptom management. *Annual Review Nursing Research*, 17, 57–84.

Ellis, A., & Harper, R. (1974). *A guide to rational living*. North Hollywood, CA: Wilshire Book Company.

Everly, G. S., & Lating, J. M. (1995). *Psychotraumatology: Key papers and core concepts in posttraumatic stress*. New York: Plenum.

Figley, Charles R. (Ed.). (1978). *Stress disorders among Vietnam veterans: Theory, research & treatment*. New York: Brunner/Mazel.

Figley, Charles R. (1995). *Compassion fatigue: Coping with secondary traumatic stress disorder in those who treat the traumatized*. New York: Brunner/Mazel.

Figley, C. R., & Carbonell, J. (1995). The "Active Ingredient" Project: The systematic clinical demonstration of the most efficient treatments of PTSD, a research plan. Tallahassee: Florida State University Psychosocial Stress Research Program and Clinical Library.

Frueh, B. Christopher, De Arellano, Michael A., & Turner, Samuel M. (1997). Systematic desensitization as an alternative exposure strategy for PTSD. *The American Journal of Psychiatry*, 154, 287–288.

Gallo, Fred P. (1996a). Reflections on active ingredients in efficient treatments of PTSD, part one. *Traumatology* [online], 2(2). http://www.fsu.edu/~trauma/art2v2i1.html.

Gallo, Fred P. (1996b). Reflections on active ingredients in efficient treatments of PTSD, part two. *Traumatology* [online], 2(2). http://www.fsu.edu/~trauma/art2v2i2.html.

Gershon, Robyn. (1999). *The public health implications of law enforcement stress*. Research in Progress Seminar, National Institute of Justice.

Gottman, John M., & Silver, Nan. (1999). *The seven principles of making marriage work*. New York: Crown.

Haley, J. (1973). *Uncommon therapy: The psychiatric techniques of Milton H. Erickson, M.D.* New York: Norton.

Hammond, D. Corydon. (1990). *Handbook of hypnotic suggestions and metaphors*. New York: Norton.

Harvey, Lintz Terry, & Tidwell, Romeria. (1997). Effects of the 1992 Los Angeles civil unrest: Posttraumatic stress disorder symptomatology among law enforcement officers. *The Social Science Journal*, 34(2), 171–183.

Hobfoll, Steven E., Spielberger, Charles D., Breznitz, Shlomo, Figley, Charles, Folkman, Susan, Lepper-Green, Bonnie, Meichenbaum, Donald, Milgram, Norman A., Sandler, Irwin, Sarason, Irwin, & van der Kolk, Bessel. (1991). War related stress: Addressing the stress of war and other traumatic events. *American Psychologist*, 46(8), 848–855.

Jimerson, S. (1987). In J. Haber, P. Hoskins, A. Leach, & B. Sideleau (Eds.), *Comprehensive Psychiatric Nursing* (3rd ed.) New York: McGraw-Hill.

Johnson, David Read, Rosenheck, Robert, & Fontana, Alan. (1996). Outcome of intensive inpatient treatment for combat-related posttraumatic stress disorder. *American Journal of Psychiatry*, 153, 771–777.

Klein, Ron. (1986). Ericksonian Hypnosis Training Seminar. American Hypnosis Training Academy. Silver Spring, MD.

Kopel, Heidi, & Friedman, Merle. (1997). Posttraumatic symptoms in South African police exposed to violence. *Journal of Traumatic Stress*, 10(2), 307–317.

Linton, John C. (1995). Acute stress management with public safety personnel: Opportunities for clinical training and pro bono community service. *Professional Psychology, Research & Practice*, 26, 566–573.

Long, Phillip W. (1996). Post-traumatic stress disorder. *The Harvard Mental Health Letter*. Part 1. http://www.health.harvard.edu/newsletters/mtltext.html.

Mann, J. P., & Neece, J. (1990). Worker's compensation for law enforcement related post traumatic stress disorder. *Behavioral Sciences and the Law*, 8, 447–456.

Marcey, Marcella. (1995). *A comparison of the long-term effects of bereavement after four types of death: Anticipated death, sudden death, drunk driver crash and homicide.* Unpublished doctoral dissertation, George Mason University.

Martin, C. A., McKean, H. E., & Veltkamp, L. J. (1986). Post traumatic stress disorder in police and working with victims: A pilot study. *Journal of Police Science and Administration*, 14(2), 98–101.

McMains, Michael J. (1991). The management and treatment of postshooting trauma: Administration and programs. In James T. Reese, James M. Horn, & Christine Dunning (Eds.), *Critical incidents in policing*. Washington, DC: Federal Bureau of Investigation.

Mellman, Thomas A., Kulick-Bell, Renee, Ashlock, Lawrence E., & Nolan, Bruce. (1995). Sleep events among veterans with combat-related posttraumatic stress disorder. *American Journal of Psychiatry*, 152, 110–116.

Mitchell, Jeffrey T. (1999). Personal communication.

Mitchell, J. T., & Bray, G. (1990). *Emergency services stress.* Englewood Cliffs, NJ: Prentice Hall.

Mitchell, J. T., & Everly, G. S. (1995). *Critical incident stress management: An operation manual.* Baltimore, MD: Chevron Publishing.

Mitchell, J. T., & Everly, G. S. (1997). The scientific evidence for critical incident stress management. *Journal of Emergency Medical Services*, 22(1), 87–93.

Ochberg, Frank M. (1991). Posttraumatic therapy. In James T. Reese, James M. Horn, & Christine Dunning (Eds.), *Critical incidents in policing*. Washington, DC: Federal Bureau of Investigation.

Ochberg, Frank M. (1993) Posttraumatic therapy. In John P. Wilson and Beverly Raphael (Eds.), *International handbook of traumatic stress syndromes*. New York: Plenum.

Ott, K., & Henry, P. (1995). *Critical incident stress management at Goulburn Correctional Centre.* Sydney, NSW: Department of Correctional Services. Sidney, Australia.

Ott, Karen. (2000, February). Peer support maintenance programs—A basic survey. *Critical Incident Stress Management & Peer Support.* http://www2. dynamite.com.au/ottdk/page12.html.

Pastorella, Richard. (1991). Posttraumatic stress disorder and the police experience. In James T. Reese, James M. Horn, & Christine Dunning (Eds.), *Critical incidents in policing.* Washington, DC: Federal Bureau of Investigation.

Perry, Bruce D. (1999). *Memories of fear: How the brain stores and retrieves physiologic states, feelings, behaviors and thoughts from traumatic events.* http:// www.bcm.tmc.edu/civitas/Memories.htm.

Pinizzotto, Anthony J., Davis, Edward F., & Miller, Charles, E. (1997). *In the line of fire: A study of felonious assaults on law enforcement officers.* Washington, DC: Federal Bureau of Investigation.

Rauch, S., van der Kolk, B. A., Fisher, R., Alpert, N., Orr, S., Savage, C., Jenike, M., & Pitman, R. (1996). A symptom provocation study of posttraumatic stress disorder using positron emission tomography and script driven imagery. *Archives of General Psychiatry, 53*(5), 380–387.

Reese, James T., & Hodinko, Bernard M. (1991). Police psychological services: A history. In James T. Reese, James M. Horn, & Christine Dunning (Eds.), *Critical incidents in policing.* Washington, DC: Federal Bureau of Investigation.

Reese, James T., & Horn, James M. (1988). *Police psychology: Operational assistance.* Washington, DC: Federal Bureau of Investigation.

Robinson, Holly M., Sigman, Melissa R., & Wilson, John P. (1997). Duty-related stressors and PTSD symptoms in suburban police officers. *Psychological Reports, 81*(3.1), 835–845.

Robinson, R., & Murdoch, P. (1998). *Guidelines for establishing and maintaining peer support programs in emergency services.* Baltimore, MD: Chevron Publishing.

Ross, R. J. (1999). Rapid eye movement sleep changes during the adaptation night in combat veterans with posttraumatic stress disorder. *Biological Psychiatry, 45*(7), 938–941.

Ross, Richard J., Ball, William A., Sullivan, Kenneth A., & Caroff, Stanley N. (1989). Sleep disturbance as the hallmark of posttraumatic stress disorder. *American Journal of Psychiatry, 146,* 697–711.

Scheck, M. M., Schaeffer, J. A., & Gillette, C. (1998). Brief psychological intervention with traumatized young women: The efficacy of eye movement desensitization and reprocessing. *Journal of Traumatic Stress, 11*(1), 25–44.

Self-Awareness. The empty chair technique: A simple means of exploring your feelings. (2000). *Self-awareness, gestalt techniques for insight-psychological self help.* http://mentalhelp.net/psyhelp/chap15/chap15e.htm.

Shalev, A. Y., Brandes, Peri T., Freedman, S., Orr, S. P., & Pitman R. K. (2000). Auditory startle response in trauma survivors with posttraumatic stress disorder: A prospective study. *American Journal of Psychiatry, 157*(2), 255–261.

Shapiro, F. (1995). *Eye movement desensitization and reprocessing: Basic principles, protocols and procedures.* New York: Guilford Press.

Shapiro, Francine, & Solomon, Roger. (1996). Eye movement desensitization and reprocessing: Neurocognitive information processing. In G. S. Everly Jr.

(Ed.), *Innovations in disaster and trauma psychology: Applications in emergency services and disaster response.* Baltimore, MD: Chevron Publishing.

Sheehan, Donald C. (1999). Stress management in the Federal Bureau of Investigation: Principles of program development. *International Journal of Emergency Management,* 1(1), 9–42.

Solomon, Roger. (1996a). Critical incident stress management in law enforcement. In G. S. Everly Jr. (Ed.), *Innovations in disaster and trauma psychology: Applications in emergency services and disaster response.* Baltimore, MD: Chevron Publishing.

Solomon, Roger. (1996b). Memory impairments in the wake of critical incidents. *International Use of Force Journal,* 1(2), 2–12.

Spiller, Roger J. (1990). Shell shock. *American Heritage,* 41, 75–87.

Stratton, John G. (1985). Employee assistance programs: A profitable approach for employers and organizations. *The Police Chief,* 52, 31–33.

van der Kolk, Bessel. (1995). Post traumatic stress disorder. Workshop presented at the conference "Third World Congress on Stress, Trauma and Coping," Baltimore, MD.

van der Kolk, Bessel. (1997a). Posttraumatic stress disorder and memory. *Psychiatric Times.* http://www.mhsource.com/edu/psytimes/p970354.html.

van der Kolk, Bessel. (1997b). The psychobiology of posttraumatic stress disorder. *Journal of Clinical Psychiatry,* 58(9), 6–24.

van der Kolk, Bessel, Hobfoll, Steven E., Spielberger, Charles D., et al. (1991). War-related stress: Addressing the stress of war and other traumatic events. *American Psychologist,* 46(8), 848–855.

van der Kolk, Bessel A., McFarlane, Alexander C., & Weisaeth, Lars (Eds.). (1996). *Traumatic stress: The effects of overwhelming experience on mind, body and society.* New York: Guilford Press.

van der Kolk, Bessel A., Pelovitz, David, Roth, Susan, Mandel, Francine S., McFarlane, Alexander, & Herman, Judith L. (1996b). Dissociation, affect dysregulation and somatization: The complex nature of adaptation to trauma. Invited paper in honor of John Nemiah, Trauma Information Pages.

Yontef, Gary (1993). *Awareness, dialogue and process: Essays on Gestalt Therapy.* New York: The Gestalt Journal Press.

Yourell, R. A. (1996). *Reprocessing for the general reader.* http://home.earthlink. net/~ryourell/Repro4Pub.

Zoler, Mitchell L. (1998). Brain imaging shows benefit of PTSD therapy. *Clinical Psychiatry News,* 26(8), 14. http://pharmacotherapy.medscape.com/IMNG/ ...PsychNews/1998/v26.n08/cpn2608.14.01.html.

Chapter 10

The Use of Neuro-Linguistic Programming and Emotionally-Focused Therapy with Divorcing Couples in Crisis

Jeanne M. Bertoli

Over 1 million couples divorce each year (Amato & Keith, 1991). The effects of divorce on both adults and children have been widely reported and are generally accepted (Furstenberg, 1990; Hetherington, 1989; Hetherington, Cox, & Cox, 1982, 1985; Seltzer, 1994; Wallerstein & Blakeslee, 1989). Children of divorce generally have lower educational and occupation attainment, lower incomes, higher divorce rates, and higher rates of depression (Wallerstein & Blakeslee, 1989). What causes the damage done to children, and how might we intervene to minimize that damage? According to the literature, the most influential factor affecting children's adjustment to divorce is parental hostility. That is, when parents legally divorce they often do not divorce emotionally. Parents often remain tied to their ex-spouses emotionally, expressing anger, hostility, and sometimes revenge toward this person they have loved and lost. When parents are struggling to cope with their own issues, they often find themselves incapable of tending to the logistical and emotional needs of their children. We must find a way to help parents deal with this struggle for the sake of themselves, their children, and all of society.

Concern over this issue has led many states to adopt laws requiring a parent education course for all those divorcing who have children (Kramer & Washo, 1993). Also, a model of divorce therapy has been developed using a solution-focused approach. In this model, parents are asked to control their feelings and refocus on the needs of their children (Beck & Biank, 1997). While these are steps in the right direction, there has been no evidence suggesting that they have reduced interparental hostility.

Offered here is a new model of divorce therapy. It combines Neuro-Linguistic Programming (NLP) and Emotionally-Focused Therapy (EFT) in an attempt first to replace the attachment to the ex-spouse (and thereby remove the emotional connection) and then to reengage ex-spouses to form new interactional patterns aligned with their new roles as co-parents. EFT, which is based on systems theory and attachment theory (each will be discussed below), has been shown to be effective in many empirical studies. NLP, although not as theoretically or empirically sound, is based on physiology and cognitive processes, and offers hundreds of cases of anecdotal evidence of effectiveness.

THEORY

This model is based on systems and attachment theories. Both will be described briefly here. For those unfamiliar with these theories, a more complete description is available through the citations offered.

Attachment Theory

First as children and again as adults, people seek to feel safe by having someone to whom they are the most important thing in the world, called a primary attachment object (Bowlby, 1969). The bond created with the attachment object serves to regulate closeness to the object and creates working models of the object's dependability and whether the self is worthy and lovable. A healthy, loving bond is created when the attachment object makes the person a priority in life, gives positive attention, and shows support. As in mother–child or adult love relationships, the result of this attachment is that people feel safe in the world and good about themselves; they feel loved and important. The bond between people in this type of relationship has been shown to maximize physical and mental health, resilience, adaptability, and personality development in those involved (Burman & Margolin, 1992; Willis, 1991).

When one's attachment object is perceived as inaccessible or unresponsive, the person often responds with anger, anxiety, fear, and sadness, and will seek to reestablish the connection (Bowlby, 1988). As in divorce, this separation is often painful and leaves the person feeling unsafe and insecure.

Through the lens of attachment theory, divorced parents may be seen as coping with the loss of their primary attachment object (Bowlby, 1969, 1988). This loss is generally viewed as devastating whether it is the loss of a parent, a child, or a spouse. People experiencing this loss are often overwhelmed with emotions; they may feel depression, fury, desire for revenge, confusion, and anxiety (Bloom-Feshbach & Bloom-Feshbach, 1987; Bowlby, 1988). The need to mourn the loss of this object has been addressed in at least one existing model of divorce therapy (Bloom-Feshbach & Bloom-Feshbach, 1987), but the mourning suggested by these authors traditionally takes time, more time than children of divorce can afford to relinquish.

Systems Theory

A system is made up of components (called subsystems), each of which is a system itself, as well as being considered a subsystem of the original system (Klir, 1988). Organs and the circulation and respiratory systems (among other systems) form a body; car parts together form an automobile; people form relationship systems. Despite each of these being components of the larger system, they are also systems themselves with subsystems and functions of their own.

A system is greater than the sum of its parts and cannot be comprehended by only examining its parts (Klir, 1988; von Bertalanffy, 1950, 1968). Exploring the parts of a car or a human being will not allow full understanding of what that car or person is like when functioning as a system. As the elements of each system are interrelated, what affects one facet of the system impacts all other facets and the entire system.

Systems strive to maintain homeostasis, the status quo, and are in a constant state of regulation to maintain that stability. This is a function of the system, whether that system is an automobile or a marital relationship. They tend to resist change and monitor their environment for any need to self-correct back to homeostasis. This helps explain why people and relationships find change so difficult; they are systems. Systems function for some purpose, and their actions are controlled by each system's laws.

One final aspect of systems is the idea of circular causality. Unlike linear causality where A causes B causes C, with circular causality these elements are seen as interactive: A leads to B leads to C leads to A leads to B, and so on. Any point in this process could be considered the beginning. The idea of one system *causing* the event is removed because these systems interact with each other to create all events. In human relationships, if interactions were subject to linear causality then people would react the same way to the same behavior from different people. The reaction would be causal, the fault or responsibility of the initiator of the interaction. Instead, under the parameters of circular causality, people react to similar situations differently when interacting with different people. People are nice to some while not nice to others and tolerate similar behavior from some while not from others. This is not because that person is just not nice (linear causality), but rather, it is due to some manifestation of relational interactions between those people (circular causality).

In relation to the current model, systems theory explains why people get entangled in and appear unable to release themselves from interactional patterns. Through the lens of systems theory, relationship interactions become organized over time, forming patterns that maintain themselves (called homeostasis) (Steinglass, 1987). As the relationship system strives to maintain homeostasis, partners may get caught up in the system (act in accordance with the system's rules), and without understanding these dynamics, may feel controlled by their partners. In treating the couple systemically, neither person is seen as "right" or "wrong" or "good" or "bad." No one causes the problem; the negative cycle is the problem in which they both get trapped. Systems theory does not address issues concerning motivation and the internal dynamics of the person (Johnson & Greenberg, 1995).

TRADITIONAL TREATMENT APPROACHES

Three treatment approaches can be considered traditional regarding divorce therapy: psychoeducational models, solution-focused models, and a third (Bloom-Feshbach's) divorce therapy model. While the first two models ask parents to ignore or redirect their anger/hostility, the third acknowledges and attempts to deal with the anger by taking time to allow for the natural grieving for the loss of the marital partner. Psychoeducational courses are usually taught in groups while the other two types are done using individual or family therapy.

The most common course of treatment for divorcing parents is psychoeducational courses aimed at helping parents understand what children go through when parents divorce (Kramer & Washo, 1993). Although these courses are offered widely and are even required by some states, their effectiveness has been called into question (Braver, 1996). Each program contains a different curriculum lasting a different length of time, which makes evaluation difficult. Most parents are legally compelled to be present, and so often resist the process. Others take advantage of the opportunity that mostly encourages parents to look at divorce through the eyes of their children, to see their needs and feelings. With this new perspective, the goal is to motivate parents to put their anger aside for the sake of their children. Although these ideas seem admirable, evidence that they lead to behavior changes remains weak (Braver, 1996).

Solution-focused divorce therapy models have the parents focus on what goals they would like to reach and how they would get there (Kramer & Washo, 1993). As a cognitive-behavioral approach, like psychoeducational courses, it does not directly address parental anger other than to ask what would be needed to transcend those feelings. This approach often makes already overwhelmed parents feel more guilty, defeated, and incapable (Bloom-Feshbach & Bloom-Feshbach, 1987). This model, like the previous one, has little evidence of effectiveness.

One type of divorce therapy model does address parents' anger/hostility, viewing it as the loss of a primary attachment object. Practitioners of this therapy warn that extensive time may be required to allow the client to grieve the loss (Bloom-Feshbach & Bloom-Feshbach, 1987). Unfortunately, children do not realistically have time to wait months and years for their parents to mourn. By that time, battle lines may have already been drawn, damage may have already been done, and troubled trajectories for the children may already have been established.

THE NLP-EFT MODEL

The literature consistently states that conflict or hostility between parents after divorce contributes more than any other factor to a decline in parents' and children's well-being (Amato & Keith, 1991). Traditional divorce therapy models have not found a way to address this factor quickly and effectively. This new model (hereafter called the NLP-EFT Model) offers a two-component therapy based on NLP and EFT, specifically tailored to divorcing or divorced families.

Centrally examined using attachment theory, the problem is viewed as follows. Divorce leads to parental hostility because of the loss of the primary attachment object (for at least one parent). This hostility is expressed when parents: speak badly of their former spouses to their children (including expressing disgust or contempt through gestures such as folding arms, facial gestures, and tones of voice); send messages to their former spouses through their children (e.g., to request money or be critical of some lifestyle or habit); or seek vengeance through actions like withholding visitation rights or not allowing children the freedom to call the noncustodial parents. These are just a few examples of the innumerable stories children tell about living with divorced parents. That such hostility damages children is clear (Wallerstein & Blakeslee, 1989).

The NLP-EFT divorce therapy model proposes to deal with and minimize this hostility by: (1) acknowledging the normality of feelings of anger and hostility (due to the removal of the primary attachment object), (2) using NLP to remove the attachment to the ex-spouse, and (3) using EFT to restructure the parents' interactions based on their new relationship and attachments. This model uses a constructivist philosophy and systems and attachment theories to conceptualize the solution.

The NLP-EFT model is not appropriate for couples where violence has eroded the possibility of feeling physically safe in the presence of the offender. Many people feel anger or fury but do not act on those feelings; these people still may be appropriate clients for this therapy. This model is predicated on non-abusive parents who want to be in their children's lives. Both NLP and EFT will be described in detail in the following sections, concluding with a case example.

NLP

Neuro-Linguistic Programming (NLP) was created by Richard Bandler and John Grinder in the 1970s as a way to help people have what they wanted in their lives through hypnosis and special communication skills. They based this technique on the skills they observed in three therapists: Virginia Satir, Milton Erickson, and Fritz Perls. From speaking to and observing these three, Bandler and Grinder extrapolated characteristics which made these practitioners so successful. Some of these characteristics included their way of speaking gently and methodically and matching the client's mode of speech, as well as specific uses of language including reframing problems into possibilities. NLP combines a hypnotic use of language with specific details of the client's story (i.e., a tendency toward visual, audio, or kinesthetic terms). After a session of discussing the issue, the therapist creates a visualization script based on Erickson's hypnotic techniques and Satir's empathetic way of communicating to expand the choices currently available in the client's unconscious. As Linden (1997) states, "It offers a paradigm of how the brain works (neuro), about how language interacts with the brain (linguistic), and how we use this interaction to get the results we want for ourselves and others (programming)" (p. 31).

NLP sees all problems as rooted to a limited number of choices in the unconscious. When clients have more choices, they are assumed to make more effective choices for themselves. These limited choices are rooted in childhood where they faced some similar dilemma and had access to few, severely limited options. At the time an option was chosen which allowed survival, but it is no longer functional.

In short, NLP therapists' goals are to understand a person's subjective experience by learning how the person has internally represented the information, and to help him change that experience to one that will be more effective in his life. After an understanding about the internal representation is acquired by the therapist through the consultation phase, the therapist guides the client through a visualization process by which new images or metaphors replace old ones which are no longer working for the client. Other NLP processes, which are beyond the scope of this text, may be done by the client himself. Each NLP script tends to focus on different issues and different types of internal representation. Many examples can be found in and modified from existing literature (e.g., Andreas & Andreas, 1992).

Underlying Theories and Assumptions

Theories and assumptions on which NLP is based are not directly stated by the founders. Others have noted that this model is based on Freud's concept of the unconscious mind, systems theory, and Milton Erickson's hypnotherapy, and the philosophical framework is constructivist in this author's opinion. Beyond these concepts, basic assumptions expressed by NLP practitioner Peter Wryckza (Linden, 1997) include: (1) mind and body are part of the same cybernetic system (assumes systems theory); (2) every behavior serves a positive intention; (3) all behavior is useful in some context; (4) all the resources we need are inherent to our own physiology; (5) human interaction is systemic in nature; (6) the meaning of my communication to another is reflected in the response it elicits; (7) there is no failure, only feedback; (8) if something is possible for one person, it is possible for everyone; and (9) since experience is mediated through each person's body/mind, each person creates his own experience and is responsible for what happens.

Criticisms

NLP's critics have commented that this process only motivates people to take control of their lives without the practical skills of communication and behavior modification (so success would be short term). Critics also say that the bases for this therapy, namely, the unconscious mind and hypnosis, have not been established empirically. Even the critics, however, have not denied that NLP works. One critic stated that there seems to be no logical or scientific reason for NLP to work, yet it does work quite well so it may not matter why.

Empirical Evidence

All evidence of NLP's effectiveness appears to be anecdotal and from testimonies as reported throughout NLP literature (Andreas & Andreas, 1989). NLP has been used in psychotherapy for problems ranging from phobias to schizophrenia, and has been expanded outside the field of psychotherapy into the business and academic worlds (Linden, 1997). Its continued expansion and popularity also speak to some level of effectiveness.

Application of NLP to Divorce Therapy

When using NLP to treat divorce-related issues, the therapist works with attachment issues and the related emotions. In other contexts this same procedure also might be used on those struggling with issues of enmeshment or co-dependence. When people divorce, generally one or both of the parents are grieving the loss of their primary attachment object. Those feelings of attachment to or dependence on another person are often internalized as being physically connected to that person, by a cord, or like a tumor or some other representation (Andreas & Andreas, 1992). The thought of disconnecting from the object creates anxiety in the person as he fears being abandoned. Using NLP techniques, the therapist helps the client emotionally detach from the old object and reattach that connection to himself (or a higher power, depending on client's choice).

The NLP process allows the person to disconnect safely from the current object, identify the needs that attachment object was meeting, create a more evolved self, attach to the new self, respect the object, and elaborate on the new relationship with self (Andreas & Andreas, 1989). It is important to emphasize here that this procedure is not magic, but positive anecdotal evidence has suggested that it allows people emotional distance from the original object. With this distance, clients feel more in control and able to choose the options more closely aligned with their values, rather than acting out of anger or pain.

EFT

History

Greenberg and Johnson (1988) found that cognitive-behavioral and other forms of marital therapy may be missing something. That something was dealing with people's emotions. They posit that our emotional experiences are the essence of our experience and must be dealt with in order for a marital therapy to be effective in the long term.

Assumptions and Theoretical Principles

EFT founders state their assumptions and principles explicitly throughout articles and books on the subject. The model comes from a constructivist perspective using attachment theory, systems theory, and the results of John Gottman's (1991) research on marital distress. EFT uses this basis to implement experiential techniques aimed at restructuring couples' interactions. Attachment and systems theories were previously discussed. A brief discussion of Gottman's research follows.

Gottman's Research on Marital Distress

John Gottman's (1979, 1991) research found that negative interaction cycles, and the concomitant inability of couples to remain emotionally engaged, cause separation and divorce. Couples engage in a typical pattern of one partner becoming critical while the other withdraws (i.e., pursuer-distancer). If this pattern escalates to either an attack-attack or withdraw-withdraw cycle, eventually the marriage will end. Gottman (1991) concluded that for a marriage to be successful, couples must retain the ability to be emotionally engaged with each other in order to work through issues. For this to happen, people's level of anxiety (as measured through pulse rate) must be low enough that they can tolerate the discussion without exploding and can think clearly enough to solve the issues (Gottman, 1994).

Experiential Techniques

Instead of relying on insight to create lasting change in relationships, Johnson and Greenberg (1992, 1995) emphasize the need for couples to experience that change in the therapy room. Couples need to take chances in the safe environment created by the therapist and know that they will be guided through first efforts. Couples also know that an "unbiased" third person is there to guide them.

Major Concepts

Greenberg and Johnson (1988) state that couples' negative interaction cycles result from feeling a fear of losing their primary attachment object. Because of this fear, couples often become entangled in destructive ways of communicating like withdrawing or attacking, being overly rational, discounting the partner's concerns, or criticizing. In EFT, emotions are viewed as the window into people's internal world of attachment and models of self.

According to Gottman (1991, 1994), these negative interaction cycles, as they escalate and become more prevalent in the relationship, cause divorce. EFT offers a model of therapy that leads couples through a process of: (1) identifying their own core emotions, (2) communicating those emotions (thereby letting go of the less destructive ways of communicating), (3) understanding and taking responsibility for how their communication evokes responses in their partners (like anger or withdrawal), and (4) restructuring their interactions to be more genuine and vulnerable because of the renewed safety of the relationship (Greenberg & Johnson, 1988; Johnson & Greenberg, 1992, 1995).

Greenberg and Johnson (1988) emphasize that people entering therapy feel a loss of trust and connection with their partners. Therapy aims to create or recreate the accessibility and responsiveness that engender a safe environment where both partners are able to express their attachment needs.

Empirical Evidence

EFT has been studied extensively and is viewed as one of the most effective therapies for treating marital distress (Alexander, Holtzworth-Munroe, & Jameson, 1994; Dunn & Schwebel, 1995), including a study testing the creators' hypothesis of how change occurs (Greenberg & Johnson, 1988). Since shown to work, EFT has been used to treat other issues present in marriages such as depression, chronic physical illness, and post-traumatic stress disorder (Johnson, in press).

Specific Treatment Procedures

Overall, Greenberg and Johnson (1988) propose two goals of therapy: accessing and reprocessing emotional experience and restructuring the couple's interactions (Greenberg & Johnson, 1988). They created a nine-step process by which EFT could be implemented, and wrote a manual entitled *Emotionally Focused Therapy for Couples* (1988). The steps are as follows:

1. Delineating the conflict issues in the core struggle.
2. Identifying the negative interaction cycle.
3. Accessing the unacknowledged feelings underlying interactional positions.
4. Reframing the problem in terms of underlying feelings, attachment needs, and negative cycles.
5. Promoting identification with disowned needs and aspects of self, and integrating these into relationship interactions.
6. Promoting acceptance of the partner's experience and new interaction patterns.
7. Facilitating the expression of needs and wants, and creating emotional engagement.
8. Facilitating the emergence of new solutions.
9. Consolidating new positions.

Although a detailed explanation of each step is not possible here, an overall description of the process follows. The therapist begins by establishing a strong therapeutic alliance. Because EFT necessitates the exploration of clients' core emotions, they must feel safe and trust that they will be treated respectfully and fairly (Johnson & Greenberg, 1995). The clients are then guided to discuss some of their issues while the practitioner notes the interaction cycles, particularly those of pursuer/distancer and anger/withdrawal. As clients continue their discussions, the therapist facilitates a transition to discussing the underlying issues related to attachment, often asking about feelings of abandonment or rejection and the history of those feelings.

The therapist validates each person's experience and emphasizes how they unintentionally create the cycle and are currently trapped by it (through describing the cycle). The most significant parts of the therapy are when each partner can communicate his or her underlying emotional issues (e.g., "I feel like you do not need me anymore and will leave me if you become successful at work") rather than discussing the event (e.g., "I can't stand how much time you spend at work"). When one person relinquishes her defenses and speaks from her emotional core, the partner usually increases his barriers in a fearful attempt to reestablish homeostasis in the system. (Note that the originally angry partner is usually mistrusting of the changes in the originally withdrawn partner and may not respond encouragingly. This is normal as he is afraid to trust this person who has continually withdrawn from him.) Clients and the therapist must remain present and consistent, and continue to delineate the core emotions and interactions from the dialogue while the therapist encourages and validates couples' interactions at that depth.

Eventually, clients are able to acknowledge their needs and express them to their partners. Once couples begin to communicate in this manner, new solutions to old problems naturally emerge. The final step involves solidifying the new roles in couples' interactions. EFT does not follow the nine steps in a linear fashion but rather in a corkscrew-type manner, with steps repeated as necessary.

Application of EFT to Divorce Therapy

Johnson and Greenberg (1995) actually recommend that this therapy not be used for separating couples since in its current form it aims to make the primary attachment more secure. Johnson (in press) states, however, that "EFT works best for couples who still have some emotional investment in their relationship and therefore some willingness to really engage in the therapy process" (p. 12). In this light, EFT may be considered for divorced or divorcing parents, as they always will have an investment in each other's lives due to their children. In the NLP-EFT model, EFT is modified slightly to offer divorcing couples a process by which they might create a new, more superficial level of attachment that is safe.

Since EFT is normally conducted with people who seek to maintain or reestablish primary attachment with each other, couples are seen together. During therapy each person is asked to become extremely vulnerable as he expresses his underlying fears about himself as well as his emotions. This level of vulnerability is not necessary for divorced couples. The goal of this therapy is to establish minimal hostility, mutual respect, and trust regarding the children.

EFT with divorced couples differs from the traditional model in the following two ways. First, each adult is seen separately for approximately three sessions. During these sessions the therapist leads each person to identify her underlying emotions, to see the interactional pattern between the couple, and to acknowledge and take responsibility for her part in the pattern and the emotions she evokes in the other person.

Second, after seeing the parents together for four to six sessions at two-week intervals, the children are brought into therapy for two to three sessions. Here the parents express, and allow the children to experience, their new way of interacting. The purpose is for the children to hear from their parents together and to see consistency between their words and actions. The other purpose is for children to express their feelings and concerns to their parents. Further therapy is made available but not considered necessary.

CASE EXAMPLE

Tim and Sue, both 38, were married for 10 years and have recently divorced. They have two children, John (eight years old) and Sara (five years old). The couple was awarded joint legal custody, while Sue retains physical custody. Tim was ordered to pay $800 per month in child support. Sue initiated the divorce against Tim's objections. Tim wanted the couple to pursue counseling to try to save the marriage, but Sue said it was too late. Since the divorce, Tim has been very hostile toward Sue. Incidents include Tim telling the children that their mother broke up their home and that she was never really committed to the marriage, that she was just using him. Tim also told the children that Sue had left him so the children should not be surprised if she left them too. He was also sending messages to Sue through the children telling her that she better not buy anything for herself with the child support he sent and that no other man would want to go out with her as fat as she was. John began doing poorly in school, his grades declining from Bs to Ds, and he had gotten in a fight on the school playground. Sara started sucking her thumb and not wanting to leave her mother's side. She did not want to visit her father. Sue realized that the family was in trouble and sought divorce therapy with a clinic using the NLP-EFT model. Tim agreed to attend sessions without Sue present, both for his children and because he was beginning to have problems at work related to his temper.

The first and most important part of therapy with this model is the therapeutic alliance. Families must be comfortable with and trust that the therapist has their best interest in mind and would not do anything harmful. The therapists saw the parents separately for the initial consultation, NLP, and initially in EFT. Therapy with the children is not discussed in this paper.

While NLP was conducted with Sue to diminish any anger or residual attachment issues she had with Tim, Tim was the primary parent needing to rework his attachment to his ex-spouse. The session with Tim presented below was his second session. The first was used as a consultation and bonding session. To begin the session, Tim was asked to do some breathing exercises to relax and to sit in a reclining chair as the therapist guided him through the following process. For the sake of space, the session is presented as a monologue. The actual pace of the session is usually slow and deliberate but allows primarily for the flexibility of each client. This NLP section takes approximately 20 minutes.

Therapist: Tim, I want you to imagine that Sue has just walked in the room. If you have trouble seeing that, pretend that she just walked in. Now see yourself walking up to her and then walking around her. I want you to notice everything about her. What does she smell like? feel like? Now tune in to your feelings. What does it feel like to be around her? Do you feel very connected to her? How do you experience your connection to Sue? Do you experience yourself as physically attached to her in some way? Are you physically attached to some part of her body or is there some object that connects you? Where on her body is the connection, and where is it on your body? Notice how you experience this. How does it look? What does it feel like? How do you feel?

This step allowed the client to become aware of his over-connection to his ex-wife.

Therapist: Now think for a moment about breaking the connection just to know how it would be for you. You might do this with a saw or some other sharp object. Sever the connection now. Most people find this very uncomfortable which shows you that this connection was very important to you and served a significant purpose in your life. If you are uncomfortable, put the connection back. It is not time for you to end it yet; you aren't ready until you have something to replace it with.

This step allowed Tim to experience temporary independence, which would make him greatly uncomfortable given that his paradigm is that he is very attached to Sue.

Therapist: Now ask yourself what you want from Sue that would satisfy you. What do you want from her? What would that do for you? What are you looking for from her? Keep asking yourself until you reach a core answer like protection, love, security, or a feeling of value.

The therapist would continue these kinds of questions until the client signaled that he had found an answer. The purpose of this is to help the client find the positive aspects of this attachment, what he was getting out of having the attachment.

Therapist: Now turn 90 degrees either to your right or left. I want you to create a three-dimensional image of yourself as you would ideally like to be. This is you beyond your current level of functioning. This Tim knows you and loves you. This Tim appreciates you and wants to nurture and protect you. This Tim can provide you with all the needs you have just identified. Get a sense of what he is like. Notice how he looks, how he feels, how you feel around him. Does he glow? Do you feel his warmth?

Some people do not actually see this other self but get a sense of him instead. This step is called developing the evolved self.

Therapist: Turn around and see Sue. See and feel your connection to her. Now cut the connection with her and immediately connect to your new self in the same way you were to Sue. Notice how wonderful it feels to be connected to someone you can count on, someone in whom you can place all of your trust. This person will never let you down. Enjoy receiving from yourself what you had wanted from the other person.

This step transforms the connection to the other into a connection with the self.

Therapist: Now look back at Sue and see the severed connection. Take her cord and reattach it to another part of her. If there was no cord, see her connecting to a more evolved version of herself like you now are. Notice that this person is better off now just as you are. Feel that you are more able to be with her now. You now feel happy and peaceful with yourself and wish her well.

With this step the purpose is to wish the attachment object well, to be able to engage more fully and in a relaxed manner with that person, not to be emotionally reactive to her. This will allow Tim to deal with Sue more productively than was previously possible.

The final two steps in the process extrapolate on the new connection with the evolved self and go into the future to experience the new sense of security and resourcefulness in different situations. This solidifies the new attachment.

(*Note*: this procedure was modified from Chapter 3 in *Heart of the Mind*, entitled "Becoming More Independent in Relationships" [Andreas & Andreas, 1989].)

Once NLP was complete for both Tim and Sue, appointments were set up for each of them three weeks later. This lapse serves to have them both adjust to their new experience of themselves. During the first sessions after NLP both Tim and Sue expressed a big relief in the level of anger and hostility between them. Both stated that although they were still frustrated with each other and not really solving their issues together, they were more able to talk. Inevitably, their discussions ended with Sue getting angry and Tim hanging up on her. This pattern of interaction mimicked their pattern in the marriage. Now that the level of hostility had decreased the therapist could help them work to change their interactions.

EFT began with seeing the couple separately. The therapist assisted each of them in identifying their underlying emotions and understanding the parts each played in the interactions with the other. Sue came to see that her anger toward Tim was based on her fear that he would emotionally leave the children as she felt he had left her. Tim saw that his withdrawal from Sue, as well as his inconsistency with the children, centered around his fear that his children, like his ex-wife, would abandon him. Both Tim and Sue were able to see how their communication evoked the opposite of the desired response from the other. After repeatedly drawing out these feelings and patterns both Tim and Sue felt ready to meet together. A piece of that session appears below.

Therapist: So, why don't we begin this discussion by having the two of you discuss a normal issue that arises in your co-parenting situation. Tim, is there an issue that comes to your mind?

Therapist begins with Tim since he is the partner that traditionally withdraws.

Tim: Okay. A usual issue for us to deal with is when I want to see the kids when it is not a regularly scheduled day. That usually ends up in a big fight. As a matter of fact we got in a big fight because I am interested in taking them to an amusement park a week from Friday.

Therapist: Okay. Is this conversation acceptable to you Sue?

Sue: Yes it's fine.

Therapist: Okay, why don't the two of you have that discussion, beginning with Tim. Please remember your goals here. And I will be involved in the discussion as well, helping each of you process the information just like in the other sessions. Remember to focus on your underlying feelings. What happened in the fight?

Tim: All right. I don't understand what the problem is. I want to take the kids to have a great day and it's a problem. I honestly don't get it.

Sue: The kids are in summer day camp right now and you just expect them not to go to that when I'm paying for that. Why can't you take them on one of your normal days? It makes me so mad when you try to rearrange our schedules and our lives. You know you're not the only one who matters here.

Therapist: Okay, Sue, tell me how you feel when you say all that? You sound angry. Can you tell me what the anger is about?

Sue: You know we're divorced now and I don't want him trying to control our lives anymore. There's a reason this relationship is over.

Therapist: And what is that reason?

Sue: Tim cannot be counted on. I'm sorry but it's true.

Therapist: So it sounds like you are afraid that the children can't count on Tim any more than you felt you could.

Sue: Yes, that's it (begins crying). I don't want them to go through what I went through. And Tim has been so erratic with them and been telling them lies and telling them too much about adult issues. I don't feel like I can trust him. He's been mostly hurting them in the last year.

Therapist: Okay, so you didn't feel like you could count on Tim during the marriage and that left you sad and lonely, scared of losing him.

Sue: Yes, yes.

Therapist: And now that you're no longer married to him and you have some distance from that, you are still frightened that the children will not be able to rely on him? And you feel that there has been some evidence in the past year that your concerns are legitimate?

Sue: Exactly.

Tim: I understand your concerns. I've done some horrible things in the past year, and I am very sorry for that. I have been trying to make it up to the kids in the past three weeks and want to continue that. That's one of the reasons I want to take them to the park. You're going to have to start trusting me. They're not just your kids. I have a right to see them too, and not just when it's convenient for you. You don't have the power over my relationship with them.

Tim would not have been able to stay calm and take responsibility for his actions had it not been for NLP. Since Sue is no longer his primary object of attachment he can interact with her on a less emotional and more rational manner.

Therapist: Tim you speak about events of the past year and Sue mentioned that you might have been erratic with the children. Can you tell me about that?

Tim: Well, I have been hours late to pick them up sometimes and sometimes not shown up at all. They really haven't been able to count on me.

Therapist: Can you please explain what you were feeling during those times?

Tim: Fear. I don't know why, but they actually scare me.

Therapist: What do you think you were afraid of, given that you had just lost your wife?

Tim: Well . . . I guess . . . no . . . Maybe I was afraid that they would leave me too. Yeah, I guess there's part of me that's really scared that they'll leave me like Sue did. It scares the hell out of me. I actually feel like I want to run away just thinking about it.

Therapist: Okay, so you see that some of the reason you were acting erratically with the kids was because you were scared they would leave you. How are you dealing with those feelings now?

Tim: Actually it's not nearly as bad as it used to be. I don't feel nearly as insecure about it. I'm really able to have more fun with them in the last three weeks and not be so paranoid.

Therapist: So you feel like you have more control and are able to make better choices than you did in the months following the divorce?

Tim: Yeah, that's a good way of putting it. I feel like I'm not so crazed with anger and jealousy. I'm making much better decisions for myself and for the kids. I know I've got a lot of making up to do.

Sue: Yes, you do. I'm glad to see you realizing that. You did a lot of damage to them (angry tone of voice).

Therapist: So, Sue, you're still feeling angry, is that still about wanting the kids to be able to count on him?

Sue: Yeah, (calmer) I guess so. Even though I have seen some changes in him in the past few weeks, I'm really scared of them getting hurt. Bad enough it happened to me as an adult. They just don't deserve it. I'm so scared for them.

Sue is holding on to the anger and not quite ready to trust Tim's shift. This is normal; she will eventually soften as these kinds of discussions continue.

Therapist: Sue, focusing on the best interest of the children, can you ask Tim for what you would need to be able to begin trusting him again?

Sue: (looking at Tim and thinking) You know, I'm not sure. I think (in a softer tone of voice) what I need is to see you being consistent with the children. Would you consider making an effort at doing that?

Here Sue has softened significantly. She seemed realize she needed to give him a chance to prove himself to the kids and her.

They debate what that effort would look like and other logistics. At the end of the session the therapist warns the clients that their struggles will not suddenly end, and to expect themselves to sometimes slip into their old pattern of interacting. They developed those patterns over years and they would not be eradicated in a week's time.

CONCLUSION

With over a million divorces each year and the level of hostility between parents continuing after divorce, clinicians are being called upon to treat divorced and divorcing families. Hostility between parents has yet to be dealt with quickly and effectively in the traditional models of divorce therapy. This hostility often dominates those divorcing or recently divorced and interferes with parents making decisions that are in their children's best interest. A new model has been offered in this chapter that combines NLP and EFT.

Using an NLP technique, attachment to the ex-spouse would be substituted with attachment to a higher self or higher power. Dealing with hostility in this manner should diminish the overwhelming sense of loss and allow parents to make more appropriate decisions regarding co-parenting. Upon completion of NLP, EFT focuses on reworking the dynamics of the interactions between the parents. The goal is to have parents communicate the underlying meanings rather than the specifics of any problem, thereby allowing for more positive interactions. For example, an ex-husband might be encouraged to tell his ex-wife that he is scared that if she remarries the children will not need him anymore, rather than insisting that it is inappropriate for her to bring men into her home in front of their children. This combination of therapies deals effectively with the emotions and restructuring necessary for functional post-divorce relationships. Studies must be conducted to show the effectiveness of these treatments together.

REFERENCES

Alexander, J. F., Holtzworth-Munroe, A., & Jameson, P. (1994). The process and outcome of marital and family therapy: Research review and evaluation. In A. Bergin and S. Garfield (Eds.), *Handbook of psychotherapy and behavior change* (pp. 595–607). New York: Wiley.

Amato, P., & Keith, B. (1991). Parental divorce and adult well-being: A meta-analysis. *Journal of Marriage and the Family, 53,* 43–58.

Andreas, S., & Andreas, C. (1989). *Heart of the mind.* Moab, UT: Real People Press.

Andreas, S., & Andreas, C. (1992). Neuro-linguistic programming. In S. Budman, M. Hoyt, & S. Friedman (Eds.), *The first session in brief therapy* (pp. 14–35). New York: Guilford Press.

Bandler, R. (1979). *Frogs into princes.* Moab, UT: Real People Press.

Bandler, R. (1985). *Using your brain—for a change.* Moab, UT: Real People Press.

Bandler, R. (1993). *Time for a change.* Cupertino, CA: Meta Publications.

Beck, P., & Biank, N. (1997). Broadening the scope of divorce mediation to meet the needs of children. *Mediation Quarterly,* 14(3), 179–199.

Bloom-Feshbach, J., & Bloom-Feshbach, S. (1987). *The psychology of separation and loss: Perspectives on development, life transitions, and clinical practice.* San Francisco: Jossey-Bass.

Bowlby, J. (1969) *Attachment & loss: Vol. I: Attachment.* New York: Basic Books.

Bowlby, J. (1988). *A secure base.* New York: Basic Books.

Braver, Sanford L. (1996). The content of divorce education programs: Results of a survey. *Family & Conciliation Courts Review,* 34(1), 41–59.

Burman, B., & Margolin, G. (1992). Analysis of the association between marital relationships and health problems: An interactional perspective. *Psychological Bulletin,* 112, 39–63.

Dunn, R. L., & Schwebel, A. I. (1995). Meta-analytic review of marital therapy outcome research. *Journal of Family Psychology,* 9, 58–68.

Furstenberg, F. (1990). Divorce and the american family. *Annual Review of Sociology,* 16, 379–403.

Gottman, J. M. (1979). Detecting cyclicity in social interaction. *Psychological Bulletin,* 86, 338–348.

Gottman, J. M. (1991). Predicting the longitudinal course of marriages. *Journal of Marital and Family Therapy,* 17, 3–7.

Gottman, J. M. (1994). *What predicts divorce?* Hillsdale, NJ: Lawrence Erlbaum Associates.

Greenberg, L., & Johnson, S. (1988). *Emotionally focused therapy for couples.* New York: Guilford Press.

Hetherington, E. (1989). Coping with familiy transitions: Winners, losers, and survivors. *Child Development,* 60, 1–14.

Hetherington, M. E., Cox, M., & Cox, R. (1982). Effects of divorce on parents and children. In M. E. Lamb (Ed.), *Nontraditional families* (pp. 233–288). Hillsdale, NJ: Erlbaum.

Hetherington, M. E., Cox, M., & Cox, R. (1985). Long-term effects of divorce and remarriage on the adjustment of children. *Journal of the American Academy of Psychiatry,* 24(5), 518–530.

Johnson, S., & Greenberg, L. (1992). Emotionally focused therapy: Restructuring attachment. In S. Budman, M. Hoyt, & S. Friedman (Eds.), *The first session in brief therapy* (pp. 14–35). New York: Guilford Press.

Johnson, S., & Greenberg, L. (1995). The emotionally focused approach to problems in adult attachment. In N. Jacobson & A. Gurman (Eds.), *Clinical handbook of couples therapy* (pp. 121–141). New York: Guilford Press.

Klir, G. J. (1988). The role of uncertainty principles in inductive systems modelling. *Kybernetes,* 17(2), 24–34.

Kramer, L., & Washo, C. (1993). Evaluation of a court-mandated prevention program for divorcing parents. *Family Relations,* 42, 179–186.

Linden, A. (1997). *Mindworks: unlock the promise within: NLP tools for building a better life.* New York: Andrews McMeel.

Seltzer, J. A. (1994). Consequences of marital dissolution for children. *Annual Reviews of Sociology,* 20, 235–266.

Steinglass, P. (1987). A systems view of family interaction and psychopathology.

In T. Jacob (Ed.), *Family interaction and psychopathology* (pp. 25–65). New York: Plenum.

von Bertalanffy, L. (1950). The theory of open systems in physics and biology. *Science, 111,* 23–29.

von Bertalanffy, L. (1968). *General system theory: Foundations, development, applications.* New York: G. Braziller.

Wallerstein, J., & Blakeslee, S. (1989). *Second chances: Men, women, and children a decade after divorce.* New York: Ticknor & Fields.

Wills, T. A. (1991). Social support and interpersonal relationships. In M. S. Clark (Ed.), *Prosocial behavior* (pp. 265–289). Newbury Park, CA: Sage.

Chapter 11

A Brief Multiple Family Group Model for Juvenile First Offenders

William H. Quinn, David J. VanDyke, and Sean T. Kurth

Juvenile delinquency is prevalent and costly for communities, families, and youth. If current trends remain, it is estimated that juvenile crime rates will double by the year 2010 (Mulvey, Arthur, & Reppucci, 1997). Estimates in 1987 stated that 4% of all boys under 18 were diagnosable with conduct disorders and two-thirds would continue antisocial behaviors into adulthood. In 1996, an estimated 2.9 million arrests were made of youth under the age of 18. The FBI reports that juveniles account for 19% of all arrests in 1996 (*Crime in the United States, 1996*).

COST OF DELINQUENCY

The cost of adolescent crime extends across systems from federal and community governments to family and adolescent life. The federal juvenile justice system's annual budget in 1996 was approximately $1 billion. The rate of juvenile crime in the United States increased 12.5% from 1991 to 1993 and 30.1% from 1986 to 1995 (U.S. FBI, 1996). A community pays the costs of delinquent crime, ranging from repairs to reparations. These costs include replacement of materials and restoration of property damaged by vandals (i.e., each month one in four schools is vandalized at a total cost of about $200 million per year), as well as dealing with health care costs of victims of violent offenses (Emens, Hall, Ross, & Ziger, 1996; Quinn, Sutphen, Michaels, & Gale, 1994). The cost of incarceration of one youth is approximately $36,000 per year (Georgia Children and Youth Coordinating Council, 1997). Other costs are not as easily measured but are significant, such as the consequences of school failure and drop-out, unemployment, drug use, and mental and emotional instability.

A community's cost can be seen in the following hypothetical situation. Consider a small western Michigan town, population 20,000. It is a tourist town that is quite homogeneous. Due to increased delinquent offenses, security officers are hired to patrol the high school campus. Adolescents began "tormenting" the locals and tourists by "cruising the main drag" in their cars, fighting, vandalizing property, and harassing pedestrians. The community expands the police force in order to patrol the highly trafficked areas. This increases needed funds, from taxes, of the community. A youth is arrested for vandalism. The cost increases for his family. They are inconvenienced with the demands of going to meetings and appointments, paying probation, and in some cases attorney costs, not to mention dealing with the added family conflict and strain. Finally, the youth has to deal with the stigma of having become a part of the judicial system and is at risk for being involved with this system into adulthood. The compounding cost of juvenile delinquency can set a destructive trajectory for an adolescent.

There is a great need to find cost-effective methods to predict and intervene in juvenile delinquency. Interventions for delinquents range from incarceration to hospitalization to outpatient counseling. Intervention with first-time juvenile offenders is needed because of known high recidivism rates. Recidivism rates for first-time offenders are as high as 85% for those who participate in probation only (Department of Juvenile Justice, 1998). One form of intervention that is gaining popularity is family interventions. Research on delinquency and family factors demonstrates that the precursors of juvenile crime relate to family functioning and relationships. Some factors of influence include: poor parent supervision (Forgatch, 1991; Peeples & Loeber, 1994; Quinn et al., 1994; Sampson & Laub, 1994); lack of effective parenting skills (Howing, Wodarski, Kurtz, Gaudin, & Herbst, 1990); Johnson & Pandina, 1991); family transitions (Dornfield & Kruttschnitt, 1992); family history of crime (Quinn et al., 1994); and lack of parental prioritizing education (Walker and Silvester, 1991). Recent studies have tested the efficacy of treatments which include a parent focus and document that family treatment with seriously delinquent youths provides a strong potential for change (Alexander, Pugh, and Parsons, 1999; Chamberlain & Rosicky, 1995; Henggeler, Melton, & Smith, 1992).

The intervention discussed in this chapter is cost-effective because it is a relatively brief intervention (10 sessions), which is structured within a multiple family group context. Two therapists/group leaders facilitate the structure and process of the group dynamics, which minimizes the utilization of professional resources. The family group is viewed as a collaborative process with the therapists/group leaders. It is an important source of information and experience to foster change for individuals and families within the multiple family group model. An additional benefit of this intervention is that a service is provided to families who may not self-refer to services.

Although there is an acknowledgment of the value of mental health treatment, some individuals do not choose to seek assistance. This occurs for several reasons, including: a perception that personal troubles should be kept in the family, prohibitive costs of treatment, concern of a stigma, distrust of persons who deliver professional services ("How could you possibly know what my life is like?"), or fear of reprisal from an employer.

A multiple family group intervention program for first-time juvenile offenders was developed to provide support to mandated families. These are often families who are reluctant to seek help and skeptical of professional involvement (e.g., therapists, case workers) in their lives. A program liaison is present during court hearings when a referral is made to build the first bridge to the program. This time period, their first interaction with the juvenile justice system, appears to be the best moment for intervention. The framework of prevention and early intervention, not punitive in nature, is the basis of the program design. We view the incident of a juvenile coming to the attention of the court as "a family caught in society's net," in which the court is an arm of society with a mandate to protect the community. Concurrently, the multiple family group program orientation is to reach out to youth's much like the philosophy that existed when juvenile courts originated in 1899. Because the youths are entering the juvenile system for the first time they may be less rooted in negative peer-group interactions and delinquent identity processes, and not yet stereotyped as a "delinquent," in comparison to chronic repeat offenders. Intervention with first offenders has the potential for interrupting the delinquent cycle, as they may be more amenable to interventions than frequent offenders (Quinn et al., 1994). Efficacy of this brief intervention will be discussed later in this chapter.

TRADITIONAL TREATMENT APPROACHES

The causal pathway to delinquency seems to be a complex process throughout development (Dishion & Andrews, 1995; Moffitt, 1993) with many "on and off" ramps. Various disciplines place their emphasis on different "ramps." Intervention for delinquency develops out of the understanding of etiology. Four types of intervention are presented that reflect various conceptualizations.

Overview of Intervention Approaches

Not all children grow up in environments that foster positive genotype-environment interactions. Due to previous interactions, these children may be on an at-risk trajectory for delinquent behavior. If children do not have sufficient environmental and biological "protection," it is probable that they will participate in some delinquent behavior. For those who seek therapy, either self-referred or through agencies (court, social service), what are the available treatments and which treatments are effective in reducing the behavior problem? The following are four views on etiology and the interventions that "flow" from their epistemology.

Court and Punishment

Not all adolescents who participate in delinquent behavior enter into the juvenile justice system. However, it is typically through the courts that youths receive the label "delinquent." For purposes of this chapter, the focus will be on treatment for those who have a juvenile justice record. The traditional treatment for youths who get adjudicated for their first offense is probation. Probation officers and the judges determine the route for a youth. An adolescent will receive informal adjustment or probation for his or her first offense (unless the locality has specific programs for first offenders).

This sentence ranges from 30 days to one year, depending on the judge and local standards. Probation requires that the youth report to an officer of the court (juvenile probation officer) once a week and follow through with the agreed-upon conditions of probation. These conditions can vary greatly. The youth receives consequences for his or her actions in the form of punishment (probation). Unfortunately, probation officers are frequently "stretched too thin" and are only able to provide the minimal support that the youth needs. Another difficulty in probation is the lack of effective intervention. Probation remains primarily focused on creating disequilibrium in the youth's life and an expectation that the requirements for probation are inconvenient enough and the consequences unpleasant enough (i.e., stigma, family attention) to motivate behavior change. In this "treatment," punishment is the focus and the investigation. The youth's psychological needs and contexts are negligible. A recent study comparing the multiple family group approach described here with a group of juvenile first offenders placed on probation indicates that the multiple family group approach is a superior approach (VanDyke & Quinn, 2000).

Individual-Centered Therapies (Weiner, 1992)

Individual treatment conceptualizes delinquent behavior being primarily located within the individual. Individual treatment can be one-on-one interaction with a therapist or it can be with a group. Individual and family treatment differs according to the number of family members involved and the rationale behind the nature of change. Delinquency, in individual treatment, tends to be conceptualized as a result of an internal deficit of the youth. Moffitt's (1993) model implies two types of delinquents: life-course-persistent and adolescent-limited. Adolescent-limited delinquents are those youths who have delinquent behavior restricted to their teenage years. Life-course-persistent (LPC) youths have an earlier onset of delinquent behavior.

Using the DSMIV nomenclature, these youths would have had oppositional defiant disorder or conduct disorder characteristics from an early age. Patterson (1993) suggests that for these youths, their behavior is like the mythical Greek Chimera, the trait remains the same but changes in appearance throughout a child's development. Intervention must occur early in a youth's development. Previous developmental research (e.g., Aguilar & Carlson, 1998) suggests that the first three years of life are formative of delinquent behavior; therefore, the time for intervention is during the first few years of life.

Socialized and neurotic delinquents are similar to adolescent-limited delinquents. Both are a late-onset delinquency that is typically non-violent. Socialized delinquency is due to unsupervised conduct and peer influences. Neurotic delinquents originate from a response to a current stressful environment. The family has been supportive and nurturing, but at the present communication is poor. LCP delinquents are similar to Weiner's (1992) characterological and neuropsychological delinquents. These are the early onset (i.e., childhood), violent, and chronic type of delinquents. Characterological (psychopathic personality) delinquency is attributed to parental neglect and rejection as well as heredity. Neuropsychological delinquency is associated with psychotic symptoms. Typically, these delinquents have a neurochemical imbalance (e.g., ADHD, temporal lobe epilepsy). The determination of treatment is dependent on the diagnosis of delinquency. Socialized delinquency can be prevented through community-based activities to reduce the negative social environment. Other interventions are job training and placement (Shore & Massimo, 1973), and community-based behavioral interventions (Kazdin, 1987).

Intervention with characterological delinquency is long-term psychotherapy that involves therapists skilled in collusive treatment. Collusive treatment does not challenge and confront the youth, but suggests ways the antisocial actions can change into beneficial behavior (Doren, 1987). Typically, this intensive work requires residential treatment. A disadvantage in individual treatment is that it typically requires lengthy interventions that are costly to both the family and the agency that provides these services. Another disadvantage is that the youth continues to return to the similar family, peer, and community context, which could have influenced the behaviors. These disadvantages are addressed in the following treatment, family therapy.

A Family View: Family Therapy and Multiple Family Group Intervention

We believe a systems perspective is necessary in understanding the multiple influences on delinquency. Delinquency emerges through the reciprocal interaction of the biological and environmental factors through childhood and adolescence. Since there are multiple systems interacting with each individual's genetic and biological makeup, it seems reasonable that there are multiple causal paths into and out of delinquency.

The interventionist must take into account multiple contexts (e.g., family, peers, school, neighborhood, culture, cohort), domains of behavior, and the interaction between them within an adolescent's distinct (physical, emotional, social, cognitive) development (Bronfenbrenner, 1986).

Family Therapy

Intervention must reach beyond the individual, since it must address numerous contexts. Family therapists believe that there are specific processes critical to changing behavior: parenting (Schmidt, Liddle, & Dakof, 1996); family coalitions (Minuchin, 1974); and family conflict, flexibility, and positive affect (Liddle, 1996). Family therapists intervene in numerous subsystems in order to address the reciprocal nature of change (e.g., parent's influence on adolescent's behavior and adolescent's influence on parent's behavior) (Scarr & McCartney, 1983).

Chamberlain and Rosicky (1995) conducted a meta-analysis of the efficacy of family therapy in treating adolescent conduct disorder and delinquency. They continued the work of Kazdin (1987) and Shadish, Montgomery, Wilson, & Wilson (1993), investigating therapeutic interventions. Interventions are becoming more ambitious because of the multiplicity in causal paths. Chamberlain and Rosicky looked at 163 studies of family therapy from 1989 to 1994. In their analysis they found encouraging effect sizes that "family therapy interventions appear to decrease delinquent behavior compared to individual, group and no treatment" (p. 445). Due to different ages and outcomes (conduct disorder and delinquency), generalization of the findings must be done cautiously.

Three major forms of family therapy were discussed. The first two types, social learning family therapy (SLFT) (Miller & Prinz, 1990) and structural family therapy (SFT), intervene in areas of parent–adolescent patterns, parental cohesiveness, and nurturing and discipline skills (Minuchin & Fishman, 1981; Quinn et al., 1988). Both treatments locate etiology of problems in the family, not the child. Marital adjustment and conflict influence the amount of warmth parents show to a child. Their parenting style influences delinquent behavior in the child. The problem behavior must be addressed at multiple levels: the couple's communication and connection, parenting skills, and the child's expression of feelings. The third therapy is multi-target ecological treatment (MET). MET not only embraces a systems perspective, it includes cognitive restructuring and interactional change within the family. It focuses on personal development and multiple causes and reciprocal processes of a delinquent. Therefore, intervention is on multiple levels (school, family, peers, and individual). One form of this therapy is multi-systemic therapy (MST) (Henggeler, Cunningham, Pickerel, Schoenwald, & Borduin, 1996). Those using MST believe that "treatment of serious antisocial behavior in juveniles can be successful when the known determinants of antisocial behavior are intensively addressed in the natural environment with youths and families" (Henggeler, Borduin, Melton, Scherer, & Hanley, 1997). Interventions with MET/MST are intrafamilial interactions (e.g., limit setting, own personal barriers) and extrafamilial interactions (e.g., PTA, limit negative peer interaction). These activities include emphasizing positive and systemic strengths for change, promoting responsibility, and having specific task-oriented interventions. Studies have shown family therapy is more effective than individual group (Chamberlain, 1990; Chamberlain & Reid, 1991) and individual therapy (Mann, Borduin, Henggeler, & Blaske, 1990). MET appears to be the best fit of the family therapies for delinquency.

One difficulty with family intervention in treating juvenile delinquency is a family's reluctance for treatment when it is viewed as "the youth's fault." This concept of moving the onus from the identified client to a systemic perspective requires a change of attribution by the family (i.e., that I as a parent might be part of the problem and/or solution). Families with blame directed at the youth present obstacles to interventionists because they may not attend scheduled sessions, refuse to participate in discussion if they do attend, and devote their time and energy to blame or worry about the deficits of their youth.

While family therapy is a viable method of treatment, it suffers from the mistaken assumption that all families want help and that they are willing to make space in their lives to seek it. This is particularly problematic for families of youth offenders because of the ease or convenience by which parents, for example, can point blame and absolve themselves of responsibility (i.e., "I didn't do the crime so why do I have to do the time?"). Therefore, they refuse to participate in treatment without active and skillful recruitment by professional interventionists. We have found that a solution to this challenging problem is to utilize other families who become a support system and valid each other's experiences. A collaboration is established which shifts the intervention structure from hierarchical (judge/ probation officer/interventionist and delinquent/family) to a collaborative process in which the judge and probation officer are removed from the intervention and the interventionist serves as facilitator and program organizer.

Multiple Family Group Therapy

Multiple family group intervention expands on the MET. The assumptions about the etiology of delinquency and the need for addressing the multiple contexts of the adolescent's development are similar. The difference arises out of the focus of family therapy in the context of a group of families. Quinn et al. (1994) have developed a multiple family, ecological treatment within a group model for first-time offenders and their families. The reasons to develop a multiple family group were based on the following principles.

As discussed earlier from Chamberlain and Rosicky's study, many traditional methods of rehabilitation and problem-resolution have not been shown to be effective in preventing recidivism, compared to family interventions. Family interventions alter the ecological context for youths in ways that may curb delinquency and contribute to improved functioning and well-being. However, group interventions are beneficial because group processes build on the trust-relationships among families who share common problems and concerns and see value in the views/opinions of those sharing human dilemmas. This group work can create a caring and accountable community that penetrates the veneer of youth or family defensiveness that continues well past the duration of the intervention. A network of relationships is formed and strengthened which promotes support and solution-building beyond the scope of the actual program length.

Another issue a therapist must consider is the historical and cultural experiences of the adolescent and family. Disempowered and marginalized families have grown to distrust professional systems due to their costly, cumbersome, or dissimilar living circumstances; therefore, the power of a group can bridge these divides and provide a sense of understanding, validation, and hope for successful adjustment. Professional intervention is costly and institutional demands are high; therefore, multiple family group intervention is cost-effective because fewer professionals are needed to meet the needs of more families. If working in conjunction with a court system, multiple family groups also assist the juvenile court staff, which can condense their time with individual youths.

In addition to being cost-effective for family members compared to family therapy, it is cost-effective for the community compared to hospitalization or incarceration (Chamberlain & Rosicky, 1995). The goal of this intervention is to disrupt the development of delinquent behavior by dealing with cognitive and contextual factors of all family members (Dodge, 1998). Building family involvement early, including siblings, can not only provide remediation for the delinquent youth but also provide prevention for other siblings within the family by changing the context they are experiencing in the family context. Additional strengths that are intrinsic in multifamily group interventions are: utilizing the family's skills for themselves and other families, increasing a sense of efficacy, fostering a sense of collaboration through feedback for and from others, addressing relevant issues (sex, drugs, parenting, peers, education) from multiple perspectives, and providing models for change.

These sources of change can be group elements such as broader parent/adult support and guidance that increases the minimal parent presence or involvement, and conflict-resolution scenarios that resolve chronic problems of youths, such as methods to avoid drug-selling attempts by others or conflicts with a teacher. Collaboration among group leaders, adolescents, the family, the court, and the school provides opportunity for change in numerous contexts.

FAMILY SOLUTIONS PROGRAM APPROACH

Brief Description

The purpose of the Family Solutions Program (FSP) is to help juvenile offenders and their families in groups find solutions that will assist them in preventing repeat criminal offenses and achieving personal and family well-being. The program has established 10 weekly sessions that are designed to reduce juvenile crime, encourage parental involvement, increase parenting skills, increase youths' life skills, utilize families' strength and resources, increase communication skills, and promote educational success. The 10 weekly (2 hours each) session time frame was established to conform to state law disallowing any court obligation of a first-time juvenile offender to exceed 90 days, and to provide "a light at the end of the tunnel," providing a sense of completion that families could see at the outset so that their motivation would be high.

The program requires that both the adolescent and parent(s) attend all 10 sessions for successful "graduation" or completion. Each session comprises educational material, group discussion, family activities, and homework assignments. The goal is to make a systemic change in the families and the way they interact in their daily contexts. Upon successful completion of the program, there is a graduation night to acknowledge the changes that the families have made, and to celebrate a new trajectory for the youth and family's life.

History of the Family Solutions Program

The Family Solutions Program (FSP) was initiated in 1992, with a grant funded by the U.S. Office of Juvenile Justice and Delinquency Prevention and the Georgia Children and Youth Coordinating Council, to test an innovative model to deter youth crime. Using a prevention/early intervention approach, targeted for the program were juvenile first offenders and their families. Typical juvenile offenses include assault, criminal trespass, unruly behavior, and shoplifting. The program is driven by two major assumptions: (1) intervention with first offenders may provide a secondary prevention approach to curb the high rate of reoffenses committed by juvenile delinquents, and (2) confirmed family influences on juvenile behavior might be modified to provide a more nurturing, supportive, and resourceful environment for adolescent development and well-being.

A risk assessment was developed and has been administered to all first offenders referred by the juvenile court prior to the inception of the FSP. The purposes of the risk assessment were: (1) to identify factors that might make the FSP an inappropriate intervention (i.e., no parent involvement possible, drug addiction), (2) to utilize information on families to construct relevant components of the program (i.e., parent–youth conflict, academic deficiencies, recruitment of adults currently experiencing family estrangement), (3) to utilize data as preassessment on program evaluation, and (4) to provide a context for recruitment through alliance-building with families.

The FSP is a weekly 10-session, multiple family group program which youths and their parents must attend to complete their obligation to the juvenile court. Siblings and extended family such as grandparents, aunts, and uncles are encouraged to attend also. The inclusion of family members not only provides opportunities to resolve problems or alter dynamics within the family; it provides the additional benefit of reducing the likelihood that families will fail to come because of obligations of supervising younger children.

Groups comprise, on average, six to eight families. The program has established topics; however, family collaboration is emphasized and any group member can request a desired topic. An intervention manual including sections on working with families; group process; risk assessment; session topics including goals and objectives, handouts, activities, homework, and case vignettes; and evaluation instruments are provided to the group leaders for standardization and effective program implementation. To complete the program families must attend all sessions, and participate in group activities and discussion. To date, over 600 families have graduated from the FSP.

Basic Assumptions

The following beliefs are shared with the families during the first session (this set of beliefs is listed on our program brochure, which is distributed to each family in the court upon referral). We believe that:

- Families must be included in helping solve the problems of youths.
- Families coming together can provide a means to find solutions that will improve functioning within the family.
- Youths and families can do better when they express their ideas to others in a friendly and cooperative atmosphere.
- Families can learn and become hopeful with involvement from other families.
- Families and individuals do best when they feel a part of their local community.

These beliefs motivated the way we developed, organized, and implemented our intervention.

Group Process

The FSP is grounded in an ecosystemic perspective in which systems and their interactions impact an individual's behavior (Brofenbrenner, 1986, 1994). A multiple family group intervention model serves as a practical translation of this perspective because it attempts to make a wider sweep of a youth's circumstances, embedded in family, highly influenced by peers, and connected to institutions such as school and community resources.

The uniqueness of a group is that it is more than the sum of its parts (Lewin, 1931, 1935). Group discussions become a means of change in which the group context becomes a social microcosm, an opportunity for corrective emotional experience, and an interactional laboratory (Yalom, 1995). This group experience provides individuals an opportunity to reduce the distortion in their problematic view of themselves or others (e.g., a youth, other adults, or a stranger trying to help them).

The group process helps members in two ways: (1) to develop more effective social skills, and (2) to experience empathy from others as well as express empathy toward others. Members can express dreaded emotions that can be open to reality-testing and evaluation by others. This experience allows persons to reassess the appropriateness and usefulness of these emotions. With family members who are reluctant to open themselves up to a professional they are required by the court to include in their lives, the shared group experience reduces the direct interaction with a professional and encourages support and empathy from those in similar circumstances. In time, of course, an effective group leader can engender trust and create honest and genuine interaction with family members, which will serve to provide group stability, guidance, and new learning.

In the FSP, helping each person change in a manner that would improve a relationship or contribute to the other's well-being can be done when those affected are present. In a multiple family group model, parents can learn from other parents certain behaviors that are conducive to effective parenting and supportive relationships with youths.

Parents can learn from other youths that are not their children. For instance, if parents observe the struggles of other children, they may be less likely to view their own children as defective or maladjusted. Parents may also have interactions with other youths that are enjoyable. This helps remind them that children have good qualities and that these qualities might be found in their own children.

There are important characteristics of small group dynamics that contribute to good outcomes. The presence of these characteristics may depend on the nature of the group, the stage of the group process, and the training of the leader. We believe that these characteristics are significant contributors to success: cohesion, structure of the group, leadership style (collaborative instead of authoritarian), respect for everyone's views, safety in ability to share, and emotional content encouraged by the group. Group members must be active in the process. In fact, refusal to participate after many attempts using many multiple approaches to enlist active involvement makes a family ineligible to complete the FSP. Content of group experience must cast out the belief of independent selves traveling in different orbits. Instead, family members, including parents, share in a journey in which they are all important and influence each other. This new belief leads to new ways of communicating and behaving within the family.

SPECIFIC ASSESSMENT AND TREATMENT

Referral and Recruitment

The assessment phase of the FSP starts when a first-time juvenile offender is referred to our program by the juvenile court. The marriage of the juvenile court system and the FSP is crucial to the success and survival of this program. It is important to remember that the FSP is designed for first-time juvenile offenders. Most of the first-time offenders in our program are adjudicated in a process known as an Informal Adjustment.

At the Informal Adjustment, the youth admits guilt for the crime to the probation officer (or FSP liaison if sworn in as a court officer) in order to bypass standing before the judge. The family is then referred to the FSP, and a representative from the FSP is available to speak with the family. This is also the time when the families are given an introduction to the program, given a brochure, and informed about the times and meeting place for the program. After the Informal Adjustment and referral to the FSP, the family then proceeds to complete the FSP risk assessment.

Risk Assessment

The risk assessment is an instrument that both the youth and parent (both parents if possible) fill out while they are at the juvenile court. It is important to inform the parents that the information collected from the risk assessment is confidential and will not be shared with the juvenile court unless legally required. The FSP representative administering the risk assessment will inform the family that we are collecting this information for three reasons.

First, the risk assessment assesses whether or not the family is an appropriate candidate for the program. Second, the risk assessment provides some information that helps us prepare program content and process that conform to family issues and needs. Third, the FSP liaison informs families that information gathered from the the risk assessment will be used to determine what special topic areas we might address during the program (Quinn, 1998).[1] After this information has been explained to the family, the leader will divide the family so that each member can complete the risk assessment independently.

The risk assessment asks general demographic questions about age, gender, race, income, and level of education (parents), and specific areas of functioning within the family that help us conceptualize the overall risk of recidivism for the family. Constructs that the risk assessment measures are school performance and behavior, parental supervision, peer associations, alcohol usage, family involvement in crime, family functioning, delinquency index, the parental relationship, family coping skills, and transitions (e.g., death of a family member, a parent's "friend" moves in, or moves that might be affecting the family). An assessment of these areas is important in conceptualizing possible strengths or deficit areas for these families.

The risk assessment phase is an important time for joining because it is often the first face-to-face meeting with the family. This is an extremely important part of the program because the family may meet a referral by the court with ambivalence or opposition. It is important for the group leader administering the risk assessment to be both empathetic to the family's problems and to be an advocate for the program. The leader needs to be clear in explaining the program and describing how attending the program will benefit the family. For instance, the group leader will inform the family about group activities such as the name game and will inform the family about the success rate of FSP families.

A risk assessment or screening tool has several functions. The conceptualization and understanding of the various areas of the family via the risk assessment is important not only in the delivery of the treatment program, but in identifying possible risk areas that leave families susceptible to recidivism. The FSP is based on the systemic and ecological belief that various systems of their everyday lives interact with and affect the developing person and/or family. An assumption of the FSP is that the families in the program have strengths that, when accessed, can maximize each other's competencies to confront the problems that resulted in their being involved with the juvenile justice system. The FSP works under the premise that families can help themselves and other families when they are working collaboratively within the structure of the FSP.

By using the risk assessment, group leaders are better able to assess with which systems or areas a particular family might be having problems. The risk assessment also gives the program leaders information about other family members who could be included in the FSP (i.e., non-custodial fathers). Contact is made with family members such as extended family or non-custodial fathers to invite them to the FSP. One area where the group leaders have become influential is in helping parents build a positive relationship with their child's school. Often many of the parents in the FSP program have had adversarial relationships with either the school or one of their children's teachers. The leaders, as well as the other FSP group families, are able to give the family possible solutions to their problem through their own personal experiences.

FSP also assists families in their dealing with the juvenile court. We have often found that families are not well-informed and are intimidated by the juvenile court. Through conversations during the program, the families gain understanding into the process and the systemic aspects of the juvenile court.

The time when the group leader administers the risk assessment is a vital part of the program and in essence is when the program begins. This initial contact with the family is the time when the group leader begins to build an alliance with the family.

APPLICATION OF THE FAMILY SOLUTIONS PROGRAM

The FSP is a 10-session program for the offending youths and their parent(s). These sessions are conceptualized into three progressive stages: (1) joining, cohesion and trust building; (2) interpersonal/family skill building; and (3) improved decision making (see Table 11.1).

Stage One

The overall goal for stage one is to have the group leaders join with the families and help the families join with each other. Particular goals are to build trust, group cohesion, group commitment, and cooperation. This stage begins with the initial contact with the family in the court and joining is the primary goal through the first two sessions of the FSP. (These goals are of primary focus in the first few sessions but are also continuously built upon throughout the program.)

The building of trust, group cohesion, and cooperation are facilitated through activities built into the FSP. Activities, such as traffic jam, family contract, and the jail visit, are designed to help the families get to know each other and to begin the process of having different members of the group help each other.

Another activity to build group cohesion is a set of role-plays performed by the group leaders. The FSP leaders role-play stereotypes of what those in the group (parents, youths, and FSP leaders) may be thinking and feeling. The role-play of the youth includes statements such as, "I won't talk if I have to come here"; "I could be watching TV." Statements in a parent role-play might be, "I didn't do anything wrong, why do I have to come," or "I have too much to do to be here every week." Not only are there role plays of a youth and parent, but also a group leader. The statement might

Table 11.1
Three Conceptual Stages of the Family Solutions Program

Stage	Sessions	Goals of Stage	Group Activities
1	Joining, Cohesion, and Trust Building (Risk Assessment, Sessions 1 and 2)	• Joining with families • Building trust and group cohesion • Building group structure • Cooperation	• Risk assessment • Name game • Traffic jam • Toothpicks & gumdrops • Group rules • Negotiating topics
2	Interpersonal/Family Skill Building (Sessions 3–7)	• Communication • Creating a home environment for learning	• Ideal parent/ideal child • Behavioral contracts • Educational planning • Parents—parenting skills
3	Improved Decision Making (Sessions 8 and 9)	• Improve decision-making skills of youths and parents • Learn how to handle conflicts in a positive manner • Assist families in finding "solutions" to their problems • Assessing consequences	• "Multiple Choice" video • Conflict-resolution role-plays by youths • Positive interaction (e.g., decorative cards) • Jail visit
	Graduation (Session 10)	• Receive acknowledgment for participation • Celebrate all that the families accomplished during the program	• Present graduation certificates • Present cards to youths • Presentation by inspirational speaker or civic leader
Additional Group Sessions			
	Community service activity	• Have youths participate in an activity in their community	• Homeless shelter, assisted living community

be made, "I could be home with my own family, but if I can help someone here, I am willing to stay."

Parents and youths are encouraged to add to these statements. Usually at least one parent will state, "Well, do we have to say something negative?" or "I want to be here because I knew we needed help." This kind of statement provides another and more positive view of their participation in the program from other families.

Stage Two

The second stage of the FSP is focused on skill-building, which is the focus of Sessions 3 through 7. These sessions focus on topics such as communication, problem-solving, education, and an optional topic decided on by the families or the group leaders. This selection process encourages collaboration and shared responsibility among group members. For example, one of the activities that we use to help generate discussions about communication is called "Ideal Parent, Ideal Child." In this activity (the youths and parents are grouped separately), both the youths and the parents generate a list of qualities that would make up an ideal parent or child that could be placed in a "want-ad." The youths and parents are then brought together to discuss and compare their lists. This activity allows for discussions about the roles and expectations the parents and youths have for each other. This activity also allows for a time of self-reflection for the youth and the parent, in which they are able to consider their own behaviors, and evaluate possible areas for growth and change. This experience opens family members up to change.

Another activity that we employ in regard to communication is the development of a family contract. With the family contracts, the youths and parents negotiate behaviors that they would like to see more of in each other. In exchange for meeting these expectations, they reward each other with a negotiated consequence (e.g., going to the movies or shopping together). This activity helps generate discussions about the expectations, roles, and rules of the family.

The contracts encourage a different experience in the parent–youth relationship. The emergence of successful contracts provides evidence that negotiations and agreements are within the realm of possibility in the relationship. It would be simplistic to think that a contract resolves all differences; however, more enthusiastic and hopeful attitudes emerge, which help resolve other serious and conflictual issues.

The group is led to focus on the importance of education in the family's life, by having the family members complete a schedule of their weekly routines. The group leaders then assess how much time is focused on education. Often the activities parents and youths place on the schedules do not focus on education. The group leaders help the group members generate ideas of different activities in which they could engage that would be focused on education. The goal is to strengthen parental advocacy of the youth's educational experience toward success. A recent feature on a national news show portrayed a 102-year-old African-American man who learned to read at 98, yet he helped raise seven children, all of whom graduated from college. This six-minute feature was purchased from a national network and is now shown to the families as a method for initiating discussion on what parents can do to promote academic success. This video also circumvents the predictable parental frustration expressed in a group that they are too busy, have other responsibilities, or have too few skills to facilitate educational success of their children. Thus the discussion is centered on ways parents can overcome barriers to helping their children succeed, instead of ways that make it difficult or impossible to help.

Another session in the second stage is the youths' trip to the local jail, where they are educated about jail life and given a tour. The purpose of the jail visit is to make visible to them the harsh realities of being incarcerated. While the youths excitedly depart for the jail as if it were a field trip, with noise and exuberance, they are usually extremely quiet and self-reflective after the jail visit. While they are at the jail, the parents meet at the program site to discuss positive parenting skills such as appropriate ways to discipline and promote positive interaction. During this time the parents are encouraged to be advocates for their children's education and discuss the approaches that would allow them to help their children be more successful.

Stage Three

The last stage of the FSP focuses on improving decision making. This stage is usually completed during sessions 8 and 9 of the program, but there are often times when these issues arise earlier in the FSP. During one of these sessions the group members will watch and discuss a video, "Multiple Choices" (a video that has received an Emmy award in its category), the theme of which is the consequences of bad decisions youths have made related to crime and delinquency that have resulted in incarceration.

This video presents youths in incarcerated settings and illustrates the consequences of choosing a life of crime and choosing to associate with a negative peer group. This video often leads to group discussions about peer associations and decision-making markers that the youths confront in school and in their neighborhoods.

The other decision-making session focuses on conflict-resolution. During this session the youths role-play conflictual situations that they face in their everyday lives. They perform two role-plays about a specific conflict. The first demonstrates how a conflict can be handled counterproductively, and the second shows how a conflict can be handled successfully by applying appropriate "solutions" to the conflict. Solutions are solicited and generated from the entire group.

While the youths are generating and practicing role-plays, the parents complete decorative cards for the youths. The cards have each youth's name on it and state "what I like about you." The parents each sign every card, pointing out the positive qualities of the youths that they have observed during the past 10 weeks. For example, "You are a good leader," or "You have a great sense of humor" are common statements. These cards are a surprise for the youths and are presented to them at graduation.

The youths in the FSP are also required to participate in a community service activity. They participate at a community site such as volunteering at a homeless shelter or assisted-living community. One of the limitations of individual or single-family therapy is that the dimension of giving in human relationships is not required. That is, there is no expectation that the client care for the therapist, only vice versa. Therefore, the client is not typically viewed as someone who could become more productive, worthwhile, or fulfilled with the choice to contribute to the lives of others. In the multiple family group model, each individual is expected to not only contribute to the lives of others in the group, but to others in the community as well. This session usually occurs during this stage of the program, but it can be scheduled earlier in the program.

The program concludes with session 10, in which the families participate in a graduation ceremony and potluck dinner. The youths and the parents are presented a graduation certificate, and an inspirational speaker or civic leader (such as the local juvenile court judge) will speak to the families. Each youth also receives his or her card and is asked to read two things from the card to the whole group. Finally, group members are asked to provide testimonials regarding how the FSP has impacted them.

EMPIRICAL EVIDENCE OF EFFECTIVENESS

Evidence of Efficacy

A juvenile court in time will want to know whether a prevention/early intervention program for youth offenders keeps them from returning to court. The FSP has been serving juvenile delinquents and their families for the past nine years. From 1992 to 1999, there were 233 families who graduated from the FSP who had complete information and could be considered for the comparison study, while 117 had complete data who were referred but did not attend or complete the program.

Neither group, graduates or drop-outs, received any other family treatment throughout the court's processing of the juvenile offense. We developed two processes to evaluate the effectiveness of the program. The first

Table 11.2
Comparisons between Intervention Groups on Recidivism

| Variable | Percentage | | X^2 | df | p |
	No Reoffense	Reoffended			
Total (N = 542)			51.83	3	.000
FSP Graduates	78.1 (182)	21.9 (51)			
FSP Drop-outs	50.4 (59)	49.6 (58)			
Probation	44.3 (47)	55.7 (59)			
Male (N = 320)			18.94	3	.000
FSP Graduates	72.9 (97)	27.1 (36)			
FSP Drop-outs	50.9 (28)	49.1 (27)			
Probation	45.1 (32)	54.9 (39)			
Female (N = 222)			37.22	3	.000
FSP Graduates	85.0 (85)	15.0 (15)			
FSP Drop-outs	50.0 (31)	50.0 (31)			
Probation	42.9 (15)	57.1 (20)			

Note: The number of youths/families in each cell are found in parentheses.

process is measuring the recidivism rates of the youths who are remanded to the Family Solutions Program. In the juvenile courts and geographic areas where this program has been in existence for those nine years, virtually all first-time offenders are referred to this program. The data on youths presented here include both "graduates" and drop-outs ("non-graduates"). Most youths in the drop-out group never attended the FSP; however, a small percentage attended one or two sessions but did not attend the required number to be considered completers. Youths/families who did drop out (failed to attend the FSP) were placed on probation by the court. We track all youths/families who were referred to the FSP (graduates and drop-outs) the youths' involvement in the juvenile justice system from their first offense to the time they turn 17 years of age. The process of tracking since 1992 has involved receiving and reviewing, on a monthly basis, the juvenile court docket and matching it with a master list of families referred to the FSP.

During the existence of this program, the rate of recidivism for youths who graduate from the FSP is less than half compared to those that do not attend (see Table 11.2 for overall difference between "graduates" and non-attenders).

Only 22% of youths who graduate from the FSP reoffend, compared to

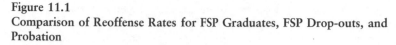

Figure 11.1
Comparison of Reoffense Rates for FSP Graduates, FSP Drop-outs, and
Probation

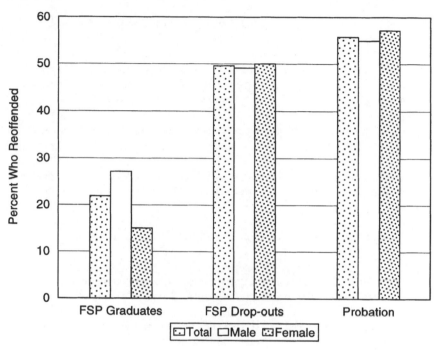

50% of the FSP non-graduates. In addition, a comparison group of juvenile first-offenders from a different juvenile court in a nearby county was formed. In this county, all first-time offenders are placed on probation (N = 106). In comparing the charts on these youths over the same period of time, the reoffense rate is even higher than both FSP groups. The reoffense rate of youths placed on probation is 56%; 44% did not reoffend. A chi-square analysis was conducted on the data to examine whether the differences on the reoffense rate for the three groups were statistically significant. Table 11.2 shows that the differences were significant. This difference holds by gender as well (see Figure 11.1). For males, FSP graduates had a 27% reoffense rate; for FSP non-graduates the reoffense rate was 49%, and the probation group had a reoffense rate of 55%. For females, the re-offense rates were 15%, 50%, and 57%, respectively. The FSP appears to be a very effective program for juvenile first-offender females.

The second method of assessment is a qualitative process at the conclusion of the program. We ask the families to answer the questions of, "Was the program of benefit to you?" and "What was/wasn't beneficial?" The following are representative excerpts from parents and adolescents:

I felt bad about having to come to this program because it was embarrassing to have your child get arrested, but the leaders and families in the program accepted and encouraged me. (parent)

The program made me feel like I wasn't such a bad person after all. (youth)

I was angry and resentful that I had to come to the program. After all, I didn't get into trouble, but before long I realized that my daughter needed me there and I knew it would help me, too. (parent)

I knew I had problems but I didn't know how to say it or who to say it to. (youth)

Before I came to this program I didn't think I could afford the time. Now I have learned that I can't afford NOT to spend time with my child. (parent)

I learned that we can be hopeful and not discouraged all the time. (parent)

Every week I learned something new. I looked forward to coming every Monday night, 6:30 to 8:30. (youth) (recorded on FSP video)[2]

All things were geared for success, not just for the youth but for the whole family. (parent) (recorded on FSP video)

CASE ILLUSTRATION

The case illustration presented here is a composite of a family that we would work with in the FSP. This family consists of a 14-year-old male, Tony, and his mom, Betty. Tony was referred to the FSP for assaulting a peer at school. While they were meeting with their probation officer who was describing the FSP, Tony was very quiet and had difficulties making eye contact with anyone in the room. Tony's stepfather was present for this meeting (he did not participate in the program because he worked in the evenings) and he and Betty did most of the talking during this meeting. Tony spoke only when directly asked a question. The family then proceeded to fill out a risk assessment. Betty was concerned about the risk assessment because she did not want any of this information to "get out." She was assured that the information on the risk assessment was kept confidential. The family eventually completed their paperwork and they were given a written reminder about the time and place of the first session. Betty looked somewhat anxious and apprehensive when the session began and Tony was sitting across the room in his chair with his arms folded and head down. As the session began, Betty started to express her anger over having to participate in a program because her son did something wrong. Betty continued to express her anger for 5 to 10 minutes, and other parent members of the group agreed with Betty. The group leader, after Betty had been given the opportunity to express her anger, discussed the philosophy of the FSP, where it is believed that the family provides valuable resources that, when accessed, can prevent negative behaviors from happening again. Betty and Tony participated minimally through the rest of the session and left quickly without talking to anyone from the group.

Betty and Tony were early for the next session, and while we were waiting for the rest of the families to arrive, Betty brought up her concerns about people in the community finding out she and her son were in the FSP. Betty stated that she was concerned because she works near the site of the program. Betty stated that she was concerned because she did not want one of the group leaders to see her with a co-worker, and say hello, because she would have to explain to her co-worker how she knew this person. We reminded Betty about how seriously the topic of confidentiality is approached, and that this subject would be discussed with the whole group. After our explanation, Betty appeared more relaxed for the rest of the session. The consequence was that Betty could trust the FSP group leaders, that they wanted to help, and they would make every effort to do so.

In this second session, Tony and Betty started to become leaders of the group. One of the activities for that session was an activity in which each family had to build a structure out of toothpicks and gumdrops. When Tony was asked how he and his mom worked together, Tony stated, "Well, when my building started to fall, my mom helped me support it." Tony was asked to repeat what he had said and while he was repeating what he had said, Tony smiled at his mom because in essence he had stated that his mom was there to help him when he needed it.

While Tony "toured" the jail, Betty participated in the group with the parents on the subject of parenting. Betty expressed her fears of Tony's becoming involved in crime. She stated that she had a brother and an uncle who were involved in the court system. Other parents expressed the same concern, and another parent shared her own personal experiences with the court system. It was at this point that Betty allowed herself to be vulnerable and use self-disclosure to the group leaders and the other families in the program.

The last half of the program is when Tony started to thrive. After seeing his mom participate and grow more comfortable, Tony started to be a leader for the youth. Tony often led group discussions, and he would generate discussion with other parents about the difficulties that young people face today, whether in their schools or in their neighborhoods. This came to the forefront during the conflict-resolution session. Tony and some other youths role-played an incident where a youth beat up another youth over a popular name-brand jacket.

Tony talked about the struggles of not wanting to appear weak in front of your peers if you surrender the jacket, standing up for yourself and taking care of what is yours, and the fear of being hurt over a piece of clothing. The parents were able to see the struggles their children faced in school and in the neighborhood. Betty told Tony and the rest of the group, "I know we have taught you to stand up for yourself and to protect yourself, but I do not want to lose you over a jacket. I can always get you another jacket, but I cannot go out and buy a new son." The youths then proceeded to resolve this conflict positively with the help and support of the parents in the group.Tony and Betty expressed joy and sadness at graduation. They stated they will miss the group, but they were happy that they got the Tuesday nights back for themselves. Graduation ended that night with Tony getting up in front of the group and saying, "I enjoyed working with you all and I will miss you, but I hope I never have to see you again," implying that he hoped that none of them will get into trouble with the law again.

CONCLUSION

The multiple family group model for treating youth offenders provides unique opportunities. Once the formidable challenge of recruitment is met, families who feel isolated or hopeless come together to provide support to each other. Reluctant families mandated by the court to attend become more enthusiastic when they encounter similar families who struggle with their own reticence and discouragement. The group process provides a setting in which interpersonal skills can be enhanced, validation can be attained, and negative and destructive feelings can be changed to create more positive family environments. Parents who began the program feeling ambivalent or opposed to participation in the program usually complete the program feeling fortunate that they had such a valuable group experience. In addition, parents continue meeting voluntarily after the completion of the FSP to further discuss and implement positive changes. The FSP is cost-effective because of its reliance on group members to help each other, as two group co-leaders create a structure and facilitate discussion for six to eight families. Finally, the recidivism rate for first-time youth offenders who complete the FSP is over 20% lower than for those who do not attend. Comparing families who have completed the FSP since 1992 with those who have not, each year of the FSP has demonstrated this consistent difference in recidivism between the two groups. Furthermore, of youths who "graduate" from the FSP who do reoffend, the rate of reoffense is only half of the reoffense rate of those who reoffend who did *not* attend the program.

NOTES

1. For the complete FSP manual, contact William Quinn, Dawson Hall, University of Georgia, Athens, GA 30602.

2. A professionally produced, 13 minute FSP video which includes actual footage of the program, comments from parents and youths, interviews with FSP group leaders, and a judge is available from the first author.

REFERENCES

Aguilar, B., & Carlson, E. (1998). *Early correlates of life-course-persistent and adolescence-limited antisocial behavior in a longitudinal, high-risk sample.* Paper presented at the Seventh Biennial Meeting of the Society for Research on Adolescence. San Diego, CA.

Alexander, J. F., Pugh, C., & Parsons, B. (1999). *Blueprints for violence prevention: Functional family therapy.* Boulder, CO: Center for the Study and Prevention of Violence.

Bronfenbrenner, U. (1986). Ecology of the family as a context for human development: Research perspectives. *Development Psychology, 22,* 723–742.

Bronfenbrenner, U. (1994). Nature-nurture reconceptualized in developmental perspective: A bioecological model. *Psychological Review,* 101, 568–586.

Chamberlain, P. (1990). Comparative evaluation of specialized foster care for seriously delinquent youths: A first step. *Community Alternatives: International Journal of Family Care, 2,* 21–36.

Chamberlain, P., & Reid, J. B. (1991). Using a specialized foster care treatment model for children and adolescents leaving the state mental hospital. *Journal of Community Psychology, 19,* 266–276.

Chamberlain, P., & Rosicky, J. G. (1995). The effectiveness of family therapy in the treatment of adolescents with conduct disorders and delinquency. *Journal of Marital and Family Therapy, 21,* 441–459.

Crime in the United States 1996. (1997). Washington, DC: U.S. Government Printing Office.

Department of Juvenile Justice. (1998). Personal communication. Winder, GA.

Dishion, T. J., & Andrews, D. W. (1995). Preventing escalation in problem behavior with high-risk young adolescents: Immediate and one-year outcomes. *Journal of Consulting and Clinical Psychology, 63,* 538–548.

Dodge, K. (1998). *The Development and prevention of serious conduct disorder.* Presentation for the Institute for Behavioral Research, University of Georgia.

Doren, D. M. (1987). *Understanding and treating the psychopath.* New York: John Wiley & Sons.

Dornfield, M., & Kruttschnitt, C. (1992). Do the stereotypes fit? Mapping gender specific outcomes and risk factors. *Criminology, 30,* 397–419.

Emens, E. F., Hall, N. W., Ross, C., & Ziger, E. F. (1996). Preventing juvenile delinquency: An ecological, developmental approach. In E. F. Zigler, S. L. Kagan, & N. W. Hall (Eds.), *Children, families, and government: Preparing for the twenty-first century.* Cambridge, MA: Harvard University Press.

Forgatch, M. (1991). Parent practices: Mediators of risk for antisocial behavior. In

J. Read (Ed.), *A social interactional model of the development and prevention of antisocial behavior and conduct disorder*. Symposium conducted at the Third Biennial Conference on Community Research and Action, Tempe, AZ.

Georgia Children and Youth Coordinating Council. (1997). *Georgia Children and Youth Statistical Report*, Atlanta, GA.

Henggeler, S. W., Borduin, M. J., Melton, G. B., Scherer, D. G., & Hanley, J. H. (1997). Multisystemic therapy with violent and chronic juvenile offenders and their families: The role of treatment fidelity in successful dissemination. *Journal of Consulting and Clinical Psychology, 65,* 821–833.

Henggeler, S. W., Cunningham, P. B., Pickerel, S. G., Schoenwald, S. K., & Borduin, M. J. (1996). Multisystemic therapy: An effective violence prevention approach for serious juvenile offenders. *Journal of Adolescence, 19,* 47–61.

Henggeler, S. W., Melton, G. G., & Smith, L. A. (1992). Family preservation using multisystemic therapy: An effective alternative to incarcerating serious juvenile offenders. *Journal of Consulting and Clinical Psychology, 60,* 953–961.

Howing, P. T., Wodarski, J. S., Kurtz, D., Gaudin, J. M., & Herbst, D. (1990). Child abuse and delinquency: The empirical and theoretical links. *Social Work, 35,* 244–249.

Johnson, V., & Pandina, R. J. (1991). Effects of the family environment on adolescent substance abuse, delinquency, and coping styles. *American Journal of Drug and Alcohol Abuse, 17,* 71–88.

Kazdin, A. E. (1987). Treatment of antisocial behavior in children: Current status and future directions. *Psychological Bulletin, 102,* 187–203.

Lewin, K. (1931). The conflict between Aristotelean and Galilean modes of thought in contemporary psychology. *Journal of Genetic Psychology, 5,* 141–177.

Lewin, K. (1935). *A dynamic theory of personality.* New York: McGraw-Hill.

Liddle, H. A. (1996). Family-based treatment for adolescent problem behaviors: Overview of contemporary developments and introduction to the special section. *Journal of Family Psychology, 10,* 1–11.

Mann, B. J., Borduin, C. M., Henggeler, S. W., & Blaske, D. M. (1990). An investigation of systematic conceptualizations of parent-child coalitions and symptom change. *Journal of Consulting and Clinical Psychology, 58,* 336–344.

Miller, G. E., & Prinz, R. J. (1990). Enhancement of social learning family interventions for childhood conduct disorder. *Psychological Bulletin, 108,* 291–307.

Minuchin, S. (1974). *Families and family therapy.* Cambridge, MA: Harvard University Press.

Minuchin, S., & Fishman, C. (1981). *Family therapy techniques.* Cambridge, MA: Harvard University Press.

Moffitt, T. E. (1993). Adolescence-limited and life-course-persistent antisocial behavior: A developmental taxonomy. *Psychological Review, 100,* 674–701.

Mulvey, E. P., Arthur, M. W., & Reppucci, N. D. (1997). The prevention and treatment of juvenile delinquency: A review of the research. *Clinical Psychology Review, 13,* 133–167.

Patterson, G. R. (1993). Orderly change in a stable world: The antisocial trait as a chimera. *Journal of Consulting and Clinical Psychology*, 61, 911–919.

Peeples, F., & Loeber, R. (1994). Do individual factors and neighborhood context explain ethnic differences in juvenile delinquency? *Journal of Quantitative Criminology*, 10, 141–157.

Quinn, W. H. (1998). *Family solutions: A group program for youth offenders and their families*. Athens: University of Georgia Press.

Quinn, W. H., Kuehl, B., Thomas, F., & Joanning, H. (1988). Systemic interventions in families with adolescent drug abusers. *American Journal of Alcohol and Drug Abuse*, 14, 65–87.

Quinn, W., Sutphen, R., Michaels, M., & Gale, J. (1994). Juvenile first offenders: Characteristics of at-risk families and strategies for intervention. *Journal of Addictions & Offender Counseling*, 15, 2–22.

Sampson, R. J., & Laub, J. H. (1994). Urban poverty and the family context of delinquency: A new look at structure and process in a classic study. *Child Development*, 65, 523–540.

Scarr, S., & McCartney, K. (1983). How people make their own environments: A theory of genotype–environment effects. *Child Development*, 54, 424–435.

Schmidt, S. E., Liddle, H. A., & Dakof, G. A. (1996). Changes in parenting practices and adolescent drug abuse during multidimensional family therapy. *Journal of Family Psychology*, 10, 12–27.

Shadish, W. R., Montgomery, L. M., Wilson, P., & Wilson, M. (1993). Effects of family and marital psychotherapy: A meta-analysis. *Journal of Consulting and Clinical Psychology*, 61, 992–1002.

Shore, M. F., & Massimo, J. L. (1973). After ten years: A follow-up study of comprehensive vocationally oriented psychotherapy. *American Journal of Psychotherapy*, 43, 128–132.

U.S. Federal Bureau of Investigation (FBI). (1996). *Crime in the United States*. Annual.

VanDyke, D. J., & Quinn, W. H. (2000). Effectiveness of a multiple family group therapy in reducing recidivism for first-time juvenile offenders. Manuscript in review.

Walker, H., & Silvester, R. (1991). Where is school along the path to prison? *Educational Leadership*, 49, 14–16.

Weiner, I. B. (1992). *Psychological disturbances in adolescence*. New York: John Wiley & Sons.

Yalom, I. D. (1995). *The theory and practice of group psychotherapy* (4th ed.). New York: Basic Books.

Chapter 12

Traumatic Incident Reduction: Moving Beyond the Wreckage of Lives

Pamela Vest Valentine

Traumatic Incident Reduction (TIR) (Gerbode, 1989) is a brief, memory-based treatment that has been found to be effective in both the increase of self-efficacy and the reduction of depression, anxiety, and post-traumatic stress disorder (PTSD) (Valentine, 1997). PTSD refers to the DSM-IV diagnosis wherein a person experiences symptoms of intrusion, avoidance, and arousal (American Psychiatric Association, 1994; Waldinger, 1990). Intrusion involves nightmares, recurring thoughts, and flashbacks. Avoidance speaks of manifestations such as the numbing of feelings, avoiding places associated with the event, and attempts to not think about the event. Arousal, among other things, pertains to an exaggerated startle response and hypervigilance. The diagnosis of PTSD means that the symptoms are more present after the traumatic event than they were before the event, and that the symptoms have existed for at least four weeks. Other symptoms associated with trauma are depression (Frank & Stewart, 1990), anxiety, low self-esteem, and a reduced sense of being in control.

TIR is most similar to imaginal flooding (Valentine, 1995). Both TIR and imaginal flooding have the client repeatedly remember and mentally reexperience the traumatic incident until the problematic symptoms are extinguished or drastically diminished.

TIR is distinct from other brief trauma treatments in various ways. First, TIR is to be conducted in an open-ended session (French & Gerbode, 1993). This means that once the procedure begins, it will continue until symptoms diminish, until the client no longer feels the emotional "charge" associated with the traumatic incident (Gerbode, 1989); the time frame for a session is generally from two to four hours.

TIR is also distinct from many trauma interventions in that it has been experimentally tested. Valentine (1997) found that TIR produced both statistical and clinical significance in the reduction of PTSD-like symptoms in female inmates after just one session. The improvement experienced by the inmates was not only maintained for three months, but actually became more pronounced after three months.

Another distinction of TIR is that it is highly structured and replicable. Instead of the traditional dialogue between client and therapist, TIR uses a script consisting of both questions and directions (French & Gerbode, 1993). The script almost never changes and is not dependent on therapist charisma. In fact, the script is so rote that the therapist should prepare the client before the TIR session that it will most likely be unlike any interpersonal interaction that the client has ever experienced before (Valentine, 1995). The script that the therapist says to the client to facilitate the client's reexperiencing the event follows: (1) When was it? (2) How long did it last? (3) Go to the beginning of the event and tell me when you are there. (4) What are you aware of? (5) Play the event through silently in your mind and tell me when you are finished, and (6) Tell me what happened. After the client and therapist go though this script once, the therapist begins again with numbers three, five, and six of the script, without making either an empathic or an interpretive remark. In the elimination of empathic and interpretive responses, TIR is also distinct from most psychotherapeutic interventions.

The differences in TIR and many therapeutic interventions can be summarized by saying that TIR leaves the vast majority of the work up to the client. The therapist does not even choose which traumatic event the client should address in the TIR session (French & Gerbode, 1993). Initially, the client may feel both incredulous about how the process works and reluctant to take responsibility for his or her recovery. The results of the TIR stance, however, are that the client most often feels relieved that there was no judgment coming from the therapist and that the client owned the event and its interpretation (Valentine & Smith, 2001). Perhaps best of all, the client feels empowered to know that he or she did all the work and therefore gets to receive all the credit for the improvement (Valentine & Smith, 2001).

CLIENT POPULATIONS

Since traumatic events are not a respecter of persons but rather cut across all races, genders, continents, and generations, TIR is appropriate for almost everyone (French & Gerbode; 1993; Gerbode, 1989; Moore, 1993). The exceptions would be persons who cannot focus on a memory for an extended period of time. Such persons could include children, mentally handicapped adults, persons who are distracted by a threat of imminent danger, persons subdued by medication, intoxicated people, and people who are actively psychotic or suicidal.

While traumatic events vary in form and substance, ranging from natural disaster to interpersonal violence, from discrete to prolonged, and from cohort trauma to individual trauma, there is no indication that TIR is more suitable for one type of trauma than another. Some traumatic events on which TIR has been shown to be effective include death of a loved one, arrest, incarceration, incest, rape, fire, assault, and accidents that maim or hurt (Bisbey, 1994; Valentine, 1995, 1997; Valentine & Smith, 2001).

THEORETICAL UNDERSTANDING OF PTSD AND OF TIR

Trauma treatment should flow from an understanding of the etiology of PTSD. Post-traumatic stress disorder is generally explained by one of four schools of thought: physiological, behavioral, cognitive, or catharsis (Valentine, 1997). Medical scientists most often conceptualize PTSD as a physiological alteration of neurotransmitters. Treatment, according to this perspective, would be pharmacological. Behavioral theory explains that the maintenance of PTSD symptoms is a matter of simple or complex conditioning (Fairbank & Brown, 1987; Spiegler & Guervremont, 1993). Rape, as an example of a trauma (Girelli, Resick, Mashoefer-Dvorak, & Hutter, 1986) is the unconditioned stimulus (UCS), and the physiological, behavioral, and cognitive responses are unconditioned responses (UCR). With classical conditioning, the unconditioned stimulus becomes a conditioned stimulus and can elicit a conditioned response to the original unconditioned response associated with the traumatic incident. While conditioning models have heuristic value for immediate fear responses, "they do not address the individual variability in responses nor provide much conceptual utility for understanding coping processes adopted spontaneously by victims" (Koss & Burkhart, 1989, p. 30).

Cognitive theory allows for more variability in responses. Cognitive theory, briefly stated, postulates that human behavior and emotions can be explained by one's thinking (Beck, 1976; Werner, 1986). Other assumptions of cognitive theory are that human beings are goal-oriented (Werner, 1986). Cognitive theorists see humans as "mini-scientists" who make hypotheses about the best way to attain a goal (Kelly, 1961). These hypotheses are based on constructs or schemas that are rooted in one's experiences. In other words, one filters past experiences, determining what was successful and what was not in attaining a goal from which a schema is built. Studies indicate that when given a choice between the familiar and the novel, humans are more likely to choose that which is familiar and fits with an established schema (Kelly, 1963). When a new experience comes along and is incongruent with an established construct, people either assimilate the experience into an existing construct or they accommodate their constructs to incorporate the new experience (Piaget, 1970).

For example, if a woman had a belief that rape happens to other people and then was raped, she might assimilate the trauma into her unaltered schema by denying that she was raped (Girelli et al., 1986; Moscarello, 1991; Rose, 1986). By contrast, she might accommodate her schema to incorporate the trauma, and believe that she is never safe and that she is likely to be raped again at any time.

According to cognitive theory, trauma is experienced forcefully, shattering old constructs (Janoff-Bulman, 1992). The victim begins operating from hastily made constructs, those formed during or immediately after the traumatic incident. Insight "is a luxury that the mind cannot afford when locked in a struggle for survival" (Everstine & Everstine, 1993, p. 18). As a result, cognitive distortions follow (Moore, 1993).

Examples of cognitive distortions that result from accommodating one's schema to include the traumatic event follow: A hypothetical rape victim realizes that the perpetrator could have killed her, and now she reasons that she owes him something; another victim engages in magical thinking, believing that she could have prevented the incident; yet another victim believes that this event was punishment for something she had done. One can easily understand how the above thoughts could readily impair rape victims' functioning.

Another explanation for PTSD comes from the catharsis school; this theory also explains TIR. Cathartic psychotherapies involve strong emotional expression. Straton (1990) explains that while mainstream psychiatry and psychotherapy have held for years that cathartic therapy has limited value, there is little research to support this "conventional wisdom." Straton (1990) points to the following people with whom cathartic psychotherapy has been associated: Gassner, a famous healer/priest of the late eighteenth century; Mesmer (1734–1815), a secularist; Charcot, who made hypnosis respectable again; Breuer; Freud; Janet, a disciple of Charcot and a chief rival of Freud's (Janet made "automatic talking," a technique similar to Neuro-Linguistic Programming, part of his practice); Rolf; Reich; Moreno; Perls (Gestalt therapy); and Lowen (Bioenergetics). Straton (1990) sees the "Human Potential Movement" as a branch of cathartic therapy. Familiar names like Perls, Satir, Rolf, and Schultz were part of that movement. Themes of catharsis are found in transactional analysis, Gestalt Therapy, Primal Therapy, Bioenergetics, Psychodrama, Encounter Groups, Neuro-Linguistic Programming, Neo-Reichian body work, and Rebirthing (Straton, 1990).

The theory underlying cathartic psychotherapy clarifies both the discussion of the origin of PTSD-like symptoms and an explanation for why TIR is effective. While four schools of thought exist within cathartic theory, the Pavlovian, the cathexis, and the holographic schools best illustrate the etiology of PTSD and TIR's efficacy. The Pavlovian model, used by Sargant (1957), shows how dogs who were trapped in cages during a flood forgot conditioned reflexes that had been recently implanted (Straton, 1990). Proponents of the Pavlovian model postulate that under severe mental distress, disturbances in the brain tend to discard old patterns of thought as new beliefs are instilled. Therefore, cathartic therapies arouse emotions in order to allow a person to embrace a new belief (Straton, 1990).

The cathexis model postulates that when aroused, there transpires an attachment between one person and another. Examples of arousal and concomitant attachment follow: the attachment a mother feels toward her newborn child after the pain of childbirth; the bonding between sexual partners after experiencing an orgasm; and the attachment some hostages have felt toward their captors (Straton, 1990).

Finally, the holographic model of cathartic theory addresses the storage and retrieval of memories (Straton, 1990). The research is based on the work of Lashley, an American neurosurgeon who experimented on animals. From his research, Lashley found that retained memories are a function of how much of the brain was affected by a trauma rather than where in the brain the memory was stored (Straton, 1990).

Straton (1990) explains that the use of the word "hologram" comes from three-dimensional pictures as used in lensless photography. One beam of light is split into two. Each is reflected toward the film. When the two intersect, an interference pattern is recorded on the film. If light that is tuned and has the same frequency is shown through the hologram, a three-dimensional image appears.

The metaphor of a three-dimensional picture points to three functions of the brain that are involved in a traumatic experience: memories, emotions, and decisions (Straton, 1990). Proponents of the hologram theory suggest that memories, emotions and decisions might be "frequency-specific" to the state the brain was in when the incident occurred. Efforts to change a life decision will be maximized if the brain is "tuned into" the same "frequency" as when the decision was made or "recorded" (Straton, 1990). This points to the importance of replicating the physiological state one experienced during the event in order to examine old ways and make a new belief pathway. This new pathway is called a redecision (Straton, 1990). The redecision is the key element. This is similar to the insight sought in psychoanalysis. In order to "redecide," one must focus one's attention after the arousal. *Where* the attention is focused is key (Straton, 1990). Since a bond may exist between the client who has been aroused and the practitioner, he or she should be careful to ensure that the client's attention is on the redecision rather than on "what a nice person the practitioner is." Lack of attention to this critical point may explain the abuses that have occurred between some practitioners and their vulnerable patients (Straton, 1990).

In summary, Straton (1990) espouses that highly arousing events may be best treated by highly arousing therapies. The arousal needs to be close to the level of arousal at the time of the incident. Finally, one should be careful to focus on the new decision, not just reliving the event or the supportive qualities of the therapist.

COMMON TRAUMA TREATMENT

Of particular interest to the subject of brief, effective trauma treatment are research studies that not only present clear hypotheses, but that systematically test for treatment effectiveness. While brief treatment is not universally defined, for the purposes of this review, brief treatment will be confined to those interventions that consist of fewer than 12 sessions. Systematic testing for treatment effectiveness means that the brief trauma treatment needs to have been empirically tested on a given population wherein a control group was used, and dependent variables were clearly stated and reliably tested. It is also helpful if the intervention is specific, simple to use, and is intuitively connected to the theory of PTSD.

The Valentine (1997) review of the trauma literature revealed that only 18 of 30 memory-based trauma studies were empirical. Of those 18, only eight fit the above criteria. Types of treatments specified in the articles were cognitive processing, prolonged exposure, hypnosis, systematic desensitization, flooding, supportive counseling, stress inoculation, assertion training, group, and eye movement desensitization (EMDR) (Shapiro, 1989). Few treatments were brief (four of eight). Group treatments were the longest form of treatment, while imaginal exposure was the shortest. Six articles reported in detail the treatment protocol. The majority of treatments chosen for the studies were treatment packages rather than simple treatments. The many facets of a treatment package make it difficult to determine which of the components are essential to the treatment and which are superfluous. It also impedes knowledge about the level of skill needed by the therapist, an element critical to the understanding of brief effective treatment. Only one of eight studies revealed how the authors controlled for treatment integrity. Five of eight studies used control groups. Random selection occurred in only one of 18 empirical studies. Most studies had no sampling frame, making generalizability impossible. Random assignment into treatment groups occurred in two studies. Of interest was the exclusion of incest victims from many of the studies. No explanation was given. Without a theoretical explanation, the exclusion of incest victims, for example, appears capricious. In light of the numbers of female victims of incest, the arbitrary exclusion of incest victims makes generalization to the larger population of trauma survivors unwise.

In summary, the current understanding of PTSD and its treatment is based on studies whose results cannot be generalized and samples whose inclusion/exclusion criteria are difficult to ascertain. However, what is known is that the studies with the most rigor had the worst theoretical foundation. Similarly, those that addressed theory stopped short of rigorous research and merely illustrated their points with case studies. The memory-focused treatments were the simplest, the shortest, and seemed to produce results at least as effective, if not more so, than anxiety management treatments (Foa, Rothbaum, Riggs, & Murdock, 1991). The two most predominant problems with the memory-focused treatments were the omission of standardized measures in an otherwise well-conceptualized study and the treatments that often extend to 12 or more sessions, taxing the endurance of clients.

RESEARCH STATUS OF TIR

To date, the research base of TIR is slight, but growing. Within the past few years, the knowledge base of TIR has moved from an anecdotal base to an experimental outcome study on the effectiveness of TIR. The first published article on TIR was a case study (Valentine, 1995). Next was a true experimental study based on victims of crime in England (Bisbey, 1994). Interspersed were an ethnographic interview study (Valentine & Smith, 2001) that examined the experience of TIR as perceived through the eyes and minds of recipients of the intervention, and a dissertation based on a quasi-experimental design (Coughlin, 1995). More recently, Valentine (1997) published a study on the effectiveness of TIR on PTSD-like symptoms in incarcerated females.

Subjects in the Valentine (1997) study were recruited from a Federal Correction Institute (FCI) located in the southeast United States. The sample was drawn from the total number of inmates at the facility (N = 730). The population (N = 730) was surveyed to determine eligibility based on whether inmates (1) had experienced a prior trauma in their lives, and if so, the nature of the trauma; (2) had experienced one or more of the trauma-related symptoms; and (3) were willing to further discuss their traumatic experience with a mental health professional. Two hundred forty-eight inmates met the initial criteria. The inmates were brought together, in groups of approximately 12, to have the study explained to them and to have them sign consent forms when they chose to participate. One hundred forty-eight agreed to participate and were randomly assigned to either treatment or control conditions. Twenty-five subsequently withdrew from the study, leaving 123 subjects.

An experimental control group design was used to evaluate the efficacy of TIR on 123 female federal inmates. The primary hypothesis of the study follows: Those inmates receiving TIR will experience significant reduction in one or more of their self-reported PTSD-related symptoms, while those in the control conditions will not.

While all subjects completed pretest, post-test, and follow-up tests, additional steps were required of those in the experimental condition. Those steps were:

1. having a one-on-one orientation to learn the nature of TIR and the roles that the inmates and the mental health practitioners would play,
2. receiving a session of TIR, and
3. completing a debriefing session.

The instruments used to determine the efficacy of TIR on trauma-related symptoms were Beck Depression Inventory (BDI) (Beck, Ward, Mendelsohn, Mock, & Erbaugh, 1961); PTSD Symptom Scale (PSS) (Rothbaum, Dancu, Riggs, & Foa, 1990); Generalized Expectancy of Success Scale (GESS) (Fibel & Hale, 1978); and Clinical Anxiety Scale (CAS) (Westhuis & Thyer, 1989). These instruments were administered in a pretest, post-test, and three-month follow-up format.

To analyze the data, an analysis of covariance (ANCOVA) (with the pretest as the co-variate) was conducted on each of the above measures, as well as on the three subscales of the PSS: intrusion, avoidance, and hyperarousal. Analysis revealed that TIR shows significant differences at the .05 level on the PSS, the BDI, the CAS, and the GESS at both post-test and the three-month follow-up. In other words, at both the post-test and the three-month follow-up, the experimental condition showed a statistically significant *decrease* in symptoms of post-traumatic stress disorder (and its related subscales) and of depression and anxiety, while those in the control condition remained approximately the same. Subjects assigned to the experimental condition *improved* on the measure of self-efficacy at a statistically significant level, while subjects assigned to the control condition did not. The null hypothesis was rejected, and the research hypothesis confirmed.

Although the results of this study were promising, care should be taken in generalizing to larger populations. For example, while this study demonstrated TIR's effectiveness in treating trauma-related symptoms in female inmates, it would be a mistake to assume that TIR is effective with male inmates, or with female inmates in different institutional settings, or with persons outside a prison setting. Additional studies should be undertaken with other populations before definitive conclusions are drawn about TIR's efficacy with those populations. Besides testing TIR's effectiveness on different populations, TIR should be compared against other brief trauma treatments. Finally, research implications involve testing TIR's effectiveness on different ethnic groups and discovering the variables associated with training therapists to deliver TIR to a variety of ethnic groups.

CASE EXAMPLE

Nancy, a 41-year-old Latino-American woman, was the mother of five and was married to her third husband. As a child, Nancy had been adopted at an early age and had experienced sexual abuse in her home.

At age 41, Nancy was referred to a TIR practitioner. For six years prior to her referral, Nancy regularly attended case management sessions. She entered into case management shortly after having experienced a traumatic incident.

Late one night, at her intoxicated husband's insistence, Nancy was driving herself and her family to another town. In the car, her husband reached for something and diverted Nancy's attention just long enough for her to run off the road and into a tree. In a dazed state, Nancy stood at the driver's door outside the car. She reached for her baby to assure that he was all right. At that moment, the car began to roll, and it rolled over Nancy's foot. Moments later, in shock, Nancy walked on her foot that had been turned totally around and was facing backwards. Ambulances came and took her to a nearby hospital.

Six years later, Nancy was still trying to regain control over her life. She met the TIR specialist, and explained that she had been referred to the specialist at her own request. Nancy felt certain that her lack of progress toward the goal of driving and becoming gainfully employed had everything to do with the accident.

The first time that Nancy met the TIR practitioner, the hour was spent preparing Nancy for the TIR session. Often, on first meeting, the practitioner will lead the client through a life-review to ascertain the number of traumatic events in the client's past (Figley, 1989) and to facilitate the client's choosing which event he or she wants to work on in the TIR session. In this case, the practitioner did not do a life-review since Nancy arrived at the office knowing the traumatic event on which she wanted to work.

The preparation for TIR was thorough. In an effort to explain to Nancy how people become "stuck" after a traumatic event, the practitioner explained cathartic theory and why TIR might be effective in her case. The practitioner also explained the roles that both she and Nancy would take in the session. The practitioner warned Nancy that there would be an absence of empathic remarks and interpretations during the session. The practitioner set the stage for TIR in the following manner:

Imagine going to a Tuesday afternoon matinee when no one else is in the movie theater. You get the seat of your choice. You look up on the screen, and there you are as well. Now, I'm in the back in the projection room. I can't really see your movie, but I can give you directions. I will tell you to roll the movie back, to go to the beginning, etc. In other words, I can give you instruction, but I can't add or subtract from your movie. I will be very careful not to make comments during the viewing of your movie. I was not present at the time of the incident, and I should not become a part of your movie now.

Then, the practitioner had Nancy remember either a pleasant or benign event, something as simple as getting dressed that morning or a stroll on the beach. The two of them role-played the simple event. The practitioner asked Nancy to go to the beginning of the event, to tell her when it was, to tell her of what she was aware, and to play the event through to the end. After Nancy indicated that she was at the end of the event, the practitioner asked Nancy to tell her what had happened. After Nancy described the event, the practitioner started over with the rote script. She did this to give Nancy a taste of what it is like to talk and to have no content response offered after she finished talking.

The practitioner finished the thorough joining session by advising Nancy that the practitioner would not even engage in interpretative dialogue after the "movie" was over. In other words, the client owns the event both during the showing and afterwards.

The joining session was thorough for two reasons: (1) The interaction allowed the client time to see if she felt comfortable working with the therapist. Valentine and Smith (1998) write that the clients report feeling the need for safety during a TIR session. This joining session is the first step in creating an atmosphere in which the client feels safe enough to go back and face a troubling memory. (2) The client should have the procedure so thoroughly explained to him or her that there is slight possibility that the procedure will unpleasantly surprise the client. Traumatic events are always unpleasant surprises. Care to avoid another unpleasant surprise, especially associated with the therapeutic process, needs to be taken.

Nancy stated that she understood the procedure and was desirous of an actual TIR session. The practitioner scheduled an appointment and told Nancy to be sure to return fed, rested, and ready to focus on the event. The practitioner also instructed Nancy that the success of the session would be the responsibility of the practitioner—that Nancy's only responsibilities were to arrive ready to focus and to become emotionally reengaged in the event. Even this instruction allowed Nancy to cease being concerned about being a "good" client and to channel all her energy on becoming emotionally reengaged in the event.

When Nancy arrived at the TIR session, she reported being rested, fed, and ready to go. When she said that she had no other questions or concerns, the practitioner began the session. Nancy replayed the event several times, showing more distress and emotions with each repetition. More details about the event surfaced with each repetition. Sometimes Nancy's focus was on the circumstances that led her to be driving at that late hour;

other times her focus was on her baby. Frequently, her focus was on the cold metal hospital doors that closed behind her, leaving her all alone.

Midway through the session, Nancy's focus changed to an early childhood event in which she was locked in a chicken coop with chickens pecking her and getting their feathers all through her hair. (In remembering this, Nancy would pull at her hair and duck in her chair to avoid the onslaught of the chickens.) Nancy escaped the chicken pen and ran to a nearby hill. She began throwing rocks off a cliff, down onto a house below. She reported that she knew that she should not be doing that, but that she was angry with her stepmother for putting her in a chicken pen. Suddenly, a man was before her, cursing her, and swinging a machete at her. She ran for her life; Nancy ran home and hid behind a flour barrel in the kitchen. The man followed her into the kitchen and told the curious stepmother what the confusion was about. The stepmother moved the barrel to expose Nancy, and said, "Here, take her." Fortunately, once again Nancy escaped.

Next in the TIR session, Nancy's mind went to her father's arrival at home later that evening. Nancy was in bed but was not asleep. She heard her father and stepmother talking in bed. Her stepmother was telling Nancy's father what an impossible child Nancy was and how she could no longer stand to rear Nancy. The father assured his wife that he would "take care of it." The following morning, Nancy's bags were packed, and she was sent to live with a relative.

The childhood scene was reviewed for approximately an hour and fifteen minutes. Then with a frown on her face, Nancy looked at the practitioner and said, "I feel at peace."

Reading Nancy's body language, the practitioner responded and asked, "Is that a problem?" Nancy said, 'Yes." The practitioner said, "Yes? Tell me more."

Nancy proceeded to explain. "You see, I've been going to case management every week for six years. Every week I tell my story. Every week we don't finish. Every week I reschedule to finish telling my story. I've been angry each and every week."

The therapist noted that the client was comparing the six-year anger that she had felt with the peace that she was currently feeling. The therapist ventured to ask the following question: "If any good has come out of today's session, to whom do you have to credit the improvement?"

Nancy paused to think about her response. Meanwhile, the therapist was regretting having asking the question, fearing that six years of case management would have trained Nancy to be reliant on a therapist and to automatically give the therapist the credit. Finally, Nancy broke the silence and said, "I guess I'd have to give the credit to me because you did not do anything!" With that, the therapist sighed with relief and knew that the

TIR process had not only relieved the symptoms, but had instilled ownership of improvement in the client.

The client came to the specialist for a follow-up interview. After reporting that her peaceful state of mind was still maintaining itself, Nancy returned to the referring case manager for closure. At last inquiry, Nancy had gone on to relearn to drive and to seek employment.

SUMMARY

TIR is a brief intervention that has been proven to be effective in the reduction of troubling symptoms associated with PTSD in both incarcerated females (Valentine, 1997) and British victims of crime (Bisbey, 1994). Case examples such as the one above point to its effectiveness with other populations. However, such claims need to be substantiated through further experimental testing.

The practice implications for TIR are multiple. TIR is simple and straightforward. While no study exists that demonstrates the lowest level of education necessary for therapists training in TIR, there are anecdotal stories of non-degreed therapists using TIR with success (Valentine, 1995). If this is true, it means that TIR could be used by agency workers in a variety of settings.

Second, the case illustration points to the need to screen for prior traumatic events and to include the resolution of such events into client treatment plans. Many practitioners believe that trauma resolution is beyond the scope of their practice, believing the process to be lengthy and complicated. TIR demonstrates that neither is a given.

Another implication is that clients may never reach the more "pragmatic goals" like driving and seeking employment without first addressing prior traumatic events. If practitioners are not careful to assess for and treat prior traumatic events, they will be intervening on the pragmatic goals, perhaps in vain. The result of this might be the practitioner's misjudging the client as "resistant" or unmotivated. The practitioner becomes frustrated with the client, and, as illustrated in this case example, the client becomes angry with the practitioner.

Finally, while TIR needs to be tested in a variety of settings with a variety of populations, it looks as if it has enormous promise of both alleviating PTSD-like symptoms and increasing clients' sense of self-efficacy. More encouraging yet is the simple treatment protocol associated with TIR. Its simplicity means at least two things: (1) that the changes observed in clients are more likely to be the effect of the intervention than confounding variables; and (2) the procedure can be readily taught to a variety of mental health practitioners in a variety of settings, thus bringing assumed relief to a wide range of mental health clients.

REFERENCES

American Psychiatric Association. (1994). *Diagnostic and statistical manual of mental disorders* (DSM-IV) (4th ed.). Washington, DC: Author.

Beck, A. (1976). *Cognitive therapy and the emotional disorders.* New York: International Universities Press.

Beck, A. T., Ward, C. H., Mendelsohn, M., Mock, J., & Erbaugh, J. (1961). An inventory for measuring depression. *Archives of General Psychiatry, 4,* 561–571.

Bisbey, I. G. (1994). *No longer a victim: A treatment outcome study of crime victims with post-traumatic stress disorder.* Doctoral dissertation, California School of Professional Psychology, San Diego. University Microfilms International publication number 952269.

Costello, T. B. (Ed.). (1994). *The American Heritage Concise Dictionary* (3rd ed.). Boston: Houghton Mifflin.

Coughlin, W. E. (1995). *Traumatic incident reduction: Efficacy in treating anxiety symptomatology.* Unpublished doctoral dissertation, Union University, California.

Everstine, D., & Everstine, L. (1993). *The trauma response: Treatment for emotional injury.* New York: W. W. Norton & Company.

Fairbank, J. A., & Brown, T. A. (1987). Current behavioral approaches to the treatment of post-traumatic stress disorder. *The Behavior Therapist, 5*(1), 22–36.

Fibel, B., & Hale, W. D. (1978). The Generalized Expectancy of Success Scale: A new measure. *Journal of Consulting and Clinical Psychology, 46*(5), 924–931.

Figley, C. (1989). *Treating stress in families.* New York: Brunner/Mazel.

Foa, E., Rothbaum, B., Riggs, D., & Murdock, T. (1991). Treatment of posttraumatic stress disorder in rape victims: A comparison between cognitive-behavioral procedures and counseling. *Journal of Consulting and Clinical Psychology, 59*(5), 715–723.

Frank, E., & Stewart, B. (1990). Depressive symptoms in rape victims. *Journal of Affective Disorders, 1,* 269–277.

French, G. D., & Gerbode, F. A. (1993). *The traumatic incident reduction workshop* (2nd ed.). Menlo Park, CA: IRM Press.

Gerbode, F. (1989). *Beyond psychology: An introduction to metapsychology.* Palo Alto, CA: IRM Press.

Girelli, A. A., Resick, P. A., Mashoefer-Dvorak, S., & Hutter, K. (1986). Subjective distress and violence during rape: Their effects on long-term fear. *Victim Violence, 1,* 35–46.

Janoff-Bullman, B. (1992). *Shattered assumptions.* New York: The Free Press.

Kelly, G. (1961). *A nonparametric method of factor analysis of dealing with theoretical issues.* Unpublished manuscript. Mimeograph, Ohio State University.

Kelly, G. (1963). *A theory of personalities: The psychology of personal constructs.* New York: Norton.

Koss, M., & Burkhart, B. (1989). A conceptual analysis of rape victimization: Long-term effects and implications for treatment. *Psychology of Women Quarterly*, 13, 27–40.

Moore, R. H. (1993). Cognitive-emotive treatment of the posttraumatic stress disorder. In W. Dryden and L. Hill (Eds.), *Innovations in rational-emotive therapy*. Newbury Park, CA: Sage Publications.

Moscarello, R. (1991). Posttraumatic stress disorder after sexual assault: Its psychodynamics and treatment. *Journal of the American Academy of Psychoanalysis*, 19(2), 235–253.

Piaget, J. (1970). *Structuralism*. New York: Basic Books.

Riggs, D., Dancu, C., Gershuny, B., Greenburg, D., & Foa, E. (1992). Anger and post-traumatic stress disorder in female crime victims. *Journal of Traumatic Stress*, 5(4), 613–625.

Rothbaum, B. O., Dancu, C., Riggs, D. S., & Foa, E. (1990). *The PTSD Symptom Scale*. Presented at the European Association of Behavior Therapy Annual Conference, Paris, France, September.

Rose, D. (1986). Worse than death: Psychodynamics of rape victims and the need for psychotherapy. *American Journal of Psychiatry*, 143, 817–824.

Sargant, W. W. (1957). *Battle for the mind, a physiology of conversion and brainwashing*. Garden City, NY: Doubleday.

Shapiro, F. (1989). Efficacy of the eye movement desensitization procedure in the treatment of traumatic memories. *Journal of Traumatic Stress*, 2(2) 199–223.

Spiegler, M., & Guervremont, D. (1993). *Contemporary behavior therapy*. Pacific Grove, CA: Brooks/Cole.

Straton, D. (1990). Catharsis reconsidered. *Australian and New Zealand Journal of Psychiatry*, 24, 543–551.

Valentine, P. (1995). Traumatic incident reduction: A review of a new intervention. *Journal of Family Psychotherapy*, 6(2), 73–78.

Valentine. P. V. (1997). Traumatic incident reduction: Treatment of trauma-related symptoms in incarcerated females. In *Proceedings of the Tenth National Symposium on Doctoral Research in Social Work*. Columbus: Ohio State University College of Social Work.

Valentine, P. V., & Smith, T. E. (1998). A qualitative study of client perceptions of traumatic incident reduction (TIR): A brief trauma treatment. *Crisis Intervention and Time-Limited Treatment*, 4(1), 1–12.

Valentine, P. V., & Smith, T. E. (2001). Evaluating traumatic incident reduction (TIR) therapy with female inmates: A randomized controlled clinical trial. *Research on Social Work Practice*, 11(1), 40–52.

Waldinger, R. J. (1990). *Psychiatry for medical students* (2nd ed.). Washington, DC: American Psychiatric Press.

Werner, H. D. (1986). Cognitive theory. In F. J. Turner (Ed.), *Social work treatment: Interlocking theoretical approaches* (pp. 239–275). New York: The Free Press.

Westhuis, D., & Thyer, B. A. (1989). Development and validation of the Clinical Anxiety Scale: A rapid assessment instrument for empirical practice. *Educational & Psychological Measurement*, 49(1), 153–163.

Chapter 13

Interventions for Couples with Post-traumatic Stress Disorder

Victoria Tichenor, Keith Armstrong, Vickie Vann, and Robert-Jay Green

Martin, a 47-year-old unemployed man diagnosed with post-traumatic stress disorder (PTSD) from his service in Vietnam, and his partner of two years, Marie, a 46-year-old administrative assistant, came into therapy wanting to improve their communication. Both Marie and Martin had children, who were not living with them, from prior marriages. This was Martin's third marriage and Marie's second.

In a discussion about what improving communication meant, Marie stated, "I can't ever have an opinion about anything. Whenever I say what I think, he walks out the door or tells me I'm yelling at him." Martin's view of the problem was that "she's always trying to control me and tell me what to do. When she goes at me, it just sets me off." Although not physically violent, Martin and Marie conducted arguments as if their lives depended on winning every battle. When the argument became heated and Marie began to voice her ideas in a forceful manner, Martin would become very tense and angry because he would experience intrusive thoughts of Vietnam combat and early childhood scenes of being physically abused by his father. Martin would then scream at Marie to leave him alone or would walk out of the house. Marie would "back off" and leave Martin alone. Martin eventually returned, but the couple would not talk. They would sleep in separate areas for two to three days until one of them would start a conversation about something benign, never having anything to do with the original disagreement.

The fights usually focused on how Martin was conducting his affairs with his children or managing his finances. Marie felt that her opinions didn't count when they differed from Martin's. This left her feeling shut out of the relationship and distant from her husband.

As illustrated by the case example above, working with couples where one partner has been diagnosed with PTSD can present unique dilemmas to the couples therapist. When a member of a couple experiences a traumatic event that results in behavior consistent with PTSD, the entire family is affected. In this chapter, we will discuss, from a systems perspective, the effects of PTSD in couples where one of the adult partners has experienced trauma. We will briefly review the relevant empirical literature on families and PTSD, and will then describe the assessment and treatment of couples in which one of the partners has been diagnosed with PTSD.

For the past twelve years, the authors have coordinated a family clinic for war veterans who have combat-related trauma. The fourth author, an academic psychologist, has acted as consultant to the clinic. We train social workers, psychologists, and psychiatric residents in work with traumatized families. The authors also maintain private practices in which they see couples and families with trauma-related problems.

TRAUMATIC STRESS

The diagnostic symptoms of PTSD fall into three main categories: intrusions, avoidance, and arousal (American Psychiatric Association, 1994, p. 424). Intrusive symptoms include nightmares and daytime memories of the traumatic event. Avoidance symptoms include attempts to stay away from intimate relationships, particular activities, or memories of the event. Arousal symptoms involve difficulties such as becoming unusually irritable or jumpy, and having difficulty concentrating. In order to warrant a diagnosis of PTSD, an individual must have been exposed to a traumatic event and intrusion, avoidance, and arousal symptoms must have been present for at least one month.

During a traumatic event, avoidance and arousal symptoms may be adaptive, especially if the trauma is prolonged or repeated. After the completion of a traumatic event however, these symptoms may continue to be used to handle non-traumatic situations and become maladaptive coping strategies. Most individuals who experience stress reactions following a traumatic event improve without intervention. However, when the traumatic event is severe, prolonged, or is experienced by someone who has been previously exposed to trauma, difficulties can develop for the individual and consequently for the couple.

Impact on the Family

When an individual exhibits the symptoms of PTSD, other family members may be influenced by the distance, isolation, and irritability on the part of the traumatized individual. Common symptom patterns in addition to the diagnostic criteria include survivor guilt and shame, hypervigilance for or denial of danger, and externalization of responsibility. These reactions negatively impact the couple system and the family's ability to participate in the larger community (see Table 13.1).

Table 13.1
Symptoms of Post-traumatic Stress Disorder

The symptoms of post-traumatic stress disorder can manifest in some of the following behavioral difficulties:

PTSD Symptoms	Manifestations of Difficulties in the Couple Relationship
1 Intrusions	Appearing self-absorbed.
	Feeling different: "You cannot possibly understand."
	Emotional withdrawal from family members because of preoccupation with intrusive memories.
2 Avoidance Symptoms	Lack of intimacy or difficulty in sustaining intimacy.
	Withdrawal during times of emotional intensity between members.
	Increased isolation.
	Non-trauma partner attempts to engage partner, and may feel that the distance has been created as a result of something they did.
3 Arousal Symptoms (including hypervigilance for danger or denial of danger)	Irritability toward partners and the larger community.
	Explosive anger. Violence.
	Separate sleep arrangements/sexual difficulties.
	Non-trauma partner "walking on eggshells" in an attempt not to upset traumatized partner.
	Overly concerned about the welfare of the family unit ("Bad things can happen"), contrasted with no overt concern about the family.
4 Survivor Guilt/Shame	Feelings of not deserving happiness and good things in a relationship.
5 Externalization of Responsibility	"The PTSD made me do it" explanation of problems.

For example, a woman who has been raped may stay up at night because she has trouble sleeping, thus disrupting the couple's traditional bedtime routine. She may have a difficult time telling her partner about the experience and what is disturbing her sleep. She may fear that such disclosure would negatively affect his view of her. Her distancing keeps her from obtaining comfort and support from her partner and keeps him in the dark about her emotional experience. The distancing may be a response to her belief that the partner would have difficulty in dealing with the trauma and her emotions. The manner in which the couple handles the trauma sequelae will influence stress symptoms and may cause or perpetuate difficulties within the relationship.

PTSD AND SYSTEMS THEORY

The etiology of PTSD has been explained by biological, psychodynamic, and cognitive behavioral theories (Marmar, Foy, Kagan, & Pynoos, 1993). However, these explanations do not emphasize understanding traumatized individuals in their social context. Systems theory helps to explain how maladaptive interactional patterns between partners may reinforce the symptoms of PTSD.

A system is defined as an interconnected group of parts which, when taken together, make up more than each part added individually (Nichols & Schwartz, 1991, p. 101). Systems can be conceptualized to include the individual, couple, family, and larger community (Peterson, Prout, & Schwartz, 1991, p. 100). Individuals participate in a number of systems in their daily lives. A person's co-workers are often members of one system, whereas the people with whom the individual lives are typically members of another. Friendships, ethnic groups, and religious affiliations are all examples of systems. Each system of which the couple is a part will impact the expression of stress symptoms as well as the relationship as a whole.

Couples Systems

We believe that the ways in which partners in a couple treat one another (i.e., their interactional patterns) can serve to increase, decrease, or maintain the symptoms of stress in the traumatized partner as well as affect the couple's well-being in the community.

Family patterns preceding the trauma may help set the stage for the couple's symptomatic response to the trauma. Difficulties with adjustment to post-trauma life may become chronic problems because the couple's system fails to adapt to the changes the trauma precipitates in the individual. The couple may attempt to cope with the sequelae of the trauma in various ways which become habitual feedback loops. Some feedback loops help to maintain the existence of the problem and, over time, become maladaptive.

For example, a man traumatized from a car accident in which another driver ran a stop sign begins refusing to allow his wife to leave his sight because "bad things can happen at any time." This overprotectiveness is at first tolerated by the partner, but as she grows weary and experiences a greater need to reconnect with the larger system, she is increasingly irritated by his behavior. This irritation may fuel his fear that he is losing her, thus increasing his insecurity and creating a greater desire on his part to keep her close to him. The maladaptive interactional pattern maintained by the feedback loop ultimately crystallizes the PTSD symptoms as part of a mutual reinforcement cycle between the spouses.

Larger Community Systems

The manner in which traumatized persons' social systems respond to them will impact their symptoms. For example, the combat veterans who returned from Vietnam experienced varying degrees of hostility from people in their communities, a phenomena labelled by Donald Catherall as secondary trauma (Catherall, 1989, p. 290). Veterans who returned to non-supportive or hostile communities may experience an increase in trauma symptoms, while those who returned to communities which honored their service and welcome them home appear to have fewer symptoms, in spite of significant wartime trauma exposure.

As the larger community affects an individual's trauma symptoms, trauma influences a couple's ability to participate in the larger community. Couples who have experienced trauma, especially idiosyncratic traumas which are not widely shared, often feel defective or different from other members of their community and fear that they will be misunderstood or rejected. The traumatized partner's desire for isolation makes it difficult for the couple to access the social supports in their communities. Without social support, the survivor's symptomatology may increase (Flannery, 1990, pp. 604–605). The couple may have difficulty trusting others outside the relationship.

In our work, we often see couples who have withdrawn from all relationships outside the marriage. This withdrawal permits some sense of safety from the dangers of the world and control over symptoms at the cost of the social support which may be otherwise available. The non-traumatized partner, perhaps feeling less need for isolation, may particularly suffer through loss of these supports. For example:

Sam, a World War II Prisoner of War, had been unable to discuss the details of his captivity with anyone. After spending most of his life working and commuting 12 hours each day, retirement was a frightening time with "nothing" to do. Sam worked at the post office, surrounded almost entirely by men. While working, he had occasionally discussed his war-zone experiences with his colleagues but did not maintain any contact with them after he retired. Troublesome thoughts about his war experiences increased following his retirement. His thoughts of being held prisoner in the war reawakened the belief that he was a coward and should never have surrendered. He became anxious, slept poorly, and was jumpy.

Eventually, he disclosed detailed information about his POW experience to his wife, Nancy, in therapy. To his surprise, she was able to listen to his painful experience. She did not judge him harshly as he had feared, and, in fact, stated that she loved him for the courage it took to tell her. The experience of sharing information and receiving support helped Sam to see himself as the courageous person he was. Telling Nancy and receiving her support helped to reduce the intensity of Sam's intrusive symptoms and his shame for having surrendered. This experience gave Sam the courage to participate more in community organizations and to become more vocal about asking for support from friends. He began to speak at the local high school about his war experiences as a way to help the "new generation" learn about war.

Studies on Family Systems and PTSD

Empirical studies on the effects of PTSD on families of male war veterans have demonstrated that veterans' PTSD or acute stress reactions negatively affect the functioning of their partners and families. Zahava Solomon studied couples who were together prior to the male partner going to war in the 1973 Arab–Israeli conflict (Solomon et al., 1992). Partners of veterans who were diagnosed with war-related PTSD or stress reactions reported more psychiatric problems than did partners of veterans without stress-related symptoms. On a symptom checklist questionnaire, the partners of veterans diagnosed with an acute stress reaction and later with PTSD indicated more psychiatric problems than did partners of veterans with either an acute stress reaction or PTSD alone. None of these couples had significant problems prior to the veteran's war experience.

In a second study, Kathleen Jordan and her colleagues (Jordan et al., 1992) found that families with PTSD-diagnosed veterans had more problems in marital and family adjustment, parenting, and violent behavior than did families of veterans in which there was no diagnosable PTSD. The wives of partners with diagnosable PTSD also were more likely to report lower levels of happiness and life satisfaction than partners of veterans not diagnosed with current PTSD. Children of PTSD-diagnosed veterans were more likely to exhibit behavioral problems than children of veterans who were not diagnosed with PTSD.

In the third study, Lisa Caselli and Robert Motta (1995) examined the effects of Vietnam veterans' PTSD on their partners and children, and found that both the partner relationship and the childrens' behavior were affected by PTSD. Individuals in couples in which the male veteran had been diagnosed with PTSD indicated that they agreed less, were less satisfied with their relationship, expressed less affection, and had fewer common interests than did individuals in couples where the veteran did not have diagnosable PTSD. Finally, couples where the veteran was diagnosed with PTSD reported more behavioral problems in their children than did couples without a PTSD diagnosis.

These reports support our clinical observation that trauma adversely affects not only the person who experiences it, but also the entire family system. Families deal with significant stressors caused by the systems' attempts to adapt to the problems created by the trauma. Although empirical work has been done on the families and partners of male war veterans, the same cannot be said of female survivors of trauma such as rape or childhood sexual abuse. There is a clear need to study the impact of this type of trauma on the relationships, partners, and children of women who have survived these kinds of events.

SETTING THE STAGE FOR COUPLES THERAPY

To set the stage for therapy with couples who have experienced trauma, we have found it helpful to provide them with general background information about the therapy process and general information about couples in which a member has been diagnosed with PTSD. The issues we discuss include natural family crises, vocational issues, trauma reminders, nightmares, and litigation. Not every couple has needs in all of these areas, but this information may help the couple select a problem focus and convey a sense of expertise on the part of the therapist.

Natural Family Crises

Ordinary stages in the family life cycle create stress for families in which a member has the symptoms of PTSD (Scaturo & Hayman, 1992). These stages include courtship, marriage or commitment, childbirth, parenting, leaving the household (launching), retirement, dying, and divorce.

Couples may come in for therapy with courtship or commitment problems. The traumatized partner may create situations to test the commitment to the relationship. Deepening the intimacy and investment in a relationship is often frightening for trauma survivors due to their fears of loss or abandonment. Childbirth, with issues around bonding and remaining attached, is another stress point. Bonding may stir fears of loss and result in the trauma survivor distancing him or herself from a loved child. The child's increasing independence and entrance into the outside world through school may bring up fears in the traumatized parent that the child will be exposed to uncontrollable and dangerous situations. The trauma survivor may become rigidly rule-bound in an attempt to ensure the safety of loved ones. In addition, a larger community must be managed, creating the need for parents to negotiate new relationships. Each new relationship presents the risk of triggering the symptoms exhibited by the traumatized individual and his or her family.

As the child grows, the conflicts of the teenage years may be accentuated by the parents' difficulties in letting the child become responsible for his or her own well-being. The young person's increasing independence and imminent launching are often troubling for couples dealing with the aftermath of trauma. Fears for the safety of the adult child and difficulty dealing with the emotional consequences of a child leaving home often lead to problems in the family. Faced with a loss of intensive daily parenting, the couple may be confronted with unaddressed issues in their own relationship. The therapist should screen for the possibility of traumatization in the children and make appropriate recommendations, which may range from education to a therapy referral.

Aging can also present a challenge to trauma survivor couples. Severely stressed couples often experience vocational problems, but retirement can present a challenge even for couples who have dealt well with the effects of trauma. No longer able to structure their relationship around work, the partners have no buffer between them. Physical disability as well as deaths of friends and family members in later life may increase PTSD symptoms. For couples who have focused on survival in the face of trauma and its sequelae, accepting the ending of life may be difficult. Couples in later life may need to rework the meaning of the trauma in their relationship and come to a new understanding of their own life goals.

Divorce may occur at any point in the developmental life cycle of a family. The endings and loss that come with divorce can be particularly painful for trauma survivors. There may be a tendency to avoid difficult feelings by quickly pushing through with the divorce and not saying goodbye to one another. The divorcing couple may benefit from working through their goodbyes in therapy. Here is an illustration:

We worked with a couple, Alice and George, who came to treatment a year after their divorce. At the time of therapy, Alice was living with a new partner and the children from her marriage with George, while George, a trauma survivor, was living alone. Because of his anger and grief about the dissolution of the marriage, George was inconsistent in seeing the children. Alice, in turn, felt guilty for leaving George. We met with Alice and George and intermittently with their two children for several sessions. The couple was able to express their regrets about the marriage not having worked out, and finally expressed caring and respect for one another in front of the children. This communication helped to reduce the bitterness and guilt between the couple and led the way for George to visit his children more consistently.

Vocational Issues

Vocational problems often accompany stress disorder for couples who have experienced trauma. The traumatized partner may have difficulty with interpersonal functioning at work and with taking on positions of responsibility or dealing with authority. Trauma survivors may feel emotionally distanced and isolated at work as they do in other arenas of their lives. They may feel a need to control for unwanted outcomes, either attempting to take on too much responsibility or refusing to put themselves in a responsible role. Often, trauma survivors feel or believe that someone in authority should have acted to protect them from the traumatic experience. This feeling can result in the trauma survivor becoming hostile and mistrustful with authority figures. Sometimes the trauma survivor restricts his or her behavior, which may in turn impair job performance. Someone who has experienced an airplane disaster, for example, may have great difficulty with the air travel required by his or her employment.

Job loss may result either directly from the trauma or indirectly from its emotional sequelae. Job loss or a decrease in the ability to achieve vocationally often has significant effects on the couple system. The traumatized partner may see job difficulties or job loss as confirmation of the damage caused by the trauma. The non-traumatized partner may have to carry a new level of financial responsibility for the couple. This financial responsibility, in combination with frequently increased emotional responsibility, adds to the stress of a system already dealing with a crisis.

Trauma Reminders

Sensory experiences such as smells, feeling states, sights, or sounds may remind the survivor of the traumatic event. For former combatants, reminders of wartime such as news coverage of conflicts may be deeply disturbing. Rape survivors may be reminded of the rape trauma by events that disempower individuals. The trauma survivor often experiences an increase in symptoms in response to such reminders or triggers. If the survivor uses negative patterns of coping that are injurious to the self or relationships in an attempt to manage the symptoms, both the symptoms and the maladaptive interactional patterns connected with them may increase.

During the assessment phase, it may be appropriate to advise the client to limit exposure to television news or other known triggers in order to reduce stress. Helping the couple understand which events act as triggers and what interactional patterns they engage in when triggered will provide the basis for further treatment.

Nightmares

Nightmares are one of the hallmark symptoms of PTSD and are discussed in greater detail elsewhere in this volume. It is important to note that nightmares impact not only the dreamer but also his or her spouse. Trauma survivors may not tell their partners about their nightmares or may physically act out portions of the nightmares. When the trauma survivor does not explain his or her difficulties sleeping, the partner is left to speculate as to the cause. The result tends to be increased emotional distance between the couple. The trauma survivor may engage in checking behaviors or, in the case of war veterans, walking the perimeter, in an effort to ensure the safety of the children and security of the home. At times, the trauma survivor may act out portions of dreams, either assaulting or being extremely fearful of the partner. All these behaviors affect the partner, resulting in disrupted sleep, stressful feelings, and, not infrequently, separate sleeping arrangements.

Litigation

Litigation is a special issue, particularly with people who have recently experienced trauma. It is our experience that engaging in litigation accentuates the traumatic event and exacerbates its negative effects. Successful litigation may provide a feeling of empowerment. Even in successful litigation, however, couples may experience feelings of depression during and after extensive depositions, negotiations, and trial proceedings. The experience of retelling the story to a skeptical and disbelieving audience can cause an increase in PTSD symptoms. If the case is not decided in the traumatized individual's favor, the litigation may be experienced as another traumatic event.

BEGINNING STAGE OF THERAPY

Establishing the ground rules in the early phases of treatment sets the stage for successful therapy. As a problem focus is slowly identified, the couples therapist simultaneously assesses both the strengths of the couple and the interactional patterns associated with the problem. Education about the effects of PTSD on families and individuals is useful in the early part of treatment. Homework may be assigned and discussed throughout the treatment to encourage the couple to focus on the maladaptive interactional patterns that are maintaining the problems. We will now describe each of these therapeutic tasks in detail.

Ground Rules

Confidentiality should be discussed at the outset of couples therapy. The couple should be informed of the limits of confidentiality under state law. Confidentiality of information given by one of the partners can be a tricky issue. Generally, we do not encourage disclosures which may draw the therapist into an alliance with one of the partners, as such an alliance can result in a therapeutic impasse. However, be aware of potentially important information that a member of the couple may have difficulty communicating. Discussion of violence may be conducted most usefully with each partner individually. Whatever your decision regarding confidentiality between partners, it is critical to attend to the consequences of such disclosures or secrets. Here is an example:

We met with a Vietnam veteran and his wife separately during therapy because we felt there was something he was holding back. In an individual session, he told a wrenching story of having killed a child in Vietnam and expressed his torment over the incident and his fear that he would not be able to fulfill his role as a new father.

We felt it would betray a deep confidence with this veteran to bring the information into the therapy with his wife, who did not know what had happened. Consequently, we acknowledged that terrible events can occur which challenge one's belief in oneself as a good person and parent. We then focused on ways the veteran, with help from his wife, could work to establish, both to himself and to others, his goodness as a father.

When the male partner has been diagnosed with PTSD, violence and threats of violence may be directed toward the spouse. The physical safety of both partners must be established and maintained throughout the course of therapy. We require that couples agree to refrain from physical violence at home. In addition, threats such as suicide, provocative behavior, verbal retaliation, or leaving the relationship must be negotiated for the duration of the therapy so that these threats do not hinder the accomplishment of the couple's therapeutic goals.

Assessment

We take a relationship history as part of the assessment. We look at family of origin, length of relationship, how the couple met, their original expectations of the union, and how they functioned as a couple prior to the trauma. Trauma may significantly change expectations and functioning, leading couples to reevaluate their relationship contract. We discuss with the couple their commitment to the relationship, indicating that difficult issues will arise and that without commitment it will be impossible to deal with these issues.

Once we have taken a relationship and family history, we consider role functioning in the relationship, examining who performs what tasks within the relationship. We look at how rigidly the tasks are divided and at the distribution of power in the relationship. We use the information about the family of origin and present role functioning to help the couple understand their current problems in the relationship.

For example, in relationships where one member has a chronic disability and the other member is working, the disability may serve the function of balancing the economic imbalance in the system. If one partner is using his or her PTSD symptoms as a source of power in the relationship, this partner may be reluctant to work on symptom reduction, even in the service of his or her own health. Likewise, the caretaking partner may have an investment in maintaining the power afforded by the caretaking role.

Jackie confronted Tom, a Persian Gulf War veteran, about not doing more at home when she was working. He became irritated with her, stating, "She just doesn't understand how my PTSD keeps me from doing more around the house." When questioned further, Tom expressed anger at himself and at his wife for asking that he do more. He would then feel guilty and begin to think about his war experiences.

Tom was receiving a service-connected disability check from the Department of Veterans Affairs, and said he was concerned about losing his income if he took a chance on finding employment. He and Jackie were able to see that his sense of himself as disabled enabled him to maintain a level of control which would be threatened if he attempted, and possibly failed, to obtain employment. Together they explored Tom's fears of failure and loss and Jackie's fears that giving up control would result in disappointment.

Individuals may be explicit about their partner's role in maintaining problems, but may have difficulty acknowledging their own contribution to the problem. We attempt to negotiate an explanation with the couple that takes into account each member's perspective on the problem. We also ask about social support systems, including friends and extended families, to help clarify which relationships are helping the couple resolve their problems and achieve their desired goals.

We explore any history of trauma, including physical or sexual abuse experienced by the individuals. An assessment of substance abuse is crucial, since in our clinic approximately 70% of the clients diagnosed with PTSD have past or present substance abuse. We also look at prior treatment, whether or not it was useful, and what did or did not work. With signed permission, we contact former therapists, and we contact the individual therapist if either partner is working with one.

When determining the level of functioning of a couple system, we find it useful to gather information about a family's strengths, or what continues to work in the family in spite of its problems (de Shazer, 1985; Walter & Peller, 1992). Focusing on strengths may help the couple to remobilize coping behaviors, return to their previous level of functioning, or modify negative patterns of interaction. Traumatized couples often feel hopeless and demoralized, and it can be therapeutic for them to identify healthy behaviors they are already using.

Obtaining an Agreed-Upon Problem Focus

We use the information gathered in the assessment phase to reach a mutually agreed-upon problem focus. We determine whether the trauma is acute or chronic, and look at the maladaptive interactional coping patterns which have developed as a result of the trauma. We examine what these patterns are, how long they have been going on, and which are most problematic to the couple. Some couples come in with a list of problems, so the therapist helps them to prioritize the focus.

The problem is examined in terms of frequency, duration, and intensity. Once the problem has been explored in detail, the couple is asked to define their goals in behavioral terms. Both the partners and the therapist work out these goals in a way agreed upon by all parties. The therapist becomes a part of the treating system, and his or her viewpoint can function to amplify a couple's strengths or their problems, thus creating change or creating impasse (Green, 1988, pp. 383–384).

Our best outcomes have occurred with couples whose problem definition has been constructed with a focus on both members working together to change a recurring pattern. Once the problem is defined in specific behavioral terms, length of treatment and outcome are negotiated. The couple is asked to describe how they will know that the problem has improved. Improvement is defined in specific behavioral terms, and this definition is set as the outcome goal.

Jeff complained that Martha was controlling and always wanted to know where he was going or where he had been. Martha complained that Jeff would never call to let her know when he would be late, and at times stayed out all night drinking. We worked with the couple to come up with the following problem explanation: Martha's controlling behavior encouraged Jeff to be dishonest, and Jeff's irresponsible behavior pushed Martha to be controlling.

Education

As we join with the couple and explore a problem focus, we use our knowledge of stress symptoms to educate the couple. Education helps to normalize the couple's experience, to help them learn to make a set of behavioral observations, and to indicate the therapist's understanding of their situation, engendering hope for change. We discuss the symptoms of PTSD as an adjustment reaction to trauma and elicit the couple's ideas for strategies to minimize the impact of the symptoms on the relationship. The couple may find it useful to become aware of which symptoms are affecting them and how the partners are working together to increase, decrease, or maintain the symptoms. Throughout this process, the therapist should ensure that the trauma survivor does not become either the exclusive focus of change or the person expected to be unable to change.

Use of Homework

During the problem formulation phase, we use homework to help the couple observe and focus on the problem. This intervention in itself may encourage a new behavior pattern which results in some improvement. Later in the therapy, homework may be used to implement change, monitor progress, or assist the couple in gaining a sense of independence from therapy.

In assigning homework, we have found it most effective to ask a couple to increase some behavior rather than to reduce a behavior. We have been more successful at increasing positive behaviors than at reducing negative ones.

The therapist can tailor homework to address a specific aspect of the problem. However, it is important to consider the couple's ability to complete the assignment successfully and to provide homework that can be accomplished. We discuss the results of the assigned homework during the following session, in order to convey a sense of the importance of the task. If the couple does not do the homework, we help them explore the reasons in a way that does not shame them. Usually, couples who do not do the homework have at least thought about the assignment and can provide useful information about their interactions. A plan to reduce the likelihood of future non-compliance with homework, such as revising or changing the assignment in response to the information elicited from the couple, may be helpful.

MIDDLE STAGE OF THERAPY

Once the problem has been defined and a goal has been set for treatment outcome, we work with the couple to move toward the chosen goal. For some couples, this process may be as straightforward as increasing some behavior that already exists, such as spending more enjoyable time together. For others, this part of the therapy may be complicated by issues that get in the way of the desired changes. Blocks to achieving the goal need to be examined carefully as they arise in therapy, and resolved in order to proceed toward the goal.

Couples with a chronic adjustment to trauma often have multiple problems and present a complicated treatment dilemma due to the length of time they have been using maladaptive coping strategies. However, therapists cannot assume that the degree of complexity in the adaptation to trauma always requires a complex therapy. We have had cases with difficult adjustments to trauma that have done very well with a single-problem focus and intervention.

At age 16 Richard had watched his mother shoot and kill his physically abusive father. Mary, his partner, grew up in a single-parent home with an extremely critical mother who had been diagnosed with bipolar disorder. The couple found themselves in a recurring pattern in which Mary would feel neglected and would criticize Richard for not paying enough attention to her. The criticism frightened Richard, and he would withdraw. Mary would then criticize him for his withdrawal, which would perpetuate the cycle.

The couple agreed on a goal of increasing the time they spent together. Helping Mary point out to Richard the moments when he wasn't neglecting her allowed Richard to come out of his protective shell and give her the intimate contact she wanted. Mary began to attempt new ways of communicating about what she needed in the relationship. Richard began to express his needs to Mary and his discomfort at her criticisms. He listened carefully to what she was saying and began to hear not only a critical message but also a message of "I need you."

Although both partners had a history of trauma, the intervention focused primarily on changing the current maladaptive pattern within the relationship. This focus helped the couple obtain their stated goal.

If the therapy becomes stuck due to a persistent maladaptive interactional pattern, we have found it useful to examine the behavioral sequence involved. The interaction can be explored for the meanings attributed by each partner to their own and their partner's words and behavior. Communication skills may be useful to help clarify the interactions and help the couple work on possible solutions. The therapist can help the partners to speak in simple, direct terms which request specific behavioral change. Trauma-exposed couples often benefit from practicing basic communication skills such as paraphrasing what the other has said, adhering to the condition of no rebuttals or criticism, and making "I" statements.

Difficulty in Talking about Trauma

Talking about the trauma is difficult for couples and therapists. When the couple says they want to talk about the trauma and are unable to do so, we assess the reasons for wanting to discuss the event and what they hope to accomplish by talking about it. It is useful to ascertain whether both members of the couple want to discuss the event.

We do not encourage the discussion of the trauma in all couples' therapies. Discussion of the trauma may set the couple up for a disappointing experience, which may include re-traumatizing one partner. Prior to discussing the traumatic event, it is helpful to conduct a brief psychosocial history and create a genogram for each member of the couple, identifying any traumas that have been experienced by each party. This information can help illuminate the significance of the traumatic event in relation to each partner. It is usually the case that discussing the traumatic event is helpful to the family. When the trauma has occurred recently, or if it has never been discussed and the partner appears supportive, we recommend talking about the event. However, when a member of the couple is significantly impaired or when a partner cannot be supportive, discussion of the traumatic event in couples therapy may not be the intervention of choice.

The rules for talking about these events and issues of safety should be discussed clearly. The couple may want to place a time limit on the discussion or make an agreement that the partners either share or not share their reactions. The partners may give each other permission to stop talking if they feel unsafe or uncomfortable. We ask them to determine what they want from their partner while they are talking about the trauma. We generally begin discussion of the trauma in the session and encourage discussions to begin at home gradually. This method will also work with discussions unrelated to the retelling of the trauma. The non-traumatized partner often has not discussed the difficulties in dealing with the relationship problems resulting from the trauma. Providing this partner with a safe forum to begin discussing feelings may open the door for increased intimacy.

The sense of separateness about having gone through a trauma leads to a sense of aloneness for both members of the couple. In dealing with this issue, we have found it important to acknowledge and work with the survivor's attachment and loyalty to other survivors and any sense of betrayal about sharing the events with the spouse. Other couples' success stories in negotiating this potential impasse are extremely helpful at this point.

Therapeutic Systems

Coordination among the treatment personnel involved with any member of the system is a crucial element to providing successful care. A couples therapist must consider the involvement of other health care providers. Clients often form strong alliances with their individual or group therapists; the couples therapist must understand these alliances in order to be effective. It is helpful to think of other treatment personnel as part of the larger family or social system in which the clients' problems are situated. Discussing and understanding the explanations by other treatment personnel as to the nature of the problem can help inform successful treatment interventions.

Donna and Jim came into couples therapy because of issues of trust in their marriage. Jim had chronic problems with drinking, and, although he had some recent periods of sobriety, continued to go on two- or three-day binges. Jim was in therapy with an individual therapist but had not told her about his drinking. After we obtained Jim's consent to talk with his therapist, Jim told the therapist about his drinking problem. We contacted the therapist, and it was agreed that we would work with Jim on his binge drinking in both the individual and couples therapy.

When to Refer

The treatment of acute or chronic PTSD may involve referring individuals to other forms of treatment in addition to couples therapy. An individual who has chronic sleep problems and irritability may benefit from a psychopharmacological assessment and intervention. There may be issues that cannot be addressed in the couple's work. Individual or group treatment should be considered if the individual diagnosed with PTSD appears to need something different from what the couples treatment is providing.

ENDING STAGE OF THERAPY

As the couple moves toward achievement of their goals, it is important for them to understand and acknowledge their strengths. Each time an accomplishment is made, it helps to consolidate the new behavior if the therapist focuses on how that change happened, the choices and behaviors of each partner, and the meaning of the change in relation to the couple and the trauma. Surviving a trauma often results in issues around feeling ineffective, out of control, and out of community. One of the functions of couples therapy can be to encourage both partners to see the couple and the trauma survivor as efficacious in achieving their goals. The therapist can help the couple understand the positive changes they have made and attribute these changes to their work in therapy and at home. Understanding the changes as the result of their own efforts can strengthen the couple's ability to build on these changes.

Getting Stuck

If, instead of improving, the couple becomes stuck or gets worse, the therapist needs to return to the problem formulation. It may be that the problem has not been formulated clearly and therefore has not been understood or agreed upon by all parties. When the problem is clarified, it may emerge that one partner actually wants to separate, but has been unable to voice this goal. Treatment may then focus on how to separate in the best way possible. The manner in which the separation occurs will be important to the well-being of the couple and any children of the partnership. Couples who are going through separation may experience great pain and vulnerability. Issues around loss are particularly difficult for survivors of trauma. Many couples will want to cut off their relationship abruptly. The couples therapist can help them see the benefit of working together on the issues of connection and disconnection around the separation, in order to become more clear and comfortable with their changed relationship and to move on in their lives.

PTSD SYMPTOMS IN COUPLES

In this section, we will discuss how the symptoms that are the diagnostic hallmarks of PTSD—intrusions, avoidance, and arousal—are expressed in couples' relationships. We will also address particular issues we frequently encounter in couples with PTSD: sexuality, guilt and shame, responsibility, and rigidified gender roles. While all of these problems will not be seen in each couple, they represent a range of possible problems to look for when treating couples who have experienced trauma.

Intrusions

The person with PTSD can seem very self-absorbed, and the spouse may be unsure how to respond. Early attempts to coax the partner into talking about the problem may cause the traumatized partner to withdraw, with the spouse feeling that it is his or her fault. If the couple wants to deal with how the intrusions disrupt the relationship, we help them articulate what they would like to be doing when the intrusive memories occur. Helping the spouse understand that the intrusions may not be a sign of disinterest opens the possibility for changed communication and new interactional patterns between the partners.

We also help the survivor become more aware of when and why he or she wants to be left alone. We then help the survivor tell the partner about this need to be alone, in a way that the partner can hear. Couples may want to put a time limit on separateness or schedule a later time to discuss why the traumatized partner needed separateness.

Mary and Don came into treatment complaining of a lack of intimacy in their relationship. Don frequently spent time alone in the garage, and often left Mary abruptly. Although she felt rejected, Mary had learned not to question these departures in order to avoid an ensuing argument. After the parameters of therapy were well established, Mary felt safe enough to ask Don about this behavior. He was able to tell her that unbidden memories of his service in Korea sometimes came to him and that he needed to be alone during these times.

Mary felt relief to hear this, because she had thought that Don was reacting to her behavior. Don was surprised that Mary was able to listen to him without criticizing what he perceived as his failures. Once the interactional pattern and the meanings behind it were clear, the couple was able to make some progress toward greater intimacy.

Avoidance

We often see couples who have lost the ability to talk intimately with one another. Strong feelings are often frightening for trauma survivors, and thus they may avoid them in relationships. Emotional intensity between the partners may be experienced as either positive or negative. Any intense or powerfully experienced feeling may bring up fears of loss of control. The trauma survivor may avoid these feelings through withdrawal, which the

partner may interpret as a rejection. Often the couple becomes more distant, with angry feelings on both sides, as a result.

We find it helpful to join with the couple by acknowledging the difficulty
of the decision to seek help. Isolation or avoidance is no longer working
for them, and they are willing at least to think about trying something
different. The therapist can build on this willingness to reach for help by
asking the couple why and how they were able to come to an outsider for
help, and by pointing out the strength and flexibility they have shown by
this effort.

After the assessment, the therapist should have a working hypothesis or
theory about the couple's interactional patterns and the meanings attributed to them by the partners. For example, the therapist may hypothesize
that the male partner's withdrawal is preceded by the female partner's push
for closeness, and that the female partner chooses to push for intimacy
when she experiences his withdrawal. He may explain his withdrawal as a
response to PTSD and fears of intimacy; she may believe that it expresses
his feeling that she is inadequate. Clarifying the meaning of each individual's behavior often results in relief and renewed commitment to work on
the relationship.

In couples with avoidant interactional behaviors who desire to become
closer, it is useful to ask the partners to describe the behaviors they believe
will bring them closer. We begin by having the couple attempt to become
closer in session. Later, we assign homework to help them to practice the
changes on their own. It is critical to ensure that the couple is adequately
prepared to talk about issues of importance at home before this is assigned
as homework. Assigning homework without adequate preparation is des-
tined to fail.

With couples who want to talk about a particular issue they have been
avoiding, we ask them to discuss the issue in session for 10 minutes. The
therapist can observe and then help the couple alter the maladaptive interactional patterns that have been causing them trouble. The therapist can
explore with the couple what did and did not work about the interactions
until the couple and therapist feel that the couple is ready to try a discussion
at home. Homework assignments may feature structured activities. A couple that has trouble talking about feelings of shame or fear might, for
example, be assigned to watch a movie which deals prominently with these
feelings and to discuss it afterward. If they want to discuss more sensitive
issues, they can work up to these over time. For example:

Ann came into therapy wanting her husband, Fred, to talk to her about his war
experiences. As her desire was explored, it turned out that she really wanted him
to reveal more of his feelings to her so that she could feel closer to him. She knew
that he had strong feelings about the war and had seen him express them, so she
thought this was the key for them to talk more intimately and become closer. As

she clarified what she wanted from him, he was able to talk more emotionally with her about other things, although not in the cathartic, intense way he talked about the war. He too wished to become closer, and eventually expressed his fears that he would lose control and cry if he revealed his feelings.

Arousal

When one member of a couple is traumatized, arousal symptoms often lead to a heightening of emotions, including irritability. Arousal symptoms occur in both response to the outside world and in interactions between partners. Trauma survivors tend to be vigilant to the possibility of threat. Concern for the welfare of family members may cause the individual to take precautionary steps perceived as protecting the family from some unknown danger. Being on guard can be stressful for the spouse, who may become frustrated when his or her assurances that the family is safe are not easily accepted. For example, one survivor of an airplane crash became so worried every time his family members flew that he was not able to function effectively at work. He requested that his family call him immediately upon landing. This concern became so annoying that his wife would refuse to tell him about any of her work-related flights.

Maladaptive interactional patterns used by partners to deal with arousal symptoms typically increase emotional distance through ignoring or withholding communication about stressful topics. Such patterns can become chronic, keeping the couple at a distance. We often see avoidance of anger in couples in which the man's trauma is war-related. Because they avoid discussing angry feelings, these couples do not learn how to identify incremental anger, and therefore notice it only when they are close to being out of control. Conflict between the partners is avoided, and there is a "walking on eggshells" quality to their interactions because the stakes in situations of conflict seem so high. Partners may hide conflictual feelings from one another, increasing the distance and mistrust between them. These situations often culminate with an explosion of anger resulting in violence.

Therapy involves helping the couple talk about what is most troubling in their interaction and notice when they start to feel irritated. The therapist can help the partners recognize the difference between irritation, anger, and rage. As the couple understands the feelings behind their anger, which is often based in fear and sadness, we help them find constructive ways to express these feelings to each other. We also help them identify themes and develop communication skills to talk about problematic issues when they are not angry. Many couples do not want to "rock the boat" when things are going well, and thus are at risk for having built-up anger spill out when they discuss a small problem. Helping them with communication skills gives them a chance to defuse problems as they arise. Here is a good example:

Cathy, an administrative assistant, and Louis, a Korean War veteran who was involved in group therapy at the Department of Veterans Affairs Hospital, had been married for six years when they came to treatment to work on decreasing the intensity of their verbal fighting. Louis would become angry during fights and would walk out of the house, staying away for days. Cathy had experienced a number of losses early in her life, and felt that his leaving was an abandonment of her; when she saw him again, she would immediately become furious with him. Her anger sent Louis out the door again. With our help, Louis acknowledged his concern about becoming violent during these arguments.

Once Cathy communicated her understanding of this fear to Louis, he found he was able to telephone her to let her know where he was (usually at a motel alone). This phone call and her understanding of Louis's fear of becoming violent allowed Cathy to manage her anger toward him when he returned. They worked toward Louis's staying in the house during the arguments by using short time-outs. These techniques helped Cathy decrease her anger and remain more patient during their disagreements.

Here is another illustration:

Sandy and Bob had been married for four years when Sandy was mugged and severely beaten. The couple worked well together during the recovery, with Bob showing understanding of Sandy's frequent angry outbursts. As time wore on, Bob had less patience with Sandy and began to avoid areas of conflict in their relationship. They both experienced distress at the increasing distance in their relationship.

In therapy, they explored the function of Sandy's arousal symptoms in their relationship. Instead of withdrawing in response to Sandy's harsh words, Bob learned to draw her attention to the conflict. Sandy, in turn, would then discuss the problem or indicate that she needed some distance and would discuss it later. Sandy became more aware of her irritability and was able to decrease its frequency as she felt Bob's support and acceptance of her struggle.

Sexuality

Trauma and its sequelae often affect sexual intimacy in the couple. Persons exposed to trauma may have performance anxiety, aggressive impulses, or fears being hurt or of strong feelings. If the trauma was sexual or particularly intimate, the therapist may worry that she or he is being sadistic in encouraging the couple to talk about the trauma and the sexual difficulties. Therapists must deal with their own feelings so that they can treat couples who want help with their sexual problems.

In a review of the rape trauma literature, Theresa Foley (1985) discussed reactions of male partners of rape survivors, including guilt or self-blame, a desire for revenge, anger, attribution of sexual overtones to the rape, a sense of loss, and the need to protect or confine the victim. These reactions from partners may arise either from the traumatic event or from the interaction between the couple.

Carolyn Maltas and Joseph Shay (1995) observed a trauma contagion that occurs with intimate sexual partners of childhood abuse survivors. When the childhood survivor first tells the partner about his or her experiences of abuse, the partner's assumptions that the world is a just, benevolent, and orderly place are shattered. Partners commonly respond by attempting to overprotect the family, decrease sexual contact, and deny the importance of the information. Partners may also have a difficult time seeing themselves as in need of any help since they often perceive themselves as the caretakers in the relationship.

The traumatized partner may become withdrawn, labile, or repulsed by sex. The intimacy and physicality of the sexual relationship itself may trigger flashbacks or body memories in the survivor, and this may be confusing to both the survivor and the partner (Maltas & Shay, 1995, p. 531). The partner is caught between a need for sex and the survivor's need to avoid it. Sexual activity between partners may unwittingly reenact the trauma, as the trauma survivor attempts to gain mastery over the situation. Therapy with these couples involves helping them become aware of how the trauma enters into their sexual relationship and then helping them to change these destructive patterns, as in this case:

Sam and Ginger came in to therapy due to the infrequency of their lovemaking. We encouraged Ginger to request that Sam hold her hand and listen as she spoke of the rape she had endured two years earlier, rather than become enraged at the man who raped her. Sam, a quiet and reserved man with difficulty in expressing his affection directly, was able to do this. As a result, the couple was able to explore some of their reactions to the trauma. Ginger felt responsible for the incident. Sam's rage covered his fears of being unable to protect Ginger from what had happened to her and from her overwhelming feelings about it. His rage allowed Ginger to avoid her own anger at the perpetrator. The interaction of holding hands and listening was helpful to both Ginger and Sam.

Guilt and Shame

Survivors of trauma commonly experience guilt and feelings that they do not deserve to enjoy life. Guilt and shame from surviving a life-threatening event often occur once the survivor is safe. This feeling may be hard for the non-traumatized partner to understand. The trauma survivor may have difficulty experiencing success or positive feelings. This can be frustrating to the partner, who often tries to push or cheer the survivor into having more fun or accepting earned rewards. A parent/child dynamic may develop where the partner plays the role of the carefree child and the survivor the controlling parent. If the trauma occurred during the relationship, the non-traumatized partner may experience guilt at not having prevented the event or at being unable to eradicate its emotional consequences. Therapy can help survivors to see how the guilt is affecting their partners.

Jake and Diane came into couples therapy while both were in their thirties. Six years earlier, when they were dating and uncertain about the future of the relationship, Diane went to pick up Jake from a bar late at night and was raped. The couple ended up getting married that year, but experienced much bitterness and constant arguing. As they explored the issues in therapy, Diane became aware that she felt like "damaged goods" after the rape and did not think anyone else would want her. Jake felt guilty about the rape, and he married Diane because of this guilt. The couple was frozen in their trauma and had been unable to talk about the feelings of guilt and resentment toward one another. The unspoken fear was that if they talked about the rape, they would break up. As they began slowly to talk about the trauma, they were gradually able to heal from the rape and forgive each other. They did, however, eventually break up as the guilt that had held their relationship together lessened.

Responsibility

Survivors of trauma often have an extreme sense of responsibility and a belief that anything can go wrong if they are not extremely careful. The trauma survivor may react to the trauma by becoming either overly responsible or irresponsible. Reactions to trauma include the feeling that the survivor did not perform well enough to prevent the trauma. The desire to protect loved ones from similar traumas may lead to a fear of making any mistakes because of the terrible consequences. This fear may be expressed through rigid expectations or criticism. The partner may feel constricted by and angry about the trauma survivor's need for perfection and safety.

Our approach to this issue involves helping the couple discuss the situation and change the responsibility pattern in one very specific interaction that they identify. We examine with the partners the ways in which that interaction does and does not serve them. We encourage discussion of the possible losses that may result from either taking responsibility or letting go of it. We have found it helpful to identify and discuss realistic concerns of making a mistake in a specific situation, and to assist the partner in communicating in a non-blaming manner about the impact of the responsible or irresponsible behavior. The couple can continue to work on situations in which one partner is taking too much or too little responsibility until they feel able to resolve these situations.

Bill served in Vietnam in 1968. He and Terry were in their late forties and had been married 20 years. They had one child, Susan, age 14. Their complaint was that Bill and Susan were fighting. Upon exploration, it was revealed that this fighting had begun fairly recently and tended to focus on Susan's homework. The couple would then argue about how to parent their daughter. We were able to help Bill and Terry look at how Susan's increasing desires for autonomy since beginning high school fanned Bill's fears that she might be hurt if she made a mistake. His demands had become too much for Susan, and she began to fight back. The couple worked together to differentiate realistic from unrealistic fears and to determine new freedoms, limits, and expectations for their daughter. The couple also decided to have Bill discuss his concerns with Susan, explaining how they were amplified because of his experiences in Vietnam. Susan became much more responsive to Bill's direction as Bill became less demanding of her.

Rigidified Gender Roles

Sometimes in the aftermath of traumatic events, gender roles become polarized. The survivor may feel set adrift and need an anchor for his or her identity in a world that has become unpredictable and unsafe. Gender identity may provide this anchor. In heterosexual couples, gender identity is often polarized. Becoming rigidified in their gender roles often leads people to mishandle the intense feelings brought up by trauma. Men may be angry and unwilling to express softer feelings toward achieving intimacy. Women may become dependent and very emotional. These behaviors may force the partner into a complementary gender role. Neither partner is able to behave without the gender constrictions, resulting in rigid behavioral patterns, and providing a convenient focus for fights. The partners can become consumed with their arguments, unable to attempt unique solutions, and locked into behavioral patterns which intensify the symptoms of PTSD.

If rigidified gender roles appear to be a problem for the couple, questioning them about their interactions and the meaning they place on them is the beginning of therapy (Brooks, 1991, pp. 457–458). Gentle questioning about the behaviors can bring forth the possibility of alternative ways of behaving. The therapist can guide the couple in exploring the pros and cons of rigidified roles in the relationship. Men are often terrified of talking about intense feelings. It is important to convey to the couple that there is a continuum of feelings and that the milder feelings are important in and of themselves and as necessary stepping-stones to talking about more terrifying feelings. Women may be reluctant to communicate about their needs, feeling angry and deprived when the needs are not met. The therapist can convey to them the necessity of communicating their needs and observing their reactions in order to increase the chances of receiving the desired response from their partner. An examination of how culture reinforces particular gender roles may help free the couple to look at what is best for them as individuals and as a couple in a more flexible manner. Questioning each partner about gender roles in their family of origin may provide information that also helps with that decision. For example:

Paul and Judy had been living together for two years. Both were committed to their relationship, but they were arguing frequently over housework. Although both were employed, Paul did not feel that the house was his responsibility. Judy felt unfairly burdened with the housework. We discussed with them their respective histories regarding family roles and responsibilities. Paul had been brought up in a family where his mother remained home and did all the housework. He was raised with a strong masculine identity, and his belief in the importance of "taking it like a man" was reinforced by his military service. His trauma experience in Vietnam led him to fall back on this identity as a protection against overwhelming feelings. Judy had been raised with several brothers and, along with her mother, had been exclusively responsible for the household chores. Exploring this background helped the couple approach the problem from a non-judgmental perspective. As Paul recognized Judy's burden and Judy acknowledged Paul's difficult feelings, they were able to begin to discuss changes in their roles in the relationship.

Working with couples where a member is diagnosed with PTSD presents many challenges to the couples therapist. The key to our work has been the establishment of a well-defined problem focus and the refusal to allow weekly disasters or other chaos within the couple to derail the process. Understanding the manifestation of the symptoms of PTSD in couples relationships is key to defining the problem, to establishing an alliance with the couple, to guiding the gathering of information during assessment, and to choosing appropriate interventions.

Working with trauma survivors can be emotionally strenuous. The impact of hearing about and working with trauma survivors and the long-term difficulties that they experience can engender feelings of horror, responsibility, fear, and helplessness. Monitoring and managing your own reactions to this work as well as obtaining support will be critical to your success in working with traumatized couples and individuals.

REFERENCES

American Psychiatric Association. (1994). *Diagnostic and statistical manual of mental disorders* (DSM-IV) (4th ed.). Washington, DC: Author.

Brooks, G. (1991). Therapy pitfalls with Vietnam veteran families: Linearity, contextual naivete and gender role blindness. *Journal of Family Psychology*, 4(4), 446–461.

Caselli, L., & Motta, R. (1995). The effect of PTSD and combat level on Vietnam veterans' perceptions of child behavior and marital adjustment. *Journal of Clinical Psychology*, 51(1), 4–12.

Catherall, D. (1989). Differentiating intervention strategies for primary and secondary trauma in posttraumatic stress disorder: The example of Vietnam veterans. *Journal of Traumatic Stress*, 2(3), 298–305.

de Shazer, S. (1985). *Keys to solution in brief therapy*. New York: Norton.

Flannery, R. B. (1990). Social support and psychological trauma: A methodological review. *Journal of Traumatic Stress*, 3(4), 593–611.

Foley, T. (1985). Family response to rape and sexual assault. In A. Burgess (Ed.), *Rape and sexual assault: A research handbook* (pp. 159–188). New York: Garland.

Green, R. J. (1988). Impasse and change: A systemic/strategic view of the therapeutic system. *Journal of Marital and Family Therapy*, 14(4), 383–395.

Jordan, B. K., Marmar, C. R., Fairbank, J. A., Schlenger, W. E., Kulka, R. A., Hough, R. L., & Weiss, D. S. (1992). Problems in families of male veterans with post-traumatic stress disorder. *Journal of Consulting and Clinical Psychology*, 60(6), 916–926.

Maltas, C., & Shay, J. (1995). Trauma contagion in partners of survivors of childhood sexual abuse. *American Journal of Orthopsychiatry*, 65(4), 529–539.

Marmar, C. R., Foy, D., Kagan, B., & Pynoos, R. S. (1993). An integrated approach to treating posttraumatic stress. In J. M. Oldham, M. B. Riba, & A. Tasman (Eds.), *American Psychiatric Press review of psychiatry* (vol. 12). Washington, DC: American Psychiatric Press.

Nichols, M., & Schwartz, R. (1991). *Family therapy concepts and methods* (2nd ed.). Boston: Allyn and Bacon.

Peterson, K. C., Prout, M. F., & Schwarz, R. A. (1991). *Family and couples therapy in post-traumatic stress disorder: A clinician's guide.* New York: Plenum.

Scaturo, D. J., & Hayman, P. M. (1992). The impact of combat trauma across the family life cycle: Clinical considerations. *Journal of Traumatic Stress*, 5(2), 273–288.

Solomon, Z., Waysman, M., Levy, G., Fried, B., Mikulincer, M., Benbenishty, R., Florian, V., & Bleich, A. (1992). From front line to home front: A study of secondary traumatization. *Family Process*, September 31, 289–302.

Walter, J., & Peller, J. (1992). *Becoming solution focused in brief therapy.* New York: Brunner/Mazel.

Chapter 14

Crisis Debriefings for Emergency Service Workers

Cheryl Regehr and John A. Hill

OVERVIEW OF THE PRESENTING PROBLEM

The effects of disaster and horrifying life events on victims is well established in the professional literature and has led to a myriad of self-help books and treatment manuals for professionals. This attention to the experiences of victims has been important for the development of effective treatment modalities and the funding of programs aimed at reducing distress. In addition, awareness of traumatic responses has led to the modification of legislation and case law dealing with victims (Regehr, Bryant, & Glancy, 1997; Regehr & Glancy, 1995).

More recently, it has been recognized that rescue workers who are exposed to mutilated bodies, mass destruction, and life-threatening situations may become hidden victims of disaster. Recent research has identified acute stress reactions in many situations involving emergency service workers. These include police officers following a shooting incident (Gersons, 1989; Solomon & Horn, 1986); firefighters following large blazes (McFarlane, 1988); nurses following the death of a child or colleague (Burns & Harm, 1993); and ambulance workers recovering bodies following mass disasters (Thompson, 1993). Symptoms described include recurrent dreams, feelings of detachment, dissociation, guilt about surviving, anger and irritability, depression, memory or concentration impairment, somatic disturbances, alcohol and substance use, and reexperiencing of symptoms when exposed to trauma stimuli (Gersons, 1989; Solomon & Horn, 1986). These reactions have important implications for individual workers and their families who are attempting to deal with the aftermath of a traumatic event. In addition, these physical, emotional, cognitive, and behavioral reactions in emergency responders have a profound effect on the ability of emergency service organizations to continue to be responsive to the needs of the public.

In response to concerns about the mental health implications of exposure to work-related trauma, the Crisis Debriefing (CD) model has arisen as an early intervention strategy designed to mitigate post-traumatic stress reactions (Mitchell, 1982; Raphael, 1986). While the debriefing model was designed to deal with a single traumatic event such as a plane crash or building collapse, recent modifications to the model address the possibility of multiple stressors (Armstrong, O'Callahan, & Marmar, 1991; Charboneau, 1994). This model offers a brief group treatment approach that is usually limited to a single session. It is based on the premise that emergency service professionals possess the internal resources to deal with most work-related events but can benefit from limited extra assistance in extreme circumstances. The group modality allows for ventilation of feelings, encourages mutual aid within the organization and reinforces innate abilities to cope. Follow-up individual sessions are available to workers experiencing acute distress.

This chapter reviews the CD model and its application to workers in various emergency fields. It also addresses issues concerned with efficacy of the model and the research conducted by the authors on the efficacy of debriefings with firefighters in Australia. Further, we propose an expansion of the model to include not only a group intervention aimed at enhancing the emotional health of individual workers, but, in addition, an organizational intervention aimed at making the workplace a more hospitable and supportive environment.

TRADITIONAL TREATMENT APPROACHES

Traditional approaches for dealing with trauma in emergency workers tended to ignore the problem or attribute the traumatic reactions to inherent character flaws. These tendencies are most evident when one considers the history of awareness of traumatic reactions related to exposure to horrifying events in the line of duty in the military. During World War I, armies responded to psychiatric symptoms caused by what is now recognized to be battle fatigue by executing soldiers. In the Canadian army, 25 soldiers were executed for cowardice. Current analysts now assume that the label cowardice was applied to dysfunction caused by psychological distress (Copp & McAndrew, 1990). By World War II, army medical corps had begun to deal with stress reactions. However, commanding officers still asked whether "demoralizing malingering cases cropping up whilst in action should be shot on the spot as an example" (Birenbaum, 1994, p. 1484). While no Canadians were executed for cowardice in World War II, controversy continued about whether to treat soldiers with battle fatigue.

In the end, many received a dishonorable discharge on the grounds of LMF—lack of moral fiber (Copp & McAndrew, 1990). As stated by Colonel F. H. van Nostrand, an army neuropsychiatrist in 1947, "Although we are interested in rehabilitation . . . our primary function is early diagnosis, early treatment, and above all, early disposal of the mentally unfit" (Birenbaum, 1994, p. 1489).

The Vietnam War and concern for military personnel in the aftermath sparked a new interest in the issue of traumatic stress reactions and the impact of combat exposure (Figley, 1978, 1980; Keane, 1993; McFarlane, 1990). In 1970, two New York psychiatrists initiated "rap groups" with recently returned Vietnam veterans in which they talked about their war experiences. These groups spread throughout the country and formed the nucleus of a network of professionals concerned about the lack of recognition of the effects of war on these men's psychological health (van der Kolk, Weisaeth, & van der Hart, 1996). Information gathered formed the basis for development of the diagnostic category post-traumatic stress disorder (PTSD) in the 1980 edition of the *Diagnostic and Statistical Manual of Mental Disorders* (American Psychiatric Association, 1980). Concern about the well-being of these veterans resulted in a wide array of services, including, in 1995, 25 programs that were officially recognized as specialized inpatient PTSD units for veterans (Fontana & Rosenheck, 1997).

To a lesser degree, other researchers documented the effects of traumatic events on rescue workers. In 1967, Lifton described the emotional distress of rescue workers following the Hiroshima devastation. It was not until the 1980s, however, that attention to this issue became widespread. As a result, treatment approaches in this area are very new and until recently have not been subject to empirical scrutiny.

OVERVIEW OF THE CRISIS DEBRIEFING MODEL

The CD model of intervention has its roots in early crisis intervention theory (Caplan, 1961; Lindemann, 1979). From this perspective, a crisis is an event which, by the nature of its magnitude, overwhelms an individual's customary coping mechanisms and results in a period of turmoil or disequilibrium. During the course of crisis, the individual perceives that the event (1) is a threat to his or her needs or autonomy; (2) represents a tangible loss or a perceived loss of ability or self-esteem; or (3) is a challenge to survival, growth, or mastery. The central tenet of crisis intervention is that "a little help, rationally directed and purposefully focused at a strategic time is more effective than more extensive help given at a time of less emotional accessibility" (Golan, 1959, p. 389).

The theoretical foundation supporting the use of crisis debriefings for emergency workers suggests that these individuals have the required coping mechanisms to manage most aspects of the job, even those which the general public would find gruesome or disturbing. Nevertheless, on occasion a tragic event occurs such as a mass tragedy or the loss of a colleague in the line of duty for which normal mechanisms are inadequate. The emotional, physical, and cognitive aftermath of these events can affect an individual worker's ability to function effectively both on the job and in interpersonal relationships.

The crisis debriefing is therefore aimed at:

1. helping the participant to understand the relationship between the event and his or her reactions;
2. providing an opportunity for cathartic release of feelings, thoughts, and emotions;
3. identifying successful coping strategies; and
4. promoting utilization of various support systems.

The debriefing is not intended to be an intervention that stands on its own, but rather is considered one component of a comprehensive, integrated crisis response program (Mitchell & Everly, 1993). Other aspects of the program may include preventative education, informal group opportunities to discuss the event (defusings), individual defusings, family outreach, and follow-up counseling.

Several variations of crisis debriefings are described in the literature, including psychological debriefings (Dyregrov, 1989; Raphael, 1986); critical incident stress debriefings (Mitchell & Bray, 1990); community crisis response teams (Young, 1991); and the multiple stressor debriefing model (Armstrong, O'Callahan, & Marmar, 1991). Detailed descriptions and comparisons of these various models can be found in McCammon and Allison (1995) and Tehrani and Westlake (1994). Although the various models were developed to meet the differing needs of professionals, volunteers, and victims, they all share some common features.

Each of the CD models involves a psychoeducational group meeting. During the groups, a structured procedure is followed in order to allow individuals to process the tragic event and its aftermath. The first stage is to review the event. This includes describing the sights, sounds, and smells associated with the event, discussing each individual's involvement and the final outcome. Next, people are invited to discuss their reactions to the event, including the emotional and behavioral consequences for both themselves and their family life. Following this, the debriefer provides educational information designed to normalize reactions and reinforce coping skills. In addition, suggestions are made regarding specific stress management techniques. As the session draws to a conclusion, participants are invited to discuss their accomplishments and reinforce one another's efforts.

Finally, participants are encouraged to provide mutual aid as required, and opportunities for professional follow-up are presented.

It is important to remember that debriefing is not therapy or counseling (Mitchell & Everly, 1993). The debriefer utilizes clinical skills in order to establish rapport, encourage discussion, and manage the group process. The debriefer monitors the level of emotional intensity within the group to ensure that it remains manageable and does not become overwhelming. Members who are experiencing acute distress are offered individual assistance. Debriefers do not interpret or challenge the underlying assumptions of the behaviors, thoughts, or feelings being expressed (Tehrani & Westlake, 1994). Further, the debriefer ensures that members do not expose themselves to risk by divulging information about their actions that may result in liability.

The CD model has been designed primarily for single catastrophic events. Most iterations of this model specifically state that no discussion of individual or organizational failings will be tolerated within the debriefing. However, while several studies confirm that traumatic events encountered in the line of duty cause stress responses in rescue workers, other researchers have argued that it is organizational stressors that cause the greatest degree of distress in emergency service personnel. Events such as dealing with victims of serious accidents, being attacked by aggressive offenders, or dealing with protesters can cause stress in police officers. However, several large-scale studies in England, Australia, Canada, and the United States have concluded that the greatest source of stress for officers is the police organization, with its rules, procedures, communication paths, bureaucratic hierarchy, and management style (Brown & Campbell, 1990; Burke, 1993; Buunk & Peeters, 1994; Coman & Evans, 1991; Hart, Wearing & Headley, 1995). The outcomes of this stress include high levels of alcoholism, a suicide rate that is 30% higher than that of comparison groups, and a rate of marital problems that is double that of comparison groups (Golembiewski & Kim, 1990). Similarly, ambulance workers involved in body recovery duties following mass disasters in England identified that poor relationships with management, not being valued for their skills, and shift work were the major stressors they encountered (Thompson, 1993).

A primary mediating factor of organizational stress is social support within the organization, particularly from superiors (Burke, 1993; Buunk & Peeters, 1994; Gibbs, Drummond, & Lachenmeyer, 1993). That is, when people feel supported and valued, they experience lower levels of distress. Such evidence has led some authors to conclude that critical incidents exert little if any disruptive influence directly, but rather operate through the exacerbation of daily hassles that occur in organizations that employ emergency service responders (Gist & Woodall, 1995).

Consequently, it is our contention that a debriefing cannot adequately offer support if participants are not permitted to discuss organizational issues that are causing them distress. Great skill is required of the debriefer to ensure that the debriefing does not spiral into a pit of despair. Rather, the power of the group to begin to create an atmosphere where mutual support and acceptance of distress are evident is reinforced. In addition, strategies to advocate for support of workers within the organization are discussed.

EVIDENCE OF EFFICACY

In the past few years, controversy has arisen about the efficacy of the CD model. In large part, this has been due to the sudden popularity and widespread use of the model in the absence of supporting empirical validation. Initial reports of the efficacy of crisis debriefings have relied on anecdotal evidence, client satisfaction surveys, and clinical impressions of debriefers. Burns and Harm (1993) report the results of a survey of 682 emergency room nurses. Thirty-two percent of the nurses had attended crisis debriefings and 88% of those who had attended debriefings found them helpful. Robinson and Mitchell (1993) similarly report that 90% of 288 emergency and hospital workers who attended debriefings found them helpful. Other literature reports the clinical impressions of debriefers as evidence of efficacy (Armstrong, O'Callahan, & Marmar, 1991).

Recent review articles however, have questioned the conclusion that crisis debriefing reduces traumatic stress reactions and have expressed concern that debriefing may in fact exacerbate symptoms (Bisson & Deahl, 1994; Raphael, Meldrum, & McFarlane, 1995). Deahl, Gillhas, and Thomas (1994), for instance, studied psychological morbidity in British soldiers who were involved in body-handling duties during the Gulf War and found no difference in scores on a PTSD scale between soldiers who received debriefings and those who did not. Bisson, Jenkins, Alexander, and Bannister (1997) reported that burn victims who received debriefings had significantly higher rates of anxiety, depression, and PTSD 13 months following their injury than a group of burn victims who did not. The authors note, however, that the debriefing group did have higher rates of these problems prior to the intervention (though not significantly) and had suffered more severe injuries. Further, it may not be appropriate to compare individuals suffering from catastrophic injuries to workers exposed to traumatic events in the line of duty.

To better understand this discrepancy in the literature, the authors of this chapter conducted a study on the efficacy of crisis debriefings for 164 Australian firefighters following a critical incident (Regehr & Hill, 2000). Our study determined that the majority (86%) of firefighters attending debriefings felt subjectively better. This confirmed the findings of prior studies in which participants in crisis debriefings responded to interview questions or questionnaires (Armstrong, O'Callahan, & Marmar, 1991; Burns &

Harm, 1993; Robinson & Mitchell, 1993). However, firefighters in our study did not experience reduced levels of post-traumatic stress symptoms and depression when compared to their colleagues who did not attend. In fact, those individuals exposed to critical events who attended debriefings had significantly higher scores on the intrusion subscale of the Impact of Event Scale (Zilberg, Weiss, & Horowitz, 1982) than those who did not. We hypothesized that this may have been due to the fact that those with higher levels of PTSD in the first place were motivated to attend debriefing sessions.

When considering the issue of efficacy of debriefings, we must therefore remain cognizant of several issues. It appears that debriefings make emergency responders feel subjectively better about their ability to cope with trauma and about the support that is available to them. As debriefings are generally sponsored by the organization employing the emergency service worker, this enhances the view that the organization cares about its staff. This is important to the well-being of individual workers and for the functioning of the organization as a whole. However, no singular, simplistic approach to managing the aftermath of traumatic events can meet the needs of all affected emergency service personnel. Workers who suffer from more significant sequelae to disturbing events encountered on the job, such that they qualify for a diagnosis of PTSD, are likely to require more intensive intervention than a brief group treatment approach such as a crisis debriefing. Therefore, while in general, crisis debriefings are favorably rated by emergency workers who attend, as with all brief treatment modalities, they must not be regarded as a panacea.

SPECIFIC ASSESSMENT AND TREATMENT PROCEDURES

A crisis debriefing typically begins with a phone call from someone in the affected organization who indicates that an event has occurred and they are concerned that emergency personnel may require some type of assistance. Common events that result in such a request include a serious injury, life-threatening experience, or death of a worker; violent death, death of a child, or multiple deaths; and incidents that attract considerable media attention. Frequently, debriefings address events that contain several of these features.

The first task of the debriefer is to obtain details about the incident and the organization and determine the suitability for a debriefing. It is imperative that the organization does not view the debriefing as an opportunity to critique the incident or to defuse union agitation over particular concerns about management or occupational safety. Further, if the incident is not sufficiently severe to warrant a debriefing, other, less intensive measures may be suggested for assisting the organization and its workers.

Information that is key for planning the debriefing includes:

- the nature of the incident, including the type and duration of the traumatic event
- time elapsed since the incident
- type of organization
- number of individuals anticipated to attend
- what has happened since the incident
- group or individual symptoms causing concern
- ability of workers and the organization to continue to function
- extent of media coverage
- post-incident developments, such as further casualties
- pre-incident morale and organizational climate
- previous traumatic events experienced by the organization or its members
- pre-incident education of traumatic stress management within the organization

Debriefings normally take place 24 to 72 hours after an incident occurs. This time frame however, can be extended as much as a week to 10 days. Participation in the debriefing is limited to individuals directly involved with the incident. Concerned management, family members, or other interested staff are not permitted to attend. The number of participants should not exceed 20–25. If larger numbers of staff were involved in the incident, multiple debriefings should be held. Debriefings can also be successfully run with very small groups. The debriefing must be planned for a time when staff can be guaranteed at least two uninterrupted hours, in a place that is free of outside disturbances. Finally, the debriefing is generally led by one or two mental health professionals along with one or two emergency service professionals (often referred to as "peers") who have been specially trained in the debriefing model.

At the commencement of the debriefing, the leaders will introduce themselves and their co-leaders. Debriefing team members will describe their background and function within the debriefing. This is followed by a discussion of the ground rules for the debriefing, which include:

- participation is voluntary and those who wish to leave may do so; no attendance is taken
- only those directly involved with the incident may remain
- out of respect for yourself and others participating, everything said within the debriefing must be kept confidential
- there is no organizational hierarchy or rank structure recognized during a debriefing; everyone is equal
- within the above parameters, if anyone is uncomfortable with the attendance of anyone else, let us discuss these concerns at this time

- everyone will be given the opportunity to speak; however, it is not mandatory that you do so
- speak only for yourself but also ask questions as desired
- no mechanical recording or written notes are made during the debriefing
- do not make any comments that may result in legal liability for yourself or others
- no breaks will be taken and you are requested to remain until the end
- team members will be available after the debriefing to answer any questions or concerns

When all participants have consented to the rules, the group leader begins by asking people to describe their role in the incident. Most members of the group will participate in this phase of the debriefing, as it is non-threatening and does not require any personal disclosure. This is often the first opportunity for participants to obtain a full picture of the incident and of the various events that occurred. If, during this factual description, members do not spontaneously begin describing their immediate reactions, they are invited to do so next. This usually initiates a more general discussion of reactions as people compare their experiences and reinforce the experiences of one another. Members are then asked how the incident continues to affect them both at work and at home.

The leaders use the descriptions of how the event has impacted people on various levels to provide information about common reactions to stress and trauma. It is at this time that both the uniqueness and the normalcy of their reactions are discussed and participants are informed of possible reactions that they may encounter in the next days or weeks. Typical statements at this time may include, "Considering what you have experienced, your reactions are normal and understandable." It is also during this phase that coping strategies for traumatic stress reactions are introduced. The suggestions for dealing with stress may include:

- Utilize the support of family, friends, and co-workers to talk about the incident and bring meaning and normalcy back into your life.
- Maintain a healthy diet and participate in regular exercise.
- Assess your work and home environment so that you return to your responsibilities only as fast as your capabilities return.
- Take time out for fun.
- Avoid use of drugs, alcohol, and tobacco as a method of coping or avoidance.
- Seek support and counseling before becoming completely overwhelmed.

In the concluding phase, additional areas of the group's concerns are discussed. These may include concerns about the support available to workers within the organization. At this time, therefore, workers are encouraged to develop mutual-aid strategies. This may include developing a climate within the organization where members can discuss their concerns and stress. It may also include discussions with management about instituting a formal crisis management strategy within the organization.

The team leader initiates closure by summarizing what has taken place within the debriefing. The group is encouraged to continue the recovery process and be cognizant of additional stress reactions within themselves and others. Information pamphlets are generally distributed, which contain descriptions of normal stress reactions, coping strategies, and contact names and numbers for the debriefing team and other support services. Once the debriefing is formally terminated, team members remain for a period of time to informally address individual concerns and comments.

CASE ILLUSTRATION

In order to illustrate the CD model in action, we will describe an intervention with nursing staff in a large hospital. The incident occurred during an evening shift on a locked psychiatric admissions unit.

A male patient who was acutely psychotic became violent and aggressive toward staff. In the course of the incident, he tore apart a metal garbage can and used the sharp edge as a weapon with which to threaten the life of nursing staff members. In the ensuing crisis, several nursing staff locked themselves in the nursing station, one nurse locked herself in the bathroom, and two became barricaded in patient rooms. Police were called, as security guards in Canadian hospitals do not carry weapons. In the intervening time until police arrived, the patient began kicking the glass in the nursing station wall and attempted to climb the walls, which did not reach to the ceiling. The walls shook violently and at one point his hand was visible over the top of the partition. Nurses in various areas had no means of contacting one another and were unsure if a colleague had been injured or killed. In the end, the patient was subdued and removed. Nurses remained on duty for the duration of the shift and were instructed to complete incident reports.

Debriefers were contacted one week after the occurrence, as nursing staff remained distressed and angry about the incident and the organizational response. After obtaining information about the event, a debriefing was arranged for the following day. The debriefers insisted that the debriefing be carried out in a room far removed from the unit and that nursing staff be assured that they would not be interrupted for a two-hour period. All staff in attendance that evening were invited to attend, including nursing staff from the affected unit and nursing staff from the next unit, who watched the incident through a locked glass door. Eleven staff members participated in the session. The debriefers consisted of two mental health professionals with expertise in this area, one from within the organization and one external to the organization, and a peer debriefer from an affiliated facility.

The debriefing began with an introduction of the group leaders and their qualifications. When the leaders were assured of the group's comfort, the rules of the debriefing were reviewed and all members agreed to abide by them.

The group members were then invited to introduce themselves and describe their involvement in the event. The session moved quickly into a description of their immediate reactions to the event. Within a very short period of time several staff members became tearful as they expressed their fear that their colleagues and friends were being attacked and their frustration with their own inability to intervene in any way. In this process, many became aware for the first time of the events as they unfolded in various parts of the unit. Staff members spontaneously supported one another and reassured one another. As the debriefing continued, staff discussed ongoing fears and reactions to the event. Several were experiencing sleeplessness, nightmares, and intrusive thoughts. Others felt overwhelmed by references to violent incidents in the news. Most experienced difficulty in performing their duties at their usual level of competence and self-assurance. These reactions were normalized within the context of reactions to life-threatening experiences, and the support that they demonstrated to one another was affirmed.

A theme that continued to arise during the session, however, was anger that the safety needs of staff were not more adequately addressed by the organization. While traditional crisis debriefing approaches steer clear of any operational debriefing, avoiding this topic entirely would have reinforced their belief that no one cared about their safety. In this context, one individual, who was the union representative, became very tearful, feeling that it was her fault that these issues had not been addressed. The senior staff member on duty that evening similarly took full responsibility. Allowing this issue to be raised provided an opportunity for the other staff to assure these individuals that the responsibility did not rest on their shoulders. Out of concern for these individuals and the safety of staff in general, the leaders then moved to an organizational intervention. Staff members developed a plan about how they would advocate for themselves and work toward positive change in the organization. As often occurs at these times, some members asked whether the debriefers could take the lead in this. It was explained, however, that this would violate our agreement to keep the content of the debriefing confidential. The group appreciated this and felt that the support they received from one another and the plans they had developed in the session empowered them to collectively address their concerns in the organization.

SUMMARY AND CONCLUSIONS

The CD model can be regarded as one of the ultimate brief treatment approaches for dealing with compassion fatigue, as it is usually limited to only one group meeting. The ability of this model to deal with trauma reactions in such a limited time span is based on the assumption that emergency service professionals, as a consequence of their training and personality styles, have the innate abilities to deal with most tragic events with which they are confronted. In addition, the ongoing exposure to gruesome sights and sounds serves as a type of systemic desensitization and allows them to develop coping strategies in order to handle the job. On occasion, however, an event occurs, the intensity of which overwhelms normal coping mechanisms. At these times, the additional assistance of a crisis debriefing can serve to normalize reactions to events, allow for catharsis, and enhance the natural support systems within the organization.

Recent criticisms of the CD model have pointed to the fact that this approach does not protect individuals from post-traumatic stress reactions and may in fact exacerbate severe symptoms in the isolated few individuals who develop them. As such, it must be remembered that such a brief intervention cannot be expected to deal with severe emotional distress. While the intervention is effective in increasing the sense of support that workers feel and enhancing mutual aid, it must be seen as part of a more comprehensive organizational plan that includes an enlightened and supportive work environment and individual assistance for workers experiencing extreme levels of distress.

REFERENCES

American Psychiatric Association. (1980). *Diagnostic and statistical manual of mental disorders* (DSM-III) (3rd ed.). Washington, DC: Author.

Armstrong, K., O'Callahan, W., & Marmar, C. (1991). Debriefing Red Cross disaster personnel: The multiple stressor debriefing model. *Journal of Traumatic Stress, 4*(4), 581–593.

Birenbaum, R. (1994). Peacekeeper stress prompts new approaches to mental health issues in the Canadian military. *Canadian Medical Association Journal, 151*(10), 1484–1489.

Bisson, J., & Deahl, M. (1994). Psychological debriefings and prevention of posttraumatic stress: More research is needed. *British Journal of Psychiatry, 165,* 717–720.

Bisson, J., Jenkins, P., Alexander, J., & Bannister, C. (1997). Randomized controlled trial of psychological debriefing for victims of acute burn trauma. *British Journal of Psychiatry, 171,* 78–81.

Brown, J., & Campbell, E. (1990). Sources of occupational stress in police. *Work & Stress, 4*(4), 305–318.

Burke, R. (1993). Work-family stress, conflict, coping, and burnout in police officers. *Stress Medicine, 9,* 171–180.

Burns, C., & Harm, N. (1993). Emergency nurses' perceptions of critical incidents and stress debriefing. *Journal of Emergency Nursing,* 19, 431–436.

Butcher, J., & Hatcher, C. (1988). The neglected entity in air disaster planning: Psychological services. *American Psychologist,* 43(9), 724–729.

Buunk, B., & Peeters, M. (1994). Stress at work, social support and companionship: Towards an event-contingent recording approach. *Work & Stress,* 8(2), 177–190.

Caplan, G. (1961). *An approach to community mental health.* New York: Grune & Stratton.

Charboneau, L. (1994). Shell shocked. *Medical Post,* 30(3), 11–12.

Coman, G., & Evans, B. (1991). Stressors facing Australian police in the 1990s. *Police Studies International Review of Police Development,* 14(4), 153–165.

Copp, T., & McAndrew, W. (1990). *Battle exhaustion: Soldiers and psychiatrists in the Canadian army, 1939–1945.* Kingston: McGill–Queen's University Press.

Deahl, M., Gillhas, A., & Thomas, J. (1994). Psychological sequelae following the Gulf War: Factors associated with subsequent morbidity and the effectiveness of psychological debriefings. *British Journal of Psychiatry,* 165, 60–65.

Dyregrov, A. (1989). Caring for the helpers in disaster situations: Psychological debriefing. *Disaster Management,* 2, 25–30.

Figley, C. (1978). *Stress disorders among Vietnam veterans: Theory, research and treatment.* New York: Brunner/Mazel.

Figley, C. (1980). *Strangers at home: Vietnam veterans since the war.* New York: Praeger.

Fontana, A., & Rosenheck, R. (1997). Effectiveness and cost of the inpatient treatment of posttraumatic stress disorder: Comparison of three models of treatment. *American Journal of Psychiatry,* 154(6), 758–765.

Gersons, B. (1989). Patterns of PTSD among police officers following a shooting incident: A two-dimensional model and treatment implications. *Journal of Traumatic Stress,* 2, 247–257.

Gibbs, M., Drummond, J., & Lachenmeyer, J. (1993). Effects of disasters on emergency workers: A review with implications for training and postdisaster interventions. *Journal of Social Behavior and Personality,* 8(5), 189–212.

Gist, R., & Woodall, S. (1995). Occupational stress in contemporary fire service. *Occupational Medicine,* 10(4), 763–787.

Golan, N. (1959). When is a client in crisis? *Social Casework,* 50, 389–394.

Golembiewski, R., & Kim, B. (1990). Burnout in police work: Stressors, strain, and the phase model. *Police Studies,* 13(2), 74–80.

Hart, P., Wearing, A., & Headley, B. (1995) Police stress and well being: Integrating personality, coping and daily work experiences. *Journal of Occupational and Organizational Psychology,* 68, 133–136.

Keane, T. (1993). Symptomology of Vietnam veterans with post-traumatic stress disorder. In J. Davidson & E. Foa (Eds.), *Posttraumatic stress disorder: DSM IV and beyond.* Washington, DC: American Psychiatric Association Press.

Lifton, R. (1967). *Death in life: Survivors of Hiroshima.* New York: Random House.

Lindemann, E. (1979). *Beyond grief: Studies in crisis intervention.* New York: Jason Aronson.

McCammon, S., & Allison, J. (1995). Debriefing and treating emergency workers. In C. Figley (Ed.), *Compassion fatigue* (pp. 115–129). New York: Brunner/ Mazel.

McFarlane, A. (1988). The aetiology of post-traumatic stress disorder following a natural disaster. *British Journal of Psychiatry*, 152, 116–121.

McFarlane, A. (1990). Vulnerability to posttraumatic stress disorder. In M. Wolf & A. Mosnaim (Eds.), *Posttraumatic stress disorder: Etiology, phenomenology, and treatment* (pp. 3–45). Washington, DC: American Psychiatric Association Press.

Mitchell, J. (1982). Recovery from rescue. *Response*, Fall, 7–10.

Mitchell, J., & Bray, G. (1990). *Emergency services stress: Guidelines for preserving the health and careers of emergency services personnel*. Englewood Cliffs, NJ: Brady.

Mitchell, J., & Everly, G. (1993). *Critical incident stress debriefing*. Ellicott City, MD: Chevron Publishing.

Raphael, B. (1986). *When disaster strikes—A handbook for caring professionals*. London: Unwin Hyman Ltd.

Raphael, B., Meldrum, L., & McFarlane, A. (1995). Does debriefing after psychological trauma work? *British Medical Journal*, 310, 1479–1480.

Regehr, C., Bryant, A., & Glancy, G. (1997). Confidentiality of treatment for victims of sexual violence. *The Social Worker*, 65(3), 137–145.

Regehr, C., & Glancy, G. (1995). Battered woman syndrome defense in the Canadian courts. *Canadian Journal of Psychiatry*, 40(3), 130–135.

Regehr, C., & Hill, J. (2000). Evaluating the efficacy of crisis debriefings. *Social Work with Groups*.

Robinson, R., & Mitchell, J. (1993). Evaluation of psychological debriefings. *Journal of Traumatic Stress*, 6, 367–382.

Solomon, R., & Horn, J. (1986). Post shooting trauma reactions: A pilot study. In J. Reece & H. Goldstien (Eds.), *Psychological services for law enforcement* (pp. 383–393). Washington, DC: U.S. Government Printing Office.

Tehrani, N., & Westlake, R. (1994). Debriefing individuals affected by violence. *Counselling Psychology Quarterly*, 7(3), 251–259.

Thompson, J. (1993). Psychological impact of body recovery duties. *Journal of the Royal Society of Medicine*, 86, 628–629.

van der Kolk, B., Weisaeth, L., & van der Hart, O. (1996). History of trauma in psychiatry. In B. van der Kolk, A. McFarlane, & L. Weisaeth (Eds.), *Traumatic stress: The effects of overwhelming experience of mind, body and society* (pp. 47–76). New York: Guilford Press.

Young, M. (1991). *Community crisis response team training manual*. Washington, DC: NOVA.

Zilberg, N., Weiss, D., & Horowitz, M. (1982). Impact of event scale: A cross-validation study and some empirical evidence supporting a conceptual model of stress response syndromes. *Journal of Consulting and Clinical Psychology*, 50, 407–414.

Chapter 15

The Rewind Technique in the Treatment of Post-traumatic Stress Disorder: Methods and Applications

David C. Muss

Bonnie L. Green (1994) exhorted, "Generally speaking, we need to move away from simply documenting the presence of PTSD (Post-traumatic Stress Disorder) and other diagnoses following traumatic events to studies of treatment, prevention and basic processes, and how we can help them when that struggle leads to negative outcomes."

In the last few years there have been interesting developments in the treatment of PTSD—particularly a shift from cognitive-behavioral counseling plus or minus drugs, to cognitive-behavioral counseling plus the use of newer, imagery-based techniques, otherwise known as power therapies, such as Eye Movement Desensitization and Reprocessing (EMDR) (Shapiro, 1989), Traumatic Incident Reduction (TIR) (Moore, 1993), Visual-Kinesthetic Dissociation (VKD), and Thought Field Therapy (TFT).

In 1991, I published the results obtained with the Rewind Technique (Muss, 1991). The Rewind Technique is based on Visual-Kinesthetic Dissociation (VKD), a Neuro-Linguistic Programming technique devised to treat phobias. Bandler (1985) mentioned that the technique should be applicable to PSTD. In 1987, I set off to use the technique with the local police force, reporting subsequently a two-year follow-up of no relapses in 19 police officers treated for PTSD (Muss, 1991). It became clear in the early use of the technique that it had to be modified to treat rescuers.

In addition to these modifications I also named the technique the "Rewind Technique." Since the original report, the Rewind Technique has been successfully used for victims of road traffic accidents, industrial accidents, assault, rape, and child sexual abuse.

It is a fact that we are all different and that we all work differently. Those of us who have been in the field for some time get set in our ways and are not all that willing to take on change just for change's sake. However, if you are honest with yourself and find that trauma counseling is not as exciting as it was a few years ago, or it is beginning to drain you more than it used to, you may well be beginning to suffer compassion fatigue. Again, if you are at the stage in which you are still very excited with your work, then you should want to make certain that compassion fatigue does not insidiously set in.

If one considers how much trauma one listens to in the course of a day's work, it is not surprising that if we do not have an effective way of dealing with it we will eventually be overcome. It has always been my belief that after I have heard from the client the nature of the trauma (assault, industrial injury, road traffic accident, etc.) and the details of it once, I really do not want to hear them over and over, nor has it shown to be of any particular use to the client, except if one is using such techniques as Traumatic Incident Reduction (TIR) (See Chapter 12 this volume), where the repetition all occurs on a one-off basis in one session.

I have found over the last 10 years that using the Rewind Technique as my first approach has undoubtedly protected me from compassion fatigue. The beauty of the Rewind Technique is that it is the client who goes through all the details of the horrific event in his or her mind, usually in just one session in a couple of minutes. In reality, one does not even have to hear all the details about the event and this, of course, would certainly apply if one were trying to counsel a group of 50 or 100 people in one session, which represented your only opportunity to offer some kind of help. You would know that this particular group all had (for example, in the case of survivors of war atrocities carried out in the former Yugoslavia) something in common but each individual would have his own experiences. The cause of their trauma is known but the details are not. You can see straight away the difference this would make to you if you had a technique that could be used for the whole group, as opposed to having to counsel each individual in such circumstances.

It is not uncommon for us to go home and, due to countertransference, start to think about the unfortunate circumstances that one or two of our clients have been through. Their trauma starts to relive in our minds. In those circumstances we can simply "rewind" their traumatic event for ourselves and this will immediately free us from unwanted intrusive phenomena.

What follows is a description of the Rewind Technique as applied to the treatment of survivors of traumatic events and for emergency workers (firemen, ambulancemen, policemen, paramedics, etc.).

METHOD

The Rewind is employed when it is clear that what is preventing recovery is the inability of either the client (or the therapist) to tackle the intrusive distressing images (sounds and smells) that continue to haunt. It will clearly be up to the individual therapist whether this aspect of the post-traumatic stress disorder is dealt with initially or at another stage of the treatment.

I have found over the years that it is crucial that the client understands what the Rewind Technique is going to achieve. I adopt various approaches until I find one the client fully understands.

1. The Rewind Technique will not help you forget what happened (this must always be made clear to the client). We never really forget anything; given enough prompts we will find most things stored in our memory. What the technique does do is actually shift the traumatic event from the "front of our minds" into our memory. Once things are in our memory it is up to us whether we wish to go and look for them. In other words, the treatment is inactivating involuntary recall while allowing retention of voluntary recall.

2. In this age of computers, I frequently make references to them, having ascertained that the client does use computers. I ask, "How would you feel if everyday, when you first go to your computer, you find on the screen the image of the traumatic event?" Normally, you would expect the screen to be clear, and only after tapping in the data would something appear on it. Despite trying to remove the imagery from the screen, you find that no keypad on the keyboard seems to do that and therefore you have to use your computer with the screen partially occupied by unwanted imagery. When you stop using your current program the screen fills up again with the intrusive traumatic images. This is similar to what is going on in your mind.

The Rewind Technique will actually remove the imagery from the screen, put it into the computer database and it will only reappear when you decide to view it. In other words, the event has not disappeared but it is stored in the computer and is only accessible if wanted.

It is important to emphasize that one will retain voluntary recall, as it is well recognized that there are some people who feel that the experience has undoubtedly had some beneficial aspects (Joseph, Williams & Yule, 1993), and they would not want to forget it.

3. A final point to make is that the Rewind Technique puts one back to feeling just like before the traumatic event; a sense of integrity and control is reestablished.

THE REWIND TECHNIOUE FOR THE ACTUAL SURVIVOR OF A TRAUMATIC EVENT

The Rewind Technique consists of watching a film of your traumatic event, in the exact way that it haunts you, first forward and then backward. However, it is not quite as simple as that, and it is very important that you follow precisely all the steps described below.

Some of the things I am going to ask you to do may seem a little odd, so let's pretend that I am introducing you to a new game. As with all new games, you need to understand the rules and the setting before you play. So, before you start the treatment, learn the rules with me.

FLOATING OUT

First, learn how to float out of yourself.

Another way of saying this is: I need you to be able to watch yourself. Have you been on a boat or a car journey and felt terribly sick? Or, have you been on a roller coaster and felt frightened (or gotten a real buzz)? Stop and think about this for a moment. Have you remembered what it felt like? You probably didn't enjoy that memory, did you? This is because you didn't detach yourself (some people, on the other hand, get a buzz, e.g., from roller coasters—then focus on the good feeling).

Try now to look at the same event in a "detached" way. Float out of the boat, leaving your body in it, and watch yourself from the shore. Do you feel as bad as you did before? (Ensure the answer is no, otherwise try with another example). This is because you are watching yourself and not reliving the event as it happened.

Another way to get the concept across is to say "imagine" you were being recorded on a camcorder at the time and you are now watching the video of the day you were on the roller coaster, a boat, or something similar.

THE SETTING

I would now like to explain the setting. You will be watching two films in a cinema (movie). Let's assume that you have a completely empty cinema hired just for you. Imagine that you are sitting in the center with the big screen in front and the projection room behind you.

When you watch the first film, I would like you to float out of your body and go to the projection room to watch yourself watching the film from there. From the projection room you will be able to see the whole cinema, the empty chairs with just your head (and perhaps shoulders) sitting in the center seat, and the screen in front of you. Check that this concept is understood—draw a little sketch if necessary. Now let's consider the two films.

THE FIRST FILM

The first film is a replay of the traumatic event "as you experienced it or as you are haunted by it in your nightmares, dreams or flashbacks." In this film you will see yourself on the screen—just as if someone had taken a video recording on the day and is now showing it to you.

The only difference to this film is that it is going to have a "new starting point." I know that when you are troubled by flashbacks or nightmares you tend to start right at the most horrendous bit, correct? I would like you today, however, to start the film just before that, when in fact you were well and enjoying the day. For example, if you were involved in a car accident with a lorry, begin the film by seeing yourself driving along happily before the accident takes place. You will then see the lorry (truck) appear and finally the accident.

Include in this forward film not only all the imagery but also sounds and smells. Run the film forward at its normal pace and stop when it begins to fade.

THE REWIND

The second film is called "the rewind." You do not watch the rewind, you are actually in it, today, experiencing it in the screen, seeing and feeling everything as if it were happening to you now. The really odd thing is that you see and feel everything happening backwards.

Thus, in the case of the car accident, the rewind starts with you in the car after the impact. Then you feel yourself in your car pulling away from the lorry. You see the front of your car returning to its normal shape, as does the lorry. The vehicles move farther and farther apart as you feel you are being sucked back until the lorry disappears and you end up where the film began, that is, at the "new starting point" where you then see yourself again driving along in your car as you did at the beginning of the forward film. In effect this means that right up to the last frame you are in the film being sucked back. At the last frame you find yourself back in the projection room looking at yourself driving along happily on the screen. The rewind must be done rapidly; if it takes you two minutes to look at the forward film then it should take about 10 seconds for the rewind. In fact, if you find your client taking longer than two minutes, stop him or her and ask what he or she is doing. You will more than likely find the client is associating in the forward film and thus finding it difficult to proceed.

Whereas every single little bit of detail must be included in the forward film, the rewind, because it is rapid, does not concentrate so much on detail—you know what is going on but the detail is not terribly clear, however, you do get the gist of what is going on. Omit all sounds and smells in the rewind.

The client must be warned that going through the first film can be painful. This usually happens because the client tends to move away from the projection room and gets into the screen, during the forward film (associates). A bit of this is inevitable and acceptable. However, if done continuously, your client may get stuck and find it difficult to go forward.

Reassure your client that this should be the last time that the event will be felt in this way and encourage him or her to keep the film moving. Further comments on this aspect are discussed under "difficulties you may encounter."

Finally, the client should be told not to describe verbally what is occurring during either film.

Having said all this to the client, check that every step is clearly understood. Prior to initiating the treatment, the client is offered the choice of doing it with eyes closed or open. If the client chooses to do it with eyes open, then it is advisable to turn the client so as to face away from the therapist, looking possibly at a blank wall in front. Make sure the client understands that the first two films must be done in sequence, one after the other—often they just do the first film, look up, and then start on the rewind.

Having explained everything, now start your client off by saying:

You are now sitting comfortably, in the best seat, screen in front, projection room behind. Now, float out of your body to the projection room, look through it, see yourself sitting there amongst the empty seats: I will now turn down the lights, the screen is now lit up and there you are on the screen, driving along, walking along— happily before the event. Take it from here, go through the forward film and the rewind film.

Once the client has done the technique, always check the following points:

1. Did you leave out any of the most distressing aspects in the forward film?

2. If you try to visualize the rewind now, can you see it? If yes, what is the last thing you see? The aim here is to make sure that the client's end point is identical to the starting point. Often clients have a tendency to "overshoot" or create a completely different end point for their rewind, such as, the film starts with them in a car and ends with them at the bank!

3. Tell them that from now on they do not need to practice this technique at home but just observe what happens to them over the following weeks. You will be reviewing them in two weeks' time.

4. Assuming that the rewind has been done correctly, one can then conclude the session by telling the client that whenever, in the future, the traumatic event is sparked off by some external or internal cue, the rewind will rapidly come into play and present very quickly the "new starting point." The "new starting point" is a good image, representing restoration, integrity. This process will happen faster and faster as every day goes by.

DIFFICULTIES YOU MAY ENCOUNTER

Some clients do not have the courage to look at the forward film in all its full detail. It is fairly common to find people wanting to gloss over the really frightening or ugly part. If they do this their symptoms will not disappear completely. It is therefore important to make sure one feels the client has done the treatment correctly, that he has definitely not left anything out. One, of course, cannot always be sure about this in the first session and you will be checking this out in the next session. It is important that the rewind is done rapidly. Some clients tend to do it as slowly as the forward film.

Another problem that occasionally arises is that the rewind is not done in an associated fashion but dissociated, as if looking at a film being rewound. It is vital that the client realizes that on the day of the treatment he is actually experiencing a new traumatic event in reverse. It is only the last frame in the rewind (i.e., the "starting-point") that will be seen from a dissociated position. If your client does in fact do the film dissociated, you will find that at review your client will probably say that at first he felt better and then the improvement wore off. If you asked him to tell you what he did the last time, you would find that the client will say "I looked at myself" in the rewind as opposed to being in it.

A Word of Warning

If your client fails to remain reasonably dissociated in the forward film, he may become extremely distressed and will not be able to continue. You had already warned the client about this prior to starting the treatment. Go over the concept of the roller coaster or sail boat, thus explaining again why the distress.

If the client is too distressed, terminate the session by inducing relaxation and stabilizing the client by saying that, in fact, nothing new was seen today and that the session confirms the treatment needs to be aimed at inactivating this distressing recall.

Go over the concept of the treatment, tell him that he has done very well so far and that next time the whole thing will be a lot easier. I have to say this problem arises about once every five years or so!

Interestingly, some people can only do the forward film associated and do not become distressed. They worry, however, that they are not doing it as explained. Reassure them that if they are able to do the forward film associated without getting unduly distressed, you do not mind.

WHAT TO DO WHEN YOU REVIEW YOUR CLIENT

If your client reports great improvement, check this out in detail and repeat the Impact of Events Scale questionnaire (see conclusion). If your client does not report significant improvement but says that he initially felt better and then did not, it could be due to the fact that he did not associate during the rewind, as mentioned above, or that he neglected omitted to insert all the distressing aspects of the traumatic event.

It is a very good tactic to just ask the client to tell you what happened the last time—"What did you do?"—as if he were now telling you how to do it. In this way you often see that something was done incorrectly and it is a simple matter of putting that right; the client feels happy that you identified "what it is that went wrong" and, usually, after doing it again correctly, the client improves dramatically.

THE REWIND FOR EMERGENCY WORKERS

This adaptation of the rewind has also been used for relations or friends who have had to identify a body. "Floating out" and "The Setting" are explained in an identical manner to the survivor version. The crucial difference is in the "starting point" of the first film, which of course represents the end point of the rewind.

Whereas, in the case of the survivor the actual starting point is known, for the rescuer, this is not. Apply the following modifications to the forward film and rewind:

Let's say that your traumatic event consisted of arriving at a scene where two trains had collided and there are a lot of injured people. Obviously, those are the distressing images that you first took in but now I want you to imagine what went on before, that is, the trains travelling along prior to the collision with the passengers all seated comfortably and happy. This becomes your new starting point. Then continue the first film, to include how you imagined the trains coming into collision, followed by what you actually found on arrival. In the rewind film you are at first actually in it, experiencing everything you saw initially in the screen, as if it were happening now backwards. Once you have dealt with the part of the event you actually witnessed (by associating) then continue to rewind the film, but watching it (dissociated) from the projection room, returning to the "new starting point."

CONCLUSION

The Rewind Technique has been used as first-line treatment for patients treated at this center since 1987. All clients complete an Impact of Events (IES) questionnaire (Horrowitz, Wilner, & Alavarz, 1979) prior to treatment and again at a two-week follow-up. On the basis of the IES and clinical findings, the success rate in this unit is in the order of 94%. The average number of treatment sessions is two to three.

The Rewind Technique should also be seriously considered as part of Critical Incident Stress Debriefing (Mitchell, 1983) when it becomes obvious that some of the group are not going to do well and may not get another chance to be helped.

At times, individual counseling is not even envisaged, due to the numbers involved. For example, in Mosta, former Yugoslavia (Yule, 1995), there was a clear need to have available a technique which could be applied to a group. I would suggest that the Rewind Technique is the only technique that could be reasonably attempted for group therapy.

The Rewind has been used with children and has been successful and extremely easy to do. Perhaps more surprising to me is that it has also been successful at the other end of the age spectrum even with patients aged over 80. Experience with survivors of sexual abuse shows it to be successful if the victim is able to understand the concept of incorporating the repeated episodes of abuse into one film and then replaying back the whole film.

The rewind takes approximately 10 to 15 minutes to explain and two to three minutes for the client to do. Its ease of use and good results make a strong case for the Rewind Technique to become part of the armamentaria for all those involved in trauma counseling.

REFERENCES

Bandler, R. (1985). *Using your brain for a change*. Moab, UT: Real People Press.

Green, B. L. (1994). Psychological research in traumatic stress: An update. *Journal of Traumatic Stress*, 7, 341–362.

Horrowitz, M., Wilner, N., & Alvarez, W. (1979). Impact of Event Scale: A measure of subjective stress. *Psychosomatic Medicine*, 47, 209–218.

Joseph, S., Williams, R., & Yule, W. (1993). The preliminary development of a measure to assess positive and negative responses. *Journal of Traumatic Stress*, 6, 271–279.

Mitchell, J. T. (1983). When disaster strikes: The critical incident stress debriefing process. *Journal of Emergency Medical Services*, 8, 36–39.

Moore, R. H. (1993). Cognitive-emotive treatment of the posttraumatic stress disorder. In W. Dryden and L. Hill (Eds.), *Innovations in rational-emotive therapy*. Newbury Park, CA: Sage Publications.

Muss, D. C. (1991). A new technique for treating posttraumatic stress disorder. *British Journal of Clinical Psychology*, 30, 91–92.

Muss, D. C. (1991). *The trauma trap*. Birmingham, UK: Doubleday.

Shapiro, F. (1989). Efficacy of the eye movement desensitization procedure in the treatment of traumatic memories. *Journal of Traumatic Stress Studies*, 2, 199–223.

Yule, W. (1995). Personal Communication, 11th Annual Conference of the International Society of Traumatic Stress Studies, Boston, MA, November 19.

Author Index

Subject Index

About the Editor and Contributors

CHARLES R. FIGLEY, Ph.D. is a Full Professor in the School of Social Work and Director of the Traumatology Institute at Florida State University in Tallahassee, Florida. He received his Ph.D. and M.S. degrees in human development from Pennsylvania State University and his B.S. degree in human development from the University of Hawaii. He was voted fellow in the American Psychological Society, the American Psychological Association, the American Orthopsychiatric Association, and the American Association for Marriage and Family Therapy. He is founding member of the Academy of Traumatology and Founding President of the International Society for Traumatic Stress Studies (ISTSS); and he is winner of the ISTSS Pioneer Award, the NOVA Shaffer Research Award, the National Association for Continuing Education's 2000 Program Award (for the Traumatology Institute's Certificate Programs in Traumatology), and Psychologist of the Year by the American Psychological Association (Division 43). He is author or editor of 18 books with several translations and over 150 refereed papers.

KEITH ARMSTRONG, L.C.S.W. is an Associate Clinical Professor of Psychiatry at the University of California, San Francisco. He directs the Couples and Family Therapy program at the Department of Veterans Affairs (DVA) Hospital, San Francisco. He is also a member of the Post-traumatic Stress Disorder Program at the DVA in San Francisco. In 2000, Mr. Armstrong won the Excellence in Teaching Award given to faculty by the Psychiatry Residents Association. He received his M.S.W. from the University of California, Berkeley in 1984. He has written numerous articles and chapters on debriefing after traumatic incidents and has conducted debriefings internationally. Mr. Armstrong maintains a private practice in the Bay Area.

JEANNE M. BERTOLI, M.S., Ph.D. (candidate) attended Florida State University's Marriage and Family Therapy program, where she taught a marriage and relationships course and did research on premarital couples and what is effective in premarital education. She currently works at the American Association for Marriage and Family Therapy. Ms. Bertoli's clinical and research interests lie in reducing inter-parental hostility between divorcing/divorced parents so that they might better co-parent their child(ren).

NANCY DAVIS, Ph.D. is a therapist, author, and trainer who specializes in treating and evaluating traumatized clients and those experiencing traumatic grief. She has had a private practice for 18 years, testified as an expert witness in over 135 legal proceedings, worked as a school psychologist for 10 years, and taught undergraduate and graduate school at Towson State University. Dr. Davis is the author of *Therapeutic Stories to Heal Abused Children* and *Therapeutic Stories That Teach and Heal.* She recently served as Chief of Counseling Services for the Federal Bureau Investigation where, in treating numerous law enforcement officers traumatized by job-related experiences, she developed a treatment technique specifically designed to meet their needs. Dr. Davis's primary interests and areas of expertise are in psychological evaluations, research, and short-term treatment of traumatized clients; and training professionals in treating trauma, grief, and expert witness testimony.

ANNE M. DIETRICH is a psychologist in British Columbia, Canada, with a specialization in psychological trauma. Her professional background includes crisis intervention; individual, couples, family, and group psychotherapy; research; and teaching. She has taught psychology at Simon Fraser University and is an instructor at the University of British Columbia (UBC). She currently works for the Correctional Service of Canada and has a private practice. She has been the recipient of several UBC graduate fellowships, a three-year doctoral fellowship from the Social Sciences and Humanities Research Council of Canada (SSHRC) to study Complex Posttraumatic Stress Disorder, a Green Cross Foundation Fellowship, and an IODE War Memorial Scholarship. She was also the recipient of the 2001 International Society for Traumatic Stress Studies Student Research Award. She is a member of the Canadian Psychological Association, the International Society for Traumatic Stress Studies, the International Society for the Study of Dissociation, the American Psychological Association, and the American Psychosomatic Society. She has served as the Treasurer and is currently President-Elect for the Canadian Society for the Study of Trauma and Dissociation, and is on the Board of Directors of the Canadian Traumatic Stress Network.

ROBERT-JAY GREEN, Ph.D. is Professor, Director of Family/Child Psychology Doctoral Training, and Director of the Alternative Family Institute at the California School of Professional Psychology, Alliant International University. He also has a private practice in San Francisco. Among his many publications are two edited volumes, *Family Therapy: Major Contributions* (with J. L. Framo, 1981) and *Lesbians and Gays in Couples and Families: A Handbook for Therapists* (with J. Laird, 1996). He serves on the editorial advisory boards of *Family Process* and *Journal of Marital & Family Therapy*. Dr. Green received the 1998 award for "Significant Contributions to the Study of Family Diversity" from Division 43 (Family Psychology) of the American Psychological Association. He also received the 2001 award for "Distinguished Contributions to Family Systems Research" from the American Family Therapy Academy (AFTA).

NICOLE T. HARRINGTON, Ph.D. is a clinical psychologist and Program Supervisor at the Family Center of the Berkshires, a clinic of Mental Health and Substance Abuse Services of the Berkshires. She is also co-director of the Anxiety Disorders Treatment Team for the agency. After obtaining her doctoral degree from the University of Vermont she completed her internship and post-doctoral training at the National Center for PTSD at the Boston VA Medical Center. She has specialized in cognitive-behavior therapy and anxiety disorders, specifically focusing on panic, obsessive-compulsive, and trauma-related disorders. Dr. Harrington has taught courses on Trauma and Recovery at the University of Massachusetts at Boston and been a research and clinical consultant to the Boston Area Rape Crisis Center for four years.

NEIL C. HEADMAN, M.S.W. is a doctoral candidate in Florida State University's Marriage and Family Therapy Program, and currently teaches undergraduate-level research and statistics courses for Florida State University's School of Social Work. Mr. Headman earned a Bachelor's degree in Psychology from the University of Utah in 1995 and an M.S.W. in social work from Florida State University in 1997. His clinical experience comes from working as a Youth and Family Counselor at Capital City Youth Services in Tallahassee, Florida. He currently serves as the Assistant Director of The Family Place, Capital City Youth Service's non-residential program. Mr. Headman's primary research interests and areas of expertise are in adolescent–parent relationships, parent training, and marital relationship improvement. The client populations which he is researching include families with at-risk adolescents and perpetrators of domestic violence.

JOHN A. HILL, M.S.W. is a professional firefighter with Mississauga Fire and Emergency Services in Ontario, Canada. In addition to firefighting duties Mr. Hill coordinates the Critical Incident Stress Management Program for his fire department. Mr. Hill earned his M.S.W. from Wilfrid Laurier University in Waterloo, Ontario. In addition, Mr. Hill has a Bachelor of Arts degree in Psychology from York University in Toronto, Ontario, and a Bachelor of Science degree from Lakehead University in Thunder Bay, Ontario. In 1996, through the International Fire Service Exchange Program, Mr. Hill worked for the Melbourne Fire Brigade in Victoria, Australia for a one-year term. During that time, Mr. Hill and Dr. Cheryl Regehr studied the PTSD levels of Australian firefighters and the effectiveness of critical incident stress debriefings. From this research several studies have been published. Mr. Hill is currently conducting research with Dr. Regehr within his own fire department, studying the impact of post-mortem reviews. Mr. Hill also works as a trauma counselor and crisis worker.

SEAN T. KURTH, M.S. is currently a doctoral candidate in the Department of Child and Family Development at University of Georgia. He received his M.S. in Marriage and Family Therapy from the University of San Diego.

LOUISE MAXFIELD, M.A. is a Ph.D. candidate in Clinical Psychology at Lakehead University in Canada. She is a Certified Trauma Specialist and a Registered Clinical Counsellor who has many years of experience working with trauma survivors in Ontario and British Columbia. Ms. Maxfield was Executive Director of the Sexual Assault Center in Vernon, British Columbia, and for three years was contracted by the B.C. provincial government to train counselors working with abuse victims. She is the author of several articles and book chapters about the treatment of traumatic stress and EMDR, and has been an investigator in two clinical research studies evaluating the efficacy of EMDR. Currently, Ms. Maxfield is involved in research on the association between adverse childhood interpersonal experiences and the qualities of adult relationships. Other research interests include the processing of traumatic events, the relationship between personality and pathology, and factors influencing treatment outcome.

KEKUNI MINTON, Ph.D. is a faculty member of Naropa University in the Psychology Department. He received his doctorate from the Union Institute. He was the resident psychotherapist at the Boulder County AIDS Project. He is also a trainer at the Hakomi Somatics Institute, where he teaches trainings in Sensorimotor Psychotherapy internationally. Dr. Minton has presented for several years at the International Society for Traumatic Stress Studies, the Psychological Trauma Conference (Boston University), United States Association of Body Psychotherapy, the European Association of Body Psychotherapy, and the Naropa Somatic Psychology Conference. He also maintains a private practice in Boulder, Colorado.

DAVID C. MUSS, L.M.S.S.A. is a physician who initially qualified in Italy and subsequently in England, starting off as a pediatric/cardiac surgeon, then practicing as a family doctor for some 20 years. He became a psychotherapist in 1988 and has since dedicated himself to treating civilian victims of motor vehicle, crime, and industrial accidents. He set up a post-traumatic stress unit in Birmingham, England at a time when PTSD was just beginning to be recognized and published the first self-help book in the United Kingdom, *The Trauma Trap*, in 1991. He presently directs the Birmingham Nuffield PTSD unit, which accepts clients from both the private sector and the national health service.

PAT OGDEN, M.A. has been a pioneer in somatic psychotherapy and the treatment of trauma and developmental issues since the late 1970s. Trained in a wide variety of somatic approaches, she is a Structural Integrator (Rolf Method), a co-founder of the Hakomi Institute, and a faculty member in the departments of Contemplative Psychology and Somatic Psychology at Naropa University, Boulder, Colorado. Often a speaker for conferences in the United States and abroad, she is the originator of Sensorimotor Psychotherapy and co-founder and director of Hakomi Somatics Institute, an internationally recognized school that specializes in training psychotherapists in Sensorimotor Psychotherapy.

MONICA PIGNOTTI, M.S.W. has been working with people in destructive cults and with their families for the past 14 years. She holds a B.A. from the University of Michigan and an M.A. in Social Work from Fordham University, and has also worked as a researcher in the health field at Saint Vincent's Hospital in New York City and at the National Multiple Sclerosis Society. She trained in Thought Field Therapy and Voice Technology with the founder, Roger Callahan, and is also trained in EEG Biofeedback and Neuro-Linguistic Programming. Recently, she moved from her practice in New York City and is currently practicing Thought Field Therapy and EEG Biofeedback with Dr. Mark Steinberg in Los Gatos, California.

WILLIAM H. QUINN, Ph.D. is a Professor in the Department of Child and Family Development at the University of Georgia in Athens, Georgia. He received his M.S. from the University of Oregon and his Ph.D. from Virginia Tech University. He is a Fellow of the American Association for Marriage and Family Therapy. He is on the editorial board of the *Journal of Marital and Family Therapy* and the *Journal of Marriage and the Family*. He received the Obermann Faculty Research Fellowship at the University of Iowa and was the Visiting Hewlett Scholar at Child Trends, Inc., Washington, DC. He is the Executive Director of Families4Change, a non-profit organization providing services to at-risk youths and their families, and training to professionals in communities who wish to implement the Family Solutions Program. He has over 50 publications in refereed journals, 15 book chapters, one edited book, and a book in press, *Multiple Family Group Intervention with Youth: Juvenile Delinquency, Truancy, and Behavior Problems.*

CHERYL REGEHR, Ph.D., C.S.W. is a University of Toronto Associate Professor of Social Work and Academic Co-ordinator for the Centre for Applied Social Research in Toronto. Dr. Regehr has years of traumatology practice experience including her work in sexual assault recovery programs and sex offender treatment programs, and in administration of community and emergency mental health programs and sexual assault care centers. At present she is the Clinical Director of the Critical Incident Stress Team at Pearson International Airport. In addition, she remains involved in the practice of forensic social work, specializing in civil litigation and criminal court assessments of trauma victims and violent offenders.

DAVID S. RIGGS received his Ph.D. in clinical psychology from the State University of New York at Stony Brook in 1990. Since then his clinical and research activities have focused on the impact of traumatic events. He has worked clinically with victims of crime and combat veterans diagnosed with post-traumatic stress disorder at the Medical College of Pennsylvania and the Boston VA Medical Center. His research has focused on identifying the causes and consequences of violence, first at the Center for the Treatment and Study of Anxiety and later at the National Center for Post-traumatic Stress Disorder.

LIZABETH ROEMER, Ph.D. is an Assistant Professor in the Department of Psychology at the University of Massachusetts at Boston. She received her Ph.D. in clinical psychology from Pennsylvania State University and completed her pre-doctoral internship and post-doctoral training at the National Center for Post-traumatic Stress Disorder—Behavioral Sciences Division. Dr. Roemer has published numerous research papers and book chapters in the areas of generalized anxiety disorder, post-traumatic stress disorder, and the role of cognitive and emotional avoidance in these disorders. She is currently involved in research on emotional dysregulation, factors that influence successful or unsuccessful processing of traumatic events, and treatment development, as well as teaching and education in the areas of cognitive-behavioral therapy, anxiety disorders and traumatic stress, and research methodology.

VICTORIA TICHENOR, Ph.D. is an Assistant Clinical Professor of Psychiatry, University of California, San Francisco, working with the Couples and Family therapy program at the Department of Veterans Affairs (DVA) Hospital since 1990. She is Director of Training for the Post-traumatic Stress Disorder Program at the DVA in San Francisco. Dr. Tichenor maintains a private practice in the Bay Area.

PAMELA VEST VALENTINE, Ph.D. is an assistant professor and Director of the Social Work Program in the School of Social and Behavioral Sciences at the University of Alabama at Birmingham. Dr.Valentine received her M.S.W. and Ph.D. in social work from Florida State University in 1997. While in Tallahassee, Florida, she worked in a research institute, managing grants to evaluate Florida's Drug Courts. In Birmingham, she has been awarded grants to study therapeutic counselors of STD-positive patients and to study the impact of prior traumatic events on illicit substance use in adolescents. Her clinical experience comes from having opened an agency to serve victims of violence and having worked in a family counseling clinic in Tallahassee, Florida. Dr. Valentine's primary research interests and areas of expertise are in assessment and brief treatment of traumatized clients. The client populations which she is researching include female inmates, juvenile drug offenders, welfare recipients, and victims of domestic violence.

DAVID J. VANDYKE, Ph.D. is Assistant Professor at the Illinois School of Professional Psychology, Chicago, Illinois. He received his master's degree from Fuller Theological Seminary in Pasadena, California and his Ph.D. from the University of Georgia. He is a Clinical Member of the American Association for Marriage and Family Therapy.

VICKIE VANN, L.C.S.W. is an Assistant Clinical Professor of Psychiatry at the University of California, San Francisco. She is co-director of the Couples and Family Therapy program at the Department of Veterans Affairs (DVA) Medical Center in San Francisco and is also a staff member of the Psychiatric Outpatient Clinic at the DVA. She maintains a private practice in San Francisco.